SWORD OVER RICHMOND

An Eyewitness History of McClellan's Peninsula Campaign

RICHARD WHEELER

1817

HARPER & ROW, PUBLISHERS, New York

Cambridge, Philadelphia, San Francisco, London
Mexico City, São Paulo, Singapore, Sydney

To Kathleen Bross,
who understands the labor
and does so much to make it easier

FIRST EDITION

Designer: Sidney Feinberg

Library of Congress Cataloging-in-Publication data

Wheeler, Richard.
  Sword over Richmond.

  Bibliography: p.
  Includes index.
  1. Peninsular Campaign, 1862. 2. Peninsular
Campaign, 1862—Personal narratives. 3. McClellan,
George Brinton, 1826–1885 I. Title.
E473.6.W43 1986   973.7′32   85-45240
ISBN 0-06-015529-9

86 87 88 89 90 RRD 10 9 8 7 6 5 4 3 2 1

CONTENTS

ILLUSTRATIONS

MAPS

PREFACE

The attack on Richmond undertaken in the spring of 1862 by Union troops ferried from Washington to the Virginia Peninsula was a Civil War campaign of momentous consequences. General George B. McClellan's defeat at the hands of General Robert E. Lee dashed all prospects for a quick, low-cost end to the conflict and convinced President Abraham Lincoln he must strengthen Washington's military and moral position by issuing an emancipation proclamation, a move that brought about a radical change in the nation's development.

Aside from its significance, the campaign was one of exceptional variety and high drama. It engendered Lee's emergence as a Confederate hero, and it saw the brilliant but overcautious McClellan transform a unique opportunity into a calamitous failure. The actions included were the naval engagement between the *Monitor* and the *Merrimack*, which launched the age of metal warships; Stonewall Jackson's celebrated exploits in the Shenandoah Valley; the Siege of Yorktown and the Battle of Williamsburg; the Siege of Richmond, along with the Battles of Fair Oaks, Mechanicsville, and Gaines' Mill; Jeb Stuart's swashbuckling ride around the Union army; and McClellan's retreat, or "change of base," with the attendant Battles of Savage's Station, White Oak Swamp, and Malvern Hill.

In spite of its status as one of the most crucial and colorful episodes of American history, McClellan's Peninsula Campaign has been the topic of only a few book-length studies. This is inexplicable. Easier to understand is that the studies that do exist are concerned primarily with the campaign's political and strategic aspects, which is fitting. But there is also much to be learned from the human side of the story, which has never had an inclusive telling. Scores of participants, both Union and Confederate—politicians, officers, soldiers in the ranks, chaplains, medical personnel, newsmen, and women of Richmond—wrote vividly of their experiences and observations, the accounts in the form of reports, letters, diaries, news items, memoirs, and histories.

Sword Over Richmond links together a representative selection of quotations from this wealth of material and provides a narrative of the campaign in which politics and strategy have been given their due but human considerations are paramount. It is hoped that the book will be recognized as a fresh approach to eyewitness history. Not simply a set of loosely connected accounts unevenly furnished with basic information, it is offered as a coherent study. All of the accounts have been checked against the official records. Although most of the book's ellipses indicate the employment of condensation, some were used to eliminate passages that appeared to be faulty. In a few cases it was necessary to include clarifications enclosed in brackets.

Many of the illustrations, which were taken from *Battles and Leaders of the Civil War* and other publications of the postwar decades, are adaptations of on-the-spot sketches or photographs.

PROLOGUE

IN MID-MARCH 1862, with the Civil War eleven months old, the Potomac River between Washington and Alexandria held a curious armada, a mixture of schooners, brigs, sloops, steamers, ferryboats, tugs, canalboats, and barges. At least 500 strong, the assemblage was composed partly of official United States naval craft, but more prominently of vessels gleaned by the Government from the waterways of the Northeast under an emergency lease program. The whole was intended as transportation for the Army of the Potomac, more than 100,000 men, and a wide range of equipment, including several thousand supply wagons and other horse-drawn conveyances, 300 pieces of artillery, a vast tonnage of ammunition, mountains of folded tents and crated rations, telegraph gear, engineering essentials such as pontoons and other bridge constituents, a total of 25,000 horses, mules, and beeves, and numberless bales of forage.

After a period of rainy weather, the March sun was bright as the troops began converging on the fleet from their winter camps around Washington, some on the Maryland side of the Potomac and others in Virginia. "When, from our camp, we came to the height over Little Hunting Creek," relates the Reverend J. J. Marks, chaplain of the 63rd Regiment, Pennsylvania Volunteers, "the spectacle that burst upon our view was brilliant. The entire plain and hillside were covered with armed men; great columns of soldiers, whose guns flashed in the light, moved under the eye. Here, on the right, in the meadows of the plain, were thousands of horsemen, their polished armor reflecting the sunbeams like hundreds of mirrors. In the fields on the left were many [artillery] batteries. Here, still further to the left, stretching from the hills to the streets of Alexandria, was a long dense column of men."

On succeeding days, the pageant continued with unabating animation.

1

"The river," noted an infantry colonel from New York, "was crowded with vessels of every kind and size. The wharves were covered with troops waiting their turn to embark as soon as the steamboats came alongside the docks to receive them. The little tugboats furrowed the waves in every direction, leaving in the air their long plumes of smoke. Night . . . did not suspend the work. The embarking was continued by the light of fires kindled along the banks, in the midst of signals exchanged between the vessels. As soon as they were loaded, the steamers anchored in the stream in the position assigned to the command of which they formed a part."

The Reverend A. M. Stewart, another regimental chaplain, found the preparations stimulating. "Such a bustle, such jamming, such apparent inextricable confusion, such a grand miscellaneous mixing up—why, I really enjoyed it. . . . At the passing of some general or other exciting event, ten thousand voices would well up in shouts together, while numerous bands of martial music made river, hills, and adjacent cities vocal. The multitudes had come from their camps of long confinement and were wild with excitement."

According to Warren Lee Goss, a private from New England, the troops shared a feeling of purpose. "The general opinion among us was that at last we were on our way to make an end to the Confederacy."

The Army of the Potomac was embarking on an amphibious operation that, as a quartermaster officer said later, "had scarcely any parallel in history, and certainly none in our country."

The undertaking was the outcome of Union designs upon Richmond dating from the beginning of the war.

1

INTO THE ARENA

AFTER FIFTY YEARS of disputation over slavery and states' rights, the North and the South became military enemies at 4:30 A.M. on April 12, 1861, when Brigadier General Pierre G. T. Beauregard, commander of a provisional Confederate force at Charleston, South Carolina, ordered his artillerymen to open fire on Fort Sumter, a Federal installation in the city's harbor. The outgunned fort surrendered the next day, and people all over the South saw the triumph as marking the birth of Confederate independence. There were many celebrations, none more enthusiastic than the one at Richmond, soon to become the Confederate capital. According to a resident, Mrs. Sarah A. "Sallie" Putnam: "A hundred guns were fired, and . . . the reverberations were heard for miles around. . . . Men from the adjoining country flocked to the city to hear the wonderful story; bonfires were kindled, rockets sent up, and the most tumultuous excitement reigned. All night the bells of Richmond rang, cannons boomed, shouts of joy arose, and the strains of 'Dixie's Land,' already adopted as the national tune of the Confederates, were wafted over the seven hills of the city."

On April 15 a telegraphic message from Washington crackled through the Union states: President Abraham Lincoln wanted 75,000 volunteers to serve against the insurrection for three months. The South began its own recruiting. Going further, President Jefferson Davis, then at Montgomery, Alabama, the Confederacy's first capital, invited Southern shipowners to help "resist aggression" by operating as privateers against the North's seaborne commerce. Lincoln, in turn, ordered a naval blockade of Southern ports. But the Gosport Navy Yard at Norfolk, Virginia, had to be abandoned to the Confederates, an attempt to destroy it only partly successful. Fortunately retained was Fort Monroe, at the tip of the Virginia Peninsula, the land between the York and James Rivers.

Abraham Lincoln

On both sides, the spring of 1861 was a time of intense feeling. Even as the sap rose in the trees and shrubs, the blood sprang hot in Union and Confederate breasts. Like early flowers, flags blossomed everywhere, the Stars and Stripes in the North and the new Stars and Bars in the South. In the Union states, newspaper editors, ministers in their pulpits, and speakers at citizens' rallies denounced the secessionists and their slavocracy, and men flocked to the recruiting offices. Units were formed, and they drilled in public to the sound of fife and drum. As they marched to the railroad depots for transport to Washington, the regiments were escorted by crowds singing patriotic airs such as "It is sweet, it is sweet, for one's country to die." Most of the troops had visions not of death but of returning as heroes. Throughout the Confederacy, the atmosphere was much the same. The frenzied editors and public speakers accused the North's abolitionists—those people who wanted the slaves freed at once, regardless of the effect on the South's economy or social order—of conspiring to subjugate the seceded states, and declared the heinous task impossible. There was talk of attacking Washington. "That filthy cage of unclean birds," cried the Richmond *Examiner*, "must and will assuredly be purified by fire." The volunteers came not only from urban areas and farms, as in the North, but also from the great plantations. These departing aristocrats made gallant farewell speeches to the ladies. "When the war is over," a youthful Virginian told a group of enraptured schoolgirls, "we will return and, like the troubadours of old, sing under your windows the songs of love." It was common for a plantation man to leave home with a favorite black servant and such things as linen tablecloths, silverware, dress clothing, and embroidered slippers.

At this point, many people of the North and South alike viewed the war as little more than an exciting game. Neither side had ever given much serious thought to what a civil conflict might entail. Northern historian Joel Tyler Headley, who recorded the story of the war even while it was in progress, explained the situation this way: "Civil War was an evil we had never contemplated. Besides, we had been taught so long to regard it as a political bugbear, a mere party menace, that we looked upon it with little or no alarm. More than this, the North had been told so long by unscrupulous politicians that the South dare not fight, that at the first call to arms the slaves would rush into insurrection—that it really believed at the first show of determination the South would decline the contest. The people at the South had been beguiled in the same manner by their leaders. They had been assured over and over again that the money-loving North would never go to war with a source of their wealth—a 'race of shopkeepers' would never fight for a sentiment; and if they attempted it, would be crushed at the first onset by the chivalrous, warlike South. Thus the two sections were hurried, through ignorance and blind presumption, towards all the untold horrors of civil war."

Jefferson Davis

As for slavery, it was more of an economic issue than a moral one. The North and the South had developed along different lines. The former was a populous, bustling place with an economy based on industrial growth, while the latter was sparsely populated and geared to a slower pace, its mainstay large-scale agriculture, with cotton the leading crop, the system sustained by slave labor. Except for the Yankee shipping companies that played a prominent part in bringing the blacks from Africa, the North had never found slavery very profitable. The majority of the farms were small enough to be run by their owners, and large urban populations were available for industrial labor. Consequently, it wasn't hard for Northerners to view slavery with disapproval. Few were aware of the paradox that certain blacks on Southern plantations led richer lives than some of the North's slum-dwelling "wage slaves." There were, of course, many Southerners who saw slavery as immoral, and these people favored at least a gradual approach to emancipation. On the other hand, there was a segment that declared the practice to be morally defensible. Wrote southern diarist Mrs. Judith W. McGuire: "Under a mysterious Providence, millions of the colored race have been saved from the foulest paganism; millions mentally and morally elevated far above those of their native land, and multitudes saved in Christ forever. Is it God's purpose to break up this system?" Perhaps the most singular irony about slavery in America was that it had ever been established in the first place, since the Europeans who founded the colonies were resolute exponents of freedom.

With the opening of the great territories to the west, which led to the formation of new states, slavery had become a burning issue. The South, in order to ensure the growth of its economy and influence—with the added consideration that some of its older cotton lands were played out—strove to extend the practice, while the North wanted it restricted in favor of its own economic system. Slave labor was seen as a threat to this system. Tied in with the sectional strife was the issue of states' rights. Since the nation was formed, various political figures, Northern and Southern, had regarded the powers of the Federal Government as being limited to those explicitly mentioned in the Constitution, and the powers of the individual states as embracing all of those not explicitly denied them. In line with this doctrine, the Southern states argued that Congress had no right to regulate slavery, nor to pass any other law that infringed upon their sovereignty. By 1859, there were eighteen free states and only fifteen slave states, and the South was at a disadvantage in both houses of Congress. The climax came the following year when the Republican party, which represented Northern interests, won with Lincoln. The South now considered itself to be politically overwhelmed and began moving to set itself up as an independent nation.

Although the North was greatly superior to the South in population and material resources, the war's outcome was by no means a foregone conclu-

8

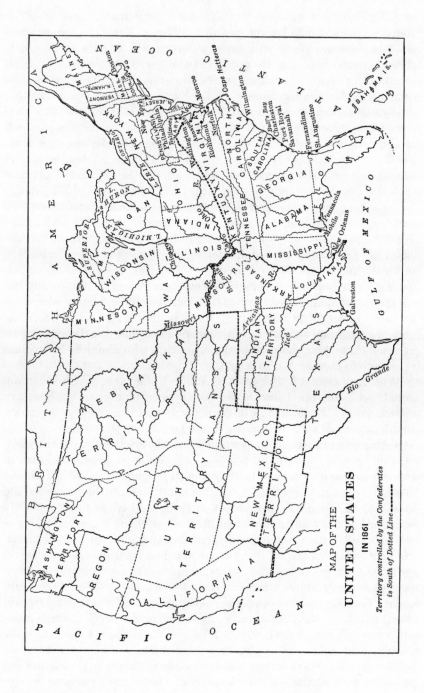

MAP OF THE
UNITED STATES
IN 1861

*Territory controlled by the Confederates
is South of Dotted Line* -------

sion. The South had many competent leaders and thousands of outdoorsmen adept with horses and firearms. Moreover, the strategy the top command settled upon would be largely a defensive one, which meant that the Confederate armies would do most of their fighting on their own ground, aided by friendly civilians. The North, on the other hand, would have to stretch its supply lines over vast regions of hostile territory. Also advantageous to the South was that the North had a strong "peace party" rooted in Lincoln's Democratic opposition. A stiff resistance might well increase the pressure on the President to end the war on terms compatible with Southern goals. Finally, since cotton was economically important in Europe, the South could look that way for aid in the form of arms and other supplies. It could even harbor a substantial hope for open intervention in its favor.

Virginia was the richest and most populous of the Southern states. Richmond, at the headwaters of the James River about a hundred miles south of Washington, was the home of 38,000 people and a number of industries, including the Tredegar Iron Works and other plants that were readily converted to the production of military supplies. The city's value to the war effort exceeded that of any other. Even while Montgomery was still the capital of the Confederacy, Richmond served as its center of operations, and troops from all parts of the South converged there. To command Virginia's own forces, Governor John Letcher chose fifty-four-year-old Robert E. Lee, who had spent his entire adult life in the Federal military service.

The Lee family had been conspicuous in Virginia for two hundred years, and Robert E. was the son of Henry "Light Horse Harry" Lee, of Revolutionary War fame. Educated at West Point, the younger Lee distinguished himself in the Mexican War and was wounded at Chapultepec. Furloughed at the close of the war, he returned to his family in Virginia, and one of his sons, Robert E., Jr., would grow up recalling: "From that early time I began to be impressed with my father's character, as compared with other men. Every member of the household respected, revered, and loved him as a matter of course, but it began to dawn on me that everyone else with whom I was thrown held him high in their regard. At forty-five years of age he was active, strong, and as handsome as he had ever been. . . . He was always bright and gay with us little folk, romping, playing, and joking with us. With the older children he was just as companiable. . . . Although he was so joyous and familiar with us, he was very firm on all proper occasions . . . and exacted the most implicit obedience."

In the early 1850s, Lee served as superintendent at West Point, and his family was with him. His son states: "My father was the most punctual man I ever knew. He was always ready for family prayers, for meals, and met every engagement, social or business, at the moment. . . . I never knew him late for Sunday service at the Post Chapel. He used to appear some minutes before the rest of us, in uniform, jokingly rallying my mother for being late,

Robert E. Lee. People who knew him considered this portrait to be
an excellent likeness.

and for forgetting something at the last moment. When he could wait no longer for her, he would . . . march along to church by himself, or with any of the children who were ready. There he sat very straight . . . and, as I remember, always becoming very sleepy, and sometimes even took a little nap during the sermon. . . .

"It was against the rules that the cadets should go beyond certain [territorial] limits without permission. Of course they did go sometimes, and when caught were given quite a number of demerits. My father was out riding one afternoon with me, and, while rounding a turn in the mountain road . . . we came suddenly upon three cadets far beyond the limits. They immediately leaped over a low wall on the side of the road and disappeared from our view. We rode on for a minute in silence; then my father said: 'Did you know those young men? But no; if you did, don't say so. . . .' He knew he would have to report them, but, not being sure of who they were, I presume he wished to give them the benefit of the doubt."

After his tour of duty at West Point, Lee became a colonel of cavalry on the Texas frontier. He made a visit back East in 1859, and on October 17 was ordered to Harpers Ferry, on the Potomac River northwest of Washington, to suppress the raid of the abolitionist John Brown. Lee handled the matter adroitly, explaining in his memorandum book: "Reached Harpers Ferry at 11 P.M. . . . Posted marines in the United States Armory. Waited till daylight, as a number of citizens were held as hostages, whose lives were threatened. . . . About sunrise, with twelve marines . . . broke in the door of the engine house, secured the insurgents, and relieved the prisoners unhurt. All the insurgents killed or mortally wounded but four." Brown was among the survivors, and Lee commanded the troops that, after the abolitionist's trial, kept the security at his hanging. Lee himself, though not in sympathy with the abolitionists, considered slavery an evil.

Lee spent another year in Texas, returning to the family home, Arlington, across the Potomac from Washington, when the Civil War began. At a meeting with one of Lincoln's aides, he was offered command of the Union forces then taking the field. "I declined the offer . . . stating as candidly and as courteously as I could that, though opposed to secession and deprecating war, I could take no part in an invasion of the Southern states." Lee went home and did some soul-searching. "I concluded that I ought no longer to retain the commission I held in the United States Army, and on the second morning thereafter I forwarded my resignation. . . . At the time, I hoped that peace would have been preserved; that some way would have been found to save the country from the calamities of war; and I then had no other intention than to pass the remainder of my life as a private citizen. Two days afterward, upon the invitation of the Governor of Virginia, I repaired to Richmond."

Even as he assumed his duties as commander of Virginia's troops (a post

Mrs. Robert E. Lee

soon to be changed to that of military adviser to Jefferson Davis), Lee was worried about his wife, his "dearest Mary," at Arlington, and wrote her: "You had better complete your arrangements and retire further from the scene of war. It may burst upon you at any time. It is sad to think of the devastation, if not ruin, it may bring upon a spot so endeared to us." Mary left Arlington, and after several more moves in Virginia, one to Hot Springs in Bath County to take treatments for arthritis, she settled at the White House plantation, a family property on the Pamunkey River about twenty miles east of Richmond. Both Arlington and the White House had only recently descended to the Lees upon the death of Mary's father, George Washington Parke Custis, Martha Washington's grandson (by her first marriage), who had been adopted by George Washington and raised at Mount Vernon. Neither General Lee nor his wife would ever return to Arlington.

Richmond and its environs became a hub of military activity. "In a very short time," relates Sallie Putnam, "the population . . . increased in wonderful ratio. Strange faces greeted the citizens at every turn. . . . Feeling that our state had become the particular object of hatred and hostility to the old government, we hastened, with all possible energy, to meet the necessities which might arise. . . . Colleges and public schools of all grades suspended operations, and our young men hastily sought instruction in the art of war. Men of all grades and professions were to be found filling up the ranks for the coming contest. . . . The most lucrative employments were cheerfully abandoned. . . .

"Every railroad train that arrived in Richmond bore its freight of soldiers. Very soon, from all directions around the city, the white tents of the soldiery were seen dotting the landscapes. . . . The Central Fair Grounds, about a mile and a half above the city, were used for the camp of instruction. Thither the volunteer companies were sent, and there they were drilled in the manual of military exercises by Colonel Smith and his corps of cadets from the Virginia Military Institute at Lexington. . . . The success which crowned the efforts to tutor the soldiers spoke volumes for the excellence of our principal military academy. . . . The raw, awkward recruit . . . soon grew soldierlike in air and bearing. . . . The camp of instruction was a place of great interest. The blunder of the well-intentioned recruit was overlooked in his evident desire to become a soldier, though not infrequently the risibilities of the spectator would be excited by the amusing scenes of the drill. The recruit's hands and arms, his feet, his head, seemed to be made for some other use. . . . We were often astonished at the patience and diligence displayed by the cadets. . . .

"All the states of the South were represented in the camps . . . and the striking characteristics of the people of each state were plainly distinguishable. Very soon it became easy to tell whence a regiment or company came, by the very appearance of the men. The glowing enthusiasm of the South

Arlington as the Lee family knew it

Carolinian was presented in striking contrast beside the cool determination of the Virginian. The fiery impetuosity of the Louisianan was vividly displayed beside the steady courage of the Arkansas man. The wild ardor of the Mississippian was visible in contrast with the active energy of the Tennesseean. The North Carolinian, the Georgian, the Alabamian, the Kentuckian, the Missourian—each had his distinctive characteristic; while from his bold, free, independent air the brave son of Texas was easily discovered. The world-wide fame of the Texas Ranger he brought with him to his new field of action. . . .

"Particularly noticeable . . . was the battalion of Washington Artillery from New Orleans. . . . The battalion of 'Tigers' from New Orleans . . . were, as their name denotes, men of desperate courage but questionable morals. . . . The troops from the northern portion of Louisiana and southern portion of Arkansas, in the vicinity of the Red River, were among the finest and most striking looking men who appeared in the city. Unusually tall, brawny, and muscular, bronzed by exposure and inured to the most active exercise, they were peculiarly fitted for the arduous duties of a soldier's life. . . . Florida, also, from her sparse population, furnished a creditable quota of troops, who were particularly distinguishable on the dress parade for their evident lack of military education, but after much patience and perseverance on the part of their officers they were drilled into a useful soldiery."

The influx of troops included one unit, a battalion of Zouaves from New Orleans, that became a liability. Mrs. Putnam explains: "It was composed of the most lawless and desperate material which that city could send forth. It is said that its colonel, with the approval of the Mayor of New Orleans, established recruiting booths in the different jails there, and each criminal was given his option either to serve out his time or join the battalion. It was a strange, mixed body of desperate men of almost every nation, guilty of almost every crime, impelled by no spirit of patriotism. . . . Dressed in their striking costume of red trousers and blue jackets, the latter adorned with fanciful embroidery, and capped by the Turkish fez, their appearance everywhere excited the greatest attention. Their bronzed complexions, countenances often disfigured by horrid scars—the marks of former desperate encounters—and the cat-like, elastic step acquired in the drill, distinguished this heterogeneous company.

"From the time of their appearance in Richmond robberies became frequent. . . . The poultry and garden stock around the city were favorite objects of depredation with these thievish soldiers. It was common with them to walk into saloons and restaurants, order what they wished to eat and drink, and then direct the dismayed proprietor to charge their bill to the government. The hall doors of private citizens were kept rigidly locked, and the strictest watch was directed upon the Zouaves as long as they tor-

mented Richmond with their presence. Always finding means to effect their
escape from their barracks at night, they roamed about the city like a pack
of untamed wildcats, and so clever were they in eluding the vigilance of the
police that few or none of them were brought to justice for the larcenies
they committed. It was found absolutely necessary to assign them to a separate encampment, where lawlessness, strife, and bloodshed became the
order of the day. No man's life was safe who dared show himself within
their encampment."

It was late in May when the provisional Confederate Congress in Montgomery voted to transfer the seat of government to Richmond. At that time
Jefferson Davis, a Mississippian, was only provisional president, but his elevation to an official status was assured, for he was both militarily and politically qualified for the task. A West Point graduate, he had campaigned in
Mexico and on the American frontier and had served in Washington as a
congressman, a senator, and as Secretary of War. His qualifications, however, did not include equanimity. Davis was insecure to the point that even
a child's disapproval upset him. Genial enough when his judgments were
accepted and followed, he became vexatious and rude when he was opposed. Indigestion and nervous exhaustion were his frequent companions. A
government clerk, John B. Jones, who met Davis for the first time just before the move to Richmond, described his physical appearance this way:
"His stature is tall. . . . His frame is very slight and seemingly frail, but when
he throws back his shoulders he is as straight as an Indian chief. The features of his face are distinctly marked with character. . . . His face is handsome, and his thin lip often basks a pleasant smile. . . . If there are no special
indications of great grasp of intellectual power on his forehead and on his
sharply defined nose and chin, neither is there any evidence of weakness, or
that he could be easily moved from any settled purpose."

When Davis boarded the train for Richmond he went directly to bed,
having been prostrated, according to his wife, Varina, by "anxiety and
unremitting labor. . . . He was quite ill. . . . The crowd that gathered at each
station would walk quietly down and look in on his sleeping face with the
greatest tenderness. One or two said, 'If only he can pull us through the
war!' "

Davis rallied by the time he reached the new capital. Sallie Putnam was
pleased to observe that "he was received with an outburst of enthusiasm. A
suite of handsome apartments had been provided for him at the Spotswood
Hotel until arrangements could be made for supplying him with more elegant and suitable accommodations. Over the hotel, and from the various
windows of the guests, waved numerous Confederate flags, and the rooms
destined for his use were gorgeously draped in the Confederate colors. In
honor of his arrival, almost every house in the city was decorated with the
Stars and Bars.

The Davis house

"An elegant residence for the use of Mr. Davis was soon procured. It was situated in the western part of the city, on a hill overlooking a landscape of romantic beauty. This establishment was luxuriously furnished, and there Mr. and Mrs. Davis dispensed the elegant hospitalities for which they were ever distinguished. . . . Mrs. Davis is a tall, commanding figure with dark hair, eyes, and complexion. . . . With firmly set yet flexible lips, there is indicated much energy of purpose and will, but beautifully softened by the usually sad expression of her dark, earnest eyes. . . . Her manners are kind, graceful, easy and affable."

With the arrival of the President, Mrs. Putnam goes on to explain, the citizens of Richmond expanded their contributions to the war effort. "There was now work for everyone to do. The effects of the blockade of our ports was very early felt. The numberless and nameless articles for which we depended upon foreign markets were either to be dispensed with or to be manufactured from our own industry and ingenuity. . . . The people set themselves to work to meet the demands made by the exigencies of the times. . . . Sewing societies were multiplied, and those who had formerly devoted themselves to gaiety and fashionable amusements found their only real pleasure . . . in providing proper habiliments for the soldier. The quondam belle of the ballroom, the accomplished woman of society, the devotee of ease, luxury, and idle enjoyment found herself transformed into the busy sempstress. The click of the sewing machine was the music which most interested them, and the 'stitch, stitch, stitch' from morning till night, as the ladies plied the needle and thread, was their chief employment. They very soon became adept in the manufacture of the different articles which compose the rough and simple wardrobe of the soldier. To these . . . they took delight in adding various other articles. . . . There were very few of the soldiers who were not furnished with a neat thread-case, supplied with everything necessary to repair his clothing . . . a visor to shield his face from the too-fierce heat of the summer sun, or, to protect him from the cold of winter, a warm scarf and a Havelock.

"The sewing operations were varied by the scraping and carding of lint [i.e., the preparation of cotton], the rolling of bandages, and the manufacture of cartridges, and many things unnecessary to mention, but which were the work of the women. . . . They employed themselves cheerfully upon anything necessary to be done. Heavy tents of cumbrous sailcloth, overcoats, jackets, and pantaloons of stiff, heavy material—from the sewing on which they were frequently found with stiff, swollen, bleeding fingers— were nevertheless perseveringly undertaken. . . .

"The usual routine of social life in Richmond had undergone a complete change. . . . We were awakened in the morning by the reveille of the drum which called the soldiers to duty, and the evening 'taps' reminded us of the hour for rest. At all hours of the day the sounds of martial music fell upon

Early volunteers parading in Richmond

our ears, and the 'tramp, tramp' of the soldiers through the streets was the accompaniment. Nothing was seen, nothing talked of, nothing thought of but the war.... Former distinctions were forgotten, old prejudices laid aside.... A little girl who had been exclusively reared ... in Richmond, though herself imbued with as much of the spirit of patriotism as could possess one so young, quite shocked at the familiarity of a soldier who had presumed to caress her, very indignantly remarked to the relative who had the charge of her, 'Why, indeed! Any man that wears a stripe on his pantaloons thinks he can speak to any lady!' The child had not then learned that the circumstances under which the soldier donned his uniform dissolved the barrier to introduction and gave the soldier a right to attention from all.

"No regiment was permitted to remain long in or near Richmond. As soon as the troops under instruction became sufficiently drilled in military exercises they were transferred to positions where their services were most likely to be needed.... As regiment after regiment passed through our streets on their way to the theaters of active engagement, cheerful adieus were waved from every window, in the flutter of snowy handkerchiefs, and bright, smiling faces beamed in blessing on the soldier—but heavy hearts were masked beneath those smiles."

During the war's first three months, while Richmond and Washington became armed camps, and while troops of both sides took up positions along the Union-Confederate border stretching from the Atlantic Ocean westward across the Mississippi River, there was only minor fighting. Early in June, several thousand Federals left Fort Monroe, marched ten miles up the Virginia Peninsula, and attacked some 1,200 Confederates at the village of Big Bethel, only to be thrown into a humiliating retreat. The Confederate defense earned Colonel John B. Magruder, formerly a career man in the U.S. Army, promotion to brigadier general and the adulation of the Southern public, which he accepted graciously. In his early fifties, Magruder was tall, dark-haired, mustachioed, and aristocratic in his bearing. Spurning "John B." as a dull name, he signed himself "J. Bankhead." He was financially reckless, and he sometimes lost his poise to the bottle. Because of a fascination for pomp and ceremony, Magruder was known to his friends as "Prince John." The new brigadier's main command was at Yorktown, about twenty miles from Fort Monroe, where his troops, aided by Negro laborers, now busied themselves with blocking the way to Richmond by establishing a line of defenses across the Peninsula. Some of these were restorations of earthworks used by Charles Cornwallis when he was besieged by George Washington and his French allies in 1781.

Additional brushes between the new armies occurred in Missouri and western Virginia, then in the political process of becoming the Union State of West Virginia. On July 11, the latter zone was host to an affair that became known as the "Battle of Rich Mountain." This was a Union success

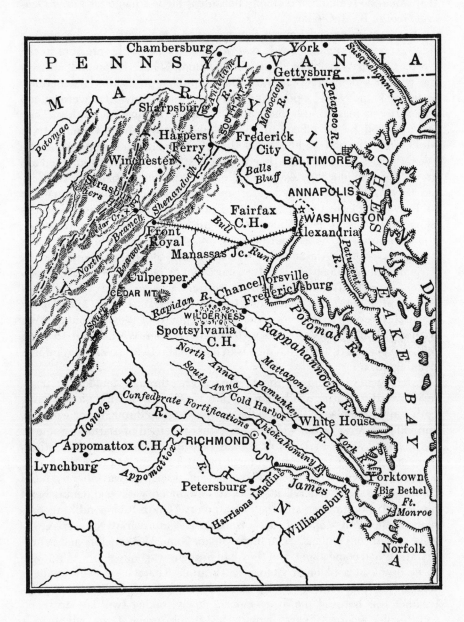

Field of operations in Virginia

that would be remembered chiefly because it made a name for Major General George B. McClellan.

Events now moved toward the war's first great battle, which neither side was really prepared for. It was precipitated by public pressure in the North. Lincoln was obliged to heed the clamor, "On to Richmond!" This is the way of a democracy at war. Sound military procedure is sometimes disregarded in favor of a popular viewpoint. By mid-July there were 35,000 Union troops massed just south of Washington, around Alexandria. They were headed by an officer in the Regular Army, Major General Irvin McDowell, who had studied war both in America and in Europe. When he asked the President for more time to prepare, McDowell was told, "You are green, it is true; but *they* are green also." Responsible for blocking the Federal approach to the Confederate capital was a West Point classmate of McDowell's, Pierre Beauregard, the captor of Fort Sumter, who had deployed his army of 22,000 men along Bull Run, a stream near Manassas, about twenty-five miles southwest of Washington. Roughly fifty miles northwest of the Alexandria-Manassas arena, at the northern end of Virginia's Shenandoah Valley, two more forces faced each other: 18,000 Federals under General Robert Patterson, a veteran of the War of 1812, and about 11,000 Confederates led by small, slender, and dapper General Joseph E. Johnston, the grandnephew of Revolutionary War patriot Patrick Henry. Patterson had orders from Washington to keep Johnston occupied, and by no means to let him slip to Manassas to reinforce Beauregard.

McDowell's march from the Alexandria area through Confederate territory toward Bull Run was begun on July 16. Groups of Virginia residents, both whites and blacks, watched the army's progress through the farmlands and villages. Most of the whites were either incensed or alarmed. Some of the blacks saw the Federals as friends bringing them hope, while others were uncertain what the development meant for them. Many of the troops were three-month volunteers whose day of discharge was already near. Good spirits were general, and the air resounded with regimental band music, patriotic singing, and the repeated cry "On to Richmond!" Accompanying the army—on foot, on horseback, and in a variety of carriages— were crowds of civilians, including women. Numerous senators and representatives had come along, and they had brought wagonloads of champagne to be drunk at a planned victory celebration. There were even civilians with tickets that someone had printed for a grand ball in Richmond. The weather was hot and the army moved slowly, taking two days to reach Centreville, where McDowell made his attack preparations, which took another two days. The time was well used by Confederate General Joe Johnston in the Shenandoah Valley. He managed to withdraw his troops from Robert Patterson's reach and start moving them, part of the way by

Richmond troops leaving for Bull Run

rail, to the Bull Run lines. Since he was senior to Beauregard, Johnston went there and assumed top command.

McDowell attacked from Centreville on the morning of Sunday, July 21, and at first the Confederates fell back. The Federals surged forward, with some of them shouting, "They're running! We'll hang Jeff Davis to a sour apple tree! The war is over!" Watching from hillsides north of Bull Run, the Union civilians clapped and cheered, and a woman said, "Isn't this a splendid battle? I suppose we'll be in Richmond by this time tomorrow." News of the success was telegraphed to Washington. The Confederates retreated up a slope to a plateau where General Thomas J. Jackson and his units were standing "like a stone wall," and there, under a blistering sun, the battle was joined in earnest. During four hours of waxing and waning gunfire, of charges and countercharges, of confusion and disorganization, and of ever-increasing casualties, the advantage seesawed from one army to the other. By three o'clock in the afternoon both sides were exhausted and the issue was still unsettled. Then fresh Confederate forces, some of them from the Shenandoah Valley, circled to McDowell's right flank and charged in shooting and giving the "rebel yell."

The Union troops, McDowell was appalled to note, began "to break and retire down the hillside. This soon degenerated into disorder for which there was no remedy." Within minutes, according to another observer, the slopes "were swarming with our retreating and disorganized forces, while riderless horses and artillery teams ran furiously through the flying crowd. All further efforts were futile. The words, gestures, and threats of our officers were thrown away upon men who had lost all presence of mind, and only longed for absence of body." A correspondent for the New York *Tribune* was amazed by the fact that "all sense of manhood seemed to be forgotten. . . . Every impediment to flight was cast aside. Rifles, bayonets, pistols, haversacks, cartridge-boxes, canteens, blankets, belts, and overcoats lined the road." The "road" was the Warrenton Turnpike, which became the main route of retreat, the troops heading back toward Centreville. The civilian observers, confounded by the reversal, came down from their hillsides and joined the rush. "Who ever saw such a flight?" asked the correspondent of the New York *World*. "It did not slack in the least until Centreville was reached." The Confederates, their own ranks disorganized, made only a limited pursuit.

Back in Washington, the people were still celebrating the earlier news when, at five o'clock that Sunday afternoon, a shocking telegram arrived: "General McDowell's army in full retreat through Centreville. The day is lost." By midnight the fugitives on horseback or in wagons or carriages began reaching the capital; and the next day, under gray and soggy skies, the thousands on foot trudged in. Drenched, worn out, hungry and dejected, the men had no quarters to seek for shelter, no kitchens to serve them ra-

Joseph E. Johnston

tions. So recently the hope of their country, they had been reduced to the status of tramps. The people of Washington rose to the emergency by opening their homes and piling their tables with food.

Nearly 3,000 casualties—killed, wounded, captured, or missing—had been inflicted on the Union army, at a cost of about 2,000 to the Confederates. As word of the disaster swept the North, the people were at first incredulous, then seized by mortification and disappointment. In the South, the joy was profound, but it was expressed not so much by wild celebrations as by special thanksgiving services in the churches. Whereas many Southerners believed that the victory had decided the war, others were not so sure. Judith McGuire wrote in her diary: "It is true that we have slaughtered them, and whipped them, and driven them from our land, but they are people of such indomitable perseverance that I am afraid that they will come again, perhaps in greater force."

Soon after making his first call for volunteers, President Lincoln had foreseen the need for a more substantial volunteer army based on longer enlistments and had issued a proclamation launching such an effort. At the same time, the Regular Army had begun enlisting at an increased pace. Thus the Union's strength was not substantially hurt by the Bull Run debacle and the disbandment of the three-month troops. Congress now legalized the President's new expedient, with its enlistment period of three years or the duration of the war, and authorized an army of 500,000 men.

Irvin McDowell stepped down as commander of the segment that would soon become known as the "Army of the Potomac" without widespread public censure, for it was realized he was not so much a failure as a victim of circumstances. "The Bull Run experiment," explains William Swinton, a newsman who covered the army's campaigns and wrote a perceptive history of them, "taught the country it was a real war it had undertaken, and that success could only be hoped for by a strict conformity to military principles. . . . The crisis was one fitted to test the mettle of the nation, for had it then shown the least supineness or hesitation, its doom had been sealed. . . . What the country *could* give—men, material, money—*that* it gave lavishly . . . but what it could not give was precisely what was most urgently needed to vitalize these sinews of war—to wit, adequate leadership . . . that soul of armies, the mind of a great commander. For this the nation, keenly alive to its need, could only breathe passionate aspirations."

There was one celebrated Army hero in the North in the summer of 1861, the commander-in-chief of the armies himself, Lieutenant General Winfield Scott. Although a Virginian by birth, Scott was a Unionist. Unfortunately, the great man was a relic of the past. Born in 1786, he was older than the capital. Scott won national acclaim as early as the War of 1812. Then a brigade commander, he helped to best the British at Chippewa and Lundy's Lane. He was active in the Indian wars of the 1830s, and he led the

Irvin McDowell

army to victory in Mexico in 1847. He was defeated, however in a bid for the presidency in 1852. A public personage for nearly fifty years, Scott was now seventy-five and was obese and ailing. Once imposing in his gold-trimmed uniform and a stately figure on horseback, the general was lately unable to rise from the couch in his Washington office without help. His days of taking the field were over.

In this crisis of leadership, a name came both to the political and to the public mind. The Battle of Rich Mountain, western Virginia, occurred only ten days before Bull Run. Right up to the time the news of the calamity broke, George McClellan's triumph was the talk of the North. It was the first victory the Union had achieved, and its importance was greatly magnified.

McClellan's appointment with destiny was not really an appointment at all—it was a happenstance. Nonetheless, the thirty-four-year-old general gave every appearance of being ready for greatness. His credentials were impeccable. The child of a Philadelphia doctor, McClellan obtained his higher learning at the University of Pennsylvania and at West Point, where he graduated in 1846, second in a class of fifty-nine. During his years at the academy he became acquainted with many youths, both Northerners and Southerners, who were destined to play roles in the Civil War. An avid military student, McClellan was also something of a Renaissance man, his other interests including history, philosophy, art, literature, and ancient and modern languages. The sandy-haired second lieutenant was only of medium height but was well proportioned and uncommonly strong. He could bend a quarter with his thumb and first two fingers, and he could heave a 250-pound man above his head. He held deep religious convictions but did not proclaim them; was dynamic, charismatic, amiable, and good at making friends. If he had an obvious flaw, it was his greater than normal need for approval, which indicated, perhaps, that he was not as self-assured as he seemed.

McClellan had scarcely graduated from West Point and entered the engineer corps before he was on his way to Mexico with Scott's army. The youth served on the general's staff with Robert E. Lee, who was nearly twenty years his senior. Twice brevetted for gallantry, McClellan was named a first lieutenant after Contreras and Churubusco, and a captain after Chapultepec. For the next ten years he served as an engineer at various stations in the United States and its Western territories. In 1855, Jefferson Davis, then Secretary of War, appointed McClellan to a commission sent to study European military affairs, including the war in the Crimea, scene of the "Charge of the Light Brigade." McClellan was a captain of cavalry when in 1857 he quit the Army to become a railroad executive. Three years later he married Ellen Mary Marcy, a soldier's daughter, and settled in Cincinnati, Ohio, establishing himself in a real home for the first

George B. McClellan

time since he left Philadelphia for West Point. As president of the Eastern Division of the Ohio and Mississippi Railroad, he was earning $10,000 a year—a princely sum for the period—when Fort Sumter fell. Giving up his new and rewarding way of life at once, he became a major general of Ohio volunteers. The commission was soon converted to one in the Regular Army.

On May 3, with the war three weeks old, General Scott sent orders from his couch in Washington for McClellan to organize a Department of the Ohio, and this came to include the states of Ohio, Indiana, Illinois, a small part of western Pennsylvania, and the bulk of western Virginia. Soon commanding 20,000 men, McClellan established his headquarters at Cincinnati. His father-in-law, Major R. B. Marcy, joined his staff as paymaster. During one of McClellan's absences from his headquarters, a fellow veteran of the Mexican War who was now down on his luck as a civilian—a short, shabbily dressed fellow named Ulysses S. Grant—stopped in to ask if there was still a staff spot open, but he left when he learned that McClellan was out of town. Grant went west and secured command of a regiment of Illinois volunteers. Had he met with McClellan, Grant would doubtless have settled into a staff job and remained in the East, and his career must have turned out differently. The course of the war itself would have been altered. But this sort of thing is an old story. History is filled with trivial incidents of major consequence.

At the end of May, McClellan determined to drive the Confederate forces, about 5,000 in number, from western Virginia, the majority of whose citizens were Unionist. The Federal army left Cincinnati by rail. "At every station where we stopped," McClellan wrote his wife, "crowds had assembled to see the 'young general': gray-headed old men and women, mothers holding up their children to take my hand, girls, boys, all sorts, cheering and crying, 'God bless you!' " He added that at Chillicothe "the ladies had prepared a dinner, and I had to be trotted through. They gave me about twenty beautiful bouquets and almost killed me with kindness. . . . I could hear them say, 'He is our own general'; 'Look at him, how young he is'; 'He will thrash them'; 'He'll do,' etc., etc. ad infinitum."

McClellan was confident he had troops enough to complete his task, and told Ellen, "I think the danger has been greatly exaggerated, and anticipate little or no chance of winning laurels." When the army, after some strenuous marching in western Virginia, neared the Confederates at Rich Mountain, McClellan rode to the front and issued an address: "Soldiers! I have heard that there was danger here. I have come to place myself at your head and to share it with you. I fear now but one thing—that you will not find foemen worthy of your steel. I know that I can rely upon you."

The enemy was in two wings, and McClellan's superior forces routed both. The Confederates lost about 1,000 men in killed, wounded, and cap-

Winfield Scott

tured, while the Federals lost but a handful in killed and wounded. McClellan told his men they had "annihilated two armies" and sent glowing reports of the victory to Washington. General Scott wired back: "The general-in-chief, and what is more the cabinet, including the President, are charmed with your activity, valor, and consequent success." McClellan wrote his wife about Scott's message, adding, "I value that old man's praise very highly." Of equal value as an assist to McClellan's career was the praise he got from Northern newspapers. At this stage of the war, editors were desperate for heroes to glorify. Almost overnight, the victor at Rich Mountain became nothing less than the "Young Napoleon."

It was while McClellan was moving to consolidate his position in western Virginia that McDowell and Johnston met at Bull Run. McClellan explains: "The first telegram I received from General Scott . . . was to the effect that McDowell was gaining a great victory. . . . Then came a despatch not quite so favorable; finally a telegram stating that McDowell was utterly defeated. . . . On the next day, the 22nd of July, I received a despatch from the adjutant-general stating that the condition of public affairs rendered my immediate presence in Washington necessary. . . . Although the telegram . . . contained no mention of the purpose in view, it was easy, under the circumstances, to divine it."

2

McCLELLAN TAKES
COMMAND

McCLELLAN reached Washington late in the afternoon on Friday, July 26. "I called on General Scott that evening, and next morning reported to the adjutant-general, who instructed me to call upon the President, by whom I was received cordially." It was a meeting that renewed an old acquaintance. "Long before the war, when vice-president of the Illinois Central Railroad Company, I knew Mr. Lincoln, for he was one of the counsel of the company. More than once I have been with him in out-of-the-way county seats where some important case was being tried, and, in the lack of sleeping accommodations, have spent the night in front of a stove listening to the unceasing flow of anecdotes from his lips. He was never at a loss, and I could never quite make up my mind how many of them he had really heard before, and how many he invented on the spur of the moment. His stories were seldom refined, but were always to the point."

The morning meeting at the White House turned out as McClellan expected. "He . . . placed me in command of Washington and all the troops in its vicinity. He directed me to return to the White House at one o'clock to be present at a cabinet meeting. I called again on General Scott . . . and, after conversing with him for some time on the state of affairs, casually remarked that I must take my leave, as the President had desired me to attend a cabinet meeting at one o'clock. Upon this the general became quite indignant and said it was highly improper that I should receive such an invitation to his exclusion, and insisted upon keeping me until too late to attend the meeting. He then instructed me to ride around the city immediately and send stragglers back to their regiments. . . .

"After leaving the general I rode around the outskirts of the city on the Maryland side towards Tennallytown, Seventh Street, etc., and examined some of the camps, buy did not devote myself individually to the police

33

work of picking up drunken stragglers. I found no preparations whatever for defense. . . . Not a regiment was properly encamped, not a single avenue of approach guarded. All was chaos, and the streets, hotels, and barrooms were filled with drunken officers and men absent from their regiments without leave—a perfect pandemonium."

McClellan saw Lincoln that evening. "I explained . . . the cause of my apparent lack of courtesy, at which he seemed more amused than otherwise."

By the next morning McClellan was hard at work. "I . . . lost no time in acquainting myself with the situation and applying the proper remedies. . . . The first and most pressing demand upon me was the immediate safety of the capital and the government. This was provided for by at once exacting the most rigid discipline and order . . . by organizing permanent brigades under regular officers, and by placing the troops in good defensive positions. . . . I lost no time in acquiring an accurate knowledge of the ground in all directions, and by frequent visits to the troops made them personally acquainted with me, while I learned all about them, their condition and their needs, and thus soon succeeded in inspiring full confidence and a good morale in place of the lamentable state of affairs which existed on my arrival. Thus I passed long days in the saddle and my nights in the office—a very fatiguing life, but one which made my power felt everwhere and by everyone."

Clandestinely, McClellan organized an intelligence service led by Allan Pinkerton, a private detective he had known since his days as a railroad executive. Pinkerton explains: "I was to have such strength of force as I might require. My headquarters were for the time located in Washington. It was arranged that whenever the army moved I was to go forward with the general so that I might always be in close communication with him. My corps was to be continually occupied in procuring, from all possible sources, information regarding the strength, positions, and movements of the enemy." Pinkerton informed McClellan that he intended to assign his detectives to "entering the rebel lines and endeavoring to obtain accurate information of the nature of their defenses, the number of troops under their command at various points, etc. . . . I propose concentrating my entire detective force of *both sexes* into this work. . . . The assumption of disguises and characters by my operatives will be a very important item in itself."

As July closed, McClellan wrote his wife that he found himself in an extraordinary position. Everyone, from the President on down, was deferring to him. "By some strange operation of magic I seem to have become the power of the land." He told of a visit he paid to the Senate: "I . . . was quite overwhelmed by the congratulations I received and the respect with which I was treated. I suppose half a dozen of the oldest made the remark I am becoming so much used to, 'Why, how young you look, and yet an old soldier!' It seems to strike everybody that I am very young. They give me my way in everything, full swing and unbounded confidence. All tell me that I am held responsible for the fate of the nation, and that all its resources shall be placed at my disposal. . . . When I . . . found those old men flocking around me; when I afterwards stood in the library, looking over the Capitol of our great nation, and saw the crowd gathering around to stare at me, I began to feel how great the task committed to me. Oh! how sincerely I pray to God that I may be endowed with the wisdom and courage necessary to accomplish the work. Who would have thought, when we were married, that I should so soon be called upon to save my country?"

McClellan was constantly busy. Along with his hundreds of concerns in the camps and defensive works, he was obliged to consult with various government committees and to take the time for courteous conversation with the many prominent citizens who sought to make his acquaintance. After attending a state dinner honoring a number of foreign dignitaries, including Prince Napoleon, he complained to Ellen that he found the affair "rather tedious, as such things generally are." He met frequently with Lincoln and his cabinet, and wrote home on August 4: "I went in to the President's last evening with the old general leaning on me; I could see that many marked the contrast."

Scott was becoming a problem. He had his own views on how the army should be organized and how the war should be fought, and these views, many of which were rooted in the past, seldom agreed with McClellan's. Ellen was informed: "The old general always comes in the way. He understands nothing, appreciates nothing. . . . I have to fight my way against him. . . . Our ideas are so widely different that it is impossible for us to work together much longer." McClellan began bypassing the general-in-chief at every opportunity, which embittered him. Lincoln did what he could to salve the old man's pride, while McClellan justified himself with Ellen: "The people call upon me to save the country, and I cannot respect anything that is in the way."

He stated further: "I receive letter after letter, have conversation after conversation, calling on me to save the nation, alluding to the presidency, dictatorship, etc. As I hope one day to be united with you forever in heaven, I have no such aspiration. . . . I feel that God has placed a great work in my hands. I have not sought it. I know how weak I am, but I know that I mean to do right, and I believe that God will help me and give me the wisdom I do not possess. Pray for me, that I may be able to accomplish my task, the greatest, perhaps, that any poor, weak mortal ever had to do."

Although McClellan was a Democrat, he and Lincoln the Republican held similar views on the war's aims. Both wanted simply to end it, not to bring the South to its knees, not even to free the slaves. The President had no love for slavery but had campaigned on a platform that only opposed its expansion into new territories, and he had said at his inauguration: "I have no purpose, directly or indirectly, to interfere with the institution of slavery in the states where it exists. I believe I have no lawful right to do so, and I have no inclination to do so." Lincoln saw the problem of slavery as being far too complicated to attack head-on.

McClellan explained himself this way: "Soon after my arrival in Washington . . . I had several interviews with prominent abolitionists—of whom Senator [Charles] Sumner was one—on the subject of slavery. I invariably took the ground that I was thoroughly opposed to slavery, regarding it as a great evil . . . but that in my opinion no sweeping measure of emancipation should be carried out unless accompanied by arrangements providing for the new relations between employers and employed, carefully guarding the rights and interests of both. . . . Mr. Sumner replied—others also agreed with him—that such points did not concern us, and that all of that must be left to take care of itself.

"My reply was that no real statesman could ever contemplate so sweeping and serious a measure as sudden and general emancipation without looking to the future and providing for its consequences; that four and a half millions of uneducated slaves should not suddenly be manumitted without due precautions taken both to protect them and to guard against them. . . . My own view was that emancipation should be accomplished gradually, and that the Negroes should be fitted for it by certain preparatory steps in the way of education, recognition of the rights of family and marriage, prohibition against selling them without their own consent, the freedom of those born after a certain date, etc. . . .

"I recognized the fact that as the Confederate States had chosen to resort to the arbitrament of arms, they must abide by the logical consequences of the stern laws of war. But, as I always believed that we should fight to bring them back into the Union, and should treat them as members of the Union when so brought back, I held that it was a matter of sound policy to do nothing likely to render ultimate reconciliation and harmony impossible, unless such a course were imperative to secure military success."

McClellan proved to be a superb organizer, and his style won him the admiration and affection of the troops. They dubbed him "Little Mac" and cheered spontaneously when he appeared among them on his black charger. As he acknowledged their homage with a smile, a bow, and a twirl of his cap, the cheering intensified. Ellen was informed: "I can see every eye glisten." During their training exercises, the men often shattered the air with a new song that included the lines "McClellan's our leader, he's gallant and strong; for God and our country we're marching along!"

McClellan continued to pursue his organizational work with feverish energy, and he talked of taking the field "with all possible speed," but he was actually not eager to tangle with the enemy. Behind his image and his record was a man who was not a true warrior. It wasn't a matter of courage but of daring; he shrank from leading any venture involving the slightest risk of failure. He had no intention of proceeding against the South until he had amassed an army of prodigious power, and he had visions of using this machine not so much for fighting as for trying to maneuver the Confederates out of Richmond. Aside from wanting to save lives on both sides, McClellan believed that an early occupation of the Confederate capital might end the fighting everywhere, with the seceded states reentering the Union and the slavery issue returning to the halls of Congress for gradual resolution. The kind of campaign McClellan had in mind, however, required not only an elaborate buildup but also complicated planning, a perfect cooperation between the army's various components, and, from start to finish, the unflagging support of the administration.

The "all possible speed" announcement was as close as McClellan came to offering a timetable for his operations; and, to protect his budding plans both from enemy spies and from government officials who might want to meddle in them, he kept their specifics a secret. He assumed that Lincoln would allow him to proceed as he wished and to take whatever time he felt he needed. But even if the President had wanted to support McClellan unconditionally, he was not in a position to do so. McClellan was emerging as a favorite of the "peace party," and this stirred discontent in the Republican party's abolitionist wing, whose members wanted to see the South decisively beaten and the blacks promptly freed and turned into Republican voters. The abolitionists had a strong voice in the party, and they urged Lincoln to be firm with McClellan. The President was also answerable to the northern people in general, most of whom were impatient to see Bull Run avenged.

By the end of August, McClellan's army had grown to 75,000 men, and Washington was well fortified, with troops stationed on both sides of the Potomac. One of the officers on the Washington side was P. Regis de Trobriand, a French soldier of fortune who was presently serving as a colonel of New York volunteers. De Trobriand relates: "In the month of September, 1861, Washington was half city and half camp. The wide extent of vacant lots, where scarcely a house was to be seen, was occupied by the tents of the infantry, stretching like an outer girdle upon all the neighboring heights. There was artillery everywhere. The wagon trains were concentrated within a smaller radius. And, finally, the commissary department had its quarters in the center of the city, where the uniform was supreme." De Trobriand's regiment was encamped near the northwest border of the District of Columbia. "Our proximity to Washington, the good condition of the roads, the beauty of the landscape caused our camp to be the favorite resort of visitors. So we did not want for company. There were high officials, politicians, members of Congress or of the diplomatic corps, foreign officers

38

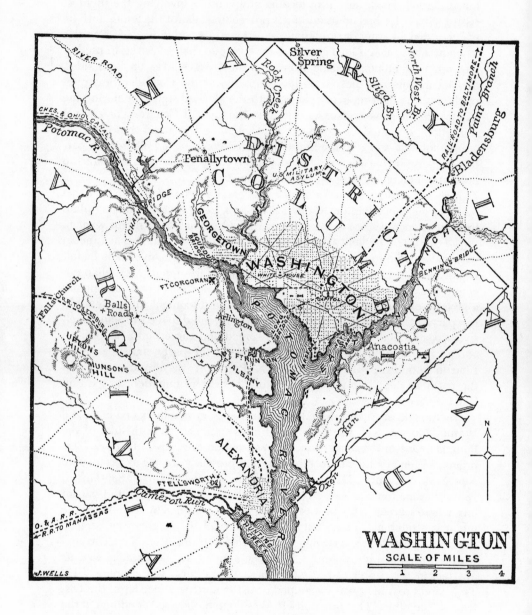

WASHINGTON

SCALE OF MILES

1   2   3   4

J. WELLS

come to offer their services or simply to study the formation of our army, newspaper correspondents, and all of them not infrequently accompanied by ladies curious to witness our drills or our reviews.

"It was altogether different [on the Virginia side] of the Potomac. . . . The bridges were guarded, and no one could cross them without a special permit. On that side, our line of defense formed an arc . . . resting its two extremities upon the river, one extremity at Alexandria, a few miles below Washington, the other covering Chain Bridge, a few miles above. It was composed of a chain of detached works, more important and better armed than the redoubts raised on the northern side of the river. These forts were on the summits of a series of heights presenting great natural advantages. . . . Within a nearer radius, other works were thrown up, defending the heights of Arlingrton, opposite the city and covering the bridgehead which protected Long Bridge.

"The estate of Arlington . . . belonged to General Robert E. Lee, of the Confederate army. . . . A great park, shaded by magnificent trees, surrounded the residence. . . . When I visited Arlington for the first time, the imprint of war had already altered its aspect. The dwelling of Lee had become the headquarters of General McDowell, now commanding a division in the army of which he had been general in chief. . . . The tents of the guard and of the servants of the staff were set up in the gardens, trampled over everywhere by men and animals. The park roads were deeply furrowed by the continual passage of artillery and ammunition wagons."

A knowledge of these things would not have disturbed Lee too much at this time, for he had other concerns. Jefferson Davis had taken him from his advisory desk in Richmond and sent him to supervise the troops in western Virginia who were trying to undo the effects of Federal victories there, including those achieved by McClellan. Plagued by hostility on the part of the region's many Northern sympathizers, by rugged mountains and muddy roads, by critical supply problems, by runaway sickness in the ranks, and by disharmony between two top commanders, Lee was failing. In the words of his chief aide, Walter H. Taylor, then a captain: "From the reputation which General Lee enjoyed, even at that [early] date, much was expected of him when he took the field. The difficulties of his situation were not properly estimated, and the press and people of Virginia became at first impatient and then indignant because the Federal army . . . was not immediately assailed by him and driven out of the state. . . . No one felt this public judgment so keenly as did General Lee; and yet, on one occasion when his attention had been directed to a fierce newspaper attack, as unjust in its conclusions as it was untrue in its statements, and he was asked why he silently suffered such unwarranted aspersions, he calmly replied that, while it was very hard to bear, it was perhaps quite natural that such hasty conclu-

Union camp on Virginia side of Potomac near Alexandria

sions should be announced, and that it was better not to attempt a justification or defense, but to go steadily on in the discharge of duty to the best of our ability, leaving all else to the calmer judgment of the future and to a kind Providence."

As for Arlington, General McClellan had issued orders against its despoliation, and against that of all other Confederate property in Virginia. But he was unable to give this matter much personal attention; he had too many other things on his mind. Among his leading concerns at this time was the enemy's strength. He believed that Confederate leader Joe Johnston and his second-in-command, Pierre Beauregard, headquartered at Manassas, had more than 100,000 men. Allan Pinkerton, analyzing the reports from his detectives, came up with this estimate; and McClellan, whose imagination had already embraced the idea that the enemy was becoming all-powerful, accepted the estimate as a true one. Actually, the Confederates numbered only about 40,000. They were strong only in audacity.

As reported by a Union newspaper correspondent, Charles Carleton Coffin, of the Boston *Journal:* "General Johnston pushed his troops almost up to General McClellan's lines, taking possession of Munson's Hill, which is only five miles from Long Bridge. . . . One bright September morning I rode to Bailey's Crossroads, which is about a mile from Munson's Hill. Looking across a cornfield, I could see the rebels behind their breastworks. Their battle flags were waving gayly. Their bayonets gleamed in the sunshine. A group of officers had gathered on the summit of the hill. With my fieldglass I could see what they were doing. They examined maps, looked towards Washington, and pointed out the position of the Union fortifications. There were ladies present, who looked earnestly towards the city and chatted merrily with the officers."

It is likely that one of the officers Coffin saw was James Ewell Brown Stuart, the twenty-eight-year-old cavalryman whose troops had taken Munson's from McClellan's pickets. Then a colonel, but in line for promotion to brigadier, Jeb Stuart was on his way to becoming one of the great personalities of the war. In the words of a subordinate officer: "Stuart was . . . rather above the middle height, of a most frank and winning expression . . . with a thick brown beard which flowed over his breast. His eye was quick and piercing, of a light blue in repose but changing to a darker tinge under high excitement. His whole person seemed instinct with vitality, his movements were alert, his observation keen and rapid, and altogether he was . . . the model of a dashing cavalry leader. Before the breaking out of hostilities between the North and South, he had served in the 1st United States Cavalry . . . against the Indians of the Far West, and was severely wounded in an encounter with the Cheyennes on the Solomon's Fork of the Kansas River in July, 1857. In that wild life of the Prairie, now chasing the buffalo, now pursuing the treacherous savage, Stuart had passed nearly all

Long Bridge over the Potomac

his waking hours in the saddle, and thus became one of the most fearless and dexterous horsemen in America, and he had acquired a love of adventure which made activity a necessity of his being. He delighted in the neighing of the charger and the clangor of the bugle, and he had something of [a] weakness for the vanities of military parade. He betrayed this latter quality in his jaunty uniform, which consisted of a small grey jacket, trousers of the same stuff, and over them high military boots, a yellow silk sash, and a grey slouch hat, surmounted by a sweeping black ostrich plume. Thus attired, sitting gracefully on his fine horse, he did not fail to attract the notice and admiration of all who saw him."

Among the Confederate infantrymen stationed near Munson's was Private Jesse W. Reid, a South Carolinian, who related in a letter to his family: "This morning I went out to the furthest point occupied by our troops . . . and there I could easily see all creation. I could see Washington City and Alexandria; at the latter could see a United States flag as high as Trinity monument; also partially see Arlington Heights. . . . Could see the enemy's position better perhaps than they could see ours from their [observation] balloon. The Potomac River is literally covered with vessels, the masts of some of them extending up considerably nearer Heaven, I fear, than the occupants of the vessels will ever be. While I was there I saw a balloon go up three times at Washington City. Suppose it went up to see what we were doing. Could see their line of tents for miles up and down the river. It was really a beautiful sight." Reid said in another letter: "The two armies are close together, and could go to fighting at any time; but it seems that each party dreads to attack the other party, and well they may; for let the attack be made by whom it may, somebody will get hurt, for I have found out long ago that the other party is about as good fighting stock as we are. We are all chips of the old block."

In overall charge of the Confederate units thrust so far forward by Joe Johnston was General James Longstreet, who was six feet two inches tall, broad-chested and well over 200 pounds in weight, had cool blue eyes and a thick brown beard, and was known for his calm demeanor, whatever the circumstances. "We were provokingly near Washington," states Longstreet, "with orders not to attempt to advance even to Alexandria. . . . We had frequent little brushes with parties pushed out to reconnoiter. Nevertheless, we were neither so busy nor so hostile as to prevent the reception of a cordial invitation to a dinner party on the other side, to be given to me at the headquarters of General [Israel B.] Richardson. He was disappointed when I refused to accept this amenity and advised him to be more careful lest the politicians should have him arrested for giving aid and comfort to the enemy. He was my singularly devoted friend and admirer before the war, and had not ceased to be conscious of old-time ties."

In Richmond at this time, according to Sallie Putnam, the people were

Confederate flag on Munson's Hill as seen from Bailey's Crossroads

generally optimistic about the military situation but were not without their concerns. The city had doubled in population and "was flooded with pernicious characters. . . . Speculators, gamblers, and bad characters of every grade flocked to the capital, and with a lawlessness which for a time bade defiance to authority pursued the rounds of their wicked professions. . . . Thieving, garrotting, and murdering were the nightly employments of the villains who prowled around the city. . . . Every man who then made his appearance in the rebel capital was by no means inspired by a patriotic principle. . . . Many were there for the sole purpose of subserving their own selfish and wicked ends. . . . Spies were there who for gold were ready at any moment to deliver the city into the hands of our enemies. . . .

"Richmond had already become a 'city of refuge.' Flying before the face of the invader, thousands sought within its hospitable walls that security they could not hope to receive in exposed and isolated places. Tales of suffering were even then the theme of thousands of tongues, as the homeless and destitute crowded into our city. . . . Richmond was taxed to the utmost extent of her capacity to take care of the surplus population. . . .

"From the extraordinary influx of population, and the existence of the blockade which prevented the importation of supplies in proportion to the demand, we were compelled to submit to the vilest extortions by which any people were ever oppressed. It was first observed in the increased prices placed upon goods of domestic manufacture. Cotton and woolen fabrics soon brought double prices. . . . The same fact was observable in regard to imported articles of food. The extraordinary increase in price was first noticeable in that demanded for coffee. An old lady, one of the most famous of the many distinguished housewives of Virginia, in great astonishment said in August, 1861: 'Only think! Coffee is now thirty cents per pound, and my grocer tells me I must buy at once, or very soon we shall have to pay double that price. Shameful! Why, even in the War of 1812 we had not to pay higher than sixty cents. And now, so soon! We must do without it, except when needed for the sick. . . .'

"Could this conscientious economist then have foreseen the cost of the berry for her favorite beverage at fifty dollars per pound, she would not grudgingly have paid the grocer his exorbitant demand of fifty cents. . . .

"With an admirable adaptation to the disagreeable and inconvenient circumstances entailed upon us by the blockade, the necessary self-denial practiced by the people was in a spirit of cheerful acquiescence and with a philosophical satisfaction and contentment that forgot the present in a hopeful looking for better and brighter days in the future. . . . The people were buoyed up with the hope and belief that their sufferings would be of short duration and that an honorable independence and exemption from the evils which surrounded them would soon compensate amply for the self-denial they were called upon to practice."

James Longstreet

Richmond's anticipation of a short war was not shared by Joe Johnston. "About the 20th of the month [of September] I became convinced that the increasing strength and efficiency of the Federal army were rendering the position of the outposts at Munson's and Mason's Hills more hazardous daily, and therefore had them withdrawn. We had been hoping, since the battle of Manassas, that the effective strength of the army would be so increased as to justify us in assuming the offensive. If such a change in policy was to be adopted, there was no time to lose, for the end of the season for active operations was near." Johnston and his top officers met with Jefferson Davis to request an expansion of the army, but were disappointed. "The President replied that no such reinforcements as we asked for could be furnished . . . that the whole country was applying for arms and troops; that he could take none from other points. . . . This, of course, decided the question of active operations *then*."

The Confederates, however, were not wholly unoccupied. They harassed Federal navigation of the lower Potomac by means of artillery batteries emplaced at several points along the Virginia bank. "So successfully was this work performed," admits Union newsman-historian William Swinton, "that early in October the flag officer of the Potomac flotilla officially reported the water highway by which a large part of the supplies for the army around Washington was brought forward from the North to be effectually closed. This event, the actual blockade of the capital, produced throughout the country a deep feeling of mortification and humiliation, and called forth bitter complaints against the Government. . . . [McClellan] was unwilling to undertake the destruction of the batteries by the only method that promised success—to wit, a movement by the right bank of the Potomac—for the reason that it would bring on a general engagement."

McClellan continued to concentrate upon building his army. As recounted by the French colonel of volunteers, Regis de Trobriand: "The first occasion which was offered to me to appreciate, with any correctness, what progress the organization of the army had already made was a grand review of the cavalry and artillery by General McClellan. It took place . . . in the field east of Washington, behind the Capitol. . . . The weather was magnificent. The people thronged upon the drill grounds and admired, without reserve, nine batteries of artillery, each having six pieces, fifty-four guns of different models, mostly new, everything in perfect order. The men appeared . . . irreproachable in bearing. Three thousand cavalry were in line, well dressed, not so well mounted, betraying their inexperience in the formation in column, and defiling.

"Quite a large number of superior officers had obtained permission to witness the review. . . . Amidst these uniforms . . . three horsemen in civil dress naturally drew to themselves the attention of all. These three . . . were the Prince de Joinville and his two nephews, the Comte de Paris and the

Duke de Chartres, scions of a dethroned royalty. The ... princes came to offer their services to the Federal Government. ...

"At this review ... there was seen a very simple open carriage mingling on terms of democratic equality with the other carriages loaded with spectators. ... It carried Mr. Lincoln and his family. It was to be observed that the eyes of the people were not upon the President of the Republic. The man upon whom more than upon any other depended the safety or the ruin of the country at that hour of supreme peril, upon whom weighed the highest responsibility, remained unnoticed in the crowd, except by those in his immediate vicinity, without guard and without attendants. All the attention was turned upon that young general with the calm eye, with the satisfied air, who moved around followed by an immense staff, to the clanking of sabers and the acclamations of the spectators."

As for the three Frenchmen, the "scions of a dethroned royalty," McClellan accepted them into his military family. The two younger men became captains, declining any higher rank. In McClellan's words: "They served precisely as the other aides, taking their full share of all duty. ... They were fine young fellows and good soldiers. ... Their uncle, the Prince de Joinville, who accompanied them as a mentor, held no official position, but our relations were always confidential and most agreeable. ... They had their separate establishment ... usually the jolliest in camp, and it was often a great relief to me, when burdened with care, to listen to the laughter and gaiety that resounded from their tents. ... The Prince de Joinville sketched admirably and possessed a most keen sense of the ridiculous, so that his sketchbook was an inexhaustible source of amusement. ... He was a man of far more than ordinary ability and and of excellent judgment. His deafness was, of course, a disadvantage to him, but his admirable qualities were so marked that I became warmly attached to him, as, in fact, I did to all the three, and I have good reason to know that the feeling was mutual."

McClellan held further reviews that autumn. "Each regiment," says newsman Charles Coffin, "tried to outdo all others in its appearance and its marching. They moved by companies past the President, bands playing national airs, the drums beating and the flags waving. ... The ground shook beneath the steady marching of the great mass of men and the tread of thousands of hoofs."

Many Northerners felt it was time McClellan's grand army began to shake the ground around Richmond. According to George Wilkes, a newsman from New York City: "Everybody wondered what could be his plan, but still they did not question his ability; and even half-misgiving minds kept hurrahing for him to their neighbors, like the schoolboy in the churchyard, to sustain their own waning faith. We, among the rest, suspecting all objection to him as disloyal, helped to domineer down the grumblers, and insisted that in due time his intentions would be wisely developed to the nation."

McClellan felt he needed more troops, more equipment, and more time to organize and train. Suggestions from government officials that he begin active operations made him angry. "I am becoming daily more disgusted with this administration," he wrote his wife. In another letter, he told her: "When I returned yesterday after a long ride, I was obliged to attend a meeting of the cabinet at eight P.M., and was bored and annoyed. There are some of the greatest geese in the cabinet I have ever seen—enough to tax the patience of Job." Lincoln, however, with his many pertinent and amusing anecdotes, was "a rare bird" who could be viewed with toleration. "The President is honest and means well."

In his memoirs, McClellan recorded: "The President . . . often came to my house, frequently late at night, to learn the last news before retiring. . . . Late one night when he was at my house I received a telegram from an officer commanding a regiment on the upper Potomac. The dispatch related some very desperate fighting [with a Confederate detachment] that had been done during the day, describing in magniloquent terms the severe nature of the contest, fierce bayonet charges, etc., and terminated with a very small list of killed and wounded, quite out of proportion with his description of the struggle.

"The President quietly listened to my reading of the telegram, and then said that it reminded him of a notorious liar who attained such a reputation as an exaggerator that he finally instructed his servant to stop him when his tongue was running away too rapidly, by pulling his coat or touching his feet. One day the master was relating wonders he had seen in Europe, and described a building which was about a mile long and a half mile high. Just then the servant's heel came down on the narrator's toes, and he stopped abruptly. One of the listeners asked how broad this remarkable building might be. The narrator modestly replied, 'about a foot.'

"I think he enjoyed these things quite as much as his listeners." The funny stories notwithstanding, McClellan at length became impatient with the President's repeated visits, sometimes keeping him waiting while he transacted business with others, and sometimes even finding ways to dodge him. This discourtesy did not escape the notice of the press. Said Lincoln: "I will hold McClellan's horse if he will only bring us success."

Although Joe Johnston had removed his outposts overlooking Washington, he had kept his main army at Fairfax Court House, about fifteen miles from the capital. Now he began to worry about his security. "The semi-circular course of the Potomac, and roads converging from different points on it to our position, made it easy for the Federal army to turn either of our flanks without exposing its own communications. As that great army became capable of maneuvering, the position of ours, of course, became more hazardous. On the 19th of October, therefore, it was drawn back to Centre-ville—a position much stronger in front, as well as less easily and safely turned."

Some 1,700 Confederate troops lingered at Leesburg, on the Virginia side of the Potomac about thirty miles northwest of Washington. McClellan felt that a "slight demonstration" against this detachment might send it packing. Advancing too boldly, the Federals involved in the mission precip-itated the Battle of Ball's Bluff (October 21) and were thrown back with heavy losses. Lincoln received the news by telegraph at McClellan's head-quarters. Included in the message was that Colonel Edward D. Baker, a member of the Senate and one of Lincoln's oldest and closest friends, had been killed. Newsman Charles Coffin, who was present when the news ar-rived, says that the President left the building unattended, with his head bowed and with tears streaming down his cheeks. "His hands were clasped upon his heart; he walked with a shuffling, tottering gait, reeling as if be-neath a staggering blow. He did not fall, but passed down the street, carry-ing not only the burden of the nation but a load of private grief which, with the swiftness of the lightning's flash, had been hurled upon him."

The Lincoln of October 1861 was not the Lincoln of legend. Still in the first year of his presidency, the awkward lawyer from Illinois was feeling his way, his grip on the war effort tentative. In a letter written by the Reverend A. M. Stewart, chaplain of the 102nd Pennsylvania Volunteers, Lincoln was rated thus: "Give the President all honor for being an honest man and a *good* president, but a *great* one he is not, nor does it seem likely that he will prove himself such. He has proved himself merely capable of honestly fol-lowing the beatings of the great Northern heart as they became manifest. Never has he said or done aught betokening the great leader—nothing to show himself capable either of originating a grand, new thought or scheme, and boldly carrying it out. Beyond all question or cavil, the President, with his generals, has the constitutional power . . . to proclaim liberty to all the inhabitants of the land at once. . . . By such a proceeding only is the present war about to be successfully ended, with the hope, at the same time, of a permanent peace. . . . Still the nation hesitates to give the decisive word or strike the fatal blow.

"Let us not, however, be over-anxious. It may be that, notwithstanding our uneasiness, things are moving in the right direction and at the right pace. It is not usual that the sentiments of a great nation on any moral question are changed in a day. A deep-seated opposition to the emancipa-tion of the slave has, no doubt, long pervaded the masses of our Northern people. The President and our generals may be right in thus moving with hesitation. The time may not yet have come for decisive action. The masses of our people—the great army now marshalled for battle—may not be suf-ficiently educated or prepared joyfully to receive a proclamation for universal emancipation. Such a course now might, perhaps, create an opposition among ourselves. Let us wait. A few more . . . defeats . . . will fully pave the way and open the eyes of all the people."

On November 1, McClellan succeeded Winfield Scott as commander-in-chief of the Union armies. Coming to terms with McClellan's ascendancy, his bitterness diminished, Scott had requested retirement. Chaplain Stewart was one of the witnesses to Scott's departure from Washington by rail. Stewart and a few friends had made it a point to be at the depot very early on the rainy and blustery morning of November 2. The group found the old general, for the moment, "almost alone" in a small side room. "We wished him God's blessing on his present journey, as well as the remainder of his pilgrimage. 'I need it much,' was the unaffected reply, 'for I am a great sinner, and have been one all my life.'

"The manner in which these words were uttered so affected each one present that no response was attempted. All were silent. Yet but for a moment. A bustle was heard at the door: the entrance of General McClellan and his staff, with all the generals of the army conveniently in reach, together with several members of the cabinet. With heads uncovered and reverent bearing, each one approached and successively greeted the worn-out giant, who, meantime, remained seated, being unable to rise without assistance. When all had paid their respects, General McClellan again drew near, as though to receive the falling mantle from the retiring commander. The old general took his hand and uttered, in the kindest and most affectionate manner, language to this effect: 'General, allow not yourself to be embarrassed by ignorant men. Follow your own judgment. Carry out your own ideas, and you will conquer. God bless you.'

"Equally brief and touching was the response of the young chieftain, upon whom the mantle of the great old man was now falling: 'Thank you, General. I will remember your counsel. May your health improve and you live to see your country again united and prosperous. God's blessing accompany you. Farewell!' The train was ready. Two assistants aided the old man to rise. As he and the young general walked side by side and in silence out to the cars, the contrast was most striking. The one appeared as a giant, the other as a little boy."

McClellan informed his wife: "He was very polite to me; sent various kind messages to you and the baby. So we parted. The old man said that his sensations were very peculiar in leaving Washington and active life. I can easily understand them; and it may be that at some distant day I, too, shall totter away from Washington, a worn-out soldier, with naught to do but make my peace with God. The sight of this morning was a lesson to me which I hope not soon to forget. I saw there the end of a long, active, and ambitious life, the end of the career of the first soldier of his nation; and it was a feeble old man scarce able to walk. . . . Should I ever become vainglorious and ambitious, remind me of that spectacle. I pray every night and every morning that I may become neither vain nor ambitious, that I may be neither depressed by disaster nor elated by success, and that I may keep one single object in view—the good of my country. At last I am 'the major general commanding the army.' I do not feel in the least elated, for I do feel the responsibility of the position. And I feel the need of some support. I trust that God will aid me."

By this time McClellan had 150,000 well-organized troops in his Grand Army of the Potomac. He was convinced that "the creation of such an army in so short a time from nothing will hereafter be regarded as one of the highest glories of the administration and the nation." The Prince de Joinville adds: "Never, we believe, has any nation created, of herself, by her own will, by her single resources, without coercion of any kind, without government pressure, and in such a short space of time, so considerable an armament. Free governments, whatever may be their faults and the excesses to which they may give rise, always preserve an elasticity and creative power which nothing can equal." William Swinton gives all due credit to McClellan: "If the Army of the Potomac afterwards performed deeds worthy to live in history, it is in no small degree due to the fact that the groundwork of victory was laid deep and broad in that early period of stern tutelage, when it learned the apprenticeship of war."

The army did not take the field in November. "I cannot move without more means," McClellan wrote his wife, "and I do not possess the power to control those means. . . . I am doing all I can to get ready to move before winter sets in, but it now begins to look as if we were condemned to a winter of inactivity. . . . I have one great comfort in all this—that is that I did not seek this position."

Swinton says that "General McClellan showed himself deficient in certain qualities of mind indispensable for one who has to deal with the larger questions of war. If, as a soldier, he was right in wishing to postpone grand military operations till spring, when the times and seasons and circumstances should all favor; when his army, strengthened in numbers and tempered by discipline, would be fit for the field . . . he certainly showed a lack of that kind of political *savoir faire* and knowledge of human nature necessary to a great commander, in remaining perfectly inactive. It was for him to consider whether the increase in numbers and improvements in discipline likely to accrue to his army in the meantime would at all compensate for that loss of confidence, that popular impatience, that political obstruction, which were certain to arise, and which actually did arise. For so soon as the period of reorganization had passed, the public and the Administration became naturally anxious to see the imposing army . . . that had grown up on the banks of the Potomac turned to some account. And this anxiety presently grew into an impatience, which at length broke out in loud

Inspection reveals Army of the Potomac to be shaping up

clamor that at once embarrassed the government and marred the harmonious relations between it and the commander of the army."

Dissatisfaction with McClellan's inertia was heightened by the fact that sickness had become rife in his camps. In mid-November, Chaplain Stewart wrote home: "On Tuesday, the 12th, as the sun was setting, we buried one of our dear young soldiers. We laid him in a lonely grave within a desolate old churchyard, where already lie, side by side, eighteen of our volunteer soldiers out of the various regiments which, for the past months, have camped in this vicinity. Not half the graves have even a board at the head. . . . Forgotten already! Such is the glory of war. Buried far from home and friends, with no tears to moisten the grave. . . . Our young soldier died of camp fever. . . . Already, perhaps, have more of our volunteers died from camp fever on the line of the Potomac than fell at Bull's Run and Ball's Bluff together."

November found official Washington agitated over the "Trent Affair." Two commissioners appointed by the Confederacy to represent its interests in England and France, having slipped through the blockade, were taken from the British mail steamer *Trent* on the high seas by a Union sloop of war. At first the North rejoiced over the capture, but England protested menacingly over this violation of her neutrality. McClellan wrote Ellen on Sunday, November 17: "I find that today is not to be a day of rest for me. This unfortunate affair of Mason and Slidell has come up, and I shall be obliged to devote the day to endeavoring to get our government to take the only prompt and honorable course of avoiding a war with England and France." The two commissioners were released to continue their journey. In the South, this was not viewed as a triumph. "The concession," states Richmond newspaper editor and historian Edward Pollard, "was a blow to the hopes of the Southern people. The . . . spectacle of their enemy's humiliation . . . was but little compensation for their disappointment of a European complication in the war."

A visitor to the Washington camps in late autumn was Julia Ward Howe of Boston, a poet and a staunch abolitionist. To her, the Union cause was nothing less than a holy one. She was thrilled by the sight of the nightly campfires, and her ears were caught by the stirring tune, originally a revival hymn, to which the soldiers sang, "John Brown's body lies a-mouldering in the grave." Urged by a friend to provide the tune with a better set of words, she wrote a poem that began, "Mine eyes have seen the glory of the coming of the Lord." Thus was born the mighty "Battle Hymn of the Republic."

By this time the twenty-mile arc of troops on the Virginia side of the Potomac had taken a further toll of the region's assets. According to F. Colburn Adams, a cavalry officer with General William B. Franklin's division, who was stationed near Fairfax Seminary: "War was writing a new and dark chapter of history on this, the fairest portion of Virginia. . . . Land-

Old Virginia estate in Washington area before its destruction by Federals. Property became part of a line of fortifications. Trees were used to make breastworks.

marks of all kinds were disappearing, fields were no longer carpeted with green—the iron hoof of war had tramped their surface into bald clay. Rude hands were destroying the dark cedar hedgerows, gardens, orchards, and even the oak forests. And much of this was done in sheer wantonness. Even the fine old shade trees, with their broad embracing branches, giving such a picturesqueness to the lawns, were being cut down and made fuel for campfires. . . . But even this desolation, as seen on the surface of the country, was not the worst punishment war was afflicting the people with. That was to be found in the almost daily acts of high-handed robbery of the private property of citizens, many of whom had had no hand whatever in the rebellion. . . . And I regret to say that some of the very worst cases of plundering on record were committed either by men in the uniform of officers, or by those who would share with them the ill-gotten gains.

"Posterity will yet do justice to Generals McClellan and Franklin for their efforts to protect private property while in the enemy's country. But even their more stringent measures to prevent plundering failed to save the helpless citizens from the acts of the mercenary wretches who had connected themselves with our army only to disgrace it, and to make enemies of men whom kindness and protection would have turned into true and substantial friends. . . . Fairfax Seminary was plundered of its valuable library, of its works of art, of its scientific and musical instruments, of its furniture, and, indeed, everything of value found within its walls. There was nothing sacred to the despoilers. Even the wardrobes of the professors, who had left with the expectation of returning soon, did not escape the fingers of the mercenary wretches. . . .

"Private houses shared the same fate. Some of these had been left in charge of housekeepers or perhaps a few old servants. This afforded an excuse to some of the field officers of our division for taking 'military possession' of them and setting up an elegant headquarters. It was not infrequently said that the object of this 'military possession' was to protect the property from injury by the soldiers. But I invariably noticed that . . . but a few weeks would pass after these gentlemen had set up their elegant headquarters when the books, pictures, furniture, and even those little treasures so dear to [families] would mysteriously disappear, and there would be nothing left but the blank walls."

As for the main body of the Confederate army, it had been fortifying at Centerville. On November 18, Private Jesse Reid of South Carolina wrote his family: "If Abraham . . . undertakes to drive us out, he will find it harder work than splitting rails. When our lines are fully established, they will be about twenty-five miles long; and this is the place most likely to be attacked, as it is on the main turnpike road, the only one over which heavy artillery could be brought at this season of the year. . . . We are now in plain view of the mountains, which are covered with snow. It was snowing there the whole night before last and all day yesterday, and it still keeps up. A stormy wind is blowing, and a colder day I never saw or want to see. It is a bad time in camp; every man is wrapped up in blankets and handkerchiefs (or shirttails) tied around their jaws and ears. And this is only the beginning of winter. While sitting in my tent writing this letter, my fingers are stiff with cold. My nasty cold nose keeps dropping, and the blots nearly freeze before I can wipe them off the paper. . . . Yesterday, while no one was in the tent, a coal [from our] fire blew into our baggage and burnt a hole in the narrative of my broadcloth coat. It also burnt holes in several other garments unnecessary to mention. So far as my smoked eyes can see there are nothing but tents and encampments. We are some ten miles from Manassas Junction, three miles from our old battlefield and some twenty-five miles from Washington city."

Reid wrote on November 24: "Our officers still persist in saying that we will have a fight soon, but I see no more prospect of it now than I did two months ago. My private opinion is that we will do nothing more than a little skirmishing before next spring." November 26: "We had a big time here yesterday, and all the troops were called out and reviewed by General Beauregard." November 28: "The biggest day yet. This morning at 10:30 o'clock everybody and the cook was called out, and each regiment was presented with a battle flag. General Beauregard was again present and so was everybody else. It was the grandest time we ever had. We were told that the flags were made and sent to us by our wives, mothers, and sisters, with an order from them to defend them. We will most assuredly obey that order. We were drawn up in a hollow square and several speeches were made. There were several bands of music on hand, and, as each regiment filed off toward their quarters, every band struck up 'Pop Goes the Weasel.' I have never heard or seen such a time before. The noise of the men was deafening. I felt at the time that I could whip a whole brigade of the enemy myself, but after due reflection I concluded that I couldn't." November 30: "Another big day today. General Johnston was present this time. We had a big muster. Our line was three-fourths of a mile long. We are to have an inspection of arms tomorrow at 10 o'clock. . . . There are one or more buried here every day. . . . The mountains are again covered with snow, and if we have to remain in these old tents all winter it will hurt us worse than the Federal army. My captain, A. T. Broyles, and a man named Rochester, of my company, were sent off to the hospital today. There is another one too sick to be carried off. He will die."

Similar concerns about shelter afflicted the Federals. "As damps, chills, snows, and cold increased apace," explains Chaplain Stewart, "and no orders for marching, fighting, or building came—the tents moreover presenting such seeming inadequate shelter—our boys became uneasy and fidgety. Young America is, however, not easily cast down, slow to put on a

Union army in winter quarters

long face, full of expedients; and possessing, moreover, a marvellous facility for adaptation. Matters were duly discussed and weighed. . . . On their own hook, it was determined to prepare winter quarters . . . and charge Uncle Sam nothing for the job. . . . Without asking leave of Uncle Abe, General McClellan, Congress, or even the owner of the wood, [a] beautiful young grove was speedily invaded, axe in hand, by hundreds of sturdy assailants. The poetry of 'Woodman, spare that tree' had no power to save. . . . The whole pine grove seemed to be in motion towards our camp. . . .

"The model pattern of structure is after this fashion. A log cabin about seven feet square, just the size of the tent, is erected about four feet high. On the top of this, the tent is set and securely fastened down. . . . The openings between the logs are chinked . . . with mortar made from the red siliceous earth beneath our encampment, with the addition of a little straw . . . in order to give consistence. In most, a regular cabin door is made. . . . To some, the entrance is effected by climbing over the four feet wall. . . . Some have procured small sheet iron stoves. The larger portion, however, have followed the model of the pioneer, having an outside chimney constructed of clay, straw and sticks. A few, despising all this effeminacy, are braving the changes of weather without any place for fire. Think of five grown men wintering in such a little pen!"

According to a Union color sergeant named D. G. Crotty: "Winter life in camp is very weary, as it is but one routine over and over again—reveille in the morning, breakfast call, sick call, guard mount call, drill call, dinner call (which is the best of all the calls), the battalion or brigade drill call . . . dress parade call, supper call, roll call, and taps—which means lights out and cover up in blankets. All this is gone through day after day. . . . But we are to have something by way of a change, and the order comes to be ready to march on a reconnaissance in force, to feel of the enemy and try to find out where he is. . . . Accordingly on Christmas we take up our line of march, pass through the picket lines, and halt in front of an old church on the crest of a hill, where we have a beautiful view of the country for miles around. Our commander, General [Samuel P.] Heintzelman, takes a ride out on the crest of the hill, peers through his field glass, but no rebel is in sight. So, of course, nothing is left but to get back to camp."

Even while this return march was in progress, South Carolinian Jesse Reid was writing in a letter to his family: "Well, Christmas is here. . . . In spite of . . . Law and Gospel, most of the boys managed to get a wee drop today, but all has been very quiet—there being no more noise than three earthquakes and a cyclone, and that is nothing unusual here. For my part, I have not tasted a drop. One reason for it is that the stuff is too high, being five dollars a quart for the worst kind of 'rot skull.' Having drunk none myself, I will miss the supreme felicity of the blues and a headache."

Another account of Confederate activities on Christmas Day is given by

Georgia's John B. Gordon, then a major commanding a company of Alabamians: "My men were winter-quartered in the dense pine thickets on the rough hills that border the Occoquan [about twenty miles southwest of Washington]. Christmas . . . was to be made as joyous as our surroundings would permit by a genuine Southern eggnog with our friends. The country was scoured far and near for eggs, which were exceedingly scarce. Of sugar we still had at that time a reasonable supply, but our small store of eggs and other ingredients could not be increased in all the country round about. Mrs. Gordon superintended the preparation of this favorite Christmas beverage, and at last the delicious potion was ready. All stood anxiously waiting with camp cups in hand. The servant started toward the company with full and foaming bowl, holding it out before him with almost painful care. He had taken but a few steps when he struck his toe against the uneven floor of the rude quarters and stumbled. The scattered fragments of crockery and the aroma of the wasted nectar marked the melancholy wreck of our Christmas cheer."

In Richmond, according to Sallie Putnam, the week of the holidays was observed in a muted fashion. "The friendly congratulations of the season were followed by anxious inquiries for dear boys in the field, or husbands or fathers whose presence had ever brought brightness to the domestic hall, and whose footsteps were music to the hearts and ears of those to whom they were so dear. . . . New Year's day was bright, balmy, and beautiful as spring. The first day of the year has never been observed in Richmond as one of public reception for ladies and of visiting for gentlemen. The usual arrangements of the household under the regime of slavery would have forbidden such a custom. Christmas week was an undisputed holiday for our domestics. Those who owned their servants could not, by time-honored and regularly established usage, claim regular duties from them, and New Year's day usually found a Southern housewife altogether unprepared for entertaining friends. . . .

"It had been, however, from time almost immemorial, a custom with our Governors. Members of the Legislature, officials of the government, and any gentlemen who desired, were expected to pay their respects to his Excellency. . . . Governor Letcher received, as usual, on . . . the anniversary that ushered in the year 1862. His guests were welcomed with the broad, good-humored hospitality and dignified courtesy which ever distinguished this gallant son of Virginia. . . . As may be supposed, on this occasion Bacchus asserted his triumph over Mars, and the devotees at his convivial shrine were many of them oblivious . . . . to the sterner mandates of the God of War.

"The President of the Confederacy, for the first time since its existence . . . had his New Year's reception. The officers, civil, naval, and military, the members of Congress and the State Legislature, and admiring crowds of less note pressed forward to testify their admiration and esteem of the first President of the South. . . .

"As the year 1862 dawned upon us, it was not spanned by the rainbow-tinted arch of future happiness to us as a nation . . . but . . . Hope stood by, and with her syren song lulled the weary mind to repose as she pointed onward and whispered, 'Liberty!' "

3

———◆———

A PLAN BEGINS
TO FORM

IN WASHINGTON, the arrival of 1862 found General McClellan seriously ill with typhoid fever. He had not yet approached the President with a proposal for putting the Army of the Potomac into action. Secretly, however, he had been working on plans for flanking Johnston by transporting the army down the Chesapeake. By this time, according to William Howard Russell, correspondent for the London *Times*, Lincoln was a man to be pitied. He was "trying with all his might to understand strategy, naval warfare, big guns, the movements of troops, military maps, reconnaissances, occupations, interior and exterior lines, and all the technical details of the art of slaying. He runs from one house to another, armed with plans, papers, reports, recommendations, sometimes good-humored, never angry, occasionally dejected, and always a little fussy."

These were days when the perplexed Lincoln would have preferred to dispense with social contacts but was obliged to be host at traditional functions. In the words of the observant Frenchman Regis de Trobriand: "Never did a more elegant multitude crowd to the receptions at the White House. Everyone knows that on these occasions the democratic usage opens the doors to whosoever wishes to enter. A cruel trial for the President, forced, for an entire evening, to a painful hand-shaking with a multitude.... Mr. Lincoln, instantly recognized from his tall and spare form, stood near the entrance door of the first parlor, his two secretaries by his side, who gave him the names of the callers, which he repeated as well as possible in the inevitable form of salutation when he thought he had heard correctly. In vain would one, on these occasions, look on his bony face for a trace of the humor so well known by numerous anecdotes and sayings. One saw there only the strain of absorbing thought, struggling with a vulgar cermony. Inwardly a prey to the heaviest cares, bending under the burden of a formidable responsibility, he must smile on all as if he had really been 'charmed to see you.' The talk imposed on Mrs. Lincoln was much easier. Always dressed with elegance, a thing she enjoyed, surrounded by feminine attentions, she escaped the crowding of the multitude, sheltered by the trains of the dresses of her entourage. . . .

"In January, 1862, I had the honor to dine at the White House, where twenty guests were assembled. The conversation was varied by the observations of men who had had different careers. . . . Mr. Lincoln took no part in it. Neither the lively sallies of Mr. N. P. Willis [a noted author] nor the inciting remarks of some of the ladies could distract him from his interior reflections, or lighten the moral and physical fatigue to which he visibly yielded.

"It was at the time when public opinion, tired of the long inaction of the Army of the Potomac, began loudly to demand some revenge for the check of Ball's Bluff, and that measures be taken to reestablish the navigation of the river, impudently interrupted by the batteries of the enemy. . . . A direct pressure was made upon the President, whose anxiety was increased by the illness of General McClellan, with whom he could not come to an understanding."

Lincoln's concerns went beyond the stalemate with McClellan over the advance against Richmond. The North's strategy for victory included efforts to keep not only western Virginia but also the disputed border states of Kentucky and Missouri in the Union, and to gain control of the Mississippi River in order to cut the Confederacy in two. At the beginning of 1862, with the war nine months old, nothing in the picture looked very promising.

On January 10, General Irvin McDowell was having dinner at his headquarters in the Lee mansion when he received word that Lincoln wished to see him. "Repaired to the President's house at eight o'clock P.M. Found the President alone. Was taken into the small room in the northeast corner. Soon after, we were joined by Brigadier General Franklin, the Secretary of State . . . the Secretary of the Treasury, and the Assistant Secretary of War. The President was greatly disturbed at the state of affairs. Spoke of the exhausted condition of the treasury, of the loss of public credit . . . of the delicate condition of our foreign relations, of the bad news he had received from the West, particularly as contained in a letter from General [Henry W.] Halleck on the state of affairs in Missouri; of the want of cooperation between Generals Halleck and [Don Carlos] Buell; but more than all, the sickness of General McClellan. The President said he was in great distress, as he had been to General McClellan's house and the general did not ask to see him; and as he must talk to somebody, he had sent for General Franklin and myself to obtain our opinion as to the possibility of soon commencing active operations with the Army of the Potomac. To use his own expression, 'If something was not done soon, the bottom would be out of the whole affair; and if General McClellan did not want to use the army, he would like to *borrow* it, provided he could see how it could be made to do something.' "

The discussion that ensued was continued at similar meetings on succeeding days. "This information," explains McClellan, "reached me when the crisis of my malady was over. . . . I mustered strength enough on Sunday morning, January 12, 1862, to be driven to the White House, where my unexpected appearance caused very much the effect of a shell in a powder magazine. It was very clear from the manner of those I met there that there was something of which they were ashamed. . . . I took advantage of the situation to explain to the President in a general and casual way what my intentions were; and before I left he told me that there was to be a meeting at the White House next day, and invited me to attend." At the Monday meeting, Lincoln asked McClellan to reveal the specifics of his intentions. "To this I replied, in substance, that if the President had confidence in me it was not right or necessary to entrust my designs to the judgment of others, but that if his confidence was so slight as to require my opinions to be fortified by those of other persons it would be wiser to replace me by someone fully possessing his confidence; that no general commanding an army would willingly submit his plans to the judgment of such an assembly, in which some were incompetent to form a valuable opinion, and others incapable of keeping a secret, so that anything made known to them would soon spread over Washington and become known to the enemy. . . . I declined giving any further information to the meeting unless the President gave me the order in writing and assumed the responsibility of the results. This was probably an unexpected *d'nouement.* The President was not willing to assume the responsibility, and . . . the meeting adjourned. . . . I . . . walked up to the President, begged him not to allow himself to be acted upon by improper influences, but still to trust me, and said that if he would leave military affairs to me I would be responsible, that I would bring matters to a successful issue and free him from all his troubles."

McClellan, of course, considered himself to be superior to Lincoln in both intelligence and judgment. The general feared that the President, with his limited comprehensions, was falling under the spell of the abolitionists, who did not like McClellan's approach to the war, who wanted the Southern states crushed and not simply maneuvered into a position where they would be brought back into the Union with the slavery issue unsettled. Although McClellan was brilliant beyond question, he suffered, like many brilliant men, from a shortage of common sense. He did not realize that it was his own attitude toward taking action that was eroding Lincoln's support and fueling abolitionist power.

Mid-January saw a significant change in the President's cabinet. Edwin M. Stanton, who had served as Attorney General under the previous administration, replaced Simon Cameron as Secretary of War. Stanton was asthmatic yet tireless, power-hungry, crafty, arbitrary, irascible, a Democrat who shared at least one of the views of the radical Republicans: He wanted to see the war pursued vigorously. McClellan relates: "I had never seen Mr. Stanton . . . before reaching Washington in 1861. Not many weeks after arriving I was introduced to him as a safe adviser on legal points. From that moment he did his best to ingratiate himself with me, and professed the warmest friendship and devotion. I had no reason to suspect his sincerity, and therefore believed him to be what he professed. The most disagreeable thing about him was the extreme virulence with which he abused the President, the Administration, and the Republican Party. He carried this to such an extent that I was often shocked by it. He never spoke of the President in any other way than as the 'original gorilla.' . . .

"At some time during the autumn of 1861 Secretary Cameron made quite an abolition speech to some newly arrived regiment. Next day Stanton urged me to arrest him for inciting to insubordination. He often advocated the propriety of my seizing the government and taking affairs into my own hands. As he always expressed himself in favor of putting down the rebellion at any cost, I always regarded these extreme views as the ebullitions of an intense and patriotic nature, and sometimes wasted more or less time in endeavoring to bring him to more moderate views, never dreaming that all the while this man was in close communication with the very men whom he so violently abused. . . .

"Finally, one day when I returned to my house from my day's work and was dressing for dinner . . . Mr. Stanton's card came up, and as soon as possible I went down to see him. He told me that he had been appointed Secretary of War and that his name had been sent to the Senate for confirmation, and that he had called to confer with me as to his acceptance. He said that acceptance would involve very great personal sacrifices on his part, and that the only possible inducement would be that he might have it in his power to aid me in the work of putting down the rebellion; that he was willing to devote all his time, intellect, and energy to my assistance, and that together we could soon bring the war to an end. If I wished him to accept he would do so, but only on my account; that he had come to know my wishes and would determine accordingly. I told him that I hoped he would accept the position."

Thus did Stanton make certain that McClellan would not oppose his confirmation. McClellan goes on: "Soon after Mr. Stanton became Secretary of War it became clear that, without any reason known to me, our relations had completely changed. Instead of using his new position to assist me he threw every obstacle in my way, and did all in his power to create difficulty and distrust between the President and myself. I soon found it impossible to gain access to him. Before he was in office he constantly ran after

Edwin M. Stanton

me and professed the most ardent friendship; as soon as he became Secretary of War his whole manner changed, and I could no longer find the opportunity to transact even the ordinary current business of the office with him."

There were now about 200,000 Federal troops in the Washington area. Those that had arrived soon after Bull Run had begun to feel like permanent fixtures. Wrote Chaplain Stewart: "Our men came here in August with the desire and expectation of getting right at these rebels, chastising them speedily into order and obedience, and then return home. Had it been told our impetuous young men when volunteering for this work that more than five months would be dragged out in the monotonous routine of camp life without any active service, it may be safely affirmed that hardly one in ten would have been here. But in order to make the best of a supposed bad bargain, very praiseworthy efforts have been, and still are making, in order to introduce into camp life, so far as possible, all the wonted and familiar arts of domestic life.

"Almost every known trade, profession, or calling has its representative in our regiment—tailors and carpenters, masons and plasterers, moulders and glassblowers, pudlers and rollers, machinists and architects, printers, bookbinders, and publishers; gentlemen of leisure, politicians, merchants, legislators, judges, lawyers, doctors, preachers. Some malicious fellow might ask the privilege of completing the catalogue by naming jailbirds, idlers, loafers, drunkards, and gamblers—but we beg his pardon and refuse the license. . . .

"So far as matters have yet developed themselves, no evidence exists that the whole of our three years' enlistment may not be spent in this locality. . . . But whatever be in the womb of the future, it is both pleasing and instructive to witness among our men a full determination to make the best of every condition. That which enables the American people to excel all others in the pursuits of life is a ready *adaptation*. . . . All the appliances of home life which are possible or befitting are being introduced into our encampment. . . .

"For some time we have enjoyed the presence and active operation of a neat portable printing press, together with a corps of practical printers, editors, publishers, and contributors both in prose and poetry. . . . A weekly newspaper called *The Thirteenth Regiment* is published, which has now reached its tenth number. It is almost exclusively filled with original matter and items of interest connected with the history of the regiment. . . . Job printing is also neatly executed in camp. . . .

"A photograph establishment, with all the modern appliances of this wonderful art, has also been introduced and operated by practical artists who are members of the regiment. The design is to have not only the whole regiment photographed but also each individual member, together with the camp, its connected objects and scenery, with incidents and places on the march, thus obtaining a living history of the campaign for future use.

"Various singing clubs may often be heard exercising the vocal organs; while, in addition to the [official] regimental music, a string band discourses, evening by evening, pleasing and merry melodies. A temperance league has been formed, in connection with which a goodly number both of officers and privates stand pledged wholly to abstain from the use of intoxicating drinks during the campaign. Our 'Christian Association' . . . is combining and bringing into active exercise all the existing religious elements of the regiment. . . .

"Our postal arrangements for the regiment demand special notice and commendation. We have a post office, letter box, postmaster and mail carrier. Each morning at 9 o'clock our postman leaves camp for Washington with all the mail matter accumulated in twenty-four hours. A horse and buggy are needed for its conveyance. In the afternoon, that for the regiment is brought out . . . that for each company in a parcel by itself. Each company has a member appointed to receive and distribute its own package. Thus, in a few minutes after arrival, each letter or paper finds its proper destination. The only cause of complaint is that letters enough do not come through. . . . Our boys write vastly more letters than they receive. . . . You can hardly imagine the eagerness with which the mailman's return is looked for, the delight on the reception of a letter, the sadness, sometimes even to tears, with which those who are disappointed turn away."

The new year had opened with moderate weather cordial to camp life, but inclemency soon followed. "Today it would be freezing cold," says cavalry trooper F. Colburn Adams. "Tomorrow a drenching rain, filling the streams and overflowing roads, would be accompanied by hail, sleet, and a fierce, cutting wind. Then snow would cover the ground, and the Army of the Potomac would lay . . . buried in a mud drench. Mud churned up everywhere. . . . Picket reliefs struggled and picked their way over fields and through woods to get to the outposts. Subsistence wagons stuck in the mud; teamsters labored in mud knee deep; and the poor animals plunged and struggled in vain to do their work. Mud covered cavalrymen, and their jaded animals, reeking and dripping, presented the most forlorn appearance as they dragged and struggled in mud. Mud dragged into headquarters, mud filled the log cabins and disfigured the tents; the whole army struggled in mud. Artillery could not be moved, forage teams were stuck fast in the road, and our poor animals suffered and died for want of something to eat. . . . Our hospitals . . . became filled with the sick. A peculiar feature of this effect of the climate was that its first victims were among those apparently the most robust and strong. Young men tenderly brought up and accustomed to the indulgencies of city life seemed to preserve their health and endure the hardships of camp best."

The Confederates, of course, had their own problems with the weather. Company commander John Gordon noted that "the men suffered greatly— not only for want of sufficient preparation, but because those from farther south were unaccustomed to so cold a climate. There was much sickness in camp. It was amazing to see the large number of country boys who had never had the measles. Indeed, it seemed to me that they ran through the whole catalogue of complaints to which boyhood and even babyhood are subjected. They had everything almost except teething, nettle-rash, and whooping cough. I rather think some of them were afflicted with this latter disease."

Sallie Putnam talked with a number of the soldiers who had occasion to visit Richmond. They told "rare stories of misery. . . . But they were cheerful. Enduring hardship, disease, and suffering with uncomplaining heroism, declaring they could endure much more for the independence they were seeking. It is easy to imagine the moral courage, the heroic bravery with which the soldier is inspired on the field of battle, where the sublimity of excitement would glory in courting death; but we have yet to learn the secret of cheerfulness and fortitude when it comes in the stealthy breath of the pestilence and cuts down its victims silently but not less surely than the sabre thrust or the Minié ball."

In Washington, Edwin Stanton, the new Secretary of War, had lost no time in urging Lincoln to take personal charge of the military situation, a course the President had already decided was necessary. At the end of January he published two orders, both of them concerned with getting things moving by February 22, the one a general order affecting all of the nation's forces, land and sea, and the other specific: "*Ordered*, That all the disposable force of the Army of the Potomac, after providing safely for the defense of Washington, be formed into an expedition for the immediate object of seizing and occupying a point upon the railroad southwestward of what is known as Manassas Junction, all details to be in the discretion of the commander in chief."

McClellan's reaction to the order, which ignored his desire to flank the enemy by water and called for a direct overland march, was to hurry to Lincoln and ask permission to submit, in writing, his objections to the plan, along with a detailed analysis of his Chesapeake proposal. The President acquiesced, but reluctantly. He could not see the point in launching an elaborate and expensive amphibious operation against an enemy readily approachable by land, particularly since a land offensive would ensure the protection of Washington by keeping the army between the enemy and the city.

Under the date February 3, and addressing Edwin Stanton, McClellan wrote a paper of great length. He began by listing his achievements since his arrival in Washington after the defeat at Bull Run, adding that "many weeks—I may say many months—ago this Army of the Potomac was fully in condition to repel any attack; but there is a vast difference between that and the efficiency required to enable troops to attack successfully an army elated by victory and entrenched in a position long since selected, studied, and fortified. In the earliest papers I submitted to the President I asked for an effective and movable force far exceeding the aggregate now on the banks of the Potomac. I have not the force I asked for. . . .

"When I was placed in command of the armies of the United States I immediately turned my attention to the whole field of operations, regarding the Army of the Potomac as only one, while the most important, of the masses under my command. I confess that I did not then appreciate the total absence of a general plan . . . nor did I know that utter disorganization and want of preparation pervaded the Western armies. . . . I sent at once, with the approval of the Executive, officers I considered competent to command in Kentucky and Missouri. . . . I soon found that the labor of creation and organization had to be performed there. . . . These things required time. . . . The generals in command have done their work most creditably, but we are still delayed. . . .

"I have ever regarded our true policy as being that of fully preparing ourselves, and then seeking for the most decisive results. I do not wish to waste life in useless battles, but prefer to strike at the heart."

McClellan next discussed the two plans for operating against Richmond, the President's and his own. He argued that the best move would be to float the army down the Potomac and up the Rappahannock for a landing at Urbanna, some forty miles east of Richmond and some ninety miles southeast of Johnston's lines at Centreville. Using Urbanna as a supply base, he would make a rapid march to West Point, at the head of the York River, then press for Richmond, which he could probably occupy without major fighting. Johnston, of course, would hurry down from Centreville to contest the occupation, but would be disorganized by the march and could be beaten. The capture of Richmond would lead to the collapse of the Confederacy's other bastions, east and west, and the war would end.

McClellan proposed to use a force numbering between 110,000 and 140,000, leaving sufficient troops behind to provide for the safety of the capital. Whichever plan was decided upon, he stated, *time* would be an important consideration. "It is possible, nay, highly probable, that the weather and state of the roads may be such as to delay the direct movement from Washington . . . far beyond the time required to complete the second plan. . . . It is by no means certain that we can beat them at Manassas. On the other line I regard success as certain by all the chances of war. We demoralize the enemy by forcing him to abandon his prepared position for one which we have chosen, in which all is in our favor, and where success must produce immense results." He had so much faith in the Chesapeake plan, he said, that he would prefer floating the army all the way down to Fort Monroe (the Union-held installation at the tip of the Virginia Peninsula) to attacking the Confederates at Manassas. The movement upon Richmond from Fort Monroe, however, would be "less brilliant than that from Urbanna." Whatever point was selected as a base, "a large amount of cheap water transportation must be collected, consisting mainly of canal-boats, barges, wood-boats, schooners, etc., towed by small steamers."

McClellan's paper became the subject of days of discussion at meetings attended by Lincoln and his cabinet and McClellan and his generals. At the same time, the President was smitten by a personal worry. His youngest son, Willie, fell critically ill with typhoid fever. On a brighter note, the general military situation improved substantially. In the East, an amphibious force under General Ambrose E. Burnside established a base on Roanoke Island, off the coast of North Carolina, while in the West, Ulysses Grant, then an obscure brigadier general, captured two Confederate bastions near the northern border of Tennessee—Fort Henry on the Tennessee River and Fort Donelson on the Cumberland.

"The Army of the Potomac," writes Regis de Trobriand, "received all this good news in its winter quarters, where the hesitations of the general-in-chief and the irresolution of the President, relative to the final adoption of a plan of campaign, continued to hold it. The great question was to know if the enemy should be attacked from the front, as Mr. Lincoln evidently thought, or if their position should be turned by means of Chesapeake Bay, to throw upon their rear all the forces which were not absolutely necessary for the security of Washington, as was proposed by General McClellan. The difference of opinion was so great that the secret was soon known through the army. Thus it was known that the President had given an order for a general movement of forces, both on land and sea, on the 22nd of February. . . . The idea of such an order was not happy, and its execution subject to so many plausible objections that General McClellan had no trouble in getting it revoked. The 22nd of February passed by without any other demonstration than the salvos of artillery in commemoration of the birthday of Washington. But, rightfully or wrongly, the impression remained that the President had been compelled to exercise his authority to force the general-in-chief from his inaction."

The vacillation in Washington had given Joe Johnston (lately working without Beauregard, who had been transferred to Tennessee) time to build his Centreville forces to 50,000; and in Richmond the new government was able to consolidate without interference. Only now, on February 22, was Jefferson Davis inaugurated as President of the Confederacy. According to Sallie Putnam: "The weather had been precarious for some days, and on the morning of the 22nd the rain fell in torrents and the streams and the gutters were like the flowing of little rivers. Yet the friends of the President, and the curious crowds of residents and strangers in the city, were not to be deterred from witnessing the scene of the inauguration by the rain and mud, which was in some places so deep as almost to render the crossings impassable. The square of the Capitol was crowded with a dense throng of old and young—men, and women, and children—soldiers and citizens—mingled with carriages and umbrellas, dripping hats, and cloaks, and blankets, and oil cloths, and draggled skirts, and muddy boots, and all other accompaniments of mud and rain upon such a dense mass of human beings in the singular panorama of the occasion.

"A covered platform had been erected just underneath, or beside the Washington Monument, where the brazen image of 'the Father of his Country' looked down upon this singular sight in the capital of his native state, seeming to watch with interest the novel proceedings—with his arm outstretched to shield the platform beneath, and his finger pointed southward. It seemed to us, of the hopeful class, significant.

"Very few heard the inaugural address. The pattering of the rain on the carriages and the umbrellas ... prevented the sound of the human voice from reaching our ears."

A newsman who was near Davis noted that the address was "characterized by great dignity, united with much feeling and grace, especially the closing sentence. Throwing up his eyes and hands to heaven he said, 'With humble gratitude and adoration, acknowledging the Providence which has so visibly protected the Confederacy during its brief but eventful career, to Thee, O God, I trustingly commit myself, and prayerfully invoke Thy blessing on my country and its cause.' "

Varina Davis was watching her husband closely at this moment and couldn't help but feel that he might be on the way to nothing more than martyrdom. "As he stood pale and emaciated, dedicating himself to the service of the Confederacy, evidently forgetful of everything but his sacred oath, he seemed to me a willing victim going to his funeral pyre, and the idea so affected me that, making some excuse, I regained my carriage and went home."

Sallie Putnam says that the rest of the viewers "with patient enthusiasm ... remained until the ceremonies were over, and retired to their homes— the gentlemen to prepare for the reception at the house of our President, and the ladies who were not fortunate enough to have a carriage, to doff garments wet and muddy. . . .

"Never was there a man put into power so nearly by public acclamation as Mr. Davis. . . . No other was mentioned as his competitor for office."

For the President in Washington, and for his wife, this was a time of personal tragedy. Willie had died and the distraught couple was preparing for his funeral. Those who were close to Lincoln worried about his ability to carry on, but Willie was scarcely buried before the President managed to

Washington Monument in Richmond

resume a full schedule. The New York *Evening Post* reported that "Mr. Lincoln . . . is again . . . spending, not infrequently, eighteeen out of the twenty-four hours upon the affairs of the nation."

The President never became convinced that McClellan's plan for a flanking maneuver upon Richmond by way of the Chesapeake was superior to his own plan for an overland approach through Manassas. When he learned that McClellan had the support of the majority of his generals, Lincoln felt obliged to submit, but only tentatively, and his patronage of the preparations was wary and hesitating. During this period, according to William Swinton, "grave faults were committed both by the Administration and by General McClellan. While we are bound to believe that each was moved by the sincere desire to bring the war to a successful issue, each did much to frustrate the very object they had mutually at heart. . . . When McClellan presented his scheme of a change of base to the lower Chesapeake, the project should either have been frankly approved or frankly disapproved. . . . General McClellan should either have been removed from command, or he should have been allowed to work out his own plans of campaign. . . . If there be any sure lesson taught by the military experience of nations, it is that when extrinsic influences, whether from councils, or congresses, or war offices, intrude into the direction of military affairs, all hope of success is gone. . . . True, it was inevitable that, in a war such as that which fell upon the United States, considerations of a kind that may be called *political* should have a great part to play; and the determination of the policy of the war was certainly a question that came within the province of statesmanship, and which, when adopted in the councils of the Government, the commander in the field was bound to adhere to and carry out. But beyond this, and in the sphere of the actual conduct of the war, the general must be head and supreme. . . .

"On the other hand, it is to be admitted that General McClellan, too, committed grave faults. He had already put the patience of the public and the Administration to severe strain by his six months' inactivity; and in proposing to remove his army from the front of Washington he made another and peculiarly heavy draft upon their confidence. In this he again exposed himself to the criticism already made respecting his deficiency in those statesmanlike qualities that enter into the composition of a great general. Granting that the lower Chesapeake was the true line of approach to Richmond, yet finding the project of a removal of the army from the front of Washington so peculiarly repugnant to the wishes and convictions of the President and his councillors as to have suggested grave doubts as to the possibility of his obtaining a cordial support in its execution, he should have considered with himself whether he could follow the wishes of his superiors by operating against the enemy at Manassas; and if not, he should have resigned."

McClellan did not resign, he explained later, because he underestimated the resolve of his radical opposition, and because he had formed a special relationship with his command. "I had become warmly attached to the soldiers, who already had learned to love me well. All my pride was wrapped up in the army that I had created, and I knew of no commander at all likely to be assigned to it in my place who would be competent to conduct its operations."

Edwin Stanton had been busy consolidating his power and establishing a firm working relationship with Lincoln, losing few chances to critize McClellan, and even going so far as to question his loyalty to the Union. The result was that early one morning the general was called to a private interview at the White House. The President "appeared much concerned about something, and soon said that he wished to talk with me about a very ugly matter. I asked what it was; and, as he still hesitated, I said that the sooner and more directly such things were approached the better." Lincoln hedged for another few moments by discussing a minor grievance he had with McClellan. "He then adverted to the more serious—or ugly—matter, and now the effects of the intrigues by which he had been surrounded became apparent. He said that it had been represented to him . . . that my plan of campaign . . . was conceived with the traitorous intent of removing the defenders from Washington, and thus giving over to the enemy the Capital and the Government, thus left defenseless. . . . I was seated when he said this. . . . I arose, and, in a manner perhaps not altogether decorous towards the chief magistrate, desired that he should retract the expression, telling him that I could permit no one to couple the word treason with my name. He was much agitated, and at once disclaimed any idea of considering me a traitor, and said that he merely repeated what others had said, and that he did not believe a word of it. I suggested caution in the use of language, and again said that I would permit no doubt to be thrown upon my intentions; whereupon he again apologized and disclaimed any purpose of impugning my motives."

The first step in the implementation of McClellan's Chesapeake plan was the gathering of water transportation from private sources in the Northeast, a task assigned to John Tucker, Assistant Secretary of War. Tucker chartered 113 steamers, 188 schooners, and 88 barges. Many of the acquisitions were old and dilapidated, and some were even recalled from barnacled retirement. The larger ones were chartered at an average price of $215.10 per day, and the smaller, from $14.27 to $24.45. Early March found the first of the vessels making their way down the East Coast toward the Chesapeake. In Washington, carpenters waited to make the necessary repairs and alterations.

McClellan's plan depended not only on these makeshift transports but also on the cooperation of the U.S. Navy. During this period in naval history, steam was replacing sail, but most of the world's vessels were still

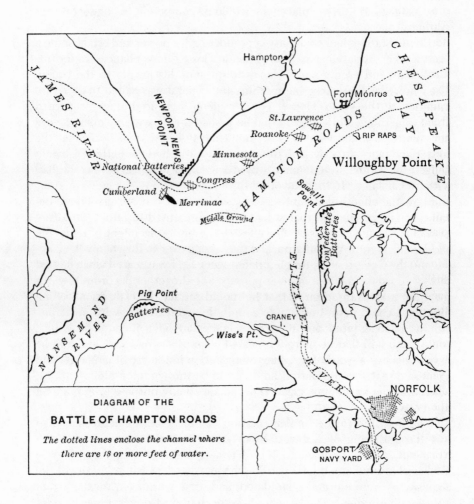

Hampton

Fort Monroe

St. Lawrence

Roanoke

RIP RAPS

Minnesota

Willoughby Point

National Batteries

Congress

Cumberland

Merrimac

Middle Ground

Pig Point
Batteries

CRANEY

Wise's Pt.

NORFOLK

DIAGRAM OF THE
BATTLE OF HAMPTON ROADS

*The dotted lines enclose the channel where
there are 18 or more feet of water.*

GOSPORT
NAVY YARD

CHESAPEAKE BAY

JAMES RIVER

NEWPORT NEWS POINT

HAMPTON ROADS

Sewell's Point

Confederate Batteries

ELIZABETH RIVER

NANSEMOND RIVER

wholly wooden. Only lately had experiments with iron sheathing been gaining prominence. The advent of the age of metal warships was to have its effect on McClellan's campaign. In the summer of 1861, even before the Battle of Bull Run, the Confederate Navy Department had launched work on a ten-gun ironclad as a response to the wooden-ship blockade of Hampton Roads, the channel through which Virginia's James, Nansemond, and Elizabeth rivers flow into the mouth of the Chesapeake. On the channel's northern shore were Fort Monroe and Newport News, manned by Union forces, while the shores to the south held Norfolk and the Gosport Navy Yard, occupied by the Confederates since the Federals had moved out at the beginning of the war. It was necessary to the success of McClellan's campaign for the U.S. Navy to retain control of the channel's waters. The ironclad with which the Confederates planned to contest this control was the *Virginia*, a remodeling of the Union frigate *Merrimack* (then better known as the *Merrimac*), scuttled and sunk during the Gosport evacuation but salvaged soon afterward. The remodeling was being done at the navy yard, the plating provided by the Tredegar Iron Works at Richmond.

The Confederates tried to keep their project a secret, but the news presently reached Washington, and the Government was quick to respond with plans for an ironclad of its own, to be built at New York City. In the words of Gideon Welles, the Secretary of the Navy: "When the contract for the *Monitor* was made in October [1861], with a primary condition that she should be ready for the sea in one hundred days, the Navy Department intended that the battery should, immediately after reaching Hampton Roads, proceed up Elizabeth River to the navy yard at Norfolk, place herself opposite the drydock, and with her heavy guns destroy both the dock and the *Merrimac*. This was *our* secret. . . . But one hundred days expired, weeks passed on, and the *Monitor* was not ready. Late in February [1862] a Negro woman who resided in Norfolk came to the Navy Department and desired a private interview with me. She and others had closely watched the work upon the *Merrimac*, and she, by their request, had come to report that the ship was nearly finished, had come out of the dock, and was about receiving her armament. The woman had passed through the lines, at great risk to herself, to bring me the information." This development, of course, put an end to plans for destroying the *Merrimack* in drydock, but it increased the Government's anxiety to get the *Monitor* into action. The modest-sized vessel began her water trials on February 27, and undertook the trip southward along the coast, towed by a tug, on the morning of March 6. Although she had beaten the *Merrimack* to completion by two days, she was 300 miles from Hampton Roads, and had to be towed cautiously because she rode low and took on water when the sea broke over her.

The *Monitor* was still five hours north of Hampton Roads at 11 A.M. on Saturday, March 8, when the *Merrimack* cast loose from her moorings at

Gosport. It was a bright day, and the Elizabeth River was calm and blue. Crowds of Confederate troops and civilians lined the shore, cheering and waving, as the vessel, accompanied by two small wooden steamers, began its ten-mile journey toward the Union fleet anchored in the waters between Newport News and Fort Monroe. The fleet included five major warships and their auxiliaries, and was backed by land batteries.

At Newport News, the Union tugboat *Zouave* had completed her morning duties and was tied up at the wharf. "A little after dinner, about 12:30," relates the tug's master, Henry Reaney, "the quartermaster on watch called my attention to black smoke in the Elizabeth River, close to Craney Island. We let go from the wharf and ran alongside the *Cumberland*. The officer of the deck ordered us to . . . find out what was coming down from Norfolk. It did not take us long to find out, for we had not gone over two miles when we saw what to all appearances looked like the roof of a very big barn belching forth smoke as from a chimney on fire. We were all divided in opinion as to what was coming. The boatswain's mate was the first to make out the Confederate flag, and then we all guessed it was the *Merrimac* come at last." Back on the anchored *Cumberland,* the pilot, A. B. Smith, studied the approaching vessel with his glass. "As she came ploughing through the water . . . she looked like a huge half-submerged crocodile. Her sides seemed of solid iron, except where the guns pointed from the narrow ports. . . . At her prow I could see the iron ram projecting straight forward, somewhat above the water's edge."

By this time, large numbers of soldiers, sailors, and civilians were hurrying to vantage points on the shores between Newport News and Fort Monroe. On the Confederate side, the crowds grew thickest at Pig Point and Sewell's Point, commanding spots that held artillery batteries.

Henry Reaney's little tug was armed with a thirty-pound Parrott gun, and the tense silence hanging over the broad expanse of water was soon broken by its booming. Ignoring the fire, the *Merrimack* came on, obviously headed for the two warships off Newport News, the *Cumberland* and the *Congress.* The other three—the *Minnesota, Roanoke,* and *St. Lawrence*— lay to the east, in the bight between Newport News and Fort Monroe. Says Henry Reaney: "We fired, I think, about six shots when our recall signal was hoisted on the *Cumberland.* By this time the batteries at Newport News had commenced firing; the *Congress* had gone to quarters and opened fire. When we got close to the *Cumberland* she also began firing. The *Merrimac* kept on until abreast of the *Congress,* when she opened fire, pouring a broadside in passing, and came right on for the *Cumberland,* which vessel was using her guns as fast as they could be fired."

Adds the *Cumberland*'s pilot, A. B. Smith: "Still she came on, the balls bouncing upon her mailed sides like India-rubber, apparently making not the least impression, except to cut off her flagstaff and thus bring down the

Confederates on Craney Island cheering the *Merrimack* as she advances
upon the Federal fleet

Confederate colors. . . . We had probably fired six or eight broadsides when a shot was received from one of her guns which killed five of our marines. It was impossible for our vessel to get out of her way, and the *Merrimac* soon crushed her iron horn, or ram, into the *Cumberland* . . . knocking a hole in the side . . . and driving the vessel back upon her anchors with great force. The water came rushing into the hold."

On board the *Merrimack*, according to Lieutenant John Taylor Wood, the impact of the collision was hardly perceptible. "Backing clear of her, we went . . . up the river . . . and turned slowly. . . . As we swung, the *Congress* came in range . . . and we got in three raking shells. She had slipped her anchor . . . and tried to escape, but grounded. Turning we headed for her and took a position within two hundred yards, where every shot told. In the meantime, the *Cumberland* continued the fight, though our ram had opened her side wide enough to drive in a horse and cart."

Pilot Smith describes the *Cumberland*'s plight: "The water was all the while rushing in the hole. . . . Broadsides swept our men away . . . and also set our vessel on fire in the forward part. The fire was extinguished. . . . We fired constantly, and the *Merrimac* occasionally, but every shot told upon our wooden vessel and brave crew." The *Cumberland*'s decks became slippery with blood; and heads, arms, legs, parts of torsos, and strings of intestines were strewn about. One small measure of revenge was achieved. A *Merrimack* sailor appeared on deck, presumably meaning to reestablish the Confederate colors, and was instantly cut in two by a *Cumberland* ball. After about forty-five minutes, the wooden ship went down, the Stars and Stripes still waving. "That flag was finally submerged," says Smith, "but after the hull grounded on the sands, fifty-four feet below the surface of the water, our pennant was still flying from the topmast above the waves." Many of the crew were drowned.

While boats loosed from the *Cumberland* and other boats from shore were picking up the swimming survivors, the *Merrimack* turned her full attention to the *Congress*. Aiding the ironclad with their fire were not only the two wooden steamers from Gosport but also two that had come down the James. Suffering heavily both in material damage and in slaughter, and unable to keep even a single gun firing, the *Congress* soon struck her colors and ran up a white cloth. Two of the wooden steamers moved in to accept the surrender and help the wounded, but were met by artillery shells and small-arms fire from shore. One of the soldiers on shore said to the commanding general, Joseph Mansfield, "Since the ship has surrendered, has not the enemy the right to take possession of her?" The general snapped back, "I know the damned ship has surrendered, but we haven't!"

Suffering casualties, and unable to retain their prize, the Confederates drew off. Commodore Franklin Buchanan, commander of the *Merrimack*, determined to destroy the *Congress* with heated shot, and she was soon aflame, fore and aft. Some of the surviving crewmen scrambled into the vessel's boats, while the rest jumped overboard and swam for shore. Among the survivors was a brother to the Confederate commodore, Paymaster McKean Buchanan, who had remained loyal to the Union. The commodore himself became a casualty at this time. While standing on the deck of the *Merrimack* directing the firing of the heated shot, he was seriously wounded by General Mansfield's small-arms fire. The command devolved upon Lieutenant Catesby Jones.

It was about five o'clock in the afternoon when the *Merrimack* and two of her consorts turned their attention to the *Minnesota*, about two miles to the east. This vessel had been trying to reach the scene of action under tow of a tug but had run aground. Relates her commander, G. J. Van Brunt: "Very fortunately, the iron battery drew too much water to come within a mile of us. She took a position on my starboard bow, but did not fire with accuracy, and only one shot passed through the ship's bow. The other two steamers took their position on my port bow and stern, and their fire did the most damage in killing and wounding men."

Aided by tugboats, the *Roanoke* and *St. Lawrence* were now approaching from Fort Monroe. Their route brought them within distant range of the Confederate batteries at Sewell's Point, and a duel resulted. The overall picture at this time is given by a Confederate observer, General R. E. Colston: "The bright afternoon sun shone upon the glancing waters. The fortifications of Newport News were seen swarming with soldiers . . . and the flames were . . . bursting from the abandoned *Congress*. The stranded *Minnesota* seemed a huge monster at bay, surrounded by the *Merrimac* and the gunboats. The entire horizon was lighted up by the continual flashes of the artillery of these combatants, the broadsides of the *Roanoke* and *St. Lawrence*, and the [fire from] the Sewell's Point batteries. Clouds of white smoke rose in spiral columns to the skies, illumined by the evening sunlight, while land and water seemed to tremble under the thunders of the cannonade.

"The *Minnesota* was now in a desperate situation. It is true that, being aground, she could not sink; but, looking through the glass, I could see a hole in her side, made by [one of] the *Merrimac*'s rifle shells. She had lost a number of men, and had once been set on fire. Her destruction or surrender seemed inevitable, since all efforts to get her afloat had failed. But just then the *Merrimac* turned away from her toward the *Roanoke* and the *St. Lawrence*. These vessels has suffered but little from the distant fire of the Sewell's Point batteries, but both had run aground and had not been floated off again without great difficulty, for it was very hazardous for vessels of deep draught to manoeuvre over these comparatively shallow waters. When the *Merrimac* approached, they delivered broadsides and were then towed back with promptness. The *Merrimac* pursued them but a short distance—for by this time darkness was falling upon the scene of action, the tide was ebbing, and there was great risk of running aground." The ironclad swung around and steamed back toward the mouth of the Elizabeth River. She anchored for the night under the batteries of Sewell's Point.

"The day," lamented a Union news correspondent, ". . . closed most dismally for our side, and with the most gloomy apprehensions of what would occur the next day. The *Minnesota* was at the mercy of the *Merrimac,* and there appeared no reason why the iron monster might not clear the Roads of our fleet, destroy all the stores and warehouses on the beach, drive our troops into the fortress, and command Hampton Roads against any number of wooden vessels the Government might send there. Saturday was a terribly dismal night at Fortress Monroe."

On the Confederate shores, the night was one of exultation. The *Merrimack,* ventured as an experiment, had proved to be a great success. Viewed historically, the ironclad had achieved one of the most remarkable triumphs the world's waters had ever seen. In a half-day's action, she had accounted for two vessels carrying a total of three times her number of crewmen and six times her weight of armament. She had slain about 250 of the enemy and had wounded many more. In return, she and her consorts had taken about twenty killed and wounded. The effect of the fight on the ironclad herself is described by crewman John Taylor Wood: "The armor was hardly damaged, though at one time our ship was the focus on which were directed at least one hundred heavy guns afloat and ashore. But nothing outside escaped. Two guns were disabled by having their muzzles shot off. The ram was left in the side of the *Cumberland.* One anchor, the smokestack, and the steam-pipes were shot away. Railings, stanchions, boat-davits—everything was swept clean. The flagstaff was repeatedly knocked over, and finally a boarding-pike was used." Although battered, the vessel had lost but little of her original strength. She was still quite ready for anything the Union chose to pit against her.

While the *Merrimack* had been wreaking her havoc that afternoon, the *Monitor* was drawing closer. She entered the mouth of the Chesapeake at about four o'clock, at which time her crew could hear the distant booming of heavy guns. While she was still ten miles from Fort Monroe, according to her executive officer, S. Dana Greene, the *Monitor* met the Union fleet's pilot boat and was told the fate of the *Cumberland* and *Congress:* "We could not credit it at first, but as we approached Hampton Roads we could see the fine old *Congress* burning brightly; and we knew it must be true. Sad indeed did we feel to think those two fine old vessels had gone to their last homes with so many of their brave crews. . . . At 9 P.M. we anchored near the frigate *Roanoke,* the flagship . . . and received orders to proceed to Newport News and protect the *Minnesota*—then aground—from the *Merrimac.* We got under way and arrived at the *Minnesota* at 11 P.M. I went on board in our cutter." Greene promised Captain Van Brunt that the *Monitor* would do everything in her power to save his vessel. "He thanked me kindly and wished us success. Just as I arrived back to the *Monitor* the *Congress* blew up, and certainly a grander sight was never seen; but it went straight to the marrow of our bones."

Alert for any emergency, the *Monitor* spent the night anchored near the *Minnesota*. Three miles away, the crew of the *Merrimack* slept at their guns, "dreaming," according to one man, "of other victories in the morning."

News of the terrible Saturday at Hampton Roads reached Washington by telegraph at an early hour on Sunday. Lincoln hastened to call a cabinet meeting at the White House. Secretary of the Navy Gideon Welles says that he arrived to find Secretary of State William Seward, Secretary of the Treasury Salmon Chase, and Secretary of War Edwin Stanton already there, consulting with the President in much alarm: "Each inquired what had been, and what could be done, to meet and check this formidable monster, which in a single brief visit had made such devastation, and would . . . repeat her destructive visit with still greater havoc, probably, while we were in council. I stated that I knew of no immediate steps that could be taken. . . . I had expected that our new ironclad battery, which left New York on Thursday, would have reached the Roads on Saturday, and my main reliance was upon her. We had, however, no information, as yet, of her arrival. . . .

"Mr. Stanton, impulsive and always a sensationalist, was terribly excited, walked the room in great agitation, and gave brusque utterances and deprecatory answers to all that was said, and censured everything that had been done or was omitted to be done. Mr. Seward, usually buoyant and self-reliant, overwhelmed with the intelligence, listened in responsive sympathy to Stanton and was greatly depressed, as, indeed, were all the members, who, in the meantime, had arrived, with the exception of Mr. Blair [i.e., Postmaster General Montgomery Blair], as well as one or two others— naval and military officers. . . . 'The *Merrimac*,' said Stanton, who was vehement and did most of the talking, 'will change the whole character of the war. She will destroy, seriatim, every naval vessel. She will lay all the cities on the seaboard under contribution. . . . I will notify the governors and municipal authorities in the North to take instant measures to protect their harbors.' It is difficult to repeat his language, which was broken and denunciatory, or to characterize his manner, or the panic under which he labored, and which added to the apprehension of others. He had no doubt, he said, that the monster was at this moment on her way to Washington, and, looking out of the window, which commanded a view of the Potomac for many miles: 'Not unlikely, we shall have a shell or cannonball from one of her guns in the White House before we leave this room.'

"Most of Stanton's complaints were directed to me, and to me the others turned—not complainingly, but naturally for information or suggestions that might give relief. I had little to impart, except my faith in the untried *Monitor* experiment, which we had prepared for the emergency, [and] an assurance that the *Merrimac*, with her draught and loaded with iron, could not pass Kettle Bottom Shoals in the Potomac and ascend the river and surprise us with a cannonball; and [I] advised that, instead of adding to the general panic, it would better become us to calmly consider the situation and inspire confidence by acting, so far as we could, intelligently and with discretion and judgment. Mr. Chase approved the suggestion, but thought it might be well to telegraph Governor Morgan and Mayor Opdyke at New York, that they might be on their guard. Stanton said he should warn the authorities in all the chief cities. I questioned the propriety of sending abroad panic missives, or adding to the alarm that would naturally be felt, and said it was doubtful whether the vessel, so cut down and loaded with armor, would venture outside of the Capes; . . . nor was she omnipresent to make general destruction at New York, Boston, . . . etc., at the same time; . . . and repeated that my dependence was on the *Monitor*, and my confidence in her great.

" 'What,' asked Stanton, 'is the size and strength of this *Monitor?* How many guns does she carry?' When I replied two, but of large caliber, he turned away with a look of mingled amazement, contempt, and distress that was painfully ludicrous. Mr. Seward said that my remark concerning the draught of water which the *Merrimac* drew . . . afforded him the first moment of relief and real comfort he had received. It was his sensitive nature to be easily depressed, but yet to promptly rally and catch at hope. Turning to Stanton, he said we had, perhaps, given away too much to our apprehensions. He saw no alternative but to wait and hear what our new battery might accomplish. Stanton left abruptly after Seward's remark. The President ordered his carriage and went to the Navy Yard to see what might be the views of the naval officers."

Down at Hampton Roads, the dawn had brought new action. "On that morning when we went out," relates a *Merrimack* crewman named Littlepage, "we thought to finish the *Minnesota*, which had been unable to get itself off the bar. Our first intimation of the presence of the *Monitor* was when we saw her run out from behind the *Minnesota* to attack us before we could begin the onset." *Merrimack* officer John Taylor Wood says that the *Monitor*, whose existence was known to the Confederates and whose appearance that morning was not altogether a surprise, was "but a pigmy compared with the lofty frigate which she guarded." Another Confederate spectator, getting his first glimpse of the Union ironclad as she was touched by the sun's earliest rays, exclaimed, "A tin can on a shingle!" Watching from the Union shore, Naval Medical Director Charles Martin was aware of the moment's historical significance: "David goes out to meet Goliath, and every man who can walk to the beach sits down there, spectators of the first ironclad battle in the world."

Lieutenant John L. Worden was the *Monitor*'s commander. The vessel's executive officer, S. Dana Greene, had a friend on the *Merrimack*, a roommate of his days at Annapolis. "Little did we think at the Academy we should ever be firing 150-pound shot at each other, but so goes the world." Greene says further: "The physical condition of the officers and men of the two ships at this time was in striking contrast. The *Merrimac* had passed the night quietly near Sewell's Point, her people enjoying rest and sleep.... The *Monitor* had barely escaped shipwreck twice within the last thirty-six hours, and since Friday morning, forty-eight hours before, few if any of those on board had closed their eyes in sleep or had anything to eat but hard bread, as cooking was impossible. She was surrounded by wrecks and disaster, and her efficiency in action had yet to be proved."

John Worden lost no time in putting the *Monitor* to the test, taking her straight toward the *Merrimack*. The larger vessel was already firing as Greene, assisted by a crew of eight brawny men, ran out one of the two guns in the revolving turret, took deliberate aim, and pulled the lockstring. "The *Merrimac* was quick to reply, returning a rattling broadside ... and the battle fairly began. The turret and other parts of [our] ship were heavily struck, but the shots did not penetrate. The tower ... continued to revolve. A look of confidence passed over the men's faces." The *Monitor*'s second gun was soon in action.

The power of the fire coming from the "tin can" on the small vessel's deck surprised the *Merrimack*'s crew, one of whom exclaimed, "Damn it, the thing is full of guns!"

From his seat on the Union beach, Charles Martin took in the general situation as the fight opened. "The day is calm, the smoke hangs thick on the water, the low vessels are hidden by the smoke. They are so sure of their invulnerability, they fight at arm's length. They fight so near the shore, the flash of their guns is seen, and the noise is heard of the heavy shot pounding the armor." Deeply thrilling to the Union spectators was the realization that the little *Monitor* was holding her own against the South's "monster." The shoreline rang with cheers. Although the Confederate spectators did their share of cheering as the *Merrimack*'s guns puffed and thundered, the mood was less exuberant than that of the day before.

Watching from the grounded *Minnesota*, along with the hundreds that made up her crew, was Captain Van Brunt, who was astonished by the battle's novelty. "Gun after gun was fired by the *Monitor*, which was returned with whole broadsides from the rebels, with no more effect, apparently, than so many pebble-stones thrown by a child.... When they struck the bomb-proof tower, the shot glanced off ... clearly establishing the fact that wooden vessels cannot contend successfully with ironclad ones, for never

The *Monitor* and the *Merrimack*

before was anything like it dreamed of by the greatest enthusiast in maritime warfare."

The contest developed into one of maneuvering and firing, with neither vessel gaining the advantage. The *Monitor* was the more agile of the two, the *Merrimack* being handicapped not only by her size and draft, but also by defects in her machinery, which was old and had been ravaged by fire and water at the time of her abandonment by the Union. According to John Taylor Wood, she was "as unwieldy as Noah's ark."

In the words of the *Monitor*'s S. Dana Greene: "The fight continued . . . as fast as the guns could be served, and at very short range. . . . Worden skillfully manoeuvered his quick-turning vessel, trying to find some vulnerable point in his adversary. Once he made a dash at her stern, hoping to disable her screw, which he thinks he missed by not more than two feet. Our shots ripped [into] the iron of the *Merrimac*, while the reverberation of her shots against the tower caused anything but a pleasant sensation." Adds Union seaman Peter Truskitt: "The din . . . was something terrific. The noise of every solid ball that hit fell upon our ears with a crash that deafened us. About that time an unexpected danger developed. The plates of the turret were fastened on with iron bolts and screw-heads on the inside. These screw-heads began to fly off from the concussion of the shots. Several of the men were badly bruised by them."

Switching to the *Merrimack* and John Taylor Wood: "More than two hours had passed, and we had made no impression on the enemy so far as we could discover, while our wounds were slight. Several times the *Monitor* ceased firing, and we were in hopes she was disabled, but the revolution again of her turret and the heavy blows of her 11-inch shot on our sides soon undeceived us."

When one of the *Merrimack*'s gun crews took an unauthorized break, the vessel's commander, Catesby Jones, inquired of the crew chief: "Why are you not firing, Mr. Eggleston?" The chief replied: "Why, our powder is very precious; and after two hours' incessant firing I find that I can do her about as much damage by snapping my thumb at her every two minutes and a half."

It was about this time that the grounded *Minnesota* became a part of the action. Relates Captain Van Brunt: "The *Merrimac*, finding that she could make nothing of the *Monitor,* turned her attention . . . to me. . . . I opened upon her with all my broadside guns and ten-inch pivot—a broadside which would have blown out of the water any timber-built ship in the world. She returned my fire with her rifled bowgun, with a shell which passed through the chief-engineer's stateroom, through the engineers' messroom amidships, and burst in the boatswain's room, tearing four rooms all into one, in its passage exploding two charges of powder, which set the ship on fire, but it was promptly extinguished. . . . Her second shot went through the boiler of

the tugboat *Dragon*, exploding it. . . . I had concentrated upon her an incessant fire . . . and . . . at least fifty solid shot struck her . . . without producing
any apparent effect. By the time she had fired her third shell, the little
Monitor had come down upon her, placing herself between us, and compelled her to change her position, in doing which she grounded, and again I
poured into her all the guns that could be brought to bear upon her. As soon
as she got off, she stood down the bay, the little battery chasing her with all
speed."

The *Merrimack* soon made a sweeping turn back toward the *Monitor*,
her intention to try either to ram or board the vessel. "For nearly an hour
we manoeuvred for a position," says John Taylor Wood. "At last an opportunity offered [to ram her]. . . . But before the ship gathered headway the
Monitor turned, and our disabled ram only gave a glancing blow, effecting
nothing. Again she came up on our quarter, her bow against our side, and at
this distance fired twice. Both shots struck about halfway up the shield . . .
and the impact forced the side in bodily two or three inches. All the crews
of the after guns were knocked over by the concussion, and bled from the
nose or ears. Another shot at the same place would have penetrated. While
alongside, [our] boarders were called away, but she dropped astern before
they could get on board."

The battle continued at close quarters. Soon after twelve noon, a shell
from a *Merrimack* gun, at a range of about thirty feet, struck the pilothouse,
whose exposed portion, constructed of iron logs bolted together, rose four
feet above the *Monitor*'s forward deck, near the prow. The shell exploded,
according to S. Dana Greene, "directly in the sight-hole, or slit, . . . cracking
the second iron log and partly lifting the top, leaving an opening. Worden
was standing immediately behind this spot, and received in his face the
force of the blow, which partly stunned him, and, filling his eyes with powder, utterly blinded him. . . . The flood of light rushing through the top of
the pilot house . . . caused Worden, blind as he was, to believe that the pilot
house was seriously injured, if not destroyed. He therefore gave orders to
. . . sheer off."

Because the *Monitor* slipped into shallow waters, the *Merrimack* could
not follow. Greene continues: "Worden sent for me, and . . . I went forward
at once, and found him standing at the foot of the ladder leading to the pilot
house. He was a ghastly sight, with his eyes closed and the blood apparently
rushing from every pore in the upper part of his face. He . . . directed me to
take command. I assisted in leading him to a sofa in his cabin." (Worden's
injuries were not as bad as they looked; his blindness was only temporary.)
Greene resumes: "When I reached my station in the pilot house, I found
that . . . the steering gear was still intact. . . . In the confusion of the moment . . . the *Monitor* had been moving without direction. . . . During this
time the *Merrimac* . . . had started in the direction of the Elizabeth River;

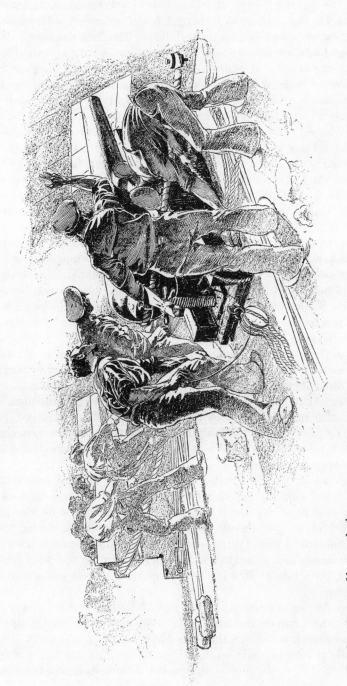

On the *Merrimack's* gun deck

and on . . . turning the [*Monitor's*] head in the direction of the *Merrimac*, I saw that she was already in retreat. A few shots were fired at the retiring vessel, and she continued on to Norfolk. . . . The fight was over."

The *Merrimack* had not left the scene in haste, but had waited for some time for the *Monitor* to return to deep water and resume the fight. But the Confederate ironclad was leaking as a result of her attempt to ram her adversary, was in need of many other repairs, and was carrying a crew now worn out from two days of work with their heavy guns, much of the time in a haze of acrid powder smoke. Moreover, the tide was ebbing and the cumbrous vessel was in danger of running aground and not getting off.

Although the battle was a drawn one, the advantage belonged to the *Monitor*. She had saved the *Minnesota* and the other ships off Fort Monroe, and the waters of Hampton Roads remained open to Federal traffic. After assuring herself that the *Merrimack* was not coming back, the *Monitor* returned to the side of the grounded *Minnesota*. As the little ironclad's crew climbed from her dark confines to her sunny deck, with the men of the turret blackened by powder and smoke, the sailors lining the rail of the wooden vessel cheered themselves breathless. Captain Van Brunt had made every preparation to destroy the *Minnesota* if the *Monitor* was bested. The joy at the battle's outcome extended to the spectators on the beach between Fort Monroe and Newport News, some of whom saluted the *Monitor* by waving flags.

Soon the word was clicking over the telegraph wires to Washington. The general feeling of relief that resulted was not shared by Secretary of War Edwin Stanton. He could not believe that the *Monitor* had handed the *Merrimack* anything but a minor setback, and he plunged into plans to deal with the matter himself, even though nautical affairs were not officially within his province. On the morning after the battle, Secretary of the Navy Gideon Welles went to the White House to see Lincoln, and found Stanton there. "He turned to me and . . . proceeded to state that he had directed the purchase of all the boats that could be procured in Washington, Georgetown, and Alexandria, which were being laden with stone and earth . . . with a view of sinking them at Kettle Bottom Shoals, some fifty miles or more below, in order to prevent the ascension of the *Merrimac*. . . . I objected, and said I would rather expend money to *remove* obstacles than to impede navigation . . . and that I should not consent to take any of the naval appropriation to cut off water communication, unless so ordered by the President."

Here Welles interjected a criticism of Stanton and the Army for not clearing the Confederate artillery batteries from the Virginia side of the Potomac. He pointed out that the Navy had been obliged to fight the blockade on its own, and that the Army, while doing nothing, was deriving great benefit from the supply transports that were breaking through.

"Our conversation was very earnest, and the President attentively listened, but with an evident inclination to guard in every way against the *Merrimac*, but yet unwilling to interrupt ocean communication, so essential to Washington. Giving the interview a pleasant turn, he said that it was evident that Mars [the Secretary of War] not only wanted exclusive control of military operations . . . but that he wanted a navy, and had begun to improvise one. Having already got his fleet, the President thought he might as well be permitted to finish this work, but he must not destroy communication on the Potomac, or cripple Neptune [the Secretary of the Navy]. The boats purchased might be loaded and sent down the river, but not sunk in the channel until it was known that the *Merrimac* had entered the river, or was on its way hither. Whatever expense was incurred must be defrayed by the War Department."

Stanton also asked permission to charter several huge old merchant steamers to station at Fort Monroe, their purpose to try to ram and sink the *Merrimack* should she make another appearance in Hampton Roads. This seemed a dubious measure to Lincoln, but he gave it his sanction. The choleric Secretary of War was not amused when the President, thereafter, referred to the nautical acquisitions—particularly the collection of battered scows and barges piled with earth and rocks—as "Stanton's Navy."

TOWARD RICHMOND
AT LAST

DURING THE SAME WEEKEND that saw the naval battles at Hampton Roads, Centreville was the scene of proceedings that upset McClellan's Urbanna plan. He had been acting under the assumption that the Confederates would be obliging enough to remain in their lines until they were cut off. But Joe Johnston, like McClellan, was a longtime student of military matters, and he was fully aware of the several routes from Washington available to the Federals. In addition to the direct one, there was the western corridor through the Shenandoah Valley, with its entrance at Harpers Ferry on the upper Potomac, as well as a choice of routes involving the lower Potomac and the Chesapeake. Using the long Shenandoah route through unfriendly territory would cause McClellan serious supply problems, so Johnston felt that he would do one of these things: make a direct approach, steal a march down the Maryland bank of the Potomac and cross near Fredericksburg, or use an eastern water route. As soon as the weather became favorable for operations, Johnston hastened to break up his camps and start heading southward. The retreat included the artillery batteries on the lower Potomac that had been harrassing the enemy's shipping. Johnston explains: "The Federal army was about to take the field, so I determined to move to the position already prepared for such an emergency—the south bank of the Rappahannock, strengthened by field works and provided with a depot for food; for in it we should be better able to resist the Federal army advancing by Manassas; and near enough to Fredericksburg to meet the enemy there, should he take that route; as well as to unite with any Confederate forces that might be sent to oppose him should he move by the lower Rappahannock or Fort Monroe."

The news that Johnston was withdrawing from Centreville reached McClellan on Sunday, March 9. "In the course of the evening I determined to move the whole army forward, partly with the hope that I might be able to take advantage of some accident and bring Johnston to battle under favorable circumstances, but also to break up the camps, give the troops a little experience in marching and bivouac before finally leaving the old base of supplies, to test the transportation arrangements and get rid of impedimenta, and thus prepare things for the movement to the Peninsula."

That evening the Prince de Joinville was walking a Washington street when a friend tapped him on the shoulder and said, in tones loud enough to transcend his deafness, "You don't know the news? The enemy has evacuated Manassas, and the army sets out tomorrow." De Joinville relates: "Next day, in reality, the whole city of Washington was in commotion. A mass of artillery, of cavalry, of wagons, blocked up the streets, moving towards the bridges of the Potomac. On the sidewalks were seen officers bidding tender farewells to weeping ladies. The civilian portion of the population looked coldly on this departure. There was not the least trace of enthusiasm among them. Perhaps this was due to the rain, which was falling in torrents.

"On the Long Bridge, in the midst of several batteries that were laboriously defiling across this bridge which is eternally in ruins, I met General McClellan, on horseback, with an anxious air, riding alone, without aides-de-camp, and escorted only by a few troopers. He who could that day have read the General's soul would have seen there already something of that bitterness which subsequently was to accumulate so cruelly upon him.

"Beyond the bridge we found the whole army in motion towards Fairfax Court House, where a great part of it encamped."

According to Trooper Adams, the picturesque old town, from which the inhabitants had fled, began to change in appearance as the soldiers settled in. "I am compelled, reluctantly, to record scenes of plunder and wanton destruction . . . disgraceful alike to those who took part in them and those who permitted them. The spirit of mischief and plunder for a time seized upon the men, who lost all respect for discipline. . . . They broke open the venerable old court house and other buildings, destroyed the county records, tore up old and valuable parchments, and strewed the floors a foot deep with papers and books. Many papers, valuable as historical reminiscences, connected with and bearing the signatures of members of the Washington, Custis, Fairfax, and other Virginia families distinguished in the nation's history, were carried off."

Trooper Adams accompanied a cavalry reconnaissance that went on to Manassas Junction, where the Stars and Stripes was raised. "The sight of the old flag flying in triumph over Manassas called forth shout after shout of applause. Manassas presented a scene of wreck only the eye accustomed to war and its devastations can comprehend. The ruins of several buildings and the railroad depot still smouldered and smoked. Heaps of burning wagons, of stores, of cars, and of various war materials spread over the ground in all directions. A charred and disabled locomotive stood, like a helpless giant, on the track. Campfires still burned here and there, and sooty Negroes huddled round them, trying to extract warmth from the dying embers. Others hailed our appearance with expressions of joy and welcome, deep and earnest. From the more intelligent of them we got much valuable information. Many of them had been the servants of rebel officers, and had cunningly taken advantage of their hasty retreat to secure freedom.

"Long lines of ingeniously built and comfortably provided log huts were left untouched. . . . The enemy left us plenty of good rations and a large stock of curiosities which the men had manufactured during the winter, but neglected to carry away. Our men . . . took peaceable possession of the huts, and, with plenty of fuel, made themselves quite comfortable. Not a few of the troopers took their horses into the huts with them, an act of kindness the poor animals seemed to appreciate, for they had suffered much from the wet and cold. . . . The large stock of curiosities were soon appropriated and sent home as mementoes of Manassas."

On March 11, the Prince de Joinville rode with a party of horsemen who toured Manassas Junction, and he was saddened by the sight of the smoking ruins. "On our return we visited the battlefield of Bull Run. General McDowell was with us. He could not restrain his tears at the sight of those bleaching bones, which recalled to him so vividly the recollection of his defeat."

McClellan had set up his headquarters in an abandoned home at Fairfax Court House. It wasn't only Johnston's unexpected withdrawal that gave him the "anxious air" de Joinville observed. He was carrying orders from Lincoln directing him to reorganize the Army of the Potomac into four corps, each under a general of the President's selection. The order, McClellan laments, "was issued without consulting me and against my judgment, for from the beginning it had been my intention to postpone the formation of army corps until service in the field had indicated what general officers were best fitted to exercise those most important commands."

Even while McClellan was implementing the unwelcome instructions from his Fairfax headquarters, an aide handed him a newspaper containing an item that stunned him, another presidential order, one that had failed to reach him directly. "Major General McClellan, having personally taken the field at the head of the Army of the Potomac, until otherwise ordered he is relieved from the command of the other military departments, he retaining command of the Department of the Potomac. . . . Ordered, also, That . . . all the commanders of departments, after the receipt of this order by them, respectively report severally and directly to the Secretary of War."

McClellan now became convinced that "the rascals in Washington" were conspiring to subvert his campaign, and that if Lincoln was not a part of the conspiracy, he was at least guilty of condoning it. McClellan was wrong. Stanton, of course, remained solidly against him. Disgusted by the general's lack of drive, the secretary took high satisfaction in assuming a significant part of his power. But Lincoln was far from an ineffectual bystander in the matter. Stanton would have liked to see McClellan relieved of his remaining command; but the President, at this point unaware of a better leader for the Army of the Potomac, chose to sustain the general in the post.

As for Stanton's peculiar character, it was perhaps best analyzed by A. K. McClure, a Union newspaper publisher who knew him well: "He was a man of whom two histories might be written as widely diverging as night and day, portraying him as worthy of eminent praise and as worthy of scorching censure, and yet both absolutely true. . . . He was a man of extreme moods; often petulant, irritating, and senselessly unjust, and at times one of the most amiable, genial, and delightful conversationalists I have ever met. He loved antagonism, and there was hardly a period during his remarkable service as a War Minister in which he was not, on some more or less important point, in positive antagonism with the President. In his antagonisms he was, as a rule, offensively despotic, and often pressed them upon Lincoln to the very utmost point of Lincoln's forbearance; but he knew when to call a halt upon himself, as he well knew that there never was a day or an hour . . . that Lincoln was not his absolute master. He respected Lincoln's authority because it was greater than his own, but he had little respect for Lincoln's fitness for the responsible duties of the Presidency. . . .

"I have seen him at times as tender and gentle as a woman, his heart seeming to agonize over the sorrows of the humblest; and I have seen him many more times turn away with the haughtiest contempt from appeals which should at least have been treated with respect. He had few personal and fewer political friends, and he seemed proud of the fact that he had more personal and political enemies that any prominent officer of the government. Senators, Representatives, and high military commanders were often offended by his wanton arrogance, and again thawed into cordial relations by his effusive kindness. . . .

"Lincoln was not long in discovering that in his new Secretary of War he had an invaluable but most troublesome Cabinet officer, but he saw only the great and good offices that Stanton was performing for the imperiled Republic. Confidence was restored in financial circles by the appointment of Stanton, and his name as War Minister did more to strengthen the faith of the people in the government credit than would have been probable from the appointment of any other man of the day. He was a terror to all the hordes of jobbers and speculators and camp followers whose appetites had been whetted by a great war, and he enforced the strictest discipline throughout our armies. . . . He had profound, unfaltering faith in the Union cause, and, above all, he had unfaltering faith in himself. He believed that he was in all things except in name Commander-in-Chief of the armies and the navy of the nation. . . . He at times conceived impossible things and peremptorily ordered them executed, and woe to the man who was unfortunate enough to demonstrate that Stanton was wrong. If he escaped without disgrace he was more than fortunate, and many, very many, would have thus fallen unjustly had it not been for Lincoln's cautious and generous interposition to save those who were wantonly censured. He would not throw the blame upon Stanton, but would save the victim of Stanton's injustice, and he always did it so kindly that even Stanton could not complain beyond a churlish growl.

"Stanton understood the magnitude of the rebellion, and he understood also that an army to be effective must be completely organized in all its departments. . . . His constant and honest aim was to secure the best men for every important position. . . . The effect of such a War Minister was to enforce devotion to duty throughout the entire army, and it is impossible to measure the beneficent results of Stanton's policy. . . . Stanton's intense and irrepressible hatreds were his greatest infirmity. . . . Lincoln's patience and forbearance were marked in contrast. . . . Notwithstanding the many and often irritating conflicts that Lincoln had with Stanton, there never was an hour . . . that Lincoln thought of removing him. Indeed, I believe that at no period . . . did Lincoln feel that any other man could fill Stanton's place with equal usefulness to the country. . . . He was in hearty sympathy with Stanton's aggressive earnestness for the prosecution of the war."

On March 13, still headquartered at Fairfax, McClellan met with his four corps commanders: Irvin McDowell, Edwin Sumner, Samuel Heintzelman, and Erasmus Keyes. Trooper Adams describes the group as "an exquisite picture, for the men forming it possessed rare peculiarities of form and feature, and were as opposite mentally and physically as it is possible for nature, in her wildest freaks, to form men. To this council of war McClellan submitted his plan for the campaign on the Peninsula, with his reasons for urging it in preference to the line of the Rappahannock. It must be remembered that these officers were the President's choice. . . . McClellan knew . . . that at least two . . . were hostile to him [McDowell, Sumner, and Heintzelman had voted with the faction of generals who disliked the Urbanna proposal]; and he had reasons to fear that they would oppose his [new] plans. . . . He was led to believe, also, that they would support the President's plan in preference to his, unless he could overbalance their opposition with arguments of the strongest kind. . . .

"The proceedings of this council of war were of the most simple and direct kind. . . . The chief questions discussed and passed upon were: the availability of the two lines; the efficiency of the navy to neutralize the power of the enemy's steamer *Merrimac;* water transportation; the force necessary to secure the safety of Washington; and whether the navy could furnish a sufficient auxiliary force to silence the enemy's batteries on the York River [which McClellan planned to use as a supply route while marching up the Peninsula]. . . . This council of war closed its deliberations by adopting Fort Monroe as a base of future operations, the . . . reluctant generals yielding, as they were reported to have said, because they knew that General McClellan had made up his mind to transfer his operations to the Peninsula. . . .

"There can be no doubt about the feeling in the army favoring the new line by the Peninsula. . . . When news came that it had been decided to move by that route, it was received with general approbation. On the 15th orders were issued, and the main portion of the army began to move back to its old quarters on the banks of the Potomac. . . . A portion of Sumner's corps was left at Manassas to disguise our movements, as it was facetiously said, and observe the enemy. A drenching rain fell on the 15th, and although the roads were churned up into a clay bed, and the jaded animals in a sorry plight, the men were in good spirits at the prospect of taking another, and, as they believed, a better road to Richmond."

Enhancing the army's morale was an address published by McClellan, whom the great majority of the troops still idolized as "Little Mac." Dismissing the general's critics as misguided, these men remained convinced he knew what he was doing. His announcement that he was about to take them where they all wished to go, to the decisive battlefield, was inspiring. "I am to watch over you as a parent over his children; and you know that your general loves you from the depths of his heart. It shall be my care, as it has ever been, to gain success with the least possible loss; but I know that, if it is necessary, you will willingly follow me to your graves for our righteous cause. . . . I shall demand of you great, heroic exertions, rapid and long marches, desperate combats, privations perhaps. We will share all these together; and when this sad war is over we will return to our homes, and feel that we can ask no higher honor than the proud consciousness that we belonged to the Army of the Potomac."

March 16 saw various units of the army reestablished in their old camps around Washington. "The land march was therefore abandoned," explains the Prince de Joinville, "and we came back to the movement by water. But this operation . . . was no longer what it had been when McClellan had conceived it. . . . The evacuation of Manassas had *preceded* instead of *following* the opening of the Federal campaign. The movement by water could no longer be a surprise. Unfortunately, it was now also to lose the advantages of a rapid execution. A few days had been half lost in a useless pursuit of the enemy while the transports were assembling at Alexandria. At last they were assembled, and the order came to embark. But here a new misunderstanding awaited the General. He had been promised transports which could convey 50,000 men at a time. He found vessels hardly equal to

Transports on the Potomac

the conveyance of half that number. . . . A number of trips had to be made. The embarkation began March 17."

After clearing out of Centreville and Manassas, Joe Johnston's army marched first to the prepared position on the Rappahannock, but soon afterward proceeded to the south side of the Rapidan so as to be closer to Richmond. Jesse Reid wrote home: "We have traveled nearly a hundred miles, though between Centreville and this place the distance is not more than half that great by rail. We came by a very circuitous route on account of most of it being good hard road. It is a mountainous country, and we traveled some distance on the Blue Ridge. . . . Although this trip was gratifying to me, it was attended with a good many hardships, such as hard marching, heavy baggage, and for the last two or three days we came through enough mud to daub every Negro cabin in the Southern Confederacy. We carried our knapsacks, with our clothing and blankets in them, our haversacks with our provisions and canteens of water, cartridge boxes with ammunition, our bayonet belts with bayonets in them, and our muskets on our shoulders—a pretty good load. You may suppose we had little room for bottles, yet there were some along. Our entire army is falling back, some going by one road and some by another. The Federal army is also changing their position. I think they are going by water, but where they are moving I don't know or care. But let the enemy go where they will, there we will be also."

McClellan's troops found the water journey a novel adventure. The early-morning departure of one of the flotillas, which presented a scene typical of all the departures, is described by Color Sergeant D. G. Crotty: "The signal from the flagship is given, and the heavily laden transports . . . steam down the majestic river amid the firing of salutes from the navy yard and the playing of scores of bands. Passing Fort Washington, a salute is fired in our honor." No one found the trip's next highlight more impressive than George T. Stevens, surgeon of the 77th Regiment, New York Volunteers: "We passed Mount Vernon, the bells of the fleet tolling. The tomb lies in the midst of a clump of firs just south and a little below the house. The mansion and the grounds are nearly as they were left by Washington, and the whole looks down upon the river, calling upon the passerby for a thought upon the great man whose dust lies beneath the fir trees." The thought that occured to Chaplain Stewart was this: "Could the Father of His Country have looked out from his tomb on the passing pageant—a host triple in number to any he ever commanded—his exclamation would, no doubt, have been, 'What! And where are you going?'" Returning to Surgeon Stevens: "After passing Mount Vernon, nothing of special interest was seen except the broad expanse of waters of this magnificent stream. A few large mansions, a few inferior houses, and now and then a little hamlet, appeared on the banks; and at Aquia Creek could be seen the insignificant earthworks that had covered the few fieldpieces which for so many months had kept up an efficient blockade of the Potomac."

Each flotilla spent its first day negotiating the river. Speaking of the regiment of which he was a part, Chaplain Stewart relates: "Neither the novelties of our condition, the tumult of the voyage, nor the dense throng of the boat, were permitted to interfere with or interrupt our accustomed evening worship. . . . A goodly number got together, on the fore and upper deck of the boat, and united in songs of praise, in prayer, and in words of exhortation and encouragement. The position, the scenery, and the uncertainties of our journey all combined to render our evening worship peculiarly interesting and profitable."

"At night," says Surgeon Stevens, "we were on the broad Chesapeake. A stiff breeze set our fleet rocking, but we slept quietly, leaving the waves to take care of themselves and the pilots to take care of the boats."

Again in the words of Chaplain Stewart: "Waking at dawn . . . we found our old New York and Fall River boat safely anchored directly in front of Fortress Monroe. . . . The fortifications are situated on a low point of sandy beach. . . . By good engineering, enormous expense, and labor long-continued, the fort has been rendered one of the strongest in the world. . . . It is almost the only fortified place in all Dixie saved to the Union from the treachery of this rebellion. . . . Here stretches, far away towards the ocean, the beautiful Chesapeake; there the bay-like mouth of the James; yonder the misty view of Norfolk and Portsmouth; around us an immense fleet."

Adds Sergeant Crotty: "Arising from my couch on the upper deck, feeling sore about the hips, I hear laughter on the other side of the boat, and, passing thither, learn the cause of it. . . . Someone points out to me an object floating around in the water. It looks like the back of a whale just floating under the water, with a large round box on its back. . . . A man with a glass walks up and down and around the box, looking very anxiously up Hampton Roads toward Norfolk. . . . At last we solve the mysterious-looking animal and pronounce it to be none other than the Mistress of the Seas, the little *Monitor*, which is waiting for the much talked of *Merrimac* to come out and show herself again."

Although most of the flotillas arrived off Fort Monroe in clement weather, the one bearing Chaplain J. J. Marks and the 63rd Pennsylvania Volunteers made its approach in a lashing rain. "The sea became very rough, and we had to land when the waves were breaking in great billows over the beach. The vessels dashed against each other, cables were broken, and steamers full of men drifted helplessly from the docks. In the most unpitying storm we landed and gathered in shivering bands on the shore." Many of these troops were pale and weak from seasickness.

The weather was good when the flotilla carrying the New York regiment led by Regis de Trobriand arrived off the wharves, but there was much congestion, and the colonel had trouble directing his regiment's ves-

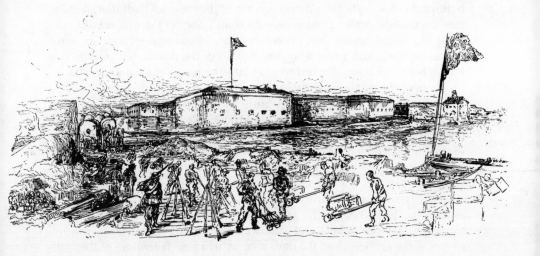

Quartermaster's dock at Fort Monroe

sel to the dock. "Hour after hour the *Croton* waited its turn and did not get any nearer, passed by the more enterprising or the more skilful. I sent my report on the difficulty which delayed me, and received simply the reply to do my best. . . . I decided . . . since it was 'everyone for himself,' to force my way to the wharf by main strength. We succeeded, thanks to our powerful engines, and thus our disembarkment on the Peninsula was effected.

"The first sight presented to our eyes was that of the ruins of Hampton. Hampton was, before the war, a charming little town, at the head of the bay bearing its name. It had its churches, its banks, its hotels, its villas, its shady gardens. Southern families flocked there during the summer to take sea baths and enjoy gayly the other pleasures of the season. Of all that, nothing now remained—nothing but masses of ruins lying on the ground, skirts of walls blackened by the fire, broken columns marking the facade of some public building, and a few straggling bushes of the devastated gardens surviving here and there. Forced to evacuate the place, the Confederates . . . had burned the village and ruined the whole population."

As vessel after vessel unloaded, Surgeon Stevens explains, "dense masses of infantry, long trains of artillery, and thousands of cavalry, with unnumbered army wagons and mules were mingled in grand confusion along the shore. The neighing of horses, the braying of mules, the rattle of wagons and artillery, and the sound of many voices mingled in one grand inharmonious concert." Private Warren Goss marveled at the scene's intermixture of colors: "The red cap, white leggings, and baggy trousers of the Zouaves mingled with the blue uniforms and dark trimmings of the regular infantrymen, the short jackets and yellow trimmings of the cavalry, the red stripes of the artillery, and the dark blue with orange trimmings of the engineers; together with the ragged, many-colored costumes of the black laborers and teamsters."

Chaplain Marks was aware that the army was entering a region of deep historical interest, and he meditated on the fact that in the spring of 1607 a small band of colonists from England, among them Captain John Smith, met with the Indians at the spot that became Hampton, then sailed into the mouth of "a beautiful river, and, in honor of the English monarch, called it James River, and laid the foundation for the first settlement in Virginia at Jamestown. . . .

"This is unquestionably one of the most interesting regions on our continent, reminding one of the rich delta of the Nile. Five rivers converge their streams and pour their waters, within fifty miles of each other, into Chesapeake Bay. . . . The largest steamers and men-of-war have ascended these rivers for more than one hundred miles. . . . In consequence of the country rising so little above the level of the sea, there is in the peninsular and tidewater counties great quantities of swampland. Many of these could be redeemed, but are now almost as impenetrable as the jungles of India. But

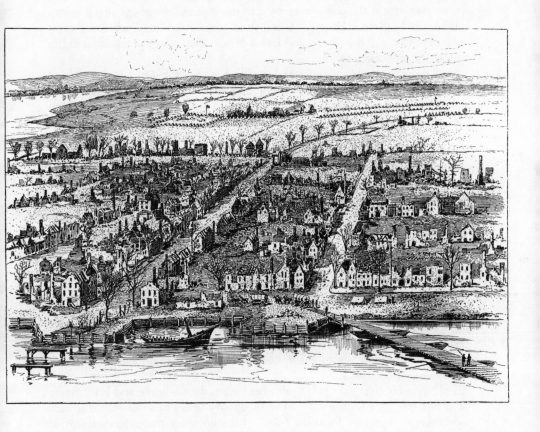

Ruins of Hampton

long tongues of the richest alluvial land pierce these heavy forests. . . . These tidewater lands had been advancing rapidly in value as their true worth became known.

"No doubt there is a great source of wealth in the . . . forest lands on the banks of the York, Chickahominy, Pamunkey, and James Rivers. Many Northern men were engaged in getting out this timber for shipbuilding and other purposes at the commencement of the war, and were opening a useful and profitable trade. Their mills and stock were abandoned, and they compelled to flee. . . . But peace and freedom will bear new enterprise and life into these unbroken wilds. . . .

"The grand army . . . collected in the green fields back of Hampton. . . . While our encampments were here, the scene was most animating and novel. . . . Here a brigade of cavalry, with waving plumes and flashing sabres, dashed across the field. In another direction were all the movements peculiar to artillery practice. On the carriage bearing each piece were seated six men . . . four horses being attached to a carriage bearing a twelve-pounder, and six and eight to the carriages bearing larger guns, and one rider to a pair of horses; a carriage . . . called a cassion, containing ammunition, following each gun. The horses were urged into the wildest gallop, as if rushing into action, wheeling around without the halt of a moment; the men sprang from their seats and unlimbered the guns; the horses were removed, and the gunners went through the pantomime show of loading and firing; and again the horses, with equal haste, were urged to the guns, attached in a second, and with furious speed rushed to another part of the field. Again . . . the guns were detached [and] brought into position. . . .

"In another field a long line of three-fourths of a mile, kneeling on one knee with presented bayonets, was a brigade waiting the dash of an enemy's cavalry. Apparently fastened to the earth . . . they reminded one of the armies sculptured on Egyptian monuments. In another field a brigade with fixed bayonets charged upon their enemies; and over brake and briar fence and bog they ran with yells on the imaginary foe. The amusement of this spectacle was greater from the fright of the horses of the officers, the wild leaps of fences and ditches, and the panting, sweltering fat officers bringing up the rear.

"In another field, companies of scouts and skirmishers were being drilled in the movements of that most dangerous but useful arm of the service. . . . In another field, a brigade that had landed but an hour before were casting their knapsacks on the ground, stacking their arms, and pitching their tents."

Simultaneously with the great migration to the Peninsula, the Shenandoah Valley saw the birth of a series of actions destined to have a dramatic effect on McClellan's campaign. The Federals who were guarding the

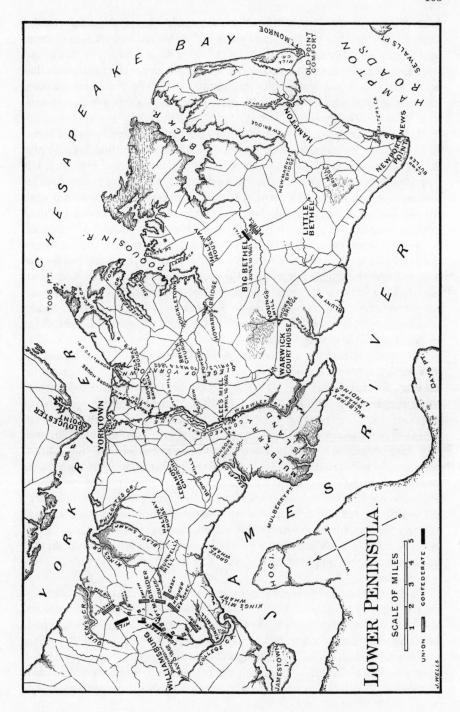

LOWER PENINSULA.

SCALE OF MILES
1 2 3 4 5

UNION ▭▭ CONFEDERATE ▬▬

J. WELLS

back-door route to Washington were commanded by Nathaniel P. Banks, one of the Union's new "political soldiers." A Massachusetts businessman and former Republican Speaker of the House of Representatives, Banks had used his influence to obtain a commission as major general. Distinguished as a civilian, Banks had neither the training nor the instinct for high military command. Worse luck for him, his opponent in the Valley was the remarkable Stonewall Jackson.

Of Scotch-Irish ancestry, Thomas Jonathan Jackson was born at Clarksburg, western Virginia, in 1824. He was raised on a farm, which he helped to run; and he became adept at riding, hunting, fishing, and trapping. His opportunities for formal education were meager. He was not robust, but his ailments, which included a form of nervous indigestion that would plague him for life, were more troublesome than serious, and his sustained physical activity seemed to help keep them at bay. "He was a youth," a cousin explained in afteryears, "of exemplary habits, of indomitable will, and undoubted courage. He was not what is nowadays termed brilliant, but he was one of those untiring, matter-of-fact persons who would never give up an undertaking until he accomplished his object. He learned slowly, but what he got into his head he never forgot. He was not quick to decide, except when excited, and then, when he made up his mind to do a thing, he did it on short notice and in quick time."

At eighteen, Jackson won admittance to West Point. He told his uneasy sponsors, "I am very ignorant, but I can make it up in study." Adopting the maxim "You can be what you resolve to be," he applied himself doggedly, often keeping at his books by firelight after "lamps out." He soon began climbing from his position near the bottom of the class, one of whose brighter members was young George McClellan. Now tall and angular, with large hands and feet, Jackson was clumsy at performing the military exercises. While striving to measure up, he was indifferent to jests about his backwoods origins, and to the inevitable practical jokes played upon him. He made no secret of the odd views he was beginning to develop regarding his health. He sat rigidly erect, he explained, to facilitate his digestion and to keep from compressing his intestines, which might dispose them to disease. To stimulate his circulation he would suddenly begin pumping an arm up and down, keeping a careful count and fretting when someone interrupted him.

Jackson's shortcomings and peculiarities were not ruinous. "I believe," recalled one of his classmates, "he went through the very trying ordeal of the four years at West Point without ever having a hard word or a bad feeling from cadet or professor. While there were many who seemed to surpass him in intellect, in geniality, and in good fellowship, there was no one of our class who more absolutely possessed the respect and confidence of all; and in the end 'Old Jack,' as he was always called, with his desperate earnest-

Stonewall Jackson

ness, his unflinching straightforwardness, and his high sense of honor, came to be regarded by his comrades with something very like affection." In this class of fifty-nine members that saw McClellan take second honors, Jackson graduated seventeenth.

Jackson served with the artillery during the Mexican War. His commanding officer was John Magruder, then a captain, who praised him in a report: "If devotion, industry, talent, and gallantry are the highest qualities of a soldier, then he is entitled to the distinction which their possession confers." Jackson's achievements under fire, performed with uncommon coolness, outshone those of McClellan and all the rest of his West Point classmates. By the end of the war he held the brevet rank of major. Asked whether he had been afraid for his life while the shells and bullets were flying, he said, "No, the only anxiety of which I was conscious during the engagements was a fear lest I should not meet danger enough to make my conduct conspicuous."

Returning to the States, Jackson was assigned to garrison duty at Fort Hamilton, Long Island. He filled much of his spare time with studies, mostly in the fields of history and religion. His stomach trouble and his other chronic discomforts led him to consult with New York City's best physicians, but he got little relief. This caused him to increase his reliance on self-treatment in the areas of exercise and diet. According to an old West Point classmate, Dabney Maury, who had become an instructor at the Point and was one day surprised by a visit from Jackson: "At that time he was convinced that one of his legs was bigger than the other, and that one of his arms was likewise unduly heavy. He had acquired the habit of raising the heavy arm straight up so that, as he said, the blood would run back into his body and lighten it." Jackson's religious studies were turning him into a zealous Christian, and he began to believe that his physical infirmities had been decreed by God to punish him for his sins and to put him on the road to salvation. Not certain he had been baptized as a child, he had this ceremony performed.

In 1850 Jackson was transferred to Fort Meade, Florida. Inclined to be somewhat restless in a peacetime army, he was soon at odds with his new commanding officer, who, he felt, was not giving him enough responsibility. Another kind of trouble developed when it was rumored that the commander was having an affair with his children's nursemaid and the strait-laced Jackson considered it his duty to undertake an investigation. The resulting scandal not only rocked the post but reached the public. The mortified commander was reassigned. Jackson himself soon left the post— and the army—for a civilian pursuit. He was accepted to fill the dual position of artillery instructor and professor of natural philosophy at the Virginia Military Institute in Lexington, at the southern end of the Shenandoah Valley. Although he proved to be a good artillery instructor, his philosophy lectures were uninspired. At least one student, writing home, called Jackson "such a hell of a fool" as a classroom teacher. Another, receiving a bad mark he blamed on the professor's ineptitude, put him down as "crazy as damnation." Jackson eventually improved his techniques, but they never advanced beyond adequate.

Jackson was thirty when he married Eleanor Junkin, daughter of a Lexington minister, in 1853. Eleanor died in childbirth, the baby with her, the following year. A crushed Jackson wrote in his notebook: "Objects to be effected by Ellie's death—To eradicate ambition; to eradicate resentment; to produce humility." Four years later Jackson married Mary Anna Morrison, also a minister's daughter, and the union presently created a baby girl he greeted with an almost delirious affection, then lost to death in a few weeks. Jackson would father another girl, a healthy one, during the war; but he would see very little of her before he was killed at Chancellorsville.

Jackson was still at the Institute when the war began. The advanced cadets were summoned to Richmond to serve as drill instructors, and Jackson accompanied them to accept from Governor Letcher a commission as colonel of Virginia volunteers. Up to this time Jackson had opposed secession but had championed states' rights. Says his wife, Mary Anna: "I am very confident that he would never have fought for the sole object of perpetuating slavery. It was for her *constitutional rights* that the South resisted the North, and slavery was only comprehended among those rights. He found the institution [of slavery] a responsible and troublesome one, and I have heard him say that he would prefer to see the Negroes free, but he believed that the Bible taught that slavery was sanctioned by the Creator himself, who maketh men to differ and instituted laws for the bond and the free. He therefore accepted slavery, as it existed in the Southern States, not as a thing desirable in itself but as allowed by Providence for ends which it was not his business to determine."

Jackson was sent to take command at Harpers Ferry, seized from the Federals just after the fall of Fort Sumter. He found the new garrison wanting in discipline; the men were performing their duties as though on a lark, and a good many of then were rosily drunk. One of Jackson's first acts was to order the garrison's whiskey stores poured into the Potomac. It was only a few days until he had all departments functioning in a military style. One of his former students who saw him at this time noted a change: "Jackson was much more in his element here as an army officer than when in the professor's chair at Lexington. It seemed that the sights and sounds of war had aroused his energies. His manner had become brusque and imperative; his face was bronzed from exposure; his beard . . . was worn unshorn."

Within a few weeks, as the Harpers Ferry garrison grew in numbers, General Joe Johnston succeeded Colonel Jackson as top commander. Jackson was placed in charge of a brigade of infantry. The Federals soon amassed a superior army on the north bank of the Potomac, and Johnston abandoned Harpers Ferry and withdrew some miles through the Shenandoah Valley. When the Federals crossed to the south bank in early July 1861, Jackson's troops, along with a few cavalrymen under Jeb Stuart, conducted a reconnaissance of the invasion. The proceedings included a skirmish during which Jackson performed smartly in the face of superior numbers. Shortly afterward he received a message from the Richmond headquarters of Robert E. Lee: "I have the pleasure of sending you a commission of Brigadier General in the Provisional Army; and to feel that you merit it. May your advancement increase your usefulness to the state." Two weeks later Joe Johnston's Shenandoah Valley army was on its way to Bull Run, where Jackson and his brigade made the stand that earned Jackson his colorful sobriquet. On the morning after the battle, he wrote Mary Anna: "Although under a heavy fire for several continuous hours, I received only one wound, the breaking of the longest finger of my left hand. . . . My horse was wounded but not killed. [My] coat got an ugly wound near the hip, but my servant, who is very handy, has so far repaired it that it doesn't show very much. . . . Whilst great credit is due to other parts of our gallant army, God made my brigade more instrumental than any other in repulsing the main attack. This is for your information only—say nothing about it. Let others speak praise, not myself." He wrote another letter at this same sitting, this one to the Lexington pastor whose church he attended. The pastor opened the letter eagerly, feeling he was about to read a firsthand report of the great battle. This was all that greeted his eye: "My dear pastor— In my tent last night, after a fatiguing day's service, I remembered that I had failed to send you my contribution for our colored Sunday school. Enclosed you will find my check for that object, which please acknowledge at your earliest convenience, and oblige yours faithfully, T. J. Jackson."

The reticent hero remained in the Centreville area for the next few months. He fretted because the powers at Richmond made no plans for an invasion of the North. His time was devoted largely to the training of his troops, with whom he was establishing a unique rapport. Confederate writer John Esten Cooke, who knew the general well, explains the relationship this way: "Jackson's appearance and manners . . . were such as conciliate a familiar, humorous liking. His dingy old coat, than which scarce a private's in his command was more faded; his dilapidated and discolored cap; the absence of decorations and all show in his dress; his odd ways; his kindly, simple manner; his habit of sitting down and eating with his men; his indifference whether his bed were in a comfortable headquarter tent on a camp couch, or in a fence corner with no shelter from the rain but his cloak; his abstemiousness, fairness, honesty, simplicity; his never-failing regard for the comfort and the feelings of the private soldier; his oddities, eccentricities, and originalities—all were an unfailing provocative to liking, and endeared him to his men. Troops are charmed when there is anything in the personal character of a great leader to 'make fun of.' Admiration of his genius then becomes enthusiasm for his person. Jackson had aroused this enthusiasm in his men."

In November 1861, Jackson was promoted to major general and sent to assume top command of the Confederate forces in the Shenandoah Valley. The opening of McClellan's Peninsula Campaign the following March found Jackson at Winchester, about twenty miles from Nathaniel Banks, who was covering Harpers Ferry. Jackson's army, which included his original "Stonewall Brigade," numbered only 5,000 men, whereas Banks had more than 35,000. Washington ordered Banks to clear the Confederates from the Valley so that the bulk of his army could be transferred eastward to help protect the capital in the absence of the Army of the Potomac. It was Jackson's mission to try to keep Banks tied up in the Valley. As Banks advanced upon Winchester, Jackson withdrew southward. The retreat convinced Banks that control of the Valley would be easily gained, and he began moving large numbers of his men toward Washington. Led by General James Shields, the Federals who continued the pursuit marched about forty miles past Winchester, then turned back. Jackson turned back, too. His cavalry commander, Colonel Turner Ashby, underestimated Shields' strength, and Jackson decided to make an attack. Shields deployed 7,000 men at Kernstown, and Jackson pressed in with 3,500. The date was March 23, 1862.

"It was the Sabbath day," relates Jackson's chief of staff, a Presbyterian doctor of divinity named Robert L. Dabney, "and if there was one principle of General Jackson's religion which was more stringent than the others, it was his reverence for its sancitity. He had yielded to the demands of military necessity, so far as to march on the sacred morning, that he might not lose the advantages which opportunity seemed to place within his reach; but now a more inexorable necessity was upon him. It was manifest that Colonel Ashby had been deceived in his estimate of the [enemy's] force. . . . Already it was doubtful whether a prompt retreat would be safely concluded. General Jackson's resolution was therefore immediately taken, to assail the enemy on the spot, and win, if not a decisive victory, at least the privilege of an unmolested retreat. . . .

"About 4 o'clock in the afternoon . . . the little army advanced against the enemy. . . . After a spirited cannonade, by which several batteries of the enemy were silenced, the infantry engaged with inexpressible fury, at close quarters. . . . In some places, the lines were advanced within twenty paces, partially shielded from each other by the abrupt little ravines, where the Confederates, lying upon their breasts behind the protuberances of the ground, or retiring a few steps into the hollow places to reload, held their enemies at bay by their scathing discharges. As regiment after regiment came into position, their heroic general led them into the hottest of the fire. . . . On the Federal side, the superior numbers enabled them perpetually to bring up fresh troops. As one regiment recoiled, reeling and panic-struck, it was replaced again and again by another; and the officers, secure of victory from their preponderating force, were seen riding madly behind the wavering lines, goading their men to the work with the saber. The Confederates, on the other hand, having no succors, fought until they exhausted their ammunition. As the men fired their last cartridge, their officers allowed them to go to the rear; and after a time the thinned lines presented no adequate resistance to the fresh crowds of enemies. Near nightfall, General Richard B. Garnett, commanding the Stonewall Brigade in the center, seeing his fire dying away for lack of ammunition and his line pierced on his right, assumed the responsibility of authorizing a retreat of his command without orders from General Jackson; and nothing now remained but to protect the movement from more serious disaster. . . .

"The infantry retreated a few miles to the neighborhood of Newtown, while the cavalry of Colonel Ashby took its station at Barton's Mills, a mile in the rear of the field of combat, and held the enemy in check. . . . General Jackson himself, begging a morsel of food at the bivouac fire of the soldiers, lay down in the field to snatch a few hours' repose, a little in the rear of his outposts. . . . This was the first pitched battle in which General Jackson had supreme command. . . . [He] was not satisfied with the results, and insisted that a more resolute struggle for the field might have won it, even against the fearful odds opposed to him. The chief error of the battle, he believed, was the unexpected retreat of the Stonewall Brigade from the center, for this necessitated the surrender of the field. His disapprobation was strongly expressed against its brave general, Garnett, nor was he willing to accept their justification that their ammunition was expended. A regiment of reserves was at hand, and the bayonet, his favorite resource, yet remained to them; and he did not consider all the means of victory as exhausted until the naked steel was employed. . . . This instance may serve to show Jackson's rigid ideas of official duty, which were always more exacting as men rose in rank."

Jackson's fight at Kernstown—which cost him 718 men killed, wounded, and missing, while the Federals suffered 590—was a tactical defeat that became a great strategic victory. Shields and Banks decided that Jackson would not have attacked unless he had strong reserves somewhere behind him in the Valley, and the Federal units that had started toward Washington were recalled. Jackson had managed to interfere with McClellan's campaign plans before they were even completed. When Jackson began retreating southward again after Kernstown, Banks followed, but ever so cautiously. The Valley would see no resumption of serious fighting for several weeks.

The Kernstown battlefield

At Fort Monroe, the last week in March found the accumulating Federals getting themselves oriented for action. They were some seventy miles southeast of Richmond, the York River to their right and the James to their left. McClellan, who was still in Washington tying up loose ends, sent word to corps commander Samuel Heintzelman to perform a reconnaissance up the Peninsula. It was known that the first enemy defenses of any substance were those under John Magruder in the Yorktown area. On March 27, Heintzelman sent two columns, a division in each, to feel out these defenses, the right column moving by way of the Yorktown Road through Big Bethel, and the left by way of the James River Road to Warwick Court House. The mission is described as it was experienced by Surgeon Stevens, who marched with the column on the left:

"All the bridges over the route had been destroyed by the enemy, but pioneers advanced at the head of the column, and as the bridges were small they were quickly repaired. A march of a few miles brought us in sight of the James River, a noble stream at least five miles wide at this point. Not far from the shore appeared the masts of the U.S. frigate *Cumberland,* sunk in the memorable fight with the *Merrimac.* As our march led us along the banks, the views were charming. On one hand was the noble river, and on the other . . . orchards and groves. Deserted houses, and gardens blooming with hyacinths and other blossoms of early spring were passed. On the opposite side of the river lay a rebel gunboat, watching our movements. . . .

"Porter's division [i.e., that of General Fitz John Porter] had marched upon Big Bethel. After a march of fifteen miles, our division was drawn up in line of battle near Warwick. Porter's division had already reached Big Bethel, on our right, and we could see huge columns of smoke rising in that direction, and hear the roar of artillery. An aide dashed up and informed General [John W.] Davidson that the enemy were in line of battle to receive us. Soon the order came to advance. The line swept onward through the woods and over a cleared field, but found no foe. A few cavalry pickets only were seen, and a shell from one of our Parrott guns set them flying. . . . We passed through the Confederate encampments where their fires were still blazing, but soon turned round and bivouacked on ground last night occupied by the rebels."

Porter's division had also routed some enemy outposts, burning a few of their buildings in the process, and pursuing them for four miles beyond Big Bethel. Although the intelligence officers of both divisions queried Confederate deserters and area residents about John Magruder's lines, they learned but little. Obtaining knowledge was made extra difficult because there were no good maps of the region. So scarce was topographical information that McClellan's mapmakers had been obliged to place considerable reliance on a yellowing British sketch of the siege lines of 1781. The reconnaissance officers estimated Magruder's strength at between 15,000 and 20,000 men.

The actual number was 11,000. These troops spanned the Peninsula, with 6,000 in flank positions on the York and James, and only 5,000 covering the ten miles in between.

The reconnaissance columns made a prompt return to Fort Monroe. Surgeon Stevens and his comrades encamped near Newport News. "The masts of the *Cumberland* greeted our eyes whenever we turned toward the river, and the rebel gunboats made short excursions toward our side of the stream. One day large numbers of men, mostly from the Vermont brigade, were on the shoals of the river bathing and gathering oysters. The gunboat *Teazer,* discovering them, steamed toward them and threw some heavy shells shrieking and cracking among them, causing great consternation among the bathers, and some confusion and much amusement on shore."

The Confederates were as yet uncertain of Federal intentions. They knew, of course, that Richmond was McClellan's ultimate goal, but they were not sure how he meant to approach. The landing at Fort Monroe was not a giveaway; it might have been made in preparation for an attack on Norfolk and the Gosport Navy Yard. Even the reconnaissance up the Peninsula did not eliminate this as a possibility. These were worrisome days for John Magruder, with his lines so thinly manned, and he wrote to Richmond asking for reinforcements. His letter was referred to General Lee, until this time a somewhat shadowy figure when it came to matters regarding the defense of Richmond. He had scarcely returned from his misadventure in western Virginia the preceding autumn before he was sent to supervise the construction of a line of fortifications along the coasts of South Carolina, Georgia, and Florida. Lee reported back from this mission on March 12, at which time he resumed his desk work under Davis, a role he found tedious but which he performed conscientiously. Now he wrote Magruder: "It is impossible to place at every point which is threatened a force which shall prove equal to every emergency. As yet the design of the enemy in your front is somewhat vague and undecided. The movement against you may be a feint, and the real attack may be on Norfolk. When it is unmistakably ascertained that he shall attempt to force his way up the Peninsula every exertion shall be made to enable you successfully to resist and drive him."

By April 2, the day McClellan arrived from Alexandria on the steamer *Commodore* to take personal command on the Peninsula, the camps around Fort Monroe held nearly 60,000 troops. Thousands of the army's members were still in transit or were in the Washington area awaiting their turn to embark. McClellan's final plans called for a peninsular force of at least 150,000 men, but such a number would be denied him. Even as the general left Washington, Lincoln detached one of his divisions, 10,000 men, for assignment to the mountain country of western Virginia, where McClellan had made his name. The present commander, General John C. Frémont, of California "pathfinder" fame, had requested reinforcements for a special

mission toward eastern Tennessee. McClellan embarked with hopes of replacing this loss with 10,000 men borrowed from Fort Monroe and its de-
pendencies, but he had barely reached the fort when he learned that this
department, at Edwin Stanton's instigation, had been removed from his
authority. Stanton seemed to feel that McClellan's numerical strength
should be sufficient and nothing more, a condition that might compel him
to abandon his visions of grand strategy and concentrate on decisive fighting.

Setting up a temporary headquarters at the fort, McClellan turned first
to matters concerning the York and James Rivers, which were not open to
his use. He expected the Navy to take care of the problem of the *Merrimack*
on the James and that of land batteries covering the mouth of the York, but
he had not obtained a commitment on such a course, nor even ascertained
its feasibility. Now came the bad news. "Flag-Officer [Louis M.] Goldsborough . . . informed me that it was not in his power to control the navigation of the James River . . . nor could he . . . furnish any vessels to attack the
batteries of Yorktown and Gloucester, or to run by them in the dark and
thus cut off the supplies of the enemy by water and control their land communication. I was thus deprived of the cooperation of the navy and left to
my own resources."

McClellan was not dismayed, since his resources seemed adequate. He
knew that celerity was essential; Joe Johnston's army was certain to be on
the March from the Rapidan to Richmond. McClellan planned to open his
campaign by marching his growing army against Magruder's defenses at
Yorktown, which he believed he could take. If he found them to be un-
yielding, Irvin McDowell's corps of about 35,000 men, still in the Washington area, would be floated down for a landing near Gloucester, on the York
River opposite Yorktown, their mission both to silence the Gloucester batteries and to turn the flank of the Yorktown defenses, making it necessary
for the enemy to fall back toward Richmond.

In a letter dated April 3, McClellan told his wife: "We move tomorrow
A.M. Three divisions to take the direct road to Yorktown. . . . Two take the
James River road. . . . The reserve goes to Big Bethel, where my headquarters will be tomorrow night. My great trouble is in the want of wagons . . .
but I cannot wait for them. . . . I hope to get possession of Yorktown day
after tomorrow. Shall then arrange to make the York River my line of supplies. The great battle will be (I think) near Richmond, as I have always
hoped and thought. I see my way very clearly, and with my [wagon] trains
once ready, will move rapidly."

Soon after dawn on April 4 the roads up the Peninsula were teeming
with military traffic. Chaplain Stewart, who traveled with the left column,
says that, hour after hour, "the immense cavalcade of many miles in
length—artillery, cavalry, infantry, baggage and ammunition wagons, am-

bulances, sutlers [i.e., civilian merchants with wagonloads of goods]—
slowly wended its way over the flat, hilless country, across worn-out fields,
over sloughs, and through pine forests."

Riding with McClellan's headquarters group, the Prince de Joinville
mused on the fact that many of the officers marching against John Magruder
had been friends of his in the prewar U.S. Army. These officers "were familiar with his habits and character, and sought to infer from them the course
he would pursue. This reciprocal knowledge which the chiefs of the two
armies possessed of each other, the result of a career begun in common in
early youth at the military school [West Point], and pursued either on the
battlefield or in the tedious life of frontier garrisons, was certainly a singular
trait of this singular war. . . .

"Another not less curious trait . . . was the complete absence of all information in regard to the country and to the position of the enemy, the
total ignorance under which we labored in regard to his movements and the
number of his troops. The few inhabitants we met were hostile and dumb;
the deserters and Negroes generally told us much more than they knew in
order to secure a welcome, and as we had no [reliable] maps and no knowledge of localities, it was impossible to make anything of their stories, and to
reconcile their often contradictory statements."

Chaplain Marks accompanied the right column, which took the road
that led through the village of Big Bethel, a dozen houses stretched over a
third of a mile. "As we came near the place, the few troops left here fled
towards Yorktown. . . . We encamped the first night on the farm of Mr.
Russel, at Rose Dale. This we found one of the finest plantations in this region. Russel himself is a timid, soulless man. Having no white wife, he lives
in the society of his Negroes. . . . He has a rare eye for beauty, for he had in
his house some of the finest specimens of octoroon girls."

The unit of the right column to which Private Warren Goss belonged
did not reach Big Bethel until the next morning. A rainstorm had come up,
and the atmosphere was dreary. "Just outside and west of town was an insignificant building [a church] from which the hamlet takes its name. . . .
Before our arrival it had evidently been occupied as officers' barracks for
the enemy. . . . There was a rude but very significant drawing on the plaster
of the walls. . . . A hotel was depicted, and on its sign was inscribed RICH-
MOND. Jeff Davis was standing in the doorway, and with an immense pair
of cowhides was booting McClellan from the door. . . .

"I visited one of the dwelling-houses . . . for the purpose of obtaining
something more palatable than hardtack, salt-beef, or pork, which, with
coffee, were the marching rations. The woman of the house was communicative, and expressed her surprise at the great number of Yanks who had
'come down to invade our soil.' She said she had a son in the Confederate
army. . . . I expressed the opinion that we should go into Richmond without

much fighting. 'No!' she said with the emphasis of conviction. 'You-all will drink hot blood before you-all get thar!'

"While wandering about, I came to the house of a Mrs. T., whose husband was said to be a captain in the Confederate service. . . . A large, good-looking woman about forty years old . . . Mrs. T. was crying profusely. . . . Her grief was caused by the fact that some of our men had helped themselves to the contents of cupboard and cellar. She was superintending the loading of an old farm wagon, into which she was putting a large family of colored people, with numerous bundles. The only white person on the load as it started away was the mistress, who sat amid her dark chattels in desolation and tears. Returning to the house after this exodus, I found letters, papers, and odds and ends of various kinds littering the floor, whether overturned in the haste of the mistress or by the visiting soldiers I could only guess. . . .

"After leaving Big Bethel we began to feel the weight of our knapsacks. Castaway overcoats, blankets, parade-coats, and shoes were scattered along the route in reckless profusion. . . . I lightened my knapsack without much regret, for I could not see the sense of carrying a blanket or overcoat when I could pick one up almost anywhere. . . . The colored people along our route occupied themselves in picking up this scattered property. They had on their faces a distrustful look, as if uncertain of the tenure of their harvest."

While the right column was approaching Yorktown, the left was nearing Warwick Court House. In the words of Regis de Trobriand: "The small number of houses, poor or fine, which were on the line of march were all abandoned. The occupants had left on our approach. . . . Near a deserted hut we met four children crouched at the side of the road. The oldest was no more than twelve. A few rags scarcely covered their feeble bodies. Their hollow eyes, their pale faces, eloquently told of what they had already suffered. Their mother was dead, and their father had abandoned them. They wept while asking for something to eat. The soldiers immediately gave them enough provisions to last them several days. Blankets were not wanting for the little ones. The weather was warm, and the sides of the road were lined with them. But what became of these children? One does not like to think about such things. This is the horrible side of war.

"That day we passed by the Young Mill, a good position and well fortified, and where the enemy might have given us much trouble if he had defended it. But he had left it on our approach, and we found there only some tents where a few regiments had passed the winter. They served us as a shelter against a pouring rain during the short halt we made there. It was, however, only a passing storm. It lasted but a short time, and the sun shone out only the warmer for it when we arrived at the Young plantation. This Young, who was then serving in the rebel army as a quartermaster, was a sort of lord in that part of the country. The house was his; the farm and mill were his; the fields and the forests were his; his were the cattle and the slaves. It seemed as though we could not get out of his domain."

Before noon that day John Magruder wrote a dispatch for transmission to General Lee in Richmond: "The enemy's pickets [have] advanced in sight of Yorktown, but it is now raining, and I think there will be no attack today. I have made my arrangements to fight with my small force, but without the slightest hope of success. If I am reinforced in time with 10,000 men I think I can block the way to Richmond."

Along the Federal routes, the intermittent rains were turning the low-land areas into lakes and the roads into mire. According to the Prince de Joinville: "The infantry could contrive to get on by marching through the water in the woods, but as soon as two or three wagons made ruts in the ground, no wheeled vehicle could move an inch. . . . Then it was that we had to make what in America are called corduroy roads. These are made by cutting down trees of the same size, a few inches in diameter, and laying them side by side on the ground. . . . The infantry . . . were employed, work-ing up to their knees in the mud and water, upon this Herculean labor, and they got through it wonderfully. Here the American pioneer was in his ele-ment; the roads were made as if by enchantment. The cannon and the wagons came in slowly indeed, but they came in where it seemed an impos-sibility they ever should do so. . . .

"Marching along in this fashion, we reached the Confederate lines, which opened on us at once with a sharp fire of artillery. We replied, but without making any impression on the well-defined works which covered the hostile cannon. The creek [the Warwick, which originated near York-town and spanned the Peninsula] had been reconnoitred and found impass-able by infantry, both on account of the depth of water and of its marshy borders, in which the troops would have been mired under a crossfire of numbers of sharpshooters concealed in the woods and behind the embank-ments. Throughout the [entirety] of the Confederate lines we encountered the same attitude of alert defense. Everywhere cannon and camps."

What the Federals did not know was that the camps had been skillfully scattered so as to present an illusion of strength. Magruder added to the show by keeping a number of his regiments marching back and forth past gaps in the woods so that each regiment seemed like several. McClellan concluded that the Confederates numbered at least 30,000 and were being rapidly reinforced. He believed that Joe Johnston's army was drawing near, when, in actuality, the bulk of these troops had not yet reached Richmond.

The Prince de Joinville's nephew, the Comte de Paris, who served as one of McClellan's aides, later analyzed the situation this way: "General McClellan . . . deceived by appearances . . . did not dare to thrust his sword through the slight curtain which his able adversary had spread before his vision. A vigorous attack . . . would have had every chance of success. The enemy could have been kept in suspense by several feints. There were men enough to attempt three or four principal attacks at once. It was easy, in short, to harass him in such a manner that his line of defense would inevitably have been pierced at the expiration of twenty-four hours. . . . The whole Peninsula would have fallen into the possession of the Federals in a few days. This is what General McClellan would not have failed to do if he had known the situation of his adversaries. . . . But at that critical moment no information was received either from spies or from other sources to convey to him the faintest idea of their weakness. . . . The army needed a daring stroke. . . . Such a success . . . would have secured to General McClellan the efficient cooperation of his government. But he would not compromise the young army entrusted to his care in an enterprise which he considered too hazardous."

5

THE SIEGE OF YORKTOWN

ON THE EVENING of April 5, even while he was weighing the matter of sending word to Washington for McDowell's corps to perform the Gloucester flanking maneuver, McClellan received this telegram from the War Department: "By directions of the President, Gen. McDowell's army corps has been detached from the force under your immediate command, and the general is ordered to report to the Secretary of War." One of Lincoln's stipulations when he consented to the Peninsula Campaign was that McClellan leave Washington perfectly secure from attack. After McClellan's departure, the President discovered that the capital's defenses held less than 20,000 troops, many of them recruits, and that there were few reinforcements within easy marching distance. Part of the trouble was that the troops under Banks in the Shenandoah Valley, supposed to be available for duty around Washington, had been tied up by Stonewall Jackson. Lincoln decided that McDowell's corps must be held before the city.

If the President acted hastily in depriving McClellan of 35,000 troops at the precise moment he went under fire, McClellan, too, was at fault. He should have cleared the Washington defense arrangements with Lincoln before he sailed. One suspects that the general purposely avoided doing this, convinced that the city was safe and hoping that the matter would not be investigated, his aim to favor his strength on the Peninsula.

Lincoln's decision astonished McClellan, and he wired back at once: "The enemy are in large force along our front, and apparently intend making a determined resistance. . . . Their line of works extends across the entire Peninsula from Yorktown to Warwick River. Many of them are formidable. Deserters say that they are being reinforced daily from Richmond and from Norfolk. Under the circumstances I beg that you will reconsider the order detaching the 1st Corps from my command. . . . If you cannot leave me the whole of the 1st Corps, I urgently ask, as a military necessity, that I may not lose Franklin and his division."

The ensuing dialogue between McClellan and Washington, conducted by telegraph and mail, was a busy one. Lincoln wired on April 6: "You now have over 100,000 troops with you.... I think you had better break the enemy's line from Yorktown to Warwick River at once." This prompted an aside to Ellen: "The President very coolly telegraphed me ... that he thought I had better break the enemy's lines at once! I was much tempted to reply that he had better come and do it himself." On April 7 McClellan wired Lincoln that he had only 85,000 men present for duty. A longer report was sent to Edwin Stanton: "It will be necessary to resort to the use of heavy guns and some siege operations before we assault. All the prisoners state that Gen. J. E. Johnston arrived at Yorktown yesterday with strong reinforcements." (This was not true. The main part of Johnston's army had not yet reached Richmond.) McClellan's letter continues: "It seems clear that I shall have the whole force of the enemy on my hands—probably not less than 100,000 men, and possibly more.... Under the circumstances that have been developed since we arrived here, I feel fully impressed with the conviction that here is to be fought the great battle that is to decide the existing contest. I shall, of course, commence the attack as soon as I can get up my siege train, and shall do all in my power to carry the enemy's works; but to do this with a reasonable degree of certainty requires, in my judgment, that I should, if possible, have at least the whole of the 1st Corps to land upon the Severn River and attack Gloucester in the rear. My present strength will not admit of a detachment sufficient for this purpose."

Upon reading McClellan's dispatch, Stanton exploded to an aide: "If he had a million men, he would swear the enemy had two millions, and then he would sit down in the mud and yell for three!"

McClellan was still basing his estimates of the enemy's strength on figures provided by his zealous but unreliable intelligence service, headed by Allan Pinkerton. The detective states: "Numerous scouts had been sent out through the rebel country.... George H. Bangs was busily engaged in examining the rebel deserters and prisoners, Southern refugees, and contrabands [i.e., slaves] who were either captured or came willingly into camp, and in preparing daily reports ... to be made to the general in command. I had accompanied McClellan upon this campaign, and gave my untiring personal supervision to the large corps of men and women, white and black, then engaged in obtaining information." Almost every member of this corps seems to have had the curious notion that it was best to credit the enemy with extra numbers. Pinkerton accepted the exaggerations as fact, and he was never disabused. "General McClellan knew, from the reports I laid before him, the fearful odds against which he had to contend." During this period, three of Pinkerton's operatives were arrested while on missions in Richmond; and one—a husky but chronically rheumatic man named Timothy Webster—was publicly hanged.

On April 9 Lincoln wrote McClellan: "Your despatches complaining that you are not properly sustained . . . pain me very much. . . . My implicit order that Washington should, by the judgment of all the commanders of army corps, be left entirely secure had been neglected. It was precisely this that drove me to detain McDowell. . . . Do you really think I should permit . . . this city to be entirely open, except what resistance could be presented by less than 20,000 unorganized troops? This is a question which the country will not allow me to evade. There is a curious mystery about the number of troops now with you. When I telegraphed you on the 6th, saying you had over a hundred thousand with you, I had just obtained from the Secretary of War a statement taken, as he said, from your own returns, making 108,000 then with you and en route to you. . . . I suppose the whole force which has gone forward for you is with you by this time. And if so, I think it is the precise time for you to strike a blow. By delay the enemy will relatively gain upon you—that is, he will gain faster by fortifications and reinforcements than you can by reinforcements alone. And once more let me tell you, it is indispensable *to you* that you strike a blow. I am powerless to help this. You will do me the justice to remember I always insisted that going down the bay in search of a field instead of fighting at or near Manassas was only shifting and not surmounting a difficulty; that we would find the same enemy and the same or equal entrenchments at either place. The country will not fail to note—is now noting—that the present hesitation to move upon an entrenched enemy is but the story of Manassas repeated. I beg to assure you that I have never written you or spoken to you in greater kindness of feeling than now, nor with a fuller purpose to sustain you, so far as, in my most anxious judgment, I consistently can. But you must act."

All of the President's sagacious counsel was disregarded. On the Confederate side, John Magruder shook his head in wonderment at McClellan's failure to attack. "In a few days, the object of his delay was apparent. In every direction in front of our lines, through the intervening woods, and along the open fields, earthworks began to appear." This portended siege operations. Only now were the main elements of Joe Johnston's army beginning to pass through Richmond on their way to the Peninsula. In the words of Richmond resident Fannie A. Beers: "Seemingly countless legions swept by with martial tread; their resounding footsteps and splended appearance, equally with the roll of many drums and the clash of regimental bands, stirred the hearts of the multitude thronging the sidewalks, crowding every doorway and gallery. . . . Among the crowd, side by side with the ladies resident in Richmond, stood mothers, wives, sisters from other Southern States, looking eagerly for the well-known uniform of *their own,* proudly pointing them out as they passed, even to utter strangers, sure of warmest sympathy. . . . Among the gayly fluttering banners borne proudly aloft, some were ragged and torn by shot or shell. As each of these appeared, men shouted themselves hoarse; women drew shuddering sighs and grew deathly pale, as if realizing for the first time the horrors of war."

Adds Sallie Putnam: "Soldiers left the ranks to grasp the hands of friends in passing, to receive some grateful refreshment, a small bouquet, or a whispered congratulation. Officers on horseback raised their hats, and some of the more gallant ventured to waft kisses to the fair ones at the doors and windows. We shall never forget the appearance of General Longstreet, the sturdy fighter, the obstinate warrior, as he dashed down Main Street surrounded by his splendid staff. Through other streets poured our cavalry, under their gallant chieftain, the pink of Southern chivalry, the gay, rollicking, yet bold, daring, and venturous Jeb Stuart. As we saw him then, sitting easily on the saddle, as though he was born to it, he seemed every inch the cavalier. . . . His genial temperament made him the idol and companion of the most humble of his men. . . . They swept through our streets . . . with their horses in good order, their own spirits buoyant and cheerful, many of them wearing in their caps bouquets of the golden daffodils of early spring, cheered on by the ringing sounds of the bugle."

Returning to Fannie Beers: "For several days this excitement was kept up. All night heavy artillery rumbled along Broad Street. At any hour of the night I could see from my window shadowy figures of mounted men, could hear the ceaseless tramp of cavalry horses. Every day the sun shone upon the glittering bayonets and gay flags of swiftly passing soldiery. The air was flooded with music until the last strain died away, and . . . calm . . . fell upon the city. The glorious scenes of the past few days had engendered a sense of protection and security. All felt that this splended army *must* prove invincible."

By April 11, John Magruder's lines had been reinforced to about 30,000 men, and additional troops were coming down the Peninsula. The general began to feel somewhat more secure. On that day he published a proclamation addressed to the citizens of the Peninsula and the south side of the James River. "McClellan, at the head of 100,000 men, is threatening our whole line. To meet this force successfully our main reliance is to be placed upon breastworks. Soldiers cannot be expected to work night and day and fight besides. Our Negro force now at work on fortifications is too small to accomplish this object before the enemy may attempt to carry us by assault. . . . Under these circumstances I am sure that no patriotic citizen, with the issue truly at heart, would hesitate to respond most cheerfully to the call which I now make, viz. one Negro man, with his ax or spade, to be furnished at once by each proprietor. Without the most liberal assistance in axes, spades, and hands to work we cannot hope to succeed, and the Northern army will be in possession of your farms in a few days. Mr. Junius Lamb is my authorized agent to receive the Negroes. Send them at once, under

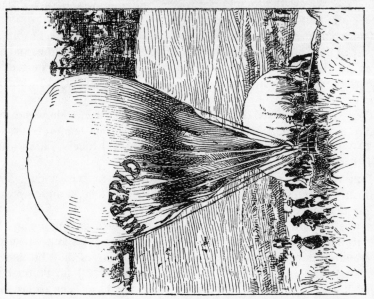

One of Professor Lowe's balloons. *Left:* replenishing its gas. *Right:* Lowe making a reconnaissance.

overseers, to Colonel [B. S.] Ewell at Williamsburg."

On the Union side, April 11 was a day that began with an episode that was pure comic opera. The siege equipment included two observation balloons under the management of Professor Thaddeus S. C. Lowe, known as the "aeronaut of the Army of the Potomac." Lowe had taught the principles of ballooning to McClellan's subordinate and friend, the handsome, soldierly, enthusiastic, and popular General Fitz John Porter, who had learned to make ascensions alone. Along with his growth in confidence, Porter had become lax regarding safety procedures. On this particular day he chose to go up at dawn. Among those who gathered close around to watch the take-off was war correspondent George Alfred Townsend, who says that the general "leaped into the car and demanded the cables to be let out with all speed. I saw with some surprise that the flurried assistants were sending up the great straining canvas with a single rope attached. The enormous bag was only partially inflated, and the loose folds opened and shut with a crack like that of a musket. Noisily, fitfully, the yellow mass rose into the sky, the basket rocking like a feather in the zephyr; and just as I turned aside to speak to a comrade a sound came from overhead, like the explosion of a shell, and something striking me across the face laid me flat upon the ground. Half blind and stunned, I staggered to my feet. . . . The air seemed full of cries and curses. Opening my eyes ruefully, I saw all faces turned upwards, and when I looked above—the balloon was adrift! The treacherous cable, rotted with vitriol, had snapped in twain. One fragment had been the cause of my downfall, and the other trailed, like a great entrail, from the receding car, where Fitz John Porter was bounding upward upon a Pegasus that he could neither check nor direct.

"The whole army was agitated by the unwonted occurrence. From . . . the brink of the York to the mouth of Warwick River, every soldier and officer was absorbed. Far within the Confederate lines the confusion extended. We heard the enemy's alarm guns, and directly the signal flags were waving up and down our front.

"The general appeared directly over the edge of the car. He was tossing his hands . . . and shouting something that we could not comprehend.

" 'O—pen—the—valve!' called Lowe in his shrill tones. 'Climb—to—the—netting—and—reach—the—valve—rope!'

" 'The valve! The valve!' repeated a multitude of tongues, and all gazed with thrilling interest at the retreating hulk that still kept straight upward, swerving neither to the east nor the west.

"It was a weird spectacle—that frail, fading oval, gliding against the sky, floating in the serene azure, the little vessel swinging silently beneath, and a hundred thousand martial men watching the loss of their brother-in-arms . . . powerless to relieve or recover him. Had Fitz John Porter been drifting down the rapids of Niagara, he could not have been so far from human assistance. But we saw him directly, no bigger than a child's toy, clambering up the netting and reaching for the cord.

" 'He can't do it,' muttered a man beside me. 'The wind blows the valve rope to-and-fro.'

"We saw the general descend, and appearing again over the edge of the basket, he seemed to be motioning to the breathless hordes below the story of his failure. Then he dropped out of sight, and when we next saw him he was reconnoitring the Confederate works through a long black spyglass. A great laugh went up and down the lines as this cool procedure was observed, and then a cheer of applause ran from group to group. For a moment it was doubtful that the balloon would float in either direction. It seemed to falter, like an irresolute being, and moved reluctantly southeastward towards Fortress Monroe. A huzza, half uttered, quivered on every lip. All eyes glistened, and some were dim with tears of joy. But the wayward canvas now turned due westward and was blown rapidly towards the Confederate works. Its course was fitfully direct, and the wind seemed to veer often, as if contrary currents, conscious of the opportunity, were struggling for the possession of the daring navigator. The south wind held mastery for a while, and the balloon passed the Federal front amid a howl of despair from the soldiery. It kept right on, over sharpshooters, rifle pits, and outworks, and finally passed, as if to deliver up its freight, directly over the heights of Yorktown. The cool courage, either of heroism or despair, had seized upon Fitz John Porter. He turned his black glass upon the ramparts and masked cannon below, upon the remote camps, upon the beleaguered town, upon the guns of Gloucester Point, and upon distant Norfolk. Had he been reconnoitring from a secure perch at the tip of the moon, he could not have been more vigilant, and the Confederates probably thought this some Yankee device to peer into their sanctuary in spite of ball or shell. None of their great guns could be brought to bear upon the balloon; but there were some discharges of musketry that appeared to have no effect, and finally even these demonstrations ceased. Both armies in solemn silence were gazing aloft, while the imperturbable mariner continued to spy out the land.

"The sun was now rising behind us, and roseate rays struggled up to the zenith, like the arcs made by showery bombs. They threw a hazy atmosphere upon the balloon, and the light shone through the network like the sun through the ribs of the skeleton ship in the *Ancient Mariner*. Then, as all looked agape, the aircraft plunged and tacked and veered, and drifted rapidly toward the Federal lines again.

"The allelujah that now went up shook the spheres, and when he had regained our camp limits the general was seen clambering up again to clutch the valve rope. This time he was successful, and the balloon fell like a stone, so that all hearts once more leaped up, and the cheers were hushed. Cavalry rode pell-mell from several directions to reach the place of descent, and the general's personal staff galloped past me like the wind, to be the first at his debarkation. I followed the throng of soldiery with due haste, and came up to the horsemen in a few minutes. The balloon had struck a canvas tent with great violence, felling it as by a bolt, and the general, unharmed, had disentangled himself from innumerable folds of oiled canvas, and was now the cynosure of an immense group of people. While the officers shook his hands, the rabble bawled their satisfaction in hurrahs, and a band of music marching up directly, the throng on foot and horse gave him a vociferous escort to his quarters."

The episode had scarcely ended before McClellan was writing his wife: "I am just recovering from a terrible scare. Early this morning I was awakened by a dispatch from Fitz John's headquarters stating that Fitz had made an ascension in the balloon this morning, and that the balloon had broken away and come to the ground . . . within the enemy's lines. You can imagine how I felt. I at once sent off to the various pickets to find out what they knew and try to do something to save him, but the order had no sooner gone than in walks Mr. Fitz just as cool as usual. He had luckily come down near my own camp after actually passing over that of the enemy. You can rest assured of one thing: you won't catch me in the confounded balloon, nor will I allow any other generals to go up in it."

In the same letter, McClellan mentioned his troubles with Washington: "Don't worry about the wretches; they have done nearly their worst, and can't do much more. I am sure that I will win in the end, in spite of all of their rascality. History will present a sad record of these traitors who are willing to sacrifice the country and its army for personal spite and personal aims. The people will soon understand the whole matter."

Even while McClellan was writing this, the "wretches" were engineering a positive response to one of his pleas. On the previous day he had wired Edwin Stanton: "The reconnoissances of today prove that it is necessary to invest and attack Gloucester Point. Give me Franklin's and McCall's divisions . . . and I will at once undertake it. If circumstances of which I am not aware make it impossible for you to send me two divisions to carry out the final plan of campaign, I will run the risk and hold myself responsible for the results if you will give me Franklin's division. . . . I have determined upon the point of attack." Now, on April 11, McClellan heard from the Adjutant General in Washington: "By direction of the President, Franklin's division has been ordered to march . . . to Alexandria and immediately embark for Fortress Monroe." McClellan telegraphed Stanton his thanks. But he changed his mind about making the Gloucester attack with a strength augmented by only one division. Death came quickly to his conceptions of moving at once, of taking risks, and of holding himself responsible for the results. The siege was continued as begun.

Confederate General Joe Johnston reached Yorktown in person on the morning of April 12, and he spent the day examining Magruder's defenses. "Before nightfall I was convinced that we could do no more on the Peninsula than delay General McClellan's progress toward Richmond.... I thought it of great importance that a different plan of operations should be adopted ... and ... I hastened back to Richmond to suggest such a one, and arrived next morning early enough to see the President in his office as soon as he entered it. After describing to him Magruder's position and the character of his defensive arrangements, I endeavored to show that, although they were the most judicious that that officer could have adopted when he devised them, they would not enable us to defeat McClellan.... Instead of only delaying the Federal army in its approach, I proposed that it should be encountered in front of Richmond by one quite as numerous, formed by uniting there all the available forces of the Confederacy in North Carolina, South Carolina, and Georgia with those at Norfolk, on the Peninsula, and then near Richmond.... The great army thus formed, surprising that of the United States by an attack when it was expecting to besiege Richmond, would be almost certain to win ... while the present plan could produce no decisive result. The President, who had heard me with apparent interest, replied that the question was so important that he would hear it fully discussed before making his decision."

Among those who joined Davis and Johnston in the presidential office for a conference later that morning were Secretary of War George W. Randolph, Robert E. Lee, and two of Johnston's division commanders, James Longstreet and G. W. Smith, whose troops were still in the Richmond area. The meeting opened with Johnston presenting his views and Smith backing them. Again in Johnston's words: "In the discussion that followed, General Randolph, who had been a naval officer, objected to the plan proposed because it included at least the temporary abandonment of Norfolk.... General Lee opposed it because he thought that the withdrawal from South Carolina and Georgia of any considerable numbers of troops would expose the important seaports of Charleston and Savannah to the danger of capture. He thought, too, that the Peninsula had excellent fields of battle for a small army contending with a great one, and that we should for that reason make the contest with McClellan's army there. General Longstreet took little part, which I attributed to his deafness."

Says Longstreet himself: "It was the first time that I had been called to such august presence, to deliberate on momentous matters, so I had nothing to say till called on. The views intended to be offered were prefaced by saying that I knew General McClellan; that he was a military engineer and would move his army by careful measurement and preparation; that he would not be ready to advance before the 1st of May. The President interrupted and spoke of McClellan's high attainments and capacity in a style indicating that he did not care to hear anyone talk who did not have the

same appreciation of our great adversary. McClellan had been a special favorite with Mr. Davis when he was Secretary of War in the Pierce administration, and he seemed to take such reflections upon his favorites as
somewhat personal. From the hasty interruption I concluded that my opinion had only been asked through polite recognition of my presence, not that
it was wanted, and said no more. My intention was to suggest that we leave
Magruder to look after McClellan, and march, as proposed by Jackson a few
days before, through the Valley of Virginia, cross the Potomac, threaten
Washington, and call McClellan to his own capital."

Joe Johnston resumes: "I maintained that all to be accomplished by any
success obtained on the Peninsula would be to delay the enemy two or three
weeks in his march to Richmond. . . . At six o'clock the conference was adjourned by the President, to meet in his house at seven. The discussion was
continued there, although languidly, until 1 A.M., when it ceased, and the
President, who previously had expressed no opinion on the question, announced his decision in favor of General Lee's opinion, and directed that
Smith's and Longstreet's divisions should join the Army of the Peninsula
[raising its number to about 50,000 men], and ordered me to go there and
take command. . . . The belief that events on the Peninsula would soon
compel the Confederate Government to adopt my method of opposing the
Federal army reconciled me somewhat to the necessity of obeying the President's order."

The first ten days of McClellan's siege, during which the weather was
often rainy and much of the ground was perpetually soggy, were spent in
general preparations for a scientific approach to the enemy's lines. "The
men," says Surgeon Stevens, "performed herculean labors on the roads and
in throwing up earthworks. No rest was allowed. When not on picket they
were cutting down trees or throwing up earthworks or building bridges."
The activities were accompanied by intermittent skirmishing. McClellan
had no wish to bring on a general engagement until his siege works were
completed and he could open up with all of his guns, but on April 16 he ordered a limited attack at a watery spot near the center of the line, his aim to
ascertain the position's strength and to prevent the enemy from building it
into a threat to his security. The action opened with long-range rifle fire and
an artillery duel. Then four companies of Vermonters were ordered to close
in. Stevens tells the story: "Down from the woods they came, rushed into
the water to their waists, and gallantly made for the rebel rifle pits. The first
line of the works was gained, and then the second. The fort was empty, but
a ditch to their left was filled with men. They poured a volley among them,
and the graycoats fled. Thus the fort was actually in their possession, and
was held for some minutes by the noble fellows, but when they looked for
support, none came. . . . The brave Green Mountain boys . . . were forced to
fall back under a galling fire from the rebels, who rushed back to their

Incident of the skirmish at Lee's Mill

pits as soon as the Vermonters had left them, pouring volley after volley into the retreating forces. . . . Before they were able to reach the shelter of the woods, sad havoc was made in their ranks. Skirmishing was kept up for some hours, by other regiments, but with no result except the loss of men. . . . Thus ended the fight known as the Battle of Lee's Mill, a battle in which two hundred men gallantly captured an important work of the enemy, and thousands of their companions burning with desire to share in their glory stood by and saw them abandon it!" The operation, however, did establish a salient, or projection, in the Federal front line, and McClellan was satisfied. "The objects . . . were completely achieved: we prevented further work at this point, prevented the enemy from using the crossing, and ascertained that the line could not be broken there without further preparation in the way of artillery, etc."

The regular siege operations are described as they were conducted on McClellan's right by the troops of Heintzelman's corps; the narrator is Captain Henry N. Blake, of the 11th Regiment Massachusetts Volunteers: "A majority of the regiment, and sometimes the whole of it, were daily detailed for fatigue duty [i.e., manual labor], and reported with arms and equipment at corps headquarters, where every man was furnished with an axe or spade, and large working parties proceeded to the different parts of the line. . . . These detachments furnished by the corps comprised 15,000 soldiers, which was more than half of its effective strength; and the picket in its front required the unceasing vigilance of 5,000 men. The first parallel was established near Wormley Creek, a sluggish stream of an irregular width that flowed between banks which were covered with a thick growth of timber. . . . Bridges and roads were constructed in the ravines for the passage of cannon and ammunition; and ditches, revetments, and parapets were built in the advance. The tract of country between the camps and the breastworks of the enemy was extremely level; but forests of pine and hemlock, and the absence of commanding hills, prevented the rebels from discerning the movements of the besieging forces. . . .

"A small number felled and split trees, but the main body of the troops was employed in the trenches. An uninjured sawmill that was located a short distance from General Heintzelman's headquarters was continually in operation in the charge of soldiers, and furnished dimension lumber to the engineers. After the first parallel had been finished in the solitude of the forest, regular approaches were made in the night . . . and strengthened during the day, until the advanced works were erected upon the plain in front of Yorktown within three hundred yards of the enemy. . . . Aided by the darkness, a small force was cautiously deployed in a certain direction, and silently labored with their shovels, placing the excavated earth upon the side nearest the enemy; and daybreak revealed an extended trench that was two or three feet in depth and width. . . . These narrow trenches were enlarged until they were ten or twelve feet in width, miles in length, and four

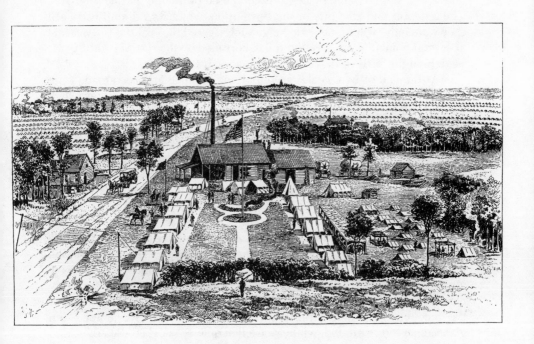

Heintzelman's headquarters on sawmill grounds

or six feet deep; and other bodies of troops built traverses and magazines, and transported the artillery and necessary supplies to the batteries that were completed. . . .

"The hostile gunners and pickets saw the earth when it was thrown upon the parapet by thousands of revolving spades, and attempted to obstruct the progress of the siege; but their constant efforts and volleys of shells and Minié balls [merely] tested the works, and the small loss that was sustained during their construction showed that they were properly executed. The soil, in many places, was composed of minute marine shells. . . . The redoubts and rifle pits of the Revolution, which had diminished until they were only twenty inches in height, intersected those of the Union army at several points. A few metallic relics, corroded by the rust of eighty years, were brought forth from their hiding places in the earth. . . .

"At the end of two weeks, an important advance had been made from the first parallel; and the massive breastworks of the enemy, upon which guns of different calibers had been mounted, could be examined. When their artillery had a good range upon an unfinished work, a man was constantly on watch, and shouted, 'Lie low!' or 'Look out for that shell!' as soon as the puff of white smoke darted forth and preceded by a few precious seconds the arrival of the iron messenger."

Private Warren Goss interjects: "We were [stationed near] Battery No. 1, not far from the York River. On it were mounted several 200-pounder guns, which commanded the enemy's water batteries. One day I was in a redoubt on the left, and saw General McClellan with the Prince de Joinville examining the enemy's works through their fieldglasses. They very soon drew the fire of the observant enemy, who opened with one of their heavy guns on the group, sending the first shot howling and hissing over and very close to their heads. Another, quickly following it, struck in the parapet of the redoubt. The French prince, seemingly quite startled, jumped and glanced nervously around, while McClellan quietly knocked the ashes from his cigar."

Captain Blake resumes: "There was . . . danger in returning to the camp after the allotted task for the day was ended . . . because the foe, who had ascertained the hour at which the 'shovel divisions' were generally relieved, opened their batteries and scattered shot and shell into every portion of the road over which they were obliged to march. . . . The national forces were not allowed to build campfires in the night because it was thought that the rebels would gain . . . information regarding their number and position; but the enemy exhibited no such fear, and the heavens above Yorktown and Gloucester Point reflected the lights that extended four or five miles in the rear of their works."

There were no campfires at the Confederate front. According to Robert Stiles, a young law student who was serving as a private in the Richmond

Howitzers: "Down in these swamps at night it was incredibly dark, and musketry never roared and reverberated as terribly anywhere else. . . . One black night a sudden outburst of fire . . . stampeded a working party of some two hundred Negroes who had just begun the much-needed strengthening of our very inadequate fortifications. The working party not only fled themselves, but the frantic fugitives actually swept away with them a part of our infantry support." Stiles cites another result of the night alarms: "One of our detachments broke down utterly from nervous tension and lack of rest. I went in as one of the relief party to bring them out and take their places. It was, of course, after nightfall, and some of these poor lads were sobbing in their broken sleep. . . . It was really pathetic. The men actually had to be supported to the ambulances sent down to bring them away." During the daylight hours, Stiles explains, "the Federal sharpshooters were . . . audacious and deadly. . . . For the most part they were concealed in the tops of tall pine trees and had down shots upon us, against which it was almost impossible to protect ourselves. When we attempted to do so by digging holes back of and beneath our works, the water rose in them and drove us out. . . . The only relief we had from the sharpshooters was when the marvelous Texan scouts got to work upon them. . . . The Texans would pass the word that it was time to go out 'squirrel shooting.' Then they would get up, yawn and stretch a little, load their rifles, and take to the water, disappearing from view in the brush. Then everything would be still a few minutes; then two or three shots and the sputter of the sharpshooters would cease. After a while the Texans would straggle back and report how many 'squirrels' they had got."

Returning to the Union side and to narrator Henry Blake: "The constant interruption of sleep by the artillery and musketry, the formation of the line of battle at all hours of the day and night, the continued labor upon the earthworks and roads, the exposure and excitement in the camp and upon picket duty, the rain which fell two days in three and increased tenfold the burdens of the troops, the quality of army rations and the absence of medical supplies, the lack of time and means to preserve habits of cleanliness, the swampy nature of the country and the character of the climate—produced disease, and thousands were afflicted with fevers. . . . The contents of two quart bottles and two pint boxes comprised the medical stores of many commands and were administered as a specific for all complaints. I have seen a surgeon give medicine from the same cup for a sore throat and a scalded foot."

It was common for an ailment to prove fatal. In a letter to his hometown newspaper, Chaplain Stewart related: "One poor lad of our regiment, overcome with wet and weariness, took a congestive chill, and presently died. We dug a hole among some pine bushes, into which the water ran as fast as the dirt was lifted out. His companions rolled up the lifeless form in a blan-

Confederate sharpshooter

ket, laid it down among the mud and water, threw in a few pine branches, then covered all up with earth. A torrent of rain was falling at the time. Wet and chilly, I tried to say a word appropriate to his messmates. Gloomy funeral. War is a barbarous thing." Writing on April 21, the chaplain questioned the progress of the siege: "Sixteen days have now been spent in this place. . . . Our grand army has again come to a halt. Whether this position is to be occupied as long as Tennally—six months—the progress of events must determine. . . . All things indicate a somewhat protracted and bloody struggle on this famous old battleground. . . . Yet what a day may bring forth, none assume to predict. In the meantime we are putting forth all the efforts after physical comfort and mental enjoyment our condition allows. It must be confessed, thus far . . . these have not been very abundant. . . . Under the dry pine leaves where we encamp, a great secesh army of wood ticks have wintered. The late warm weather has waked them into activity, and after their long fast, hungry as hyenas. Few so happy as not to find each morning half a dozen of these villainous bloodsuckers sticking in his flesh. You seize one with the fingers and pull it, but it don't come. You seize it again, with double tightness, and jerk. . . . There is a severance, yet the probabilities are the fangs of the bloodthirsty rascal have been left buried under the skin. . . . The past few nights being quite warm, though so early in the season, my extemporized shanty has been visited by picket guards and squads of full-grown mosquitoes, and so hungry as fairly to squeal when they sink their bills into me. These are, no doubt, merely a prelude to what may be expected in the coming hot weather. . . . How these fragile bloodsuckers contrived to live through the winter is a mystery. The heat and excitement of the rebellion must have kept them alive. They have . . . beyond question, joined the rebels, and possess all their venom. Determined do they seem to shed the blood of us Northern invaders."

In the same letter, Stewart sermonizes: "The filthiest of all living animals is *man*. No brute, so called, has ever yet become so debased as to chew or smoke tobacco. Three-fourths, perhaps, of our regiment either chew or smoke—many do both, and this is a sample of all other regiments in the service. . . . More than ten days since, the stock of the weed on hand became small . . . till finally all the treasury notes of Uncle Sam sufficed not to buy a single plug. Then what an outcry; what peevishness, what complaints and irritability! They were certainly the worst-used soldiers in the universe. Uncle Sam was a humbug; the sutlers were all a set of rascals and swindlers. . . . In this almost mutinous condition of affairs, our sutler, after nearly a month's absence, came up. The supply of luxuries brought along consisted principally in a limited supply of chewing and smoking tobacco. This was distributed as equitably as possible through the regiment. Then what filth and nastiness! What chewing, spitting, squirting, and whiffing! The nerves were all speedily quieted, the irritability soon gone, and a more contented set of men it was not easy to find. What strange freaks this fallen humanity of ours does exhibit!"

These were days when, for security reasons, the Federal army's regimental bands were silent, and no calls were sounded by bugle or drum. Group singing, however, went unrestricted. The pastime reached a crescendo one evening as darkness settled down after a fine sunset—one of the few that April afforded. According to an unnamed special correspondent for the Washington *National Intelligencer:* "While we were sitting in our tent, in company with several other 'specials,' one of our number, laying his hand upon our knee, suddenly said to us, 'Hark! What is that?' In a second all had ceased talking, and every ear endeavored to catch the sound. . . . There was a silence for a moment, and then there was wafted across the air the music of that glorious anthem, 'Old Hundred,' in which it seemed a thousand voices were participating. All of us immediately sought the open air, and there stood until the last note died away. . . . Never before have we heard anything so magnificently grand as that same 'Old Hundred' sung by the soldiers of the Union army on the plains of Yorktown. The air was made vocal with the music, and the woods around reverberated with the mighty strain. . . . The incident was a sublime one."

There were few sublime moments in Richmond at this time. On April 15, Judith McGuire wrote in her diary: "A panic prevails. . . . Many persons are leaving town. I can't believe they will get here, though it seems to be their end and aim. My mind is much perturbed. We can only go on doing our duty as quietly as we can." April 21: "The ladies are now engaged making sandbags for the fortifications at Yorktown; every lecture room in town crowded with them, sewing busily, hopefully, prayerfully. Thousands are wanted. . . . We are intensely anxious; our conversation, while busily sewing at St. Paul's lecture room, is only of war. We hear of so many horrors committed by the enemy in the [Shenandoah] Valley—houses searched and robbed, horses taken, sheep, cattle, etc., killed and carried off, servants deserting their homes, *churches desecrated!*" April 27: "The country is shrouded in gloom because of the fall of New Orleans! . . . Such an immense force was sent against the forts which protected it that they could not be defended. . . . Oh, it is so hard to see the enemy making such inroads into the heart of our country!"

On a brighter note, McClellan's hesitation was permitting Richmond to strengthen not only its defenses but also the Confederate government. The most important political development, according to editor-historian Edward Pollard, was "the Conscription law of the 16th of April . . . from which properly dates the military system of the Confederacy. Previous to this the Confederacy had had nothing that deserved the title of a military system, and had relied on mere popular enthusiam to conduct the war. . . . The Conscription law was barely in time to save the Confederacy. . . . The

Confederate Secretary of War stated that thirty days after the passage of this law the terms of one hundred and forty-eight regiments would have expired and left us at the mercy of an enemy which had every guarantee of success that numbers, discipline, complete organization, and perfect equipment could effect."

Through newspaper reports, the Confederate troops on the Peninsula followed the course of the Conscription law through Congress, and many were unhappy when it passed. Jesse Reid wrote home that the law would "do away with all the patriotism we have. Whenever men are forced to fight they take no personal interest in it, knowing that . . . it will be said they were forced, and their bravery was not from patriotism. My private opinion is that our Confederacy is gone up, or will go soon, as the soldiers themselves will take little or no interest in it hereafter. A more oppressive law was never enacted in the most uncivilized country or by the worst of despots." The South Carolinian was at this time stationed "within a hundred yards of the house where Washington had his headquarters previous to the surrender of Lord Cornwallis . . . a small, old-fashioned house, painted white." Reid also visited "the spot where Lord Cornwallis surrendered . . . which ended the War of Independence. I wish McClellan would surrender to us and end this war."

As April waned, not only official Washington but also the Northern public was becoming frustrated with McClellan's siege. The general was still thinking in terms of flanking the enemy, and he wrote Stanton, "Give me McCall's division and I will undertake a movement by West Point which will shake them out of Yorktown." This concept was a variation of the Gloucester plan. The troops of Franklin's division, which Lincoln had sent down in response to McClellan's earlier request, were still aboard ship. Among them was Trooper Adams. "Our division [had] left Alexandria with the expectation of landing on the Severn River, under cover of gunboats, moving on the enemy's works at Gloucester Point, opposite Yorktown, and having the first fight with the enemy. But we remained afloat day after day in Poquosin River, until both officers and men became impatient at the delay. . . . Today a report would be circulated that gunboats to cover our landing could not be got. . . . Tomorrow this report would be contradicted, and the delay charged to the engineer's department, which, it was said, had not provided the proper means of landing. . . . Both men and animals were suffering terribly. . . . The rigors of shipboard soon became more trying than those common to camp life. On the 20th, Lieutenant Colonel B. S. Alexander joined our staff. He enjoyed the reputation of being one of the most skillful engineers in the regular army. . . . He began his work by collecting a large number of barges, old canalboats, and scows with which to form landing stages. . . . When, however, the colonel got his landing stages ready, it was reported that the Navy could not furnish the recquisite number of gunboats to cooperate in our intended movement, and another delay was the result.

"Then everyone became impatient to know why General McClellan, whose seige guns had been going foward for at least a fortnight, did not open the seige [bombardment]. One attributed it to this, another to that. The general impression was that he wanted to make a grand display of his engineering skill by completing his works and opening fire along the whole line. Officers whom he had counted among his best friends became restive and impatient at the delay this policy was causing, and openly expressed their doubts of its wisdom. A few were malicious enough to say that General McClellan had again changed his mind as to the practicability of his base and was contemplating a new plan which would change the destination of our division. Again, it was whispered that there was a serious misunderstanding between General McClellan and the authorities at Washington, which had brought on an unpleasant controversy and was likely to end in a change of commanders. To this it was added that sundry mischievous politicians in Washington had so influenced the President and Secretary [of War] against General McClellan that they were doing everything in their power to destroy his plans and damage him in the eyes of the public. These reports had a very bad effect on the army, and more especially on its officers. They placed McClellan in the position of an injured man, with an army to fight in front of him and a worse enemy in his rear; and yet it did him no real good. Respect for the authorities at Washington was already too low in the Army of the Potomac, and reports like these were not calculated to promote that good understanding between the executive powers and our army so necessary to success.

"The general who seeks strength in the sympathy of his army places himself in a more unsafe position than if he were to work patiently, avoid political entanglements, and do the best he can with the means at hand. It was the misfortune of McClellan not to separate his military duties from the political entanglements of the day. He believed, and sincerely, that the fate of the nation was in the hands of the Army of the Potomac and that he was the political as well as military saviour of the republic. Indeed, all his mental energies seemed directed to the preservation of this army, which he fancied represented the political as well as the military status of the country. He seemed to forget that what strength an army gathers on the field of battle may be thrown away in inactivity as well as want of boldness and decision in its commander. . . .

"As a partial relief to the impatience of which I have before spoken, we were entertained every day with a desultory cannonading at the front. Then a rumor would pass from ship to ship that the siege [bombardment] had really opened at last. But after an exchange of ten or fifteen shots the cannonading would cease, only to increase our disappointment."

If McClellan was disinclined to do what was expected of him, so was his enemy Joe Johnston. The Confederate general had taken command at Yorktown with little intention of making a major stand there, as Davis wished, and he had not changed his mind. He knew that he was vulnerable to a flanking maneuver. "It was evident that the enemy was . . . preparing to demolish our batteries on York River. The greater range of his guns would have enabled him to do it without exposure. . . . I determined to remain in position only so long as it could be done without exposing our troops to the powerful artillery which, I doubted not, would soon be brought to bear upon them." Johnston's strength remained at about 50,000 men—scarcely half McClellan's number. Johnston wrote Robert E. Lee on April 29: "The fight for Yorktown, as I said in Richmond, must be one of artillery, in which we cannot win. . . . We must abandon the Peninsula soon. . . . I think it best . . . to do it now, to put the army in position to defend Richmond."

On that same day John Magruder, presently commanding Johnston's right wing, wrote a dispatch of a different sort, one addressed to Secretary of War George Randolph. "I have learned that complaints have been made to you of the treatment of the slaves employed in this army. It is quite true that much hardship has been endured by the Negroes in the recent prosecution of the defensive works on our lines; but this has been unavoidable, owing to the constant and long-continued wet weather. Every precaution has been adopted to secure their health and safety as far as circumstances would allow. The soldiers, however, have been more exposed and have suffered far more than the slaves. The latter have always slept under cover and have had fires to make them comfortable, whilst the men have been working in the rain, have stood in the trenches and rifle pits in mud and water almost knee-deep, without shelter, fire, or sufficient food. There has been sickness among the soldiers and the slaves, but far more among the former than the latter. I write this for your information, supposing that you might not know the facts."

For whites and blacks alike, the days of suffering in the sodden defenses were coming to a close. Davis and Lee accepted Johnston's proposal, even though its implementation meant the loss not only of Yorktown but also of Norfolk and the Gosport Navy Yard, home of the *Merrimack*, or *Virginia*, as the Confederates called her. Johnston's plans were kept from reaching McClellan. On April 30 Ellen was informed: "We are working like horses and will soon be ready to open. It will be a tremendous affair when we do begin." May 1: "Another wet, drizzly, uncomfortable sort of a day. . . . I shall be very glad when we are ready to open fire, and then finish this confounded affair. I am tired of public life; and even now, when I am doing the best I can for my country in the field, I know that my enemies are pursuing me more remorselessly than ever; and 'kind friends' are constantly . . . informing me of the pleasant predicament in which I am—the rebels on one side and the abolitionists and other scoundrels on the other. I believe in my

Union mortar battery in Yorktown works

heart and conscience, however, that I am walking on the ridge between the two gulfs, and that all I have to do is to try to keep the path of honor and truth, and that God will bring me safely through." During the night of May 2–3, he wrote: "We are now nearly ready to open. . . . I don't half like the perfect quiet which reigns now. . . . It don't seem natural. It looks like a sortie or an evacuation. If either, I hope it may be the former. I do not want these rascals to get away from me without a sound drubbing. . . . I feel that the fate of a nation depends upon me, and I feel that I have not one single friend at the seat of government. Any day may bring an order relieving me from command. If they will simply let me alone I feel sure of success; but will they do it?"

Surgeon Stevens sums up: "After a month of toil and exposure almost unprecedented, after losing nearly one-fifth of our magnificent army by disease and death, our batteries were finished, the enormous siege guns were mounted, and the 13-inch mortars in position. The army looked anxiously for the grand finale of all these extensive preparations. Men had lost the enthusiasm which had prevailed when we landed upon the Peninsula, and a smile was seldom seen; but a fixed and determined purpose to succeed still appeared on their faces. Now at length we were ready, and the countenances of the soldiers began to lighten up a little."

The Prince de Joinville elaborates: "Not only was a terrible bombardment to be directed against the city, not only were the choicest troops selected for the grand assault which was to follow the bombardment, but the steam transports waited only for the signal to pass up into the York River as soon as the place should fall, and land the forces of Franklin high up on the line of the Confederate retreat. . . . In a few hours they would have passed over the distance which it would have taken the enemy two days to traverse. Driven by storm from Yorktown, followed up step for step, intercepted on their road by fresh troops, the army of the South would have been in a very critical position, and the Federals would have found what they so greatly needed, a brilliant military success. . . . Unfortunately, the Confederate leaders and generals saw and felt this also; and like skillful men they took the best way of preventing it. . . . On the 3rd, the fire of the hostile batteries . . . greatly increased in intensity. The shells from the rifled guns flew in all directions. . . . The accuracy of their fire forced us to abandon all the signal posts we had established in the tops of the tallest trees. The balloon itself, whenever it rose in the air, was saluted with an iron hail of missiles. . . . The object of all this was to mask the retreat." Surgeon Stevens adds that during the night of the 3rd the roar of the enemy's artillery "exceeded anything that had been heard before. From one end of the line to the other the shells and shot poured into our camps, and the arches of fire that marked the courses of the shells, with flame spouting from the mouths of the guns, created a magnificent pyrotechnic display."

Returning to the Prince de Joinville: "On the 4th, at daybreak, the men in the rifle pits of the advance saw no signs of the foe before them. A few of them ventured cautiously up to the very lines of the enemy. All was silent as death. Soon suspicion grew into certainty. It was flashed upon the headquarters by all the telegraphic lines which connected them with the different corps of the army. The Confederates had vanished, and with them all chances of a brilliant victory. . . . We had spent a whole month in constructing gigantic works now become useless. . . . The Confederates fell back, satisfied with gaining time to prepare for the defense of Richmond."

Captain Henry Blake says that "loud cheers resounded along the line, from the York River to Warwick Creek, when the result was officially announced; and the bands, which had been dumb so long, again enlivened the soldiers; and the notes of a thousand drums, fifes, and bugles filled the woods with a discord of melody." The division to which Surgeon Stevens belonged was one of the first to be rushed forward. "We found ourselves in the strongholds that we had so long invested. As the 77th Regiment passed along one of the roads leading among the entrenchments, a sharp report like that of a pistol was heard at the feet of those in the center of the column. . . . The men scattered, and a piece of old cloth was seen lying on the ground at the point from which the report emanated. Colonel [J. B.] McKean, who was very near, lifted the cloth with the point of his sword, and discovered a torpedo carefully buried in the ground, except a nipple which had been filled with fulminating powder, which was covered by the old cloth. The fuse only had exploded. Had the machine itself exploded, it must have destroyed many of our men, our colonel among them. Other regiments were not so fortunate as we were." Chaplain J. J. Marks says that the torpedoes were even concealed "in green spots where soldiers would be likely to sit down to rest. In one case that I heard of, a soldier, taking his seat with his companions on a green knoll, near to a well, saw lying at his feet a pocketknife. As he picked this up he found around it a small cord. . . . He gave the knife a sudden jerk to break the cord. This was followed by an explosion which blew the soldier into a hundred fragments. . . . The prisoners who had been taken [during the siege] were immediately put to work in unearthing the concealed shells."

Among the first newsmen to enter the defenses was the special correspondent of the Boston *Journal,* who was soon writing: "The whole place is strewed with heaps of oyster shells, empty bottles, and cans of preserved fruit and vegetables, and, strange to say, there are an enormous number of sardine boxes lying around. . . . Their exit was so sudden that their bread was left in their kneading troughs, their pork over the fire, and biscuits half-baked; but attempts were made, more or less generally, to spoil the food. Here and there a bottle of turpentine or some other vile fluid was

McClellan's van marching into Yorktown

emptied over the food they could not take. The tents are standing, but are slashed by knives. The equipments and clothing of the rebel dead were of the most miserable kind. No attempt at uniformity of dress could be seen. Here and there some officer had a flannel stripe sewed to his pantaloons. . . . The men were dressed in common linsey butternut and cotton suits of the commonest and coarsest materials. They had few knapsacks, being generally supplied with a schoolboy's satchel, sometimes of flimsy leather, but more commonly of cotton osnaburg, with here and there a rope to sling over the shoulders."

The day was a busy one for McClellan. "The moment I learned that our troops were in possession of Yorktown and the line of the Warwick, I ordered General [George] Stoneman in pursuit with all the available force of cavalry and horse artillery, supported by infantry, on both the Lee's Mill and Yorktown roads to Williamsburg. . . . While keeping steadily in view Stoneman's operations and his proper support, I at once turned my attention to expediting the movement [of Franklin's division] up the York River by water." Throughout the day, McClellan paused from time to time to wire a dispatch to Edwin Stanton, saying such things as: "Yorktown is in our possession. . . . We have the ramparts; have guns, ammunition, camp equipage, etc. Hold the entire line of his works, which the engineers report as being very strong. . . . No time shall be lost. . . . I shall push the enemy to the wall. . . . The enemy's rear is strong, but I have force enough up there to answer all purposes. We have thus far [taken possession of] seventy-one heavy guns . . . large amounts of tents, ammunition, etc. All along the lines their works prove to have been most formidable, and I am now fully satisfied of the correctness of the course I have pursued. The success is brilliant, and you may rest assured that its effects will be of the greatest importance." Stanton wired back: "Accept my cordial congratulations upon the success at Yorktown, and I am rejoiced that your forces are in active pursuit. Please furnish me with the details as far as they are acquired, and I hope soon to hail your arrival in Richmond."

Because of the wet weather, the Confederate retreat was a slow one. John Gordon, now a colonel commanding the 6th Alabama, brought up the rear over a route already much used, and he saw progress at its worst. "The roads were in horrible condition. In the mud and slush and deep ruts cut by the wagon trains and artillery . . . a number of heavy guns became bogged, and the horses were unable to drag them. My men, weary with the march and belonging to a different arm of the service, of course felt that it was a trying position to be compelled to halt and attempt to move this artillery, with the Union advance pressing so closely upon them. But they were tugging with good grace when I rode up from the extreme rear. An extraordinary effort, however, was required to save the guns. As I dismounted from my horse and waded into the deep mud and called upon them to save the

Federals moving in Johnston's wake

artillery, they raised a shout and crowded around the wheels. Not a gun or caisson was lost. . . .

"At another time on this march I found one of my youngest soldiers—he was a mere lad—lying on the roadside, weeping bitterly. I asked him what was the matter. He explained that his feet were so sore that he could not walk any farther and that he knew he would be captured. His feet were in a dreadful condition. I said to him, 'You shall not be captured,' and ordered him to mount my horse and ride forward until he could get into an ambulance or wagon, and to tell the quartermaster to send my horse back to me as soon as possible. He wiped his eyes, got into my saddle, and rode a few rods to where the company of which he was a member had halted to rest. He stopped his horse in front of his comrades, who were sitting for the moment on the roadside; and, straightening himself up, he lifted his old slouch hat with all the dignity of a commander-in-chief and called out: 'Attention, men! I'm about to bid you farewell, and I want to tell you before I go that I am very sorry for you. I was poor once myself!' Having thus delivered himself, he galloped away, bowing and waving his hat to his comrades in acknowledgment of the cheers with which they greeted him."

6

FROM WILLIAMSBURG
TO McDOWELL

ACCORDING to the Army of the Potomac's chief historian, William Swinton, "Stoneman met little opposition till he reached the enemy's prepared position in front of Williamsburg, twelve miles from Yorktown. The peninsula here contracts, and the approaching heads of two tributaries of the York and James Rivers form a kind of narrow isthmus upon which the two roads leading from Yorktown to Williamsburg unite. Commanding the débouché [i.e., the starting point of the single road leading into Williamsburg] was an extensive work with a bastion front named Fort Magruder; and, to the right and left, on the prolongation of the line, were twelve other redoubts and epaulements for field guns. These works had been prepared by the Confederates many months before. Now, this position, though a strong one so long as its flanks were secured by the closing of the rivers on either side, was one which evidently General Johnston had no intention of occupying; for, by the opening up of the York, the line of Williamsburg was exposed to be immediately turned. The Confederate army had, in fact, passed through Williamsburg toward the Chickahominy, and only a rear guard remained to cover the trains."

It was still May 4 and the time was about 4 P.M. when Joe Johnston, riding with the main body of his army, learned that the rear guard was being threatened by the Federals; and he ordered two brigades to turn back in support. One of the men in the brigade of South Carolinians under Colonel J. B. Kershaw was Sergeant D. Augustus Dickert, who relates: "As we passed through the town the citizens were greatly excited, the piazzas and balconies being filled with ladies and old men who urged the men on with all the power and eloquence at their command. The woods had been felled [forming a set of abatis] for some distance in front of the earthworks and forts, and as we neared the former we could see the enemy's skirmishers

Confederate earthworks at Williamsburg. *Left:* William and Mary College as a Union hospital

pushing out of the woods in the clearing. The 2nd and 8th South Carolina Regiments were ordered to occupy the forts and breastworks beyond Fort Magruder, and they had a perfect race to reach them before the enemy did."

Although McClellan was still in Yorktown working with Franklin's division, the scene at Williamsburg included some of McClellan's aides, among them the Prince de Joinville, who noted that "Stoneman, seeing that the enemy covered the fork of the roads . . . undertook to dislodge them by a vigorous blow. He threw forward all his horse artillery, which took up its positions brilliantly in front of the abatis, and replied to the fire of the redoubts; and he then ordered his cavalry to charge. The 6th Federal Cavalry dashed forward gallantly to meet the cavalry of the Confederates, passing directly under the crossfire of the redoubts, and rode into one of those fights with the cold steel which have become so rare. . . . Nevertheless, this was all so much valor thrown away. The enemy . . . had the advantages of number and position. To carry these works with cavalry was impossible. Men, and particularly horses, began to fall. 'I have lost thirty-one men,' said Major [Lawrence] Williams, who had led the charge of the 6th, gracefully saluting General Stoneman with his saber, with that air of determination which says, 'We will go at it again, but it's no use.' Stoneman then ordered the retreat. He repassed the abatis, and, falling back to a clearing about half a mile distant, there awaited the arrival of the infantry to renew the engagement. Unluckily, in traversing the marsh a gun of the horse artillery got buried in the mud and could not be extricated. . . . As to the Federal infantry, it came up very late . . . . At night General Sumner, who had assumed command [in McClellan's absence], wished to make an attempt to carry the works. Unfortunately, it was completely dark before the troops debouched from the woods and the marshes, and everything had to be put off to the next day. . . . The rain began to fall. . . . The troops dismally bivouacked for the night where they stood."

This was a harrowing night for Confederate soldier Jesse Reid, whose battalion was settling into a wet encampment on the Richmond side of Williamsburg when orders came for the unit to join the troops at the fortifications to perform picket duty. "It was a very dark night, cloudy and drizzling rain. We nearly ran into the enemy's lines before we knew it. Three men were put at each post, with orders to stay awake all night, and for one of us to crawl out toward the enemy's lines and find out, if possible, their position. I crawled out to a fence post about one hundred yards . . . two or three times through the night. I could distinctly hear them talking . . . but could see nothing on account of the darkness. Thus we passed the night of the 4th of May. The rain descended slowly. Just at daylight the enemy commenced snapping caps on their guns—to dry the tubes, I suppose. I will admit that I never felt so nervous in my life. . . . A little after daylight they appeared in large numbers and soon attacked."

This was the beginning of the day-long Battle of Williamsburg. According to the Union Army's Alexander S. Webb, then a major commanding the Rhode Island Artillery, the attack lacked a tactical plan and was made by too few troops. "The responsibility has been laid by some upon the shoulders of McClellan because of his absence from the field; and by others upon Sumner, who seems to have directed the movements of the day without method. Whatever may have prevented McClellan's presence with the advance, one might at least expect that his senior corps commander should have been competent to fight a battle of moderate proportions."

It was the Federal division commanded by Brigadier General Joseph Hooker, a man of coarse ways and aggressive energy, that Jesse Reid and his battalion comrades were facing that misty morning. Reid goes on: "We held our ground as long as possible, giving them as good as they sent until about 7 o'clock, when they came in such overwhelming numbers as to force us back on our main lines, a distance of about six hundred yards. . . . We left several men killed or wounded, who fell into the enemy's hands. While Thomas Stacks and another man were carrying off Archibald Sadler, who was wounded, the man who was helping was shot dead and a minnie ball struck Stacks' canteen and tore it all to pieces. Stacks left Sadler . . . in the enemy's hands . . . badly wounded. A ball went through my overcoat, but did not graze the skin." The battalion entered one of the earthen forts, the artillery fire of which kept the enemy at bay.

Joe Hooker's division, located on the left of the Federal front, had begun the fight at a fearful disadvantage. It was the only division that had gone into action. Hooker had not waited for orders from the hesitating Sumner, but had attacked on his own. In fairness to Sumner, it must be stated that a large part of the Federal army was still struggling along the muddy roads from Yorktown. Only William F. "Baldy" Smith's division, which included a number of regiments under Winfield S. Hancock, was on the line (on the right) and ready for action.

As related by an unnamed soldier in Hooker's division who was among the troops that pushed Jesse Reid and his battalion back to their fortifications: "Their heavy shot came crushing among the tangled abatis of fallen timber and ploughed up the dirt in our front, rebounding and tearing through the branches of the woods in our rear. The constant hissing of the bullets, with their sharp *ping* or *bizz* whispering around and sometimes into us, gave me a sickening feeling and a cold perspiration. I felt weak around my knees. . . . These symptoms did not decrease when several of my comrades were hit. The little rifle pits in our front fairly blazed with musketry. . . . Seeing I was not killed at once, in spite of all the noise, my knees recovered from their unpleasant limpness and my mind gradually regained its balance and composure. . . .

"We slowly retired from stump to stump and from log to log, finally regaining the edge of the wood, and took our position near Webber's and Bramhall's batteries, which had just got into position on the right of the road, not over seven hundred yards from the hostile fort. While getting into position, several of the battery men were killed, as they immediately drew the artillery fire of the enemy, which opened with a noise and violence that astonished me. Our two batteries were admirably handled, throwing a number of shot and shell into the enemy's works, speedily silencing them; and by nine o'clock the field in our front, including the rifle pits, was completely cleaned out of artillery and infantry.

"Shortly afterwards we advanced along the edge of the wood to the left of Fort Magruder, and about eleven o'clock we saw emerging from the little ravine to the left of the fort a swarm of Confederates, who opened on us with a terrible and deadly fire. Then they charged upon us with their peculiar yell. We took all the advantage possible of the stumps and trees as we were pushed back, until we reached the edge of the wood again, where we halted and fired upon the enemy from behind all the cover the situation afforded. We were none of us too proud . . . to dodge behind a tree or stump. I called out to a comrade, 'Why don't you get behind a tree?' 'Confound it,' said he, 'there ain't enough for the officers.' "

Taking cover in this way during firefights was not considered dishonorable unless one was deliberately skulking. According to Captain Henry Blake, also of Hooker's division: "The facts attending the death of two skulkers may be adduced to show the folly of trying to evade a soldier's duty in the day of battle. While one was peeping over a log behind which he had concealed himself, a bullet entered his temple, which was the only part of his person that was exposed. Another, who had cautiously moved until he was ten yards in the rear of his company, was pierced by two balls which dodged between the legs of his comrades." The champion skulker known to Blake was "a captain in the regiment [who] . . . consulted a small pocket compass which led him, with a third of his company, towards Yorktown, when the reports of cannon, if he had pricked his ears, would have called him to the battlefield in the opposite direction."

Blake gained a healthy respect for Joe Hooker: "I witnessed one of the rare exhibitions of the power of a commanding presence which great exigencies demand. The remnant of a brigade, which had resisted with brilliant valor the onset of superior numbers, discouraged by its large losses in officers and men and the absence of reinforcements, retreated to escape capture; and the regiments mingled together in confusion while they fell back into the road. The yells of the exulting rebels proclaimed their success; and the gallant soldiers . . . commenced to rush to the rear in disorder. General Hooker, who was riding along the lines, at once halted his favorite white horse in the midst of the medley and exclaimed, 'Men! What does this mean? You must hold your ground!' The voice that uttered these simple words had always taught justice and patriotism in the camps; the uplifted hand had always returned the salute of every soldier in his division; the form had ever been seen in the front when the storm of bullets fell and spared not; the dress was the uniform of a brigadier general, who welcomed the dangers that belonged to his rank. The recollection of these exalted qualities flashed through the minds of all. . . . It inspired the timid with courage; the weak became strong; and every man stopped in his place and faced the enemy."

The Federal retreat had seen not only the slain but also many of the helpless wounded left on the field, and some of the latter fell into Confederate hands. As observed by Southerner Robert Stiles of the Richmond Howitzers: "During a lull in the fighting our guns were withdrawn and [we] were in column parallel to the road, in a common on the outskirts of town, resting and awaiting orders, when a number of wounded Federal prisoners were brought up in an ambulance and laid temporarily on the grass, while a field hospital was being established hard by. Among them was a poor wretch, shot through the bowels, who was rolling on the ground in excruciating agony and beseeching the bystanders to put him out of his misery. There did not appear to be anything that could be done for him, at least not in advance of the coming of the surgeons, so I was in the act of turning away from the painful spectacle when a couple of Tureos, or Louisiana Tigers, the most rakish and devilish-looking beings I ever saw, came up and peered over the shoulders of the circle of onlookers. Suddenly one of them pushed through the ring, saying: 'Put you out of your misery? Certainly, sir!' And before anyone had time to interfere, or even [to grasp] the faintest idea of his intention, [he] brained the man with the butt of his musket; and, the bloody club still in his hands, looking around upon the wounded men, [he] added glibly, 'Any other gentlemen here'd like to be accommodated?' It is impossible to express my feelings. I fear that if I had had a loaded musket in my hands I should have illustrated the demoralization of war a little further by shooting down in his tracks the demon, who suddenly disappeared as a gasp of horror escaped the spectators."

Joe Hooker and his men managed to cling to the field even though additional Confederate units, retracing their steps through Williamsburg, kept joining the fight. James Longstreet was in command, but Joe Johnston himself was now riding toward the sounds of the action. Northerner William Swinton says that the Confederate attacks "bore heavily on Hooker. That officer had taken care to open communications with the Yorktown road, on which fresh troops were to come up. Yet, notwithstanding the repeated requests made by him for the assistance he sorely needed, none came. . . . While during the morning the fight thus waxed hot in front of Fort Magruder, the troops on the right, composed exclusively of General Smith's division, had not engaged the enemy; but towards noon Sumner ordered General Smith to send one of his brigades to occupy a redoubt on the extreme right, said to be evacuated by the enemy. For this purpose, Hancock's brigade was selected. [Hancock was at that time commanding two brigades, his own and that of Brigadier General John W. Davidson, and he used elements of both.] Making a wide detour to the right, which brought him within sight of the York River, Hancock passed Cub Dam Creek on an old mill bridge and took possession of the work indicated, which he found unocccupied. Twelve hundred yards in advance, another redoubt was discovered in the same condition, and this also he quietly took possession of. The position which, through the carelessness of the Confederates, Hancock had thus seized, proved to be a very important one . . . entirely commanding the plain between it and Fort Magruder. He had, in fact, debouched on the flank and rear of the Confederate line of defense. On reconnoitring what lay beyond, there were found to be two more redoubts between the position and the fort. These seemed to be occupied by at least some force. Hancock put his battery into position to play upon these works, and a few shells and the fire of the skirmishers proved sufficient to drive the Confederates from their cover; but he did not deem it prudent to occupy them until reinforcements should arrive."

Because of his weakness, Hancock was unable to divert much of the enemy's attention from Hooker. But by this time General Sumner had sent word down the Yorktown road for Philip Kearny and his division to hasten to Hooker's support. Phil Kearny was a likely man for the emergency, for he was always eager to fight. Undaunted by the fact he had lost his left arm while leading a cavalry charge in Mexico, he was known for maintaining a smile and a spirited demeanor under the most perilous combat conditions. Kearny's division was farther down the road than many of the other Federals, all of whom were moving toward the battlefield. These included John J. Peck's brigade, and one of Peck's regimental commanders was Regis de Trobriand: "The rain had not stopped . . . . The heavens were hid by one of those thick curtains of gray clouds behind which it seemed as if the sun were forever extinguished. The roads were horrible. . . . However, the cannon were heard firing uninterruptedly at Williamsburg, indicating a serious engagement. . . . We must hurry forward. And we pushed on the best we could, through an ocean of mud, amongst the mired teams, in the midst of an inevitable disorder which left behind many stragglers. . . . The regiments, the brigades, and even the divisions became mingled in inevitable confusion. Whenever I reached a favorable place, I made a short halt of a few minutes to rally my scattered companies and give the laggards time to rejoin us. Then we again started on, following the route of the 102nd Pennsylvania, with which General Peck had taken the advance. Behind us marched General Kearny, leading the head of his division. . . . His ardor had found means of passing all the troops which were ahead of him. He urged on our stragglers. . . .

"Soon an aide of General Peck brought me the order to pass by [Silas] Casey's division, which had halted, I do not know why, in a large open field near a brick church. The sound of the cannonade did not diminish. At this point Kearny's division turned to the left to come into line by a crossroad less encumbered. A little further along I met Captain Leavitt Hunt, aide of General Heintzelman, who had been ordered to hurry forward reinforcements. He informed me that ... Hooker, strongly opposed by superior forces, had lost ground after a desperate contest of more than four hours, during which no assistance had been sent to him. The Prince de Joinville, in his turn, passed by me without stopping, urging me to hurry forward. He was mounted on an English horse and covered with mud from head to foot. He was hurrying to Yorktown to endeavor to bring up General McClellan, who, ingnorant of what was passing at Williamsburg, had not yet started."

Reaching the battlefield, De Trobriand found that "General Peck was on the edge of a strip of woods, which was all that separated us from the enemy. Learning that, on account of our hurried march and the difficulties of the road, I had left behind me half of my men, he ordered a halt of ten minutes to rest those who had come up and to give the others a chance to join us. . . . The greater part of the regiment were in the ranks before it went into action. It was then about one o'clock in the afternoon. . . .

"[Our] brigade, the first to come to the aid of General Hooker, was promptly deployed along the edge of the wood. . . . The enemy, encouraged by a first success, was reforming for a new attack, whose shock we were about to receive . . . . At the signal of a group of officers emerging at a gallop from Fort Magruder, the enemy's line started out of the woods with loud yells and marched straight for us. When they had advanced halfway, I opened upon them a fire by file, which promised well, while the 102nd fired a volley with its entire second rank. I do not know what harm we did them, but they continued to advance rapidly, with increased cries.

"There was in front of my left a natural opening in the abatis, toward which two battalions of the enemy directed their course with the evident intention of making it their especial point of attack. Unhappily, the company which was posted in front of that point was the worst commanded, and the one on which I could the least depend. I had my eyes on it when it received its first volley. Alas! It did not even wait for a second. A man in the rear rank turned and started toward me. And, like a flock of sheep after the leader, the rest followed in the twinkling of an eye. Almost immediately the next company gave way, then the third. The Zouaves, thus finding themselves left alone, broke in their turn and fell back; and, what is most shameful, some officers ran away with their men, and even without them. The 93rd [Pennsylvania], in forming the second line, could not stop the runaways. They broke through the ranks and disappeared in the woods—the cursed woods which tempted the cowards by an easy refuge, and upon which, instead of rain, I wished at that moment to see fall fire from heaven.

"However, in the breaking of the left, a handful of brave men . . . remained immovable. Posted behind the trees, they held firm and endeavored to cover the opening by a rapid and well-directed fire. . . . Some officers, taken by surprise and led away by the current, stopped of their own accord or retired slowly, rather hesitating than frightened, and as if seeking to find out what they ought to do. In spite of the density of the thicket, where my horse advanced with difficulty, I was soon amongst [the shirkers]. At my voice they stopped and formed around me. I gathered in this way a hundred, and led them quickly into line. But at the moment when I reformed them in front of the fatal opening, a strong volley broke them a second time.

"The enemy had then advanced to the end of the abatis, and rushed into a passage which he thought open to him. In the midst of the smoke I saw six or eight grayjackets advance to within a few steps of us. Are we about to be swept away? No! This time the men whom I led back under fire had not *fled*. The most of them had only taken shelter behind the neighboring trees, and from there directed a well-sustained fire upon the assailants, whom the fire of my center companies struck obliquely. Those nearest to us were killed or wounded, and the others fell back. . . .

"My right had not yielded. On that side . . . were brave officers who kept their men in position without effort. . . . When I could see clearly for myself how matters stood, through the smoke which floated over the whole line, in the midst of the rolling of the small arms and the bursting of the shells among the trees, I breathed as a man would breathe rescued from the water where he was drowning. The flag of the regiment had not receded. Our honor was safe."

De Trobriand re-formed his left; and, with Peck's other regiments participating, the enemy's ensuing attacks were persistently beaten back. "The engagement," says De Trobriand, "lasted about an hour, when, for the first time, firing was heard on my left. I could perceive nothing yet, but the fire became more and more vigorous in that part of the woods. No more doubt. Kearny had arrived. Hurrah for Kearny!"

There were now enough Federal reinforcements on the field to make it possible for Joe Hooker's exhausted division to withdraw to a reserve position. Corps Commander Samuel Heintzelman, who had been at the front with Hooker, rode among the retiring columns, with their thinned ranks, and tried to raise morale by calling out, "Halloo, men! Richmond is taken!" Some cheers were returned, but Heintzelman was not satisfied, and he gave the order, "Bring up the bands! Play 'Yankee Doodle' or anything; but make some noise!" According to Captain Henry Blake, "A squad of musicians who belonged to different regiments was collected together, and the strains of 'Dixie' and 'Yankee Doodle' mingled in the din of the musketry and can-nonade [heard from the front]. The execution of the music in a public as-sembly, if it was viewed from an artistic point of view, would be pronounced inferior; but the . . . Federal battalions . . . received new strength." Blake felt that the volume of the hurrahing that arose was intim-idating to the enemy, "who did not make another advance after the repulse which General Kearny's gallant troops had made decisive." The Confeder-ates, however, still held their line of redoubts. The fighting was merely stalemated.

For some time now, Joe Johnston had been on the field, directing Con-federate operations from a headquarters established at Fort Magruder. A young major who saw the general at work was impressed by his manner. "As report after report came in from different parts of the fight, he seemed not to be in the least excited or worried. No move of the enemy seemed to surprise him. Without seeming hesitation, he gave orders as confidently as if checking names off a list." Says Johnston himself: "About five o'clock Gen-eral [Jubal A.] Early sent an officer to report that a battery that had been firing upon Fort Magruder and the troops near it was near in his front, and asked permission to attack it. The message was delivered to General Long-street in my presence, and he referred it to me. I authorized the attempt, but enjoined caution in it."

It happened that Jubal Early was stationed on the Confederate left, and that the troublesome battery near his front belonged to Winfield Hancock, who had not received the reinforcements he needed to press his unique ad-vantage and was inflicting punishment as best he could. General Sumner, with his concern centered on Hooker's part of the field, had not only with-held support from Hancock but had also ordered him to retire to a safer po-sition. The frustrated Hancock did not obey at once, and by the time he began falling back Jubal Early's brigade was moving toward him. "Old Jube" led the left wing in person, riding hunched in the saddle because of an arthritic spine, yet waving his sword and shouting, "Follow me!" The troops chanted for Yankee ears: "Bull Run; Ball's Bluff! Bull Run; Ball's Buff!" Hancock rushed his units into defensive positions, soon opening fire both with artillery and musketry. Uncertain of the ground and the Federal dispositions, the Confederates became confused. Their attack fragmented, and Hancock started to cut them up. The fate of those elements that closed with his principal line is told by Thomas W. Hyde, a Federal soldier with the 7th Maine Volunteers: "On the Confederates came, and a fine picture of a charge they made. They were at the double-quick and were coming over a ploughed field. . . . They could not see us as we lay flat on the ground. From my place on the left of the regiment, I saw General Hancock galloping to-ward us, bareheaded, alone, a magnificent figure; and with a voice hoarse with shouting he gave us the order, 'Forward! Charge!'. . .

"Well, up we started, and the long line of sabre bayonets came down together . . . as we crossed the crest and with a roar of cheers . . . dashed on. It was an ecstasy of excitement for a moment. . . . The foe, breathless from their long tug over the heavy ground, seemed to dissolve all at once into a quivering and disintegrating mass and to scatter in all directions. Upon this we halted and opened fire, and the view of it through the smoke was pitiful. They were falling everywhere; white handkerchiefs were held up in token of surrender. No bullets were coming our way except from a clump of trees in front of our left. Here a group of men, led by an officer whose horse had just fallen, were trying to keep up the unequal fight, when . . . the crack shot of Company D ran forward a little and sent a bullet crashing through his brain. This was Lieutenant Colonel J. C. Bradburn [actually, Badham] of the 5th North Carolina, and at his fall all opposition ceased. We gathered in some three hundred prisoners." Adds Winfield Hancock: "The enemy were completely routed and dispersed. For 600 yards in front of our line the whole field was strewn with the enemy's dead and wounded." Jubal Early himself had been shot through the shoulder, and his horse had been badly wounded in the face, one eye torn from its socket. Both horse and master escaped the field, and the half-blind but loyal animal carried the tottering Early to the Confederate hospital in Williamsburg.

The day was waning and the inconclusive fighting was winding down everywhere when McClellan arrived from Yorktown. A newsman who saw him says that "the rapidity of his ride . . . had well spattered him with mud, and the drenching rain had penetrated his every garment. He, however, showed no signs of fatigue." In a letter to Ellen, McClellan described his arrival this way: "I found everybody discouraged, officers and men; our troops in wrong positions, on the wrong side of the woods; no system, no cooperation, no orders given, roads blocked up. As soon as I came upon the field the men cheered like fiends, and I saw at once that I could save the day." He made all the necessary dispositions, he explained, "for whatever might occur."

Nothing occurred, and the army settled down for the night. Now McClellan began worrying about a counterattack, and he telegraphed Stanton: "I find Joe Johnston in front of me in strong force, probably greater a good deal than my own, and very strongly entrenched. . . . I learn from prisoners that they intend disputing every step to Richmond. I shall run the risk of at least holding them in check here. . . . My entire force is undoubtedly considerably inferior to that of the rebels, who still fight well, but I will do all I can with the force at my disposal."

From the Confederate point of view, the Battle of Williamsburg was nothing more than a delaying action. It was necessary for Johnston to retard the Federals for a day in order to keep his trains moving safely. He had no

intention of disputing every step to Richmond. That night his forces quietly
packed up and resumed their march. When their absence was discovered in
the morning, McClellan's mood changed dramatically. Now he informed
Stanton: "The effect of Hancock's brilliant engagement yesterday afternoon
was to turn the left of their line of works. He was strongly reinforced, and
the enemy abandoned the entire position during the night. . . . The victory
is complete." In a follow-up telegram, he said, "Every hour proves our victory more complete." Ellen was told: "Every hour its importance is proved
to be greater. . . . In short, we have given them a tremendous thrashing."
The casualty figures alone were enough to invalidate this claim. Whereas
Johnston had lost about 1,700 in killed, wounded, and missing, McClellan's
total exceeded 2,200.

McClellan did not resume his hot pursuit of the Confederates; he sent
only an advance guard marching in their wake. It was necessary for him to
await the arrival of his supply trains, which were still winding their way
from Yorktown. Although the rains had stopped, the roads remained mired,
and progress was labored. "Thus," says Regis de Trobriand, "we had three
entire days of leisure at Williamsburg to lie around in the sun and brush up
our arms to the sound of military music, which celebrated our indolent
glory by playing from morning till night. . . . I profited by the delay to visit
the field of battle, where several detachments passed the day of the 6th in
burying the dead. Not an exhilarating spectacle. And yet, to be sincere, I
could not help feeling a little disappointed in finding only fifteen [Confeder-
ate] dead in the abatis behind which we had fought. Three hours of firing
and sixteen thousand cartridges expended to kill fifteen men and put perhaps a hundred and fifty *hors de combat!*

"Where Hooker's division had fought, our loss was much greater than
theirs. On the open ground, and especially on the sides of the road, lay
many of the dead from [Daniel E.] Sickles' New York brigade. Further
along in the woods, where the attack had begun, the New Jersey brigade
had left the thicket full of dead. Everywhere those who had been killed out-
right had retained, when fallen, the position in which death had struck
them standing. . . . The cannon which the enemy had not been able to carry
off were buried in the mud to the axles. The two wheel-horses were literally
drowned in the liquid mud, their heads half buried. The others, killed by
balls, mingled their blood with that of some artillerymen who had endeavored to release them by cutting the harness. Human remains frightfully
mutilated gave evidence here and there that the cannon had also done its
part in the bloody work. One of those lay at the foot of a fence with nothing
of the head left but the face like a grinning mask. The remainder, crushed
by a ball, adhered to the rails in bloody blotches."

Adds Captain Henry Blake: "Nearly one hundred of the enemy, in one
part of the woods, had been killed while they were lying upon the ground,

and the bullets had penetrated their foreheads. Some who had lived a few hours after they were wounded grasped photographs or letters upon which their dying eyes [had] rested. . . . The pockets of friend and enemy had been turned inside out by the army thieves . . . and the buttons of the uniforms of every traitor had been removed. 'I wish there was a battle every week,' one of those miscreants remarked in speaking of the amount he had stolen. In wandering over the field, a corporal found in the pocket of a rebel a piece of tobacco upon which the blood had been coagulated. . . . He washed the article, took a 'chaw,' and reserved the rest for future consumption."

The burials were governed by expediency rather than by ceremony. De Trobriand, impelled by a "strange curiosity, which by a natural impulse leads us toward the horrible," did not hesitate "to step on the edge of these broad trenches, carelessly dug today by those for whom others will dig trenches elsewhere, perhaps in a year, perhaps in a month, perhaps tomorrow. The first to depart on the long journey lie stretched out before us, side by side, with marble features, glassy eyes, and in their torn and bloody uniforms. The comrades who will follow them hasten to finish their duty without philosophizing on the skull of poor Yorick, whose infinite witticisms but yesterday enlivened the bivouac. A layer of men and a layer of earth. The ditch filled, it is covered over with a little hillock to provide for settling. Then they depart, leaving to a few friendly hands the pious care of marking a name and a date on small boards aligned at the head of the dead, where no one will come to read them."

De Trobriand next went in search of the men of his regiment who had been wounded, and he found them "in a neighboring farmhouse transformed into a hospital, where those of the brigade had been carried. The farm buildings were full. The patients were laid on the ground on beds of straw. Those who could walk went and came with the head bandaged or the arm in a sling, helping to take care of the others. All showed a remarkable courage and bore their sufferings with a tranquil resignation. The most boastful were even laughing, and spoke of soon retaking their places in the ranks. A few only, feeling that they were mortally wounded, groaned aloud with grief or shed silent tears while thinking of those they would never see again."

De Trobriand went on to visit a house in which a collection of Confederate wounded, at McClellan's orders, were being cared for by Union surgeons. "A little stream of coagulated blood reddened the steps coming from the half-opened door. On pushing it to enter I felt a resistance, the cause of which I soon recognized. It was a pile of amputated legs and arms thrown into a corner of the room, waiting the coming of a Negro to take them out and bury them in the garden. . . . Near the pile there lay by itself a leg white and slender, terminating in a foot almost as small as that of a child. The knee had been shattered by a ball. 'You see we have had some work to do,' said a surgeon to me. 'Come in, colonel.' Around the room . . . the amputated were on the floor in rows with the head to the wall. All these mutilated creatures turned their eyes, hollow with suffering, towards me, the greater part of them listless but a few with an air having a shade of defiance. I looked for the one to whom the leg with a child's foot had belonged. I had no trouble in recognizing him. He was, really, almost a child, with blue eyes, long blond hair, and with emaciated features. . . .

"I went into the next room. The same sight. 'Water,' cried several feeble voices. 'Wait a minute, boys,' said the doctor in a fatherly tone. . . . 'Sam is busy just at this instant. As soon as he is disengaged he will bring you some.' Sam was the Negro ordered to bury the amputated limbs. 'Think of it, colonel,' began the doctor again, 'we found here only an old black man to help us take care of these poor creatures, a good enough old fellow, but not as active as he might be, and who is hardly enough to tend to everything.'

"On the stairs I met a second surgeon, eating, with a good appetite, a piece of biscuit and some cheese. 'The surgeon-in-chief detailed me here yesterday,' said he, 'and I assure you, colonel, it is no sinecure. This is the first morsel I have eaten since I left the brigade hospital.' And, continuing his hasty repast, he introduced me to a room where a dozen patients waited their turn. One of them, whose leg had been amputated the previous evening, had been left there on a straw mattress, a privilege accorded to him on account of his rank as captain. He was a robust Georgian . . . whose morale had not been affected by the loss of a leg.

"We entered readily into conversation, and what he said to me . . . was a prediction. . . . 'Do not be in a hurry . . . to cry victory and to regard that as a great success which is really only the execution of our own plans. What we wanted at Yorktown was simply to delay your arrival before Richmond until the summer heat. We have succeeded. We kept you there, throwing up earth, digging ditches, erecting batteries, for a whole month, although we had but one-against-ten when you came. McClellan having thrown up his mountain to crush our shed, we gave him the slip without his even knowing it. You did not take Yorktown; we made you a present of it when it was no longer of use to us. You caught up with us here, but you have not beaten us. . . . What I regret the most is that I cannot be there to see your army melt away in the Chickahominy marshes, where Johnston and the fever await you. I can tell you now, if you had taken Yorktown a month ago, Richmond would perhaps be yours today. Now it is too late. . . . Go and besiege Richmond. You will find there a new adversary. . . . The season begins when the marsh fevers will do more to demoralize your men and destroy your army than all the battalions and all the redoubts we can oppose to them.'

"The Georgian captain spoke this with an animation somewhat feverish.

I thought it all an exaggeration, attributable to a sense of defeat and irritation from his wound. I left him, assuring him that, whatever might happen before Richmond, the Southern Confederation was nonetheless condemned to perish. . . .

"I went into the next room. This was the operating room—the *butchery*. Blood everywhere—on the floor, on the walls, and in the pails. An arm taken off at the shoulder joint [had been] rolled under the table more bloody than any of the rest. The table of torture. A young man lay there unconscious, from whom that arm had been taken. Under the influence of chloroform, he appeared not to suffer; but from time to time a sad smile passed over his countenance. I did not wait his revival. I had had enough of it. The surgeon told me that it was doubtful if the patient survived the operation. . . . When I went out of the house, Sam came in, having finished his work of gravedigger. He bowed very low several times. 'Sam,' said I, 'if you are a good man go immediately to the well and get some water for the wounded, who are very thirsty.' That was all I could do for them."

When they were sated with battlefield scenes, the Federal soldiers turned their attention to Williamsburg. "The ancient city," explains Captain Blake, "had lost its former importance, and was now celebrated as the seat of the College of William and Mary, in which some of the most eminent statesmen of the United States had been educated. All the desolations of war, the legitimate results of the Rebellion, were visible throughout its limits; and the public buildings, halls, churches, and many dwelling houses were filled with the wounded of both armies. The yellow flags, which indicated the rebel hospitals—red was the color of the Union hospital flag— waved in every district. . . . The people, with few exceptions, were traitors who had always encouraged those that murdered the forces that upheld the National Government; and the closed and empty stores, the absence of the ablebodied white men, the scowls of the women and children, and the delighted faces of the Negroes were perceived by the most casual observer. . . .

"One-half of the population, fearing that the troops would commit the grossest outrages, [had] fled to Richmond as destitute and terror-stricken as the settlers upon the frontier when the torch and scalping knife of the savage commenced the work of destruction. No wagons or horses were seen in the streets or stables of the town; and the slaves lived in the mansions of the fugitives and enjoyed the privileges of freedom. Persons who had refused to flee, and ignorant women who had been left helpless by their male relatives in Johnston's army, bolted the doors and closed the blinds of their domiciles, and shuddered when they thought of the 'monsters of Lincoln' who had a 'heart of iron.' The conduct of the Union soldiers, after the occupation of the place, which was humane and just . . . convinced them of the groundlessness of their apprehensions, and the shutters were once more opened to admit the rays of sunlight into their cheerless homes. . . .

"The women . . . who had been so cowardly in the time of imaginary dangers, took advantage of the uniform courtesy of the 'Yankees,' whom they despised and hated, and haughtily walked in the streets with their 'niggers,' who carried dishes and baskets of luxuries and food for 'missus,' who distributed them among the sick and wounded rebels. They compressed their dresses whenever they met an officer or enlisted man, so that the garment would not touch the persons they passed. They pulled their hats over their faces to preclude scrutiny. But these precautions were useless, for their cadaverous features and lank forms were sometimes seen; and all were satisfied that the Southern beauties about whom so much has been written did not reside in Williamsburg.

"They gladly paraded through the mud and filth of the street to avoid a squad of men upon the sidewalks. When two young rebel females were walking by some soldiers, one of them suddenly screamed . . . 'Oh! Oh! What have you done? Your skirt touched a Yankee!' "

While McClellan tarried at Williamsburg, personally lodged, as he wrote Ellen, "in a very fine house which Joe Johnston occupied as his headquarters," the Confederates continued toward Richmond, moving, according to one man, "neither by land nor water, but by a half-and-half mixture of both." Robert Stiles of the Richmond Howitzers recounts: "Our company wagon, containing a . . . supply of commissary and quartermaster stores and all our extra clothing, sank to the hubs and had to be abandoned. We feared for the guns and could not think of wasting teams on wagons. The danger was really imminent that the guns themselves would have to be abandoned. . . . By dint, however, of fine driving and heavy lifting and shoving at the wheels, we managed to save our brazen war dogs, for which we were beginning to feel a strong attachment. The poor horses often sank to their bellies, and we were several times compelled to unhitch a stalled horse, tie a prolonge around him, hitch the rest of the team to the rope, and drag him out. . . .

"We mounted upon the gun and caisson horses, for the emergency, the very best men, regard being had to the single requisite of skill and and experience in handling draft horses and heavy loads, and no regard whatever as to whether or not they had theretofore been battery drivers. In this way it happened that two of the finest soldiers in the command were driving at my gun, the one the wheel team and the other the lead, there being at the time six horses to the piece. It was stalled, and two or three unsuccessful efforts having been made to start it, the wheel driver declared that it was the fault of the leader. The latter retorted, and the war of words waxed hot, until suddenly the wheel charioteer dismounted in the thigh-deep mud and, struggling up abreast of the lead team, dared the driver of it to get down and fight it out then and there. It is possible the other would have accepted the challenge if a glance down at his friend and foe had not brought the absurdity of the entire thing so vividly before him that he simply threw his head back in a burst of laughter, saying, 'Why, Billy, you must take me for an infernal fool, to expect me to get down in that infernal mud to fight you!' Whereupon the gentleman in the mud laughed too, as did everybody within sight and hearing, and Billy struggled back to his wheelers, remounted, and with 'a long pull, a strong pull, and a pull all together,' out she came."

Added to their struggles with the mud, Robert Stiles and his comrades had trouble keeping themselves in rations. Stiles tells of a fortuitous procurement: "The column had halted at New Kent Court House, a little hamlet in the great pine forest ... boasting not over a half dozen houses in addition to the tavern and the temple of justice. The infantry had broken ranks and most of them were resting and chattering, seated or reclined upon the banks of the somewhat sunken road. On one side had been a large cabbage patch from which the heads had been cut the preceding fall, leaving the stalks in the ground, which under the genial spring suns and rains ... had greened out into what I think are termed 'collards' or 'sprouts.' They were just what the soldiers longed for and required, and an enterprising fellow sauntered up to the fence and offered an old woman who stood nearby 'a dollar for one of them green things.' The price was fixed ... by the purchaser ... under the combined influence of three considerations: he thought so much of the sprout, and so little of the dollar; and then that dollar was probably the smallest money he had.

"No sooner said than done; and by the time the fellow paid his dollar and began browsing upon his sprout, the fence, which was about breast high and a very flimsy affair, was lined with soldiers, each with his right arm extended toward the old woman, a one-dollar Confederate Treasury note fluttering in his fingers. . . . 'Here, miss, please let me have one; I'm a heap hungrier'n these other men.' 'But, mother, I'm a sick man and *such* a good boy; you ought to 'tend to me first.' And so it went. And so went the old woman, backward and forward, jerking the sprouts out of the ground with wondrous speed, and as fast as she gathered an armful, striding along the fence, distributing them, and raking in the dollars. I never witnessed a brisker trade in cabbage. But the buyers were so eager and the pressure of the leaning men became so great that the fence ... suddenly gave way, and quicker than I can tell it there wasn't a sprout left in the patch. The men had no intention of breaking into the enclosure, but Providence having removed the fence, they followed up the Providential indications by removing the sprouts. It is not easy to say just what the purchasing power of these dollars was, but ... it is easy to see that the old woman, counting only the money she actually got, made an astounding sale of her entire crop of sprouts."

Aside from the mud and the commissary problems, Joe Johnston's retreating army had little to worry about. It will be recalled that McClellan spent the greater part of the day of the Battle of Williamsburg at Yorktown, his purpose to start Franklin's division sailing up the York River in order to land these troops ahead of Johnston and on the right flank of his retreat. Intercepted, the Confederates might be held in one spot until enough Federal reinforcements could be brought up to produce a showdown battle. The endeavor was another of scant achievement. The flotilla, made up of civilian-owned transports covered by Navy warships, completed its preparations to sail on the morning of May 6, the day after Williamsburg.

Trooper Adams, of Franklin's division, says that the weather "was remarkably clear and springlike, and the river smooth. The signal was given . . . and the fleet moved in two lines, preceded by gunboats, and presented a grand appearance. . . . The landscape here was new and strange to us. . . . The beautifully sloping banks of the river, the deep green fields, the fine farm houses with their pretty gardens, their orchards in full blossom, their broad avenues and lawns dotted with shade trees, and the cattle grazing in the distance formed a pastoral picture of great beauty. The people came out at times from their houses and stood along the banks, watching the movements of the fleet. . . . Twenty miles above Yorktown the water began to shoal, and the river seemed to expand into a lake. There was a thickly wooded ridge on the south shore, and extending nearly at right angles from this, and well across the head of the stream, was a broad level plateau, at the northern extremity of which a little brick house stood. This was Brick House Point. The river here made a sweep to the right, or north, and opened into what seemed a sequestered cove. About a mile and a half beyond this, and to the west, was a narrow point of land on which stood a number of large wooden buildings or sheds. This was West Point, the buildings marking the terminus of the Richmond and West Point railroad. The Mattapony on the one side and the Pamunkey on the other swept past this point, mingled their waters in the cove below, and formed the York River.

"Our light draught steamers and sailing vessels deployed along this broad plateau, some of them within one hundred yards of the shore, and prepared to land the troops, while the gunboats took position to cover the landing. . . . In less than an hour from the time we had taken position the water swarmed with all sorts of odd craft, from pontoons to canalboats. . . . But the enemy was not inclined to let us do this work in peace. As soon as the first fleet of pontoons started to make a landing, the enemy opened from a battery concealed on the lower end of the ridge I have before described. His shells and round shot flew thick and fast, some of them exploding among the pontoons, others paying their compliments to the fleet. The pontoons kept steadily on towards the shore, which the men reached with cheers. But there was intense excitment among the fleet, and it was amusing to see the alarm created among some of the [civilian] captains. Some ran up into the rigging, thinking it a better place of safety than the deck. Others sought shelter on the outside of their vessels. A shot whizzed past one who had sought shelter in the rigging, and he came to the deck so quick that many thought him killed. But he was up in an instant, over the side of his vessel, and sculling away for dear life in his boat. . . . He was not the only New England captain ready to forsake his ship at the first sound of the enemy's guns. . . .

"Officers began to inquire what our gunboats were doing that they did not open. . . . The fact was that, owing to want of water, the gunboats found it difficult to get within range of the enemy's batteries. They however succeeded at last, and a few well-directed shells silenced the enemy and drove him from his position. The work of landing now went on unmolested. . . . When the sun went down we had one brigade of infantry and two regiments of another landed. We also had three batteries of artillery . . . and two companies . . . of the Lincoln Cavalry. Professor Lowe was up taking an airing in his balloon, but came down without bringing us any valuable information concerning the enemy. He thought he saw signs of the enemy north of West Point, but was not sure. . . .

"Drums beat, bugles sounded, and bands played on Brick House Point that night; and as the shadows of the setting sun played over the broad plateau, over the gleaming bayonets and flying banners, and over the ships on the broad river . . . the scene became grand and imposing. The troops formed in line of battle as soon as landed, the right stretching away towards the Pamunkey River, the left resting near the south bank of the York and facing the ridge of wood where the enemy had his batteries. . . . We were entirely in the dark as to the enemy's strength, position, and intentions."

Everyone, however, believed that a fight was imminent. As related by Newton M. Curtis, an officer with the 16th New York Infantry: "After supper was over, the members of Company F were engaged in general conversation when Edwin R. Bishop, a light-hearted and fun-provoking man, rose from the ground and interrupted the conversation by saying, 'Boys, if I should fall . . . as I now believe I shall, I wish you would bury me under this tree, where I indicate by these lines.' He then proceeded to mark with a pioneer's spade the outlines of a grave. Immediately Corporal George J. Love, a very sedate man, rose and picking up the spade which Bishop had used, said, 'I would like you to dig my grave beside Bishop's, but please dig it with more regularity than his crooked lines indicate. I am the son of a sexton, and have helped to dig many.' He then proceeded to draw a parallelogram, dropped the spade, and sat down. Then Peter J. Ploof, a lad of twenty, much beloved for his boyish, winsome ways, picked up the spade, and said, 'If I fall, dig my grave here beside Love's and do it as we dig graves at home. Please follow the lines I make for you.' He drew the lines . . . wider at the shoulders and tapering toward the head and foot. Conversation was resumed, and no futher attention was paid to the incident."

Returning to Trooper Adams: "Pickets were posted, and scouts were sent out, who soon returned and reported the enemy's pickets just in the edge of the wood, a few hundred yards south of us. The few people we found at Brick House Point had no information to give us. About ten o'clock at night our pickets captured and sent in two of the enemy's men, who for some time would give no particular account of themselves, except that they belonged to a Texas regiment. . . . They were both intelligent men and fine-looking soldiers. One was both silent and sullen. From the other we ascertained that the rebel General [William H. C.] Whiting, with two brigades of infantry . . . was in position in the woods in front of us, and would attack us . . . in the morining. This force consisted in that portion of the enemy's troops retreating [from Williamsburg] along the bank of the York River."

When the action opened in the morning, the 16th New York Infantry was in a forward position on the Union right. According to Newton Curtis, "Companies F and G . . . met the advancing lines of General J. B. Hood's brigade. . . . These companies could not stay the progress of the over-whelming force brought against them, but they made a manful resistance until the artillery was brought up and made ready for action. They were then ordered back, with 17% of their number among the killed and wounded. Three members of Company F were killed—Bishop, Love, and Ploof." Not only the Union right but also the center and the left were driven for a time before they began to hold and to counterattack. Some welcome support came booming from the gunboats in the river. The Confederates strove to establish a position from which artillery fire could be rained on the transports and the landing zone, but their efforts failed. At about 2 P.M. they began an orderly withdrawal. Pressing after, the Federals repossessed all of the lost ground, but they carried the contest no further. Neither side had suffered major damage.

Newton Curtis offers some additional vignettes: "Corporal James Cook . . . whose leg was broken by a musket ball, was left on the field during its temporary occupation by the enemy. A Confederate soldier took his watch, purse, and a Masonic ring. His call for help brought to his side a Confederate Mason, who caused Cook's property to be restored to him." Another Federal soldier "was found alive, but lived only long enough to tell his comrades that the Confederates had been kind to him, and had done all they could to make him comfortable." A Union man named Mummery "was found in a pool of water with the throat cut," and "great indignation-was felt by all." One of the Confederates involved in this incident said later that he always remembered the West Point battlefield as "the place where we cut the Yank's throat. . . . One, who was severely wounded and unable to stand, opened on the Confederates with a seven-shooter [a revolver], every shot of which killed or wounded a man. It was thought that a wounded man whose line of battle had been driven from the field, and who thereafter continued to fight on his own account, deserved to be summarily dealt with, so we cut his throat." As for Bishop, Love, and Ploof, Newton Curtis says that "their comrades, in paying them the martial honors due the gallant dead, gave to each the resting place he had selected on the night before the battle." Curtis himself was badly wounded in this fight; he was shot through the left breast.

While Johnston continued his retreat unmolested, and while McClellan began marching from Williamsburg toward a junction with Franklin at West Point, the Shenandoah Valley arena was the scene of another clash that was linked to the struggle for Richmond. During the weeks succeeding the Battle of Kernstown, Union General Nathaniel Banks, at the head of nearly 20,000 men, had followed the retiring Stonewall Jackson southwestward to Harrisonburg, a distance of some sixty miles. Jackson's retreat encouraged Lincoln and Stanton to consider releasing Irvin McDowell from his role as Washington's protector and sending him overland to McClellan, and he had advanced to Fredericksburg, fifty miles north of Richmond. A special plan was hatched to finish the work against Jackson. General John Frémont, commanding in Union-held western Virginia, had begun dispatching troops toward the Shenandoah Mountains at the Valley's western rim, their aim to cross at a point southwest of Harrisonburg, occupy Staunton, and unite with Banks, thus raising Federal strength to 35,000 men. The van of Frémont's forces was led by General Robert H. Milroy. By this time Jackson had been reinforced to 17,000 men. Robert E. Lee, fully aware of Jackson's potential for making a vital contribution to the defense of Richmond, had been aiding him from his adviser's desk. With Lee's blessing, but left to his own devices, Jackson entered upon a campaign designed to disrupt the enemy's plans. He was not without advantages, since he had lived in the Valley and, according to one of his officers, knew "all the distances, all the roads, even to cow paths through the woods and goat tracks along the hills." Moreover, thanks to his cavalry scouts, to spies, and to friendly civilians, he was able to keep abreast of the enemy's every move.

Jackson began his campaign by leaving a part of his army in a threatening position in front of Banks and taking the rest on a march eastward, as though beginning a general retreat upon Richmond. Contending with heavy rains and deep mire, he passed through a gap in the Blue Ridge Mountains to Mechum's River Station on the Virginia Central Railroad. In the words of John D. Imboden, then serving as one of Jackson's artillery commanders: "Despair was fast settling upon the minds of the people of the Valley. Jackson made no concealment of his flight, the news of which soon reached his enemies. Milroy advanced two regiments to the top of the Shenandoah Mountains, only twenty-two miles from Staunton, and was preparing to move his entire force to Staunton, to be followed by Frémont.

Jackson had collected, from Charlottesville and other stations on the Virginia Central Railroad, enough railway trains to transport all of his little army. That it was to be taken to Richmond when the troops were all embarked no one doubted. It was Sunday, and many of the sturdy soldiers were Valley men. With sad and gloomy hearts they boarded the trains at Mechum's River Station. When all were on, lo!, they took a westward course, and a little after noon the first train rolled into Staunton. News of Jackson's arrival spread like wildfire, and crowds flocked to the station to see the soldiers and learn what it all meant. No one knew."

Making a rapid march westward over the Shenandoah Mountains to the spur known as Bull Pasture Mountain, Jackson met Milroy near the village of McDowell. On May 8, the day after the Battle of West Point on the Peninsula, 4,000 of Jackson's men clashed with 2,500 Federals. The outnumbered Federals fought well, finally withdrawing from the field in good order under cover of darkness. Relates Robert Dabney, Jackson's chief of staff: "By nine o'clock the roar of the struggle had passed away, and the green battlefield reposed under the starlight as calmly as when it had been occupied only by peaceful herds. Detachments of soldiers were silently exploring the ground for their wounded comrades, while the tired troops were slowly filing off to their bivouac. At midnight the last sufferer had been removed and the last picket posted; and then only did General Jackson turn [toward] . . . a farmhouse at the eastern base of the mountain. The valley of McDowell lay beneath him in equal quiet. The campfires of the Federals blazed ostentatiously in long and regular lines, and their host seemed to be wrapped in sleep. At one o'clock A.M. the general reached his quarters and threw himself upon a bed. When his faithful servant, knowing that he had eaten nothing since morning, came with food, he said, 'I want none; nothing but sleep,' and in a minute was slumbering like a healthy infant. The dawn found him in the saddle and ascending the mountain again. When he reached the crest of the battlefield, he saw the vale beneath him deserted.

The Valley Campaign. From Staunton *(lower left)*, Jackson marched northwestward and defeated Frémont's van near McDowell on May 8. Turning back and heading northeastward by way of Harrisonburg, New Market, and Luray (east of New Market), Jackson hit Banks at Front Royal on May 23. Banks retreated to Winchester, was defeated there on May 25. Resuming his retreat, Banks passed through Martinsburg and crossed the Potomac into Maryland. Jackson demonstrated toward Harpers Ferry. Learning that his rear was threatened by Frémont and McDowell, Jackson turned back to Winchester and began retreating by way of Strasburg and Harrisonburg. He struck Frémont at Cross Keys (indicated on map as XKeys) on June 8, and McDowell's van, led by Shields, at Port Republic on June 9. Ten days later Jackson began marching toward Richmond by way of Gordonsville.

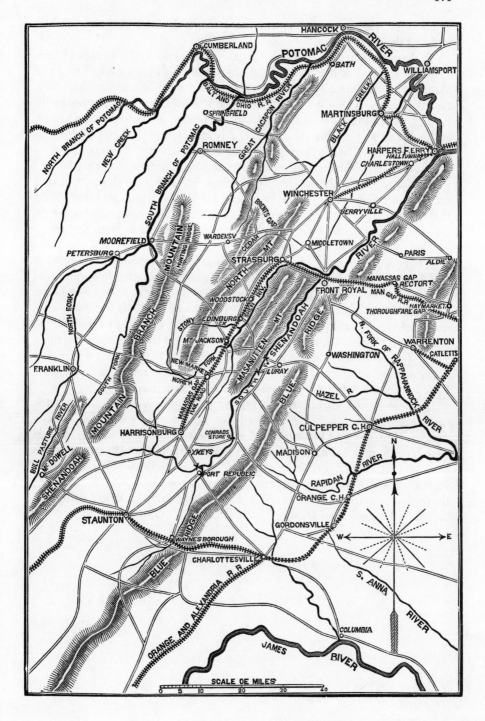

SCALE OF MILES

0 5 10   20   30   40

The foe had decamped in the night, leaving their dead, and partially destroying their camp equipage and stores."

Jackson returned to his headquarters, where John Imboden found him. "I called ... to ask if I could be of any service to him, as I had to go to Staunton ... to look after some companies that were to join my command. He asked me to wait a few moments, as he wished to prepare a telegram to be sent to President Davis from Staunton, the nearest office to McDowell. He took a seat at a table and wrote nearly half a page of foolscap. He rose and stood before the fireplace pondering it some minutes. Then he tore it to pieces and wrote again, but much less; and again destroyed what he had written, and paced the room several times. He suddenly stopped, seated himself, and dashed off two or three lines, folded the paper, and said, 'Send that off as soon as you reach Staunton. ...' I read the message he had given me. It ... read about thus: 'Providence blessed our arms with victory at McDowell yesterday.' That was all."

There was a mixed reaction to Jackson's news among the people of Richmond. In her diary, Judith McGuire quoted the terse telegram, and added: "Nothing more had been given us officially, but private information is received that he is in hot pursuit. ... The croakers roll their gloomy eyes and say, 'Ah, General Jackson is so rash!' And a lady even assured me that he was known to be crazy when under excitement, and that we had everything to fear from the campaign he was now beginning in the Valley. I would that every officer and soldier in the Southern army was crazed in the same way. How soon we would be free from despotism and invasion!"

Jackson shortly abandoned his pursuit of Milroy, who was falling back upon Frémont, but nothing was lost. The McDowell venture had been a success. Frémont and Banks were denied their junction. Moreover, a worried Lincoln and Stanton, in order to make certain that Washington was kept covered, not only ordered Banks to retire some forty miles northward through the Valley to Strasburg, but also suspended Irvin McDowell's movement toward McClellan. Now barely launched, Jackson's campaign had already scored remarkably.

7

RICHMOND INVESTED

LINCOLN AND Stanton were not running the war from Washington when the McDowell crisis occurred. Along with several other government officials, including Secretary of the Treasury Salmon Chase, the President and Secretary of War had sailed down the Potomac and Chesapeake to Fort Monroe, where they had taken rooms and set up a temporary headquarters. Lincoln had got the urge to take the field, desiring, in particular, to learn what could be done about repossessing Norfolk and the Gosport Navy Yard. The President had an eager ally in the elderly but energetic General John E. Wool, commander of Fort Monroe's army garrison. As explained by an unnamed correspondent of the New York *Times:* "For some time past General Wool has been of the opinion that Norfolk might be taken with but little cost; but nothing definite has been done in regard to it, partly because the cooperation of the Navy Department could not be secured, and partly because such a movement was not consistent with the general plan of the campaign [on the Peninsula].... After the fall of Yorktown and the withdrawal of the great body of the rebel army, it was believed that the abandonment of Norfolk would speedily follow as a necessary consequence. When General McClellan, therefore, on Monday after the fall of Yorktown, telegraphed to General Wool asking for more troops in order to make an effective pursuit of the rebels up York River, General Wool declined to send any, on the ground that it might become necessary for him to take and hold Norfolk.

"On Thursday [May 8] the little steam tug *J. B. White* came in from Norfolk, having deserted from the rebel service. She had been sent to bring in a couple of rebel schooners from the mouth of Tanner's Creek. The officers in charge of her being Northern men, and having been long desirous of escaping from the rebel regime, considered this a favorable opportunity for effecting their object. They slipped past Craney Island without attracting any hostile observation, and then steered directly for Newport News. On arriving they reported that the rebel troops were evacuating Norfolk—that very many had already gone, and that not over two or three thousand remained, and even these, it was confidently believed, would very speedily be withdrawn. They were men of intelligence and of evident sincerity, and their statements commanded full confidence."

General Wool, with Lincoln's approval, ordered an immediate move against Norfolk. While a large body of troops began embarking on transports lying in Hampton Roads, a group of warships was sent to bombard Sewell's Point. This brought the *Merrimack* steaming down the Elizabeth River. Says Commodore Josiah Tatnall, who had replaced the wounded Franklin Buchanan as the *Merrimack*'s commander: "We found six of the enemy's vessels, including the ironclad steamers *Monitor* and *Naugatuck*, shelling the battery. We passed the battery and stood directly for the enemy for the purpose of engaging him, and I thought an action certain, particularly as the *Minnesota* and *Vanderbilt* [the latter being one of the merchant steamers secured by Edwin Stanton for the purpose of trying to ram the *Merrimack*], which were anchored below Fortress Monroe, got underway and stood up to that point apparently with the intention of joining their squadron in the Roads. Before, however, we got within gunshot the enemy ceased firing and retired . . . under the protection of the guns of the fortress. . . ." The *Merrimack* herself retired as she began receiving fire from the guns of the Rip Raps, a partly finished fortification rising from the water a mile south of Fort Monroe.

The Federal effort to force a landing by way of the Elizabeth River had been checked. Returning to the New York *Times* correspondent: "The troops were accordingly disembarked on Friday morning, and the expedition was for the time abandoned. On Friday Secretary Chase . . . learned from a pilot familiar with the coast that there was a place where a landing could be effected a mile or so beyond Willoughby Point [the Confederate shore closest to Fort Monroe, a spot where the waters were too shallow for the *Merrimack*], and that a very good road led directly from that shore to Norfolk. In company with General Wool and Colonel T. J. Cram, of the Topographical Engineers, Secretary Chase . . . crossed over in the steam revenue cutter *Miami* and sent a boat to sound the depth of the water and examine the shore, with a view to a landing for troops. While doing so, they perceived signs of a mounted picket guard on the shore above, and not deeming it safe to venture too far, they pulled back for the *Miami*. On their way, however, a woman was seen in a house on shore waving a white flag. The boat's crew at once returned, and were told . . . a good deal of valuable information concerning the roads and the condition of the country between there and Norfolk. Secretary Chase and Colonel Cram went ashore and satisfied themselves that a landing was perfectly feasible. On returning to Fortress Monroe, they found that President Lincoln and Secretary Stanton, on examining the maps, had been led to [send a crew to] make a similar exploration, and had come to a similar conclusion, though the points at which the parties had struck proved to have been a mile or two apart."

When someone remarked that the shallowness of the water at the shoreline might cause some disembarkation problems, the President himself made a proposal regarding the improvisation of piers. "Those old canalboats that I saw near the wharf at the fort do not draw more than a foot of water when they are entirely empty. Those may easily be placed in such a position at high water that the ebb tide will leave them—or, rather, the one nearest the shore—entirely dry, while at the outer one, which may be securely anchored, there will be a depth of seven or eight feet—plenty for the numerous fleet of light draughts that we have at our disposal."

That evening, according to another newsman (a correspondent for the Baltimore *American*), Old Point Comfort, upon which Fort Monroe was located, presented "a very stirring spectacle. About a dozen steamers and transports are loading with troops. They will land on the shore opposite the Rip Raps and march direct on Norfolk. At the time I commence writing— nine o'clock P.M.—the moon shines so brightly that I am sitting in the open air, in an elevated postion, and writing by moonlight. The transports are gathering in the stream, and have on board artillery, cavalry, and infantry, and will soon be prepared to start. The Rip Raps are pouring shot and shell into Sewell's Point [as a diversion], and a bright light in the direction of Norfolk indicates that the work of destruction [by the Confederates] has commenced. President Lincoln, as Commander in Chief of the Army and Navy, is superintending the expedition himself. About six o'clock he went across to the place selected for the landing. It is said he was the first man to step on shore, and after examining for himself the facilities for landing returned to the Point [Fort Monroe], where he was received with enthusiastic cheering by the troops who were embarking. . . . The *Monitor* has resumed her usual position. The fleet are floating quietly at their anchorage, ready at any moment for activity."

There would be no challenge from the *Merrimack*. Aside from her inability to enter shallow water, she wasn't even aware of what was happening. Lying behind Sewell's Point, about five miles from Fort Monroe and six from Norfolk, she had no orders but to cover the mouths of the Elizabeth, Nansemond, and James Rivers against entry by Federal vessels while Norfolk was being evacuated. Strangely enough, she hadn't been informed that the evacuation was in its final stage.

The Federal transports crossed to Willoughby Point during the night, and the landing was begun at dawn. Lincoln and Stanton were on the scene for a time, then took a tug to the flagship *Minnesota*. "The President," relates the Baltimore *American* newsman, "was received by a national salute.

It is generally admitted that the President and Secretary have infused new vigor into both naval and military operations here. The President has declared that Norfolk must fall, the *Merrimac* must succumb to the naval power of the Union, and that the Government property at Norfolk must be repossessed, at whatever cost it may require.

"The point at which we are landing, with the aid of a half-dozen canal-boats, furnishes quite a fine harbor, and the troops and horses are landing with great facility. . . . Norfolk . . . is distant only seven miles, and at noon our infantry advance had accomplished half the distance without obstruction of any kind where they halted for the arrival of the artillery and cavalry. . . . I just learn that General Max Weber has advanced to within three miles of Norfolk. . . . At Tanner's Creek a small picket was stationed, with a howitzer, and a slight skirmish took place. . . . The rebels fled in great haste across the bridge, which they destroyed. Two prisoners were taken, who stated there would be no resistance at Norfolk, which was being evacuated. . . . Fires were burning all around the country, principally the destruction of barracks and camps. . . . Whilst all these active movements are progressing toward Norfolk . . . there is the utmost quiet observable on the sea side. The iron monster, the *Merrimac*, still remains moored."

By this time the crew of the Confederate ironclad were in a state of consternation. As explained by Josiah Tatnall: "At ten o'clock A.M. we observed . . . that the flag was not flying on the Sewell's Point battery, and that it appeared to have been abandoned. I dispatched Lieutenant J. P. Jones . . . to Craney Island, where the Confederate Flag was still flying, and he there learned that a large force of the enemy had landed on Bay Shore and were marching rapidly on Norfolk . . . and our troops were retreating. I then dispatched the same officer to Norfolk [by way of Gosport]. . . . He found the navy yard in flames, and that all its officers had left by railroad. On reaching Norfolk he found that . . . all the . . . officers of the army had also left, that the enemy were within half a mile of the city, and that the mayor was treating for its surrender."

While Lieutenant Jones was hurrying back to the *Merrimack* the surrender terms were completed at Norfolk's city hall. In the words of the *Times* correspondent: "Immediately after General Wool left the city hall, a large concourse of citizens assembled . . . and called loudly for a speech from the mayor. . . . He said he had nothing to do with deciding the result; that had been done by the superior authorities [at Richmond]. The citizens of Norfolk had been deserted by their friends, and all the city authorities could do was to obtain the best terms possible for themselves and their property. He was happy to assure them that in this he had been successful. . . . He enjoined upon the citizens the maintenance of peace and quiet, and exhorted them to abstain from all acts of violence and disorder. If the decision had rested with him, he would have defended the city to the last man; but their government had decided differently, and they must yield to its authority. The mayor's remarks were cheered by the crowd, who also gave three cheers for President Davis . . . and . . . three groans for Lincoln."

The Federal troops made camp at Norfolk, and as night came on their attention was drawn to the fires at Gosport, across the waters of the harbor. The Baltimore *American* correspondent noted that a few Confederates had lingered to ensure the job. "Incendiaries could be seen moving about . . . with their pitch-pine flambeaux. . . . The scene strongly reminded the spectators of the panorama of the burning of Moscow, and . . . the immense flame that it threw forth made the scene one of terrible grandeur."

In spite of his years and the strains of the past twenty-four hours, General Wool did not remain with the troops at Norfolk. He rode back to the landing and boarded a tug for Fort Monroe, where he knew that Lincoln and Stanton were awaiting a report. "That night," says Lincoln, "we went to bed, but not to sleep, for we were very anxious for the fate of the expedition. About two o'clock the next morning, I heard the heavy tread of Wool ascending the stairs. I went out into the parlor and found Stanton hugging Wool in the most enthusiastic manner as he announced that he . . . had captured Norfolk."

At that very moment, some additonal news of major importance to Lincoln and Stanton—news concerning the Confederate ironclad *Merrimack*—was in the making. The story is told by *Merrimack* officer John Taylor Wood: "Norfolk evacuated, our occupation was gone, and the next thing to be decided upon was what should be done with the ship. Two courses of action were open to us: we might have run the blockade of the forts [Monroe and the Rip Raps] and done some damage to the shipping there and at the mouth of York River. . . . On the other hand, the pilots said repeatedly if the ship were lightened to eighteen feet [in draft], they could take her up James River to Harrison's Landing or City Point, where she could have been put . . . in a position to assist in the defense of Richmond. The commodore decided upon this [latter] course. Calling all hands on deck, he told them what he wished done. Sharp and quick work was necessary; for, to be successful, the ship must be lightened five feet and we must pass the batteries at Newport News and the fleet below before daylight next morning. The crew gave three cheers and went to work with a will, throwing overboard the ballast from the fantails, as well as that below; all spare stores, water—indeed, everything but our powder and shot.

"By midnight the ship had been lightened three feet, when, to our amazement, the pilots said it was useless to do more, that with the westerly wind blowing, the tide would be cut down so that the ship would not go up even to Jamestown Flats; indeed, they would not take the responsibility of taking her up the river at all. This extraordinary conduct of the pilots rendered some other plan immediately necessary. . . . The ship had been so lifted as to be unfit for action; two feet of her hull below the shield was exposed. She could not be sunk again by letting in water without putting out the furnace fires and flooding the magazines.

"Never was a commander forced by circumstances over which he had no control into a more painful position than was Commodore Tatnall. But coolly and calmly he decided, and gave orders to destroy the ship; determining if he could not save his vessel, at all events not to sacrifice three hundred brave and faithful men. . . . She was run ashore near Craney Island, and the crew landed with their small arms and two days' provisions. Having only two boats, it took three hours to disembark. Lieutenant Catesby Jones and myself were the last to leave. Setting her on fire fore and aft, she was soon in a blaze, and by the light of our burning ship we pulled for the shore, landing at daybreak." The crew at once began marching toward Suffolk to board a train for Richmond.

It was between four-thirty and five o'clock when the light from the burning vessel was noted by the sentries at Fort Monroe. Very soon, according to the *American* correspondent, "an explosion took place which made the earth and water tremble for miles around. In the midst of the bright flame which shot up . . . the timbers and iron of the monster steamer could be seen flying through the air." The incident was reported to the commander of the fort's fleet, Flag Officer L. M. Goldsborough, who, the newsman says, "ordered two armed naval tugs, the *Zouave* and *Dragon*, to proceed toward Craney Island on a reconnoissance [*sic*]. . . . Immediately after they had turned the point, the *Monitor* and *E. A. Stevens* steamed up in the same direction, followed by the *San Jacinto, Susquehanna Mount Vernon, Seminole*, and *Dacotah*. It was a most beautiful sight, and attracted throngs of spectators along the whole line of Old Point. Some were disposed to discredit the announcement that the *Merrimac* was destroyed, and as the vessels passed up to Craney Island the excitement became intense. In the meantime [the] two tugboats were seen coming on toward the fortress at full speed, each endeavoring to outvie the other, and when nearing the wharf the radiant countenance of Captain Case of [the tug belonging to] the *Minnesota*, gave assurance that . . . the report was true; he had met parts of the floating wreck. . . . Captain Case immediately reported the fact to the President and Secretary of War, who received the confirmation . . . with great satisfaction. At the request of the President, Captain Case immediately proceeded to Craney Island to ascertain if the works were evacuated, in company with the fleet, which was then advancing."

The correspondent accompanied Case on his tug, which soon "overtook and passed all the vessels of war that had started in advance of us except the *Monitor* and *Naugatuck*, which were moving ahead on their way to Norfolk. . . . As we neared Craney Island we found this immense fortress apparently abandoned. . . . A boat was immediately lowered, and . . . I accompanied it to the shore to participate in the honor of lowering the rebel emblem and substituting the 'pride of America' in its place. . . . After spending an hour on the island, we proceeded. . . . Immediately at the upper end of the island we found a mass of blackened wreck floating on the water. . . .

"On the line of the river leading from Craney Island to Norfolk there are not less than six heavy earthworks mounting in all about sixty-nine cannon, all of which are still in position, except those near the naval hospital. These are said to have been taken to Richmond during the past week. On the opposite bank of the river is another battery, with two or three other small works. On all the works the rebel flag has been lowered by the fleet, and the Stars and Stripes substituted. . . . After cruising about for some time among the fleet, we landed at the wharf."

Across the harbor waters, the black ruins of Gosport still smoked, but the Norfolk side was pleasant in the spring sunshine. "It being Sunday, of course all business places were closed, and the city presented a most quiet aspect. The wharfs were crowded with blacks, male and female; and a goodly number of white working people with their wives and children were strolling about. Soldiers were stationed on the wharfs and picketed through the city, while the flag of the Union floated triumphantly from the cupola of the customs house. The houses through the city were generally closed, especially those of the wealthier classes. Some of the females scowled at the horrible Yankees, and some almost attempted to spit upon them. But there was a subdued quiet among the middle classes, their countenances implying a desire to wait and watch for further developments. The secessionists talked boldly of the Southern Confederacy, declaring their intention to receive nothing but Confederate money, and saying they would have nothing to do with Lincoln shinplasters. They were fully confident that in twenty days Norfolk would be repossessed and the Yankees driven out.

"President Lincoln, who had accompanied Commodore Goldsborough and General Wool in the steamer *Baltimore* on a visit of observation to Elizabeth River, did not disembark but remained on board for about an hour in front of the city, and then steamed back to the fortress." That evening Lincoln and his party from Washington began their return trip up the Chesapeake and Potomac. The President had found his few days of active campaigning a rewarding adventure.

There was, of course, nothing rewarding about the developments for Lincoln's counterpart in Richmond. A niece of the Confederate President lamented in a letter: "Uncle Jeff is miserable. He tries to be cheerful and bear up against such a continuation of troubles, but, oh, I fear he cannot live long if he does not get some rest and quiet. . . . He is so weak and feeble it makes my heart ache to look at him." Weighing most heavily on Davis at this time was the loss of the *Merrimack*. Richmond editor Edward Pollard explains that this "had left the water avenue to Richmond almost unde-

Looking down the James River from Drewry's Bluff

fended. The City Council had for months been urging upon the Confederate Government the necessity of obstructing the river [the James], and failing to induce them to hurry the work, had, with patriotic zeal, undertaken it themselves. A newspaper in Richmond—the *Examiner* [Pollard's paper]—had in good time pointed out the necessity of obstructing the river with stone, but the counsel was treated with . . . conceit and harshness. . . . The government was [as a result of Joe Johnston's retreat from Yorktown] at last aroused to a sense of danger, only to fall to work in ridiculous haste and with the blindness of alarm. . . . The only obstruction between the city and the dread *Monitor* and the gunboats was a half-finished fort at Drewry's Bluff [only eight miles below the city], which mounted four guns. Some of the Confederate officers . . . seized upon schooners at the wharves loaded with plaster of paris, guano, and other valuable cargoes, carried them to points where they supposed the passage of the river was to be contested, and in some instances sunk them in the wrong places.

"There is no doubt that about this time the authorities of the Confederate States had nigh despaired of the safety of Richmond. . . . It is true that President Davis, when invited by the Legislature of Virginia to express his intentions towards Richmond, had declared that he entertained the prospect of holding it. But . . . he at the same time suggested the fanciful possibility that even with the loss of Richmond our struggle for independence might be protracted for many years in the mountains of Virginia. In the meantime, the acts of the Confederate officials gave visible and unmistakable signs of their sense of the insecurity of the capital. They added to the public alarm by preparations to remove the archives. They ran off their wives and children into the country. . . .

"In the early weeks of May the capital of the confederacy presented many strange and humiliating spectacles. The air was filled with those rumors of treason and disloyalty which seem invariably to grow out of a sense of insecurity. Men who had been loudest in their professions of resistance . . . when the Yankees were at a distance were now engaged in secreting their property, and a few openly flattered themselves that they had not committed themselves in the war in a way to incur the enemy's resentment. . . . The railroad trains were crowded with refugees. At every extortioner's shop on Main Street [i.e., at those shops whose owners had been profiteering] . . . an array of packing trunks invited attention and suggested the necessity of flight from Richmond. At the railroad depots were to be seen piles of baggage, awaiting transportation. But the most abundant and humiliating signs of the panic were to be seen in the number of pine boxes about the departments [of the government] ticketed 'Columbia, South Carolina,' and which contained the most valuable of the public archives.

"In this condition of the public mind, a new appeal was made to it. When it was ascertained that the *Monitor, Galena,* and *Aroostook* [plus the

Naugatuck and *Port Royal*] were about to head for Richmond, the Legislature of Virginia passed resolutions calling upon the Confederate authorities to defend it to the last extremity, and to make choice of its destruction rather than that of surrender to the enemy. . . . This resolution was worthy . . . of a people who were the descendants of Washington's contemporaries, of Hampden's friends, and of King John's barons. . . . They . . . declared that 'the President be assured that whatever destruction or loss of property of the State or individuals shall thereby result, will be cheerfully submitted to.' The resolutions of the Legislature were responded to in meetings of citizens. The magical efects of the spirit which they created will long be remembered in Richmond. The Confederate authorities were stimulated by the brave lesson; inert and speculative patriotism was aroused to exertion; mutual inspiration of courage and devotion passed from heart to heart through the community, and with the restoration of public confidence came at last vigorous preparations. The James was rapidly filled up, the works at Drewry's Bluff were strenghtened, and a steady defiance offered to the Yankee gunboats, which had appeared within a few miles of the city at a moment when the last gap in our river obstructions was filled up by a scuttled schooner.

"On the 15th of May the fleet of Yankee gunboats in the James opened an attack on our batteries at Drewry's Bluff. The sound of the guns was heard in the streets of Richmond. . . . In the midst of the excitement, an extraordinary scene occurred in the city. A meeting of citizens had been called at the City Hall . . . and at the enthusiastic call of the crowd, impromptu addresses were made by the Governor of Virginia and the Mayor of the city. Each of these officials pledged his faith that Richmond should never be surrendered. Governor Letcher declared, with a peculiar warmth of expression, that if the demand was made upon him, with the alternative to surrender or be shelled, he should reply, 'Bombard and be damned!' Mayor [Joseph C.] Mayo was not less determined in the language which he addressed to the citizens. He told them that even if they were to require him to surrender the Capital of Virginia and of the Confederacy, he would, sooner than comply, resign the mayoralty; and that, despite his age, he still had the nerve and strength to shoulder a musket in defense of the city founded by one of his ancestors. These fervid declarations were responded to by the citizens with wild and ringing shouts. Nor were these the demonstrations of a mob. Among those who so enthusiastically approved the resolution of consigning Richmond to the flames rather than to the possession of the enemy were some of the most wealthy and respectable citizens of the place, whose stakes of property in the city were large."

The Confederate artillery positions and rifle pits at Drewry's Bluff were manned by the sailors of the *Merrimack*, who had been rushed to the spot upon their arrival in Richmond by train from Suffolk. The gunners registered most of their fire on the ironclad *Galena*, the flagship of the invading squadron, which was led by Commander John Rodgers. The *Galena* had anchored at a range of 600 yards and was delivering broadsides. As for the *Monitor*, her commander, Lieutenant William N. Jeffers, explains: "I endeavored to pass ahead of [the *Galena*] to take off some of the fire, but found that my guns could not be elevated sufficiently to point at the fort. I then took position on the line with the *Galena* and maintained a deliberate fire. . . . The fire of the enemy was remarkably well directed, but vainly towards [our] vessel. She was struck three times—one solid eight-inch shot square on the turret, two solid shot on the side armor forward of the pilot house. Neither caused any damage beyond bending the plates. . . . So long as our vessels kept up a rapid fire they rarely fired in return, but the moment our fire slackened they re-manned their guns. It was impossible to reduce such works, except with the aid of a land force."

A mishap on the *Naugatuck* is described by Lieutenant Davis C. Constable: "Our 100-pounder Parrott rifle-gun burst, one third of it being thrown overboard, one third falling over on the starboard side of the deck, while the remaining third retained nearly its proper position. The heavy iron gun carriage was almost entirely destroyed, our pilot house shattered, and the captain of the gun blown some fifteen feet but fortunately not killed. I was within two feet of the gun when it burst, having just trained it upon the enemy's battery. The speaking trumpet in my hand was crushed; a fragment of the gun weighing nearly a ton fell within an inch or two of me, actually tearing my coat . . . and one of the large squares of rubber attached to the gun struck me upon the head, stunning me for a moment, but still I was able to remain on deck and superintend the fighting of our broadside guns, which were engaged throwing shell and canister into the rebel rifle pits which lined the shore under cover of the woods. . . .

"A rifle ball passed through my clothing and lodged in a hammock near me. . . . At least three well-directed shots had been fired at me from one spot before I discovered where they came from. I then saw that they had been fired from a thick green bush about eighty yards from me. Once I even caught sight of the muzzle of the rifle as it was protruded through the bush to aim at me, and twice I raised a rifle to my shoulder to aim at him, but he dropped out of sight in a twinkling. Finding that I must either shoot him or get shot myself, I tried another plan. I aimed one of our 12-pounders, loaded with canister, at the bush, and directed the captain of the gun to fire at the moment I raised my signal. I then took my former position and watched the bush closely. Sure enough, when the fellow saw me standing without a rifle in my hand he again thrust the muzzle of his gun through the bush, but before he could pull the trigger I raised my hand. 'Bang!' went the 12-pounder, and when the smoke cleared away, rebel, gun, [bush] and all had been destroyed together. . . .

"For an hour and a half after the bursting of our 100-pounder we kept up the fight with our broadside guns, and only fell back when the *Galena* and *Monitor* set us example, the other two vessels of the squadron having drawn out of range of the battery at least half an hour before we moved."

The squadron dropped back down the river, the *Galena* badly battered. Four hours of fighting had cost the Federals twenty-seven in killed and wounded, the Confederates fifteen. In itself, the Battle of Drewry's Bluff was a minor affair and was destined for scant historical mention, but its effect on the Peninsula Campaign was major. The *Merimack*'s crew had saved Richmond from the Federal naval commander. As *Merrimack* officer John Taylor Wood asserts: "The obstructions would not have prevented his steaming up to the city, which would have been as much at his mercy as was New Orleans before the fleet of Farragut." When Richmond received news of the victory, according to Sallie Putnam, "the reaction of joy upon the minds of the people was quite as intense as the suspense and agony had been, in proportion, terrible. Once again we breathed freely and pursued the usual avocations of business until the next turn in the enginery of war should place us in the midst of a fresh agitation."

Robert E. Lee had been instrumental in the fortification of Drewry's Bluff; and now, unaware that the Federals had no further plans to approach Richmond by way of the James, the general saw to it that the bluff and its environs were provided with infantry. One of the brigades was commanded by Henry A. Wise, governor of Virginia between 1856 and 1860, whose official acts included authorizing the execution of John Brown for his raid on Harpers Ferry. Now a brigadier general, Wise found in the role a natural outlet for his rambunctious ways and colorful profanity. In the words of a Richmond officer who visited the brigadier on the James: "He received me most cordially, walked with me all the morning round his lines, explaining his views most eloquently, quoting from the great masters in the art of war . . . interspersing these learned and scientific disquisitions with the most scathing criticisms on men and measures, denouncing the Confederate Executive and Congress and the narrow curriculum of West Point, but winding up always with a stream of fiery invective against the Yankees.

"General Wise was encamped on the plantation of one of the richest and most influential citizens of Richmond. He annoyed Wise greatly with complaints of depredations committed by the Wise Legion on his property. Wise was greatly enraged when he presumed to charge some of his men with stealing, and after a fierce altercation ordered him out of his tent. As the gentleman was mounting his horse Wise came out and, calling him by name, said: 'Sir, before you leave, I think it due both to you and myself to make you an apology.' 'I'm glad, General Wise, that you show some sense of what is becoming to us both.' 'My apology,' replied General Wise, 'is that, having on my slippers, I could not possibly do you justice. I ought to have kicked you out of my tent, and will do so now if you will wait till I pull on my boots!' Then he poured a broadside upon his retreating enemy."

This incident had repercussions. Wise himself explains: "General Lee came down to see me. . . . My wife and several other ladies were spending the day at my headquarters. We had a good dinner and a charming time. . . . When he asked me to take a walk with him, I suspected what was coming. After telling me of the complaints made of my treatment of the Richmond man, and hearing my account of the affair, not omitting the apology and broadside, he laid his hand upon my arm, and, with that grace and cordiality which at such times tempered his usual stately dignity, said, 'Wise, you know as well as I do what the army regulations say about profanity. . . . As an old friend, let me ask you if that dreadful habit cannot be broken, and remind you that we have both already passed the meridian of life. . . .' Seeing I was in for a sermon, and one that I could not answer, I replied, 'General Lee, you certainly play Washington to perfection, and your whole life is a constant reproach to me. Now I am perfectly willing that Jackson and yourself shall do the praying for the whole Army of Northern Virginia; but, in Heaven's name, let me do the *cussin'* for one small brigade!' Lee laughed and said, 'Wise, you are incorrigible,' and we then rejoined the ladies."

Since the Battle of West Point at the head of the York River on May 7, there had been no fighting beyond an occasional skirmish between the forces under Johnston and McClellan. Johnston had been moving ever closer to Richmond. The artillery unit to which Robert Stiles belonged continued to suffer from hunger. "We overhauled a commissary train in a by-road we were traveling to escape the jam and the mud, and Captain [E. S.] McCarthy, making known the extreme need of his men, begged rations enough to give them just one meal; but the officer in charge answered, 'I cannot issue you anything, Captain, except upon the order of General Griffith, your brigadier, or my commanding officer.' To which our captain replied: 'General Griffith is somewhere between here and Richmond. I don't know where your commanding officer is. But if you can't give me anything except upon the order of one of these two officers, then I can take what my men need, on my own order, and I'll do it! Here, boys, drive a gun up here in the road ahead of this train; unlimber it, and load it. Now, sir, you shan't pass here without issuing three day's rations for my men. But I'll give you a written statement of what has occurred, signed by me!'

"We sprang with a shout to execute the captain's order, and in a few moments had our three days' rations, cooking them in the few utensils we always kept with us, and soon made a good square meal. I suppose Captain McCarthy's conduct was deemed justifiable, as no notice of a court martial or a court of inquiry was ever served upon him.

"It was, however, some days before the supply departments were thoroughly organized . . . and meanwhile not only did we artillerymen once

Confederate skirmish line under attack during McClellan's advance
up the Peninsula

more come down to hard pan and hard corn, but one evening General Griffith, who was a charming gentleman, rode over to where our battery was parked, saying to our captain that he came to beg three favors—a couple of ears of corn for himself, a feed for his horse, and a song from our glee club—to all of which he was made royally welcome; and he sat right down about our campfire and roasted and ate his corn with us."

One of the songs rendered by the glee club began with the stanza "Mynheer von Dunck/ Though he never got drunk/ Sipped brandy and water gaily/ And he quenched his thirst/ With two quarts of the first/ To a pint of water, daily." Another rendition included the lines "A pretty girl who gets a kiss and runs and tells her mother/ Does something that she should not do, and don't deserve another."

Joe Johnston had not communicated his plans to Davis and Lee, who began to wonder, with mounting concern, how close to the city the general intended to come before making a stand. Johnston was under little pressure from the Federals. Still some forty miles from Richmond when he began his march from Williamsburg on May 9, McClellan was thinking chiefly of merging with Franklin near West Point and moving toward the establishment of a base of supplies on the Pamunkey River, the York's western tributary. The roads were in fair condition, and on the second day of the march the army began coming abreast of Franklin's position. "It was here," states Franklin's cavalry trooper F. Colburn Adams "that General McClellan brought us the news of the evacuation of Norfolk and destruction of the phantom terror of our navy, the *Merrimac*, which news was received with an outburst of rejoicing that made the very woods echo. When it became known to the soldiers that General McClellan was in camp, they manifested the wildest enthusiasm, broke away from all restraint, and cheered for him in their loudest strains. When, on taking his departure, he rode through the camps, they gathered about him in crowds, impeded his progress, threw up their caps, and made the very air ring with their shouts of joy."

Such demonstrations notwithstanding, McClellan was not without his critics during this part of the march. Regis de Trobriand says that many of the soldiers were provoked by "the excess of precaution and the severity of orders to preserve from injury any object, even the smallest, belonging to the rebels. Not a farmhouse, not a cottage, not a Negro, but was furnished with a guard on our approach, by the troops of General Andrew Porter, especially ordered . . . to watch over the farmyards, the stables, the forage, the wells, and even the fences. I have seen our men, covered with dust and overcome by the heat, try in vain to get water from wells overflowing, from which stringent orders drove them away, because the supply of water for a rebel family might be diminished. I have also seen them, covered with mud and shivering with the rain, prevented by orders of the general-in-chief

from warming themselves with ... fence rails ... because the cattle of a
rebel farmer might get out and eat the grass in his fields while he was rebuilding his fences."

This was a time of particular humiliation for corps commander Erasmus
Keyes, who was not one of McClellan's favorites. Keyes relates: "At Williamsburg ... I was quartered in the house of a prominent rebel who had
abandoned it to fight against the Union. General McClellan had issued an
order against marauding. ... The rebel owner of the house had left behind
several bottles of brandy. I took for myself one bottle of wine and drank it
with my friends, and I gave a bottle of brandy to Colonel John J. Astor,
A.D.C. [aide-de-camp] to General McClellan. ... I took several bottles and
carried them along for the use of the sick. The liquor was safe with me, for I
did not drink brandy. ... On arriving at Roper's Church, two marches from
Williamsburg, I received peremptory orders to report in person to the Provost Marshal General of the army. By him I was questioned concerning the
liquor and directed to return it, in charge of a staff officer, to the place from
which it was taken. I suppressed all signs of anger and directed Lieutenant
Chetwood, A.D.C., to execute the order without delay. The Provost Marshal General to whom I, a corps commander, was ordered to report in person was my junior in rank, and the opinions he entertained in regard to the
war and its causes were ... little in smypathy with my own. ... I am greatly
mistaken if he did not feel happy in the opportunity to insult me grossly in
the line of duty."

De Trobriand has a further word about McClellan's policy: "It must not
be imagined that the people treated with such great consideration were in
the least grateful for it. They were animated with such irreconcilable hatred against us that they did not give themselves the trouble to dissemble.
The women would sometimes even take advantage of their immunity to
boast of their enmity. They were so many spies, whom we were guarding.
Everything they heard, everything they could get out of anyone, was reported to the enemy as soon as possible. The horses, cattle, hogs which we
were so scrupulously compelled to respect were sent, on the first occasion,
to the Confederates. ... [Later,] when the army was before Richmond, letters of these enemies whom we treated as friends were intercepted. They
were full of exact information as to the location of our pickets and the disposition of our forces. They designated also the farms where, under our safe-
guard, provisions were reserved for the Confederates. ... The Richmond
papers, which were filled every day with invectives against us, showed
themselves more courteous towards our general, whom they called 'the only
gentleman in his army.' It can be seen that they had very good reason to
feel so.

"So the soldiers lived poorly. ... On two occasions, the coffee failed us,
which, of all privations, is the one the soldiers feels the most. The means of

transportation are still incomplete, it was said. And the quartermasters incompetent, [it] might be added without injustice. On the general's staff they
possibly were ignorant of these things, for evidently they did not suffer from
the want of anything. Near New Kent Court House, my bivouac being near
the army headquarters, I profited by it to make a call on two of my friends,
who kept me to dinner. It was an excellent dinner . . . and we had a [memo-
rable] mixture of Bordeaux and iced champagne. . . . I finished my evening
in the tent of the Orleans princes [De Joinville and his nephews], who, influenced by their surroundings, appeared to me to see things somewhat differently from what they really were. At headquarters they had but one bell,
and consequently only one sound was heard—praises of McClellan."

It happened to be a time when McClellan felt that special praises were
due him. Yorktown and Norfolk had fallen and the *Merrimack* had perished
as the result of his grand maneuvering. He was in a good mood on the evening of May 12 when he picked up his pen and addressed Ellen: "While I
write, the 2nd Dragoons' band is serenading, and about fifty others are
playing tattoo at various distances—a grand sound in this lovely moonlight
night. My camp is at an old frame church in a grove. I differ from most of
the generals in preferring a tent to a house. . . . Are you satisfied now with
my bloodless victories? Even the Abolitionists seem to be coming around,
judging, at least, from the very handsome resolution offered by Mr. [Owen]
Lovejoy in the House. I look upon that resolution as one of the most com-
plimentary I know of; and that, too, offered by my bitterest persecutors. . . .
The union of civic merit with military success is what pleases me most. To
have it recognized that I have saved the lives of my men and won success by
my own efforts is to me the height of glory. I hope that the result in front of
Richmond will cause still greater satisfaction to the country. I still hope that
the God who has been so good to me will continue to smile upon our cause
and enable me to bring this war to a speedy close, so that I may at last have
the rest I want so much. . . . I do need rest. You know I have had but little in
my life. . . . My government, alas, is not giving me any aid. But I will do the
best I can with what I have, and trust to God's mercy and the courage of my
men for the result. . . . We march in the morning to Cumberland, gradually
drawing nearer to Richmond."

Its route through Cumberland carried the army along the south side of
the Pamunkey River. "Nothing could be more picturesque," enthuses the
Prince de Joinville, "than this military march along the banks of a fine
stream through a magnificent country arrayed in all the wealth of spring
vegetation. The winding course of the Pamunkey through the valley in
which meadows of the brightest green alternated with wooded hills offered
a perpetual scene of enchantment to our eyes. Flowers bloomed everywhere. . . . Hummingbirds, snakes, and strange birds of every hue sported in
the branches and about the trunks of the trees. Occasionally we passed a

stately habitation which recalled the old mansions of rural France, with its large windows in the roof, around it a handsome garden, and behind it the slave cabins.

"As the army was descried in the distance, the inhabitants would hang out a white flag. One of the provost marshal's horsemen would dismount at the door; and, reassured by his presence, the ladies in their long muslin dresses, surrounded by a troop of little Negresses with frizzled hair and bare legs, would come out upon the verandah and watch the passage of the troops. They were often accompanied by old men, with strongly marked faces, long white locks, and broad-brimmed hats—never by young men. All the men capable of bearing arms had been carried off, willy-nilly, by the government to join in the general defense. If an officer dismounted and made his bow to the ladies, he was civilly received. The classic cup of cold water was offered to him in a gourd fixed on the end of a stick, and a melancholy sort of conversation followed. . . .

"The ladies naturally expressed their hopes for the success of the side on which their [men] were enlisted; but they longed, above all things, for the end of the war and of the incalculable evils it had brought upon the land. 'Alas!' we would reply, 'Who is to blame? Who kindled this unhappy strife? Who fired the first gun. . . ?' They would make no answer, but their glances would wander mechanically over the black heads crowded in the doors of the Negro huts. We never spoke of slavery in those interviews. To utter the word 'slave' would have sufficed to call up into the most amiable eyes an expression of hatred.

"At other times we would find the white owners fled, and nobody left but the Negroes, with whom we spoke of other matters. . . . A mulatto woman . . . called our attention with an air of pride to her son, a fine, bright, yellow child of some four years, with these significant words: 'He is the son of a white man; he is worth four hundred dollars. I began at fifteen, and I am nineteen now. I have four already.' "

Surgeon Stevens adds that in some spots "the Negroes, gathering in crowds along the wayside, would grasp the hands of the Union soldiers, calling down all manner of blessings upon them, and leaping and dancing in their frantic delight. . . . Whatever information the slaves could give concerning the movements, numbers, or probable intentions of the enemy was communicated gladly; and although this information was not always reliable for accuracy, it was always given in sincerity, and was very often of great service."

Returning to De Joinville: "The gunboats went first and explored the country before us. Then came the topographical officers, moving through the woods with an escort of cavalry, reconnoitering the country, and sketching by the eye and the compass provisional maps, which were photographed at headquarters for the use of the generals. The next day, with the help of these maps, the army would get into motion, mingled in masses with its immense team of wagons. . . . The army stretch[ed] upon these narrow forest paths over an immense space of country. Hence followed delays equally immense. . . .

"In the evening, when we came to a halt, the camps were formed with much order and regularity. The shelter-tents of the soldiers were put up in the twinkling of an eye. The staffs planted theirs, which were larger and more commodious. The headquarters was fixed in some central position, with the tent of the General-in-Chief in the middle, and two parallel ranges of tents on either side. The cavalry officers brought in their reports of their reconnoissances and their constant skirmishes with the enemy. The telegraphers brought on their wires, fastened as usual upon posts, or enveloped in gutta percha and unrolled along the ground from a rapidly driven wagon, which was followed by the operators on horseback with the apparatus slung from their shoulders. . . . Let us do justice to the Americans. They understood this camp life better than anybody else. Their locomotive habits, the familiarity of many of them with the partriarchal spectacle of emigrant columns moving across the Western prairies, the nomadic life which their officers have led among the Indian tribes, all these things fit them beyond any other soldiers of the world for this kind of life.

"This encampment of a hundred thousand men, the establishment of this city of tents . . . recalled the descriptions of the Bible; but there was little that was biblical in the forest of transport ships, most of them steamers, which came up by water under a cloud of smoke as soon as the camp was fixed; and, blowing off steam with a loud noise, hauled in to the banks and improvised wharves, which soon became scenes of extraordinary activity. Thousands of wagons hastened in from every side by roads which the axe had opened for them in a few minutes, and returned . . . loaded with all the commodities required by an army: biscuit, salted meat, coffee, sugar, barley, hay, corn. Then the sick were embarked; and, alas, the number of these constantly increased, for the season was at once rainy and intensely hot, and these lovely meadows of the Pamunkey gave birth to deadly fever. Then night would come on, disturbed only by the tedious cry of the mockingbird. . . . The next morning the flotilla and the army would resume their march, leaving behind them nature silent but deflowered by their passage."

The army's first destination after passing through Cumberland was the landing at the White House plantation, the Lee property sought as a refuge by the Confederate general's wife some months earlier. She was still there. Trooper Adams accompanied the horsemen who led the infantry toward the plantation on the morning of May 15. The weather was rainy and the roads were as mucky as they had been at any time during the march. "A dull gray fog hung . . . over everything; and the figures moving . . . in it, now disappearing and again appearing, had a strange and shadowy appearance."

Soon the mist gave way to heavy rain. "The cavalry guard . . . after struggling for nearly four hours . . . reached the White House before the head of
the [infantry] column debouched into the [plantation's] open fields. . . . We
were all drenched to the very skin, and so hungry. [Henry W.] Slocum and
other general officers came up, dripping wet, and having given directions to
the troops where to camp, were glad to accept shelter in the dingy cabin of
an old Negro, the few smouldering embers in the great open fireplace af-
fording . . . a little warmth.

"The plantation . . . extended about five miles along the bank of the
river, and nearly three inland. There were fields of clover a foot deep, and
rye, and wheat, and corn, looking so bright and healthy, extending as far as
the eye could reach. Clumps of fine old shade trees broke the monotony
here and there, while broad avenues ran in various directions, fringed with
willows and cedars. The plantation had belonged to the Custis estate, and,
like the rest of that property, had descended to the Lee family. . . .

"The Lee house, a small, neat cottage . . . with gothic windows, pointed
gables, and little balustrades, stood at the upper end of the ridge, overlooking the river, and was surrounded by a green lawn in which there were a
few shade trees. A gravelled walk led to the front entrance. The grounds
were small but laid out with considerable taste. . . . There were also flower
and vegetable gardens nearby. . . . Then there were extensive fodder yards,
barns, and cribs, filled to their utmost capacity with wheat, corn, and other
cereals.

"Below these there was quite a village of Negro cabins, stretching along
the ridge and divided up into classes, with streets running between. The
many colored occupants of these cabins seemed well provided for and contented. According to the Custis will, they would all be free on the 4th of
July. I conversed with a number of them, found them much attached to the
place, and quite indifferent about changing their condition so long as they
could be made safe against being sold off the plantation. . . .

"Mrs. Lee . . . solicited protection from us. We at once placed guards
over the house and gardens; and the quartermaster placed a guard over the
grain and forage. . . . A large number of pigs ran loose on the plantation, and
soon became an object of envy to our soldiers . . . . A captain . . . being exceedingly hungry . . . paid an old Negro two dollars . . . for the privilege of
shooting a pig. For this grievous military offense, the . . . man was placed
under arrest and confined to his tent with a guard over him. . . . When he
had sufficiently repented of his crime, he wrote a letter to the commanding
general [McClellan], setting forth the great reform that had taken place in
his morals, and promising that if he were restored to his liberty, never to
shoot another pig without a special order from the Provost Marshal General. This had the desired effect, and the . . . man was welcomed back to liberty and his regiment by his brother officers, who complimented him on his

escape from being tried by a court-martial and shot for killing a pig in an enemy's country."

McClellan had a reverential feeling for the White House. "It was the residence of Mrs. Custis when she was married to Washington. The ceremony took place in St. Peter's Church, a lonely old building beautifully placed on a commanding hill. . . . Finding one's self alone within that historic building, it was a natural impulse to invoke the aid of God to enable me to serve the country as unselfishly and truly as did the great man who had often worshipped there. The residence at White House was not the original building of the time of Washington. That had been destroyed by fire; but the existing one was constructed on the same foundations. I neither occupied it myself nor permitted any others to do so. . . . For this natural act of respect for the memory of the greatest man our country has produced I was most violently attacked and maligned by the extreme radicals."

His feeling for the place did not prevent McClellan from using its landing. De Joinville explains: "At White House the Pamunkey ceased to be navigable [for large vessels]. The York River railroad, which unites Richmond with this river, crosses it at this point by a bridge which the enemy had destroyed, and then runs in almost a straight line to the Virginian capital. This road had been scarcely injured. . . . A few rails only had been removed, and were soon replaced. All the rolling stock had been run off, but the Federal army had locomotives and cars on board of its transports. The whole flotilla was unloaded at White House, where a vast depot was established under protection of the gunboats, and all the bustle of a seaport soon became visible."

During the three days he was headquartered at the White House, McClellan did some shifting in the makeup of his army. "In consequence of my earnest representations, the President authorized me to organize two provisional army corps, the 5th and the 6th, which soon became permanent corps, and the organization of the Army of the Potomac was now as follows: 2nd Corps, General Sumner. . . . 3rd Corps, General Heintzelman. . . . 4th Corps, General Keyes. . . . 5th Corps, General Fitz-John Porter. . . . 6th Corps, General Franklin." The missing 1st Corps was, of course the one under Irvin McDowell.

As for Joe Johnston, he had placed nearly the whole of his army, officially totaling 53,688 men, on the Richmond side (the southerly bank) of the Chickahominy River, with some of the units in the city's suburbs. Jefferson Davis, who had wanted the defense made at a greater distance, says that he approached Johnston for an explanation of the last leg of his retreat and was told that "he thought the water of the Chickahominy unhealthy and had directed the troops to cross and halt at the first good water on the southern side. . . . He also adverted to the advantage of having the river in front rather than in the rear of him." Johnston "afforded no satisfactory infor-

The White House as a Union
depot. *Right:* The house in ruins.

mation as to his plans and purposes." Davis sent Robert E. Lee, who was on more compatible terms with Johnston than he, to confer with the reticent general, and plans were made for an active defense in Richmond's environs. Johnston was at this time deploying his troops in an eastward arc extending about fifteen miles, his right at Drewry's Bluff on the James, and his left at Mechanicsville, north of Richmond and on the far side of the Chickahominy. His cavalry was thrown northward from Mechanicsville toward Fredericksburg, its chief mission to keep an eye on Irvin McDowell's corps.

In the Shenandoah Valley, Stonewall Jackson had not yet matured his preparations for the continuation of his campaign. His lack of aggressiveness since the Battle of McDowell had reduced Washington's concerns about him. Lincoln and Stanton had divested Nathaniel Banks of half his command—James Shields' division of 10,000 men—for assignment to McDowell at Fredericksburg. On May 17 Stanton wrote McClellan: "Your dispatch to the President, asking for reinforcements, has been received and carefully considered. The President is not willing to uncover the capital entirely . . . [but] in order . . . to increase the strength of the attack upon Richmond at the earliest possible moment, General McDowell has been ordered to march upon that city by the shortest route. He is ordered—keeping himself always in position to cover the capital from all possible attack—so to operate as to put his left wing in communication with your right. . . . He will move with between thirty-five and forty thousand men. . . . At your earnest call for reinforcements, he is sent forward to cooperate in the reduction of Richmond, but charged, in attempting this, not to uncover the city of Washington, and you will give no orders, either before or after your junction, which can keep him out of position to cover this city."

McClellan was far from pleased by this news from "the hounds in Washington." He had wanted McDowell sent to him by water and placed solidly under his control. In a dispatch to Lincoln, McClellan lamented: "The enemy are in force on every road leading to Richmond. . . . All accounts report their numbers as greatly exceeding our own. . . . I regret the state of things as to General McDowell's command. We must beat the enemy in front of Richmond. . . . I fear there is little hope that he can join me overland in time for the coming battle. Delays on my part will be dangerous. I fear sickness and demoralization. This region is unhealthy for Northern men, and, unless kept moving, I fear that our soldiers may become discouraged. At present our numbers are weakening from disease, but our men remain in good heart. . . . I believe that there is a great struggle before this army, but I am neither dismayed nor discouraged. I wish to strengthen its force as much as I can, but in any event I shall fight it with all the skill, caution, and determination that I possess, and I trust that the result may either obtain for me the permanent confidence of my government or that it may close my career."

Later, McClellan would claim that the orders he received concerning McDowell's overland march proved fatal to his campaign, that they forced him to conduct his siege on the York side of the Peninsula, his army divided by the Chickahominy. With the *Merrimack* out of the way, he said, he could have swung over to the banks of the James, where the waters were ideal both for supply transports and warships, and where the Chickahominy was not a threat. Unfortunately, there is no evidence to support this claim. In the beginning at least, McClellan seems to have done all of his thinking in terms of operating by way of the York. He apparently underestimated the Chickahominy as a military obstacle.

One of the civilian correspondents who covered the march from the White House to the Chickahominy was George Alfred Townsend, of the New York *World,* who noted that "there was a prodigious number of stragglers from the Federal lines. . . . They sauntered along by twos and threes, rambling into all the fields and green-apple orchards, intruding their noses into old cabins, prying into smoke-houses and cellars, looking at the stock in the stables, and peeping on tiptoe into windows of dwellings. These stragglers were true exponents of Yankee character, always wanting to know, averse to discipline, eccentric in their orbits, entertaining profound contempt for everything that was not up . . . 'to hum.' "

Although their mirthful criticisms of Southern methods of building and farming and making tools may have offended, these men were generally not destructive. However, according to Townsend, there were segments of the army in which McClellan's orders against theft and ravage were breaking down: "There was a mill on the New Bridge Road, ten miles from White House, with a tidy farmhouse, [smoke] stacks, and cabins adjoining. The road crossed the millrace by a log bridge, and a spreading pond or dam lay to the left, the water black as ink, the shore sandy, and the stream disappearing in a grove of straight pines. A youngish woman with several small children occupied the dwelling, and there remained, besides, her fat sister-in-law and four or five faithful Negroes. I begged the favor of a meal and a bed in the place one night, and shall not forget the hospitable table with its steaming biscuits; the chubby baby perched upon his high stool; the talkative elderly woman, who took snuff at the fireplace; the contented black girl, who played the Hebe; and, above all, the trim, plump, pretty hostess, with her brown eyes and hair, her dignity and her fondness, sitting at the head of the board. When she poured the bright coffee into the capacious bowl, she revealed the neatest of hands and arms, and her dialect was softer and more musical than that of most Southerners. In short, I fell almost in love with her . . . though she was the wife of a quartermaster in a Virginia regiment. For, somehow, a woman seems very handsome when one is afield, and the contact of rough soldiers gives him a partiality for females. It must have required some courage to remain upon the farm, but she hoped thereby to save the property from spoilation.

"I played a game of whist with the sister-in-law, arguing all the while; and at nine o'clock the servant produced some hard cider, shellbarks, and apples. We drank a cheery toast: 'An early peace and old fellowship!' To which the wife added a sentiment of 'always welcome,' and the baby laughed at her knee. How brightly glowed the fire! I wanted to linger for a week, a month, a year. . . . When I strolled [out] to the porch—hearing the pigeons cooing at the barn, the water streaming down the dam, the melancholy monotony of the [breeze in the] pine boughs—there only lacked the humming millwheel . . . to fill the void corner of one's happy heart.

"But this was a time of war, when dreams are rudely broken; and mine could not last. The next day some great wheels beat down the bridge and the teams clogged the road for miles. The waiting teamsters saw the miller's sheep; and the geese, chickens, and pigs rashly exposed themselves in the barnyard. These were killed and eaten, the mill stripped of flour and meal, and the garden despoiled of its vegetables. A quartermaster's horse foundered, and he demanded the miller's. . . . To crown all, a group of stragglers butchered the cows and heaped the beef in their wagons. . . .

"When I presented myself [after a ride abroad] late in the afternoon, the yard and porches were filled with soldiers. The wife sat within, her head thrown upon the window[sill], her bright hair unbound, and her eyes red with weeping. The baby had cried itself to sleep, the sister-in-law took snuff fiercely at the fire, the black girl cowered in a corner. 'There is not bread in the house for my children,' she said, 'but I did not think they could make me shed a tear.' If there were Spartan women, as the storybooks say, I wonder if their blood died with them. I hardly think so. . . .

"War brutalizes! . . . The men were thieves and brutes. . . . But they were perhaps hungry and weary and sick of camp food. . . . I . . . hated warfare, though I knew nothing to substitute for it in *crises*. Besides, the optimist might have seen much to admire. Individual merits were developed around me. I saw shopkeepers and mechanics in the ranks, and they looked to be better men. Here were triumphs of engineering, there perfections of applied ingenuity. I saw how the weakest natures girt themselves for great resolves, and how fortitude outstripped itself. It is a noble thing to put by the fear of death. It was a grand spectacle, this civil soldiery of both sections [North and South] supporting their principles, ambitions, or whatever instigated them, with their bodies. . . ."

Among the bodies that broke down at this time was that of Regis de Trobriand. "The division arrived at a brick building called Providence Church, not far from the swamps in the midst of which flowed the Chickahominy. The weather was rainy, the ground soaked. I had taken hardly any nourishment for three days. On dismounting from my horse I felt that I was falling, and that if I passed the night in that mud I should be unable to rise

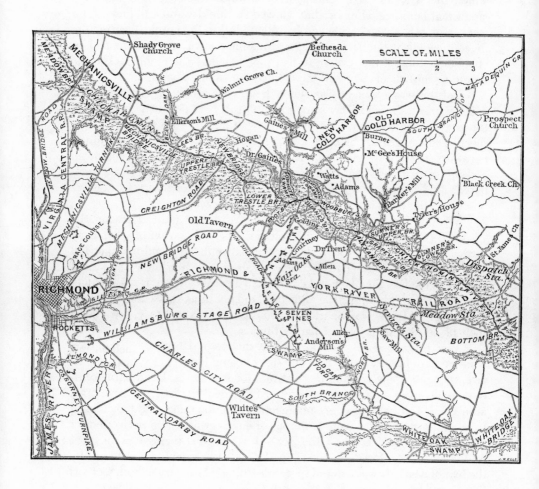

Richmond and the Chickahominy River

in the morning. There was, close by, a dilapidated barn where a few men, weakened by fever or worn out by the march, had obtained shelter. I thought myself happy to be able to lie down on a pile of corn stalks, sometimes shivering and sometimes stifled under my blankets. I thought of the sinister predictions of the Georgia captain.

"I had turned over the command of the regiment for the night to the lieutenant-colonel. In the morning, when I learned that the brigade was ordered on a reconnoissance toward Bottom's Bridge, in the direction of Richmond, I made a last effort and left on horseback at the head of my regiment. A few hours later I returned under the charge of the regimental surgeon, stricken down by the terrible malady which was soon to make such ravages in our ranks. Much was said at that time of the 'fine organization' of the Army of the Potomac. Things should be seen from a near point of view to know the truth. We have already seen how the commissary and quartermaster service was performed. I had to make trial, in my own person, of the ambulance service. In the whole division, there could not be found one available to transport a colonel to a hospital.

"I was no longer able to keep in the saddle. Shelter must be sought somewhere for me. That shelter was a miserable little house inhabited by some poor people named Turner. The husband and his wife composed the whole family. The ground floor was divided into two small rooms, the kitchen, in which they slept, and a vestibule, to which an old leather sofa furnished a pretense to call it a parlor. From the vestibule, a stairway like a ladder led directly to a garret, with sloping ceiling, where there was a bed. I should have said a cot. But, under the circumstances, it seemed like a gift from heaven. It actually had sheets.

"My orderly was left with me as nurse. He was a Zouave named Shedel, a careful and steady man, who was of great service to me. He found . . . room enough to stretch his blankets near my bed. My two servants put up their shelter tent near the door. My horses were hitched to a fence, and my installation was complete. A sorry installation. I was abandoned there like an estray from the vast current of men advancing toward Richmond."

Union narrator William Swinton takes up: "Upon McClellan's arrival on the Chickahominy, there were two objects which he had to keep in view: to secure a firm footing on the Richmond side of that stream with the view of carrying out the primal purpose of the campaign, and at the same time to so dispose his forces as to insure the junction of McDowell's column from Fredericksburg with the force before Richmond. The former purpose was accomplished by throwing the left wing of the Army of the Potomac across the Chickahominy at Bottom's Bridge, which the Confederates had left uncovered. Casey's division of Keyes' corps crossed on the 20th of May and occupied the opposite heights. Heintzelman's corps was then thrown forward in support, and Bottom's Bridge was immediately rebuilt. To

Confederates retreating through Mechanicsville as McClellan's right wing is advanced

secure the second object, McClellan extended his right wing well northward, and ... carried the village of Mechanicsville, forcing the enemy
across the Chickahominy at the Mechanicsville Bridge." By this time
McDowell was nearly ready to start southward from Fredericksburg, and
McClellan began to believe that the junction had a chance of succeeding. It
would raise his forces to about 140,000 men.

As explained by Southerner Edward Pollard: "The investment of the
line of the Chickahominy brought the two armies face to face within a few
miles of Richmond and opened one of the grandest scenes of the war, exhibiting the strength and splendour of the opposing hosts and appealing to the
eye with every variety of picturesque effect. For nearly a year an immense
labor had been expended upon the fortifications of Richmond. Earthworks
of magnitude arose on every side. They were constructed in different shapes
to suit the conformation of the ground. They swept all the roads, crowned
every hillock; and mounds of red earth could be seen in striking contrast
with the rich green of the landscape. Redoubts, rifle pits, casemate batteries, horn works, and enfilading batteries were visible in great number, in
and out of the woods, in all directions. Beyond, through the open and culti-
vated country ... stretched the camp of the enemy. Wooded heights overlooked them, and the numerous tents of the army, the vast trains of wagons,
the powerful park of artillery, together with the fleet of steamers and transports [on the distant Pamunkey], presented a striking contrast to the usually
quiet country." The situation caused much "alarm and excitement" among
the Confederate populace at the outset, but this abated somewhat as "the
tardy battle for Richmond yet lingered. Public confidence and public courage rose each day of the delay."

8

---•◆•---

JACKSON STRIKES NORTHWARD

IN WASHINGTON, President Lincoln currently had an extra reason for wanting McClellan to speed his efforts to take Richmond and deal the Confederacy a fatal blow. The cause of abolitionism, which the President did not favor, had been served by a spate of new publicity. Union General David Hunter, commanding the Department of the South from Hilton Head, South Carolina, had taken it upon himself to issue an emancipation proclamation affecting the slaves of South Carolina, Georgia, and Florida, the measure calling for the arming of the able-bodied. Lincoln was obliged to make a public repudiation of the general's work, stating that he reserved to himself the power to authorize emancipation if this became necessary to maintain the Government. He took the opportunity, in the face of abolitionist censure, to repeat his own preference for solving the slavery problem by means of a gradual, compensated emancipation. To the people of the South he said: "I do not argue; I beseech you to make the arguments for yourselves. You cannot, if you would, be blind to the signs of the times. . . . The change . . . would come gently as the dews of Heaven, not rendering or wrecking anything. Will you not embrace it? So much good has not been done by one effort in all past time as, in the Providence of God, it is now your high privilege to do. May the vast future not have to lament that you have neglected it."

The President had come to believe that unless the South agreed to his plan, or unless she were quickly conquered, he would be driven to declaring for emancipation as a military measure. This would not only give a new vitality to Northern efforts but would also lessen the chances of European intervention in favor of the South, however important her cotton was to the Old World's economy. Once the North defined the war as a moral crusade, the South would have a difficult time securing open allies.

The beginning of the fourth week in May 1862 found Lincoln in a hopeful mood. McClellan was finally at the gates of Richmond, and McDowell was poised to lend him powerful support. Criticism of the administration had subsided. Northerners meeting on the streets or at social events talked of the war in eager tones. Editorialists offered optimistic pronouncements; and on mellowly lighted threater stages vaudeville performers made scornful jests about Southern hopes. Lincoln and a party of aides journeyed by steamboat and train to Fredericksburg for a last-minute talk with McDowell, and the President was honored by a review that was expansive with pageantry and clangorous with patriotic music. McDowell then began disposing his van southward.

Unknown to the Federal leaders, their grand plan was about to become the object of a counterstroke. Stonewall Jackson was on the march in the Shenandoah Valley.

The departure of the Union division under James Shields for McDowell's camp at Fredericksburg had left Nathaniel Banks with 10,000 men deployed on a cross-valley line between Front Royal and Strasburg, about twenty miles south of Winchester and forty miles from Harpers Ferry on the Potomac. Banks himself, with the main body, was on the northwestern flank at Strasburg. The southeastern flank at Front Royal, ten miles distant, held only 1,000 men commanded by Colonel John R. Kenly.

Jackson was at Mount Solon, some sixty miles southwest of the Federal line, on May 17 when he received a dispatch from Robert E. Lee. "Whatever move you make against Banks, do it speedily, and if successful drive him towards the Potomac and create the impression, as far as possible, that you design threatening that line." Lee knew of Lincoln's fears for the safety of his capital and wanted them played upon. Lee's order was precisely in line with Jackson's own ideas. The two men were beginning to develop the strategic and tactical rapport that became a marvel in military annals. Both had the ability to see a field situation in its broadest terms, and both understood the importance of confusing the enemy and keeping him off balance.

Jackson had only half his 17,000-man army with him at Mount Solon. The other half, commanded by the jaunty, shiny pated, appealingly eccentric General Richard S. Ewell, was at Swift Run Gap, a good twenty-five miles to the east. Both wings started marching northward on May 19, and reached the New Market area, about half the distance to the Federal lines, on the twentieth. At this time one of Ewell's brigades, that of General Richard Taylor, joined the wing under Jackson's personal command. Dick Taylor, son of President Zachary Taylor, was a Louisiana planter and political figure. He had served in the Mexican War with his illustrious father, and had also established a remarkable scholastic record, having studied at Harvard and Yale and at universities abroad. Taylor tells of his arrival at Jackson's campsite: "After attending to necessary camp details, I sought

Scene near Banks' headquarters at Strasburg revealing nature of Valley terrain

Jackson, whom I had never met. . . . The mounted officer who had been sent on in advance pointed out a figure perched on the topmost rail of a fence overlooking the road and field, and said it was Jackson." During the ensuing interview, Jackson sucked on a lemon, something he did often because he believed it aided his digestion. The two were discussing the day's march when Taylor's camp began to resound with waltz music. Jackson commented, "Thoughtless fellows for serious work." Taylor says that he "expressed a hope that the work would not be less well done because of the gayety. A return to the lemon gave me the opportunity to retire. Where Jackson got his lemons no fellow could find out, but he was rarely without one. . . .

"Quite late that night General Jackson came to my campfire, where he stayed some hours. He said we would move at dawn, asked a few questions . . . and then remained silent. If silence be golden, he was a bonanza. He sucked lemons, ate hardtack, and drank water; and praying and fighting appeared to be his idea of the whole duty of man.

"In the gray of the morning, as I was forming my column on the pike, Jackson appeared and gave the route—north—which, from the situation of its camp, put my brigade in advance of the army. After moving a short distance in this direction, the head of the column was turned to the east and took the road over Massanutten Gap to Luray. Scarce a word was spoken on the march as Jackson rode with me. . . . An ungraceful horseman, mounted on a sorry chestnut with a shambling gait, his huge feet with outturned toes thrust into his stirrups, and such parts of his countenance as the low visor of his shocking cap failed to conceal wearing a wooden look, our new commander was not prepossessing."

According to Chief of Staff Robert Dabney, Jackson "had determined to march by Luray and Front Royal in order to avoid the necessity of attacking Banks in his strong fortifications [at Strasburg]. This route offered other advantages. It placed him between his enemy and eastern Virginia [specifically, Richmond and Fredericksburg]. . . . It enabled him to conceal his march from Banks more effectually until he was fairly upon his flank; and it ensured the issuing of that general from his entrenched position in order to save his communications [with Winchester and the Potomac crossings]." Jackson's two columns merged on May 22, and the entire force headed for the small band of Federals at Front Royal.

The wretched deployment of Banks' army was not entirely the general's fault. Edwin Stanton had sent orders for him to establish his main line in the vicinity of Strasburg and to detail a small force to hold the bridges over the Shenandoah River at Front Royal. Banks said later: "This force was intended as a guard for the protection of the town, and partly against local guerrilla parties that infested that locality. . . . It had never been contemplated as a defense against the combined forces of the enemy in the Valley of Virginia." But Banks should have foreseen the possibility of a major attack on Front Royal and discussed the matter with Stanton. Of course, neither Stanton the lawyer-politician nor Banks the political soldier had enough military expertise for situations like this.

When he made camp on the evening of the twenty-second, Jackson was about a ten miles south of Front Royal. "Off the next morning," relates Dick Taylor, "my command still in advance, and Jackson riding with me. The road led north between the east bank of the river [the Shenandoah's South Fork] and the western base of the Blue Ridge. Rain had fallen and softened it, so as to delay the wagon trains in rear. Past midday [after a period of uphill marching] we reached a wood extending from the mountain to the river, when a mounted officer from the rear called Jackson's attention, who rode back with him. A moment later, there rushed out of the wood to meet us a young, rather well-looking woman, afterward widely known as Belle Boyd. Breathless with speed and agitation, some time elapsed before she found her voice. Then, with much volubility, she said we were near Front Royal, beyond the wood." The woman went on to give Taylor and his party a complete report on the Federal situation in the area. Taylor noted that she spoke "with the precision of a staff officer making a report. . . . Jackson was possessed of these facts before he left New Market, and based his movements upon them; but, as he never told anything, it was news to me. . . . There also dawned on me quite another view of our leader."

Jackson shortly came galloping from the rear, followed by a troop of horsemen, and made his dispositions for the attack. He had already sent cavalry forces to the west side of the river to cut the garrison's communications with Strasburg and to threaten its flank. Now he advanced two columns down through the wood, one by the road leading into the town, and the other toward the left for a passage between the town and the northerly flowing river. As the attackers emerged from the wood with bugle calls, shouts, and volleys of musketry, the Federal outposts fell back through the town toward a wide expanse of meadows and hillocks beyond, along the river's bank. This was the spot where the North Fork of the Shenandoah came in from the west to join the South Fork for the river's northerly trip to the Potomac. In the open area, about a mile beyond the town, lay the Federal encampment. Behind the clusters of tents was a bridge over the South Fork, and behind that bridge was another over the merging North Fork. The road over the twin bridges led northward to Winchester.

"When we entered Front Royal," says an unnamed Confederate soldier, "the women and children met us with shouts of the liveliest joy. As we passed through the place in double-quick, we could not stop to partake of the hospitality so generously and profusely tendered on all hands."

As the elements of the Confederate attack deployed across the meadows just north of the town, Colonel Kenly's Federals, with their drummers beating the "long roll," rushed to form a defense line on a rise near their camp, the first bridge not far behind them. Kenly began to realize he was gravely outnumbered, but he determined to make a stand. At this point he had the advantage of artillery, for Jackson's guns had not yet come forward. One of the units on Jackson's line was the 1st Maryland Confederate Regiment, while Kenly's line included the 1st Maryland Federals. The regiments were displaying their colors, and both sides were swept by an extra excitment. Some of the opposing Marylanders were related.

Again in Dick Taylor's words: "I rode down to the river's brink to get a better look at the enemy through a fieldglass, when my horse, heated by the march, stepped into the water to drink. Instantly a brisk fire was opened on me, bullets striking all around and raising a little shower-bath. Like many a foolish fellow, I found it easier to get into, than out of, a difficulty. I had not yet led my command into action, and, remembering that one must strut one's little part to the best advantage, sat my horse with all the composure I could muster. A provident camel, on the eve of a desert journey, would not have laid in a greater supply of water than did my thoughtless beast. As last he raised his head, looked placidly around, turned, and walked up the bank. This little incident was not without value, for my men welcomed me with a cheer; upon which, as if in response, the enemy's guns opened, and, having the range, inflicted some loss on my line."

According to a Confederate staff officer, William Allan, Colonel Kenly "made a spirited resistance for a time. His artillery was well served, and his infantry kept up a steady fire.... At length Colonel [Stapleton] Crutch-field, chief of artillery for Jackson, got three guns—one of them rifled—into position and replied to the Federal battery. But the Confederate infantry had not waited for this. The 6th Louisiana was sent ... through some woods to flank the enemy's battery, while Major [Roberdeau C.] Wheat and Colo-nel [Bradley T.] Johnson ... pressed forward in front with the greatest ardor. Meantime, Colonel [Thomas S.] Flournoy, with his cavalry, was moving down between the rivers and threatening the Federal rear. Colonel Kenly, seeing himself about to be surrounded ... retreated rapidly across the two rivers, having set fire to his camp."

The Confederate infantry regiments hurried past the blazing tents, which were sending up columns of smoke, and clattered across the first bridge. As they approached the second, they saw that it had been packed with combustibles that were beginning to flare and crackle. Kenly's rear guard was still close enough to register musketry on the bridge and its envi-rons, and his artillery had found a new height from which to operate. The Confederates were not deterred. Astride his horse, Dick Taylor led his Louisianans on a rush to extinguish the flames. "Concealed by the cloud of smoke, the suddenness of the movement saved us from much loss; but it was rather a near thing. My horse and clothing were scorched, and many men burned their hands severely while throwing brands into the river. We were soon over, and the enemy in full flight. . . . Just as I emerged from flames and smoke, Jackson was by my side. How he got there was a mystery, as the bridge was thronged with my men going at full speed; but smoke and fire had decidedly freshened up his costume."

Although the bridge was saved, it had been rendered hazardous for cavalry, which happened to be the arm that Jackson wanted to use at this time. The bridge route was supplemented by a nearby ford, and Jackson and Flournoy were soon across and galloping northward with four companies, or about 250 men. Jackson had left orders for additional troops to follow as quickly as they could. "The Federals," says Robert Dabney, "were overtaken near a little hamlet named Cedarville, five miles from Front Royal, where their whole force, consisting of a section of artillery, two companies of cavalry, two companies of Pennsylvania infantry, and the 1st Maryland Regiment of Federal infantry, now placed themselves in order of battle to stand at bay. General Jackson no sooner saw them than he gave the order to charge with a voice and air whose peremptory determination was communicated to the whole party. Colonel Flournoy instantly hurled his forces in column against the enemy. . . . "

To at least one man on the Union side, the approaching troopers seemed a horde about 2,000 strong. "They closed in upon us, literally cutting us to pieces, our men fighting desperately. Colonel Kenly, seeing our position, called our men to *rally around their colors*, which was the last order I heard from him. He was fighting hand-to-hand with the rebels, receiving a saber wound in the head, which was the last I saw of our beloved colonel."

With Kenly's incapacitation, resistance ended. Returning to Dabney: "Their cavalry broke and fled, the cannoneers abandoned their guns, and the infantry threw down their arms and scattered in utter rout. Other Confederate troops speedily arriving, the fields and woods were gleaned, and nearly the whole opposing force was killed or captured. The result was the possession of about 700 prisoners, immense stores, and two fine 10-pounder rifle-guns. The loss of the Patriots, in the combat and pursuit, was twenty-six killed and wounded." One of Jackson's Marylanders found his brother among the prisoners. Although each considered the other to be "in bad company," the pair enjoyed a warm reunion.

Dabney reveled in the fact that Jackson's "dash and genius" had inspired 250 horsemen to destroy a force four times their number. "His quick eye estimated aright the discouragement of the enemy and their wavering temper. Infusing his own spirit into the men, he struck the hesitating foe at the decisive moment and shattered them. A glorious share of the credit is also due to the officers and men of the detachment. General Jackson declared with emphasis to his staff that he had never, in all his experience of warfare, seen a cavalry charge executed with such efficiency and gallantry—commendation which, coming from his guarded and sober lips, was decided enough to satisfy every heart."

As for Banks at Strasburg, he began getting sketchy news of the attack at Front Royal about four o'clock in the afternoon. He was not greatly disturbed, for he believed the attack to be merely a raid by a small force, and that Jackson and his main army were still far to the south. One of Banks' brigade commanders was Colonel George H. Gordon, who fretted over the general's views. "Nothing was done towards sending away to Winchester any of the immense quantities of public stores collected at Strasburg; no movement had been made to place our sick in safety. It did not seem as if Banks interpreted the attack to signify aught of future or further movement by the enemy, or that it betokened any purpose to cut us off from Winchester. I was so fully impressed, however, with Jackson's purpose, that as soon as night set in I sought Banks at his headquarters. I labored long to impress upon him what I thought a duty, to wit, his immediate retreat upon Winchester, carrying all his sick and all his supplies that he could transport, and destroying the remainder. Notwithstanding all my solicitations and entreaties, he persistently refused to move, ever repeating, 'I must develop the force of the enemy.' "

Gordon finally left Banks' headquarters, but he soon returned to press the matter again. He tried to convince the general that the abandonment of Strasburg would not be an ignominious flight but a maneuver designed to keep the army from being cut off. At this interview, Gordon attests, sparks began to fly. "Moved with an unusual fire, General Banks, who had met all my arguments with the single reply, 'I must develop the force of the enemy,' rising excitedly from his seat, with much warmth and in loud tones exclaimed, 'By God, sir, I will not retreat! We have more to fear, sir, from the opinions of our friends than the bayonets of our enemies!' The thought so long the subject of his meditations was at last out. Banks was afraid of being thought afraid. I rose to take my leave, replying, 'This, sir, is not a military reason for occupying a false position.' It was eleven o'clock at night when I left him. As I returned through the town I could not perceive that anybody was troubled with anticipation for the morrow. The sutlers were driving sharp bargains with those who had escaped from, or those who were not amenable to, military discipline. The strolling players were moving crowds to noisy laughter in their canvas booths, through which the lights gleamed and the music sounded with startling shrillness. I thought as I turned towards my camp, how unaware are all of the drama Jackson is preparing for us."

It wasn't until the following morning that Banks "developed the force of the enemy." Once he realized that Jackson's entire army was in a position to flank him, he acted with celerity and skill, putting his troops and trains on the pike to Winchester and assigning units to cover the roads approaching the pike from Front Royal. Jackson was at first obliged to move slowly. He had to make certain that Banks was indeed marching northward and hadn't decided upon an alternate maneuver. By the time Jackson was operating forcibly, it was too late for him to sever and shatter the Federal column. He achieved a dent by dispatching a cavalry raid, but the rest of his army was still pushing its way toward the pike as the Federal van neared Winchester.

One of the Northern people in that city was the wife of a Boston pastor, Mary A. Denison, who was serving as nurse and comforter to Federal soldiers who had been wounded in previous fights in the Valley. On the morning of Banks' retreat, Mrs. Denison had risen at her usual early hour. "When I went the rounds of the hospitals . . . how little I expected that I was looking my last upon so many of our poor wounded boys. We then looked for reinforcements by every train, having heard that General Banks and his army were coming towards Winchester. Towards noon . . . army supplies and ambulances began pouring in. . . . The Unionists there had confidence in Banks, while the secessionists put on a bolder face than ever, dressed themselves in their best, and made entertainment [preparations] for Jackson's army. Little we thought, as we heard their impertinent remarks, that we should 'see who would rule tomorrow,' that their boasting was to be verified. Soon came the foot soldiers, weary and travel-worn, by tens and fifties. People began to say, 'This looks like a retreat.' Still we had hope."

Early afternoon found only Banks' rear guard and a portion of his baggage train susceptible to Jackson's flanking maneuver. As related by Dabney: "When the little village of Middletown came in view across the broad and level fields, the highway passing through it at right angles to the direction of General Jackson's approach was seen canopied with a vast cloud of gray dust, and crowded beneath, as far as the eye could reach, with a column of troops. At the sight, the artillery dashed forward in a gallop for a rising ground, whence to tear their ranks with shell. Ashby swooped down upon the right like an eagle; cut through their path and arrested their escape on that side; while General Taylor, throwing his front regiment into line, advanced at a double-quick to the center of the village, his men cheering and pouring a terrific volley into the confused mass which filled the street. Never did a host receive a more mortal thrust. In one moment the way was encumbered with dying horses and men; and at every fierce volley the troopers seemed to melt by scores from their saddles; while the frantic riderless horses rushed up and down, trampling the wounded wretches into the dust. But the astute cowardice of the Federals made the real carnage far less than the apparent; they fell from their horses before they were struck, and were found, when the victors leaped into the road, squat behind the stone fences which bordered it . . . where they all surrendered at the first challenge. Among the remainder of the Federal cavalry the wildest confusion ensued, and they scattered in various directions. Two hundred prisoners and horses with their equipments remained in the hands of the Confederates at this spot. . . .

"As soon as the bullets ceased to fly, the astonished citizens gathered around; and when they saw the miserable, begrimed, and bloody wreck of what had just been a proud regiment of Vermont cavalry, they exclaimed with uplifted hands, 'Behold the righteous judgment of God; for these are the miscreants who had been most forward to plunder, insult, and oppress us!' By some of them, General Jackson was informed that dense columns of infantry, trains of artillery, and long lines of baggage wagons had been passing from Strasburg since early morning. Many wagons were seen disappearing in the distance towards Winchester, and Colonel Ashby, with his cavalry, some artillery, and a supporting infantry force from Taylor's brigade, was sent in pursuit."

At sight of the approaching peril, many of the Federal wagoners unhitched their horses and fled upon them. Others scurried on foot. The tardy were taken prisoner, and there was booty in abundance. Dick Taylor had had no personal part in this affair, and it was over by the time he rode toward the scene. He noted that Major Wheat's Louisiana Tigers "were looting right merrily, diving in and out of the wagons with the activity of rabbits in a warren; but this occupation was abandoned on my approach, and in a moment they were in line, looking as solemn and virtuous as deacons at a funeral."

In Washington that afternoon, Lincoln and Stanton were pondering the telegraphic reports that Banks had provided regarding Jackson's attack on Front Royal. Lincoln wired McClellan at Richmond that Banks seemed to be "in some peril" but that McDowell would be sent to McClellan as promised. McClellan, who happened to be sick at the time (he told Ellen that his "old Mexican complaint" was acting up), found the news reassuring. "I now felt confident that we would on his arrival be sufficiently strong to overpower the large army confronting us." But even as McClellan was reading the message, Lincoln and Stanton learned that Banks was in full retreat northward. Deeply alarmed, the two amateur tacticians promptly devised a plan they hoped would save the situation. Fresh troops would be sent into the Valley both from the east and the west, their mission to get behind Jackson and trap him. At 4 P.M. Lincoln wired McClellan again: "In consequence of General Banks' critical position I have been compelled to suspend General McDowell's movements to join you. The enemy are making a desperate push upon Harpers Ferry, and we are trying to throw General Frémont's force and part of General McDowell's in their rear." The ailing McClellan sighed resignedly. "I could not expect General McDowell to join me in time to participate in immediate operations in front of Richmond, and . . . I replied to the President that I would make my calculations accordingly."

After the attack at the village of Middletown, according to Dabney, Jackson became convinced "that the larger game was in the direction of Winchester . . . and the whole army advanced towards Newtown. The deserted wagon train of the enemy . . . occupied the road for a mile. Upon approaching Newtown the General was disappointed to find his artillery arrested and wholly unsupported by the cavalry; while the enemy, taking heart from the respite, had placed two batteries in position on the left and right of the village, and again showed a determined front. Nearly the whole of Colonel Ashby's cavalry present with him, with a part of the infantry under his command, had disgracefully turned aside to pillage; so that their gallant commander was compelled to arrest the pursuit. Indeed, the firing had not ceased . . . at Middletown before some of Ashby's men might have been seen, with a quickness more suitable to horse thieves than to soldiers, breaking from their ranks, seizing each two or three of the captured horses and making off across the fields. Nor did these men pause until they had carried their illegal booty to their homes, which were, in some instances, at the distance of one or two days' journey. That such extreme disorders could occur, and that they could be passed over without a bloody punishment, reveals the curious inefficiency of officers in the volunteer Confederate army.

"The rifled guns of Captain [W. T.] Poague were immediately placed in position upon arriving near Newtown, on an opposing eminence, and replied to the Federal battery upon the right of the village with effect; but it was sunset before they were dislodged and the pursuit resumed. The enemy had improved this pause to set fire to a large part of their train containing valuable stores; and, as the army advanced, the gathering darkness was illuminated for a mile by blazing wagons and pontoon boats; while blackened heaps of rice, beef, and bread, intermingled with the bands and bars of glowing iron, showed where carriages laden with these stores had been consumed."

Dick Taylor was at this time riding with Jackson and got another glimpse of his nature. "An officer, riding hard, overtook us, who proved to be the chief quartermaster of the army. He reported the wagon trains far behind, impeded by a bad road. . . . 'The ammunition wagons?' sternly. 'All right, sir. They were in advance, and I doubled teams on them and brought them through.' 'Ah!' in a tone of relief. . . . Without physical wants himself, he forgot that others were differently constituted, and paid little heed to commissariat; but woe to the man who failed to bring up ammunition!"

Again in Dabney's words; "General Jackson's perfect knowledge of the ground surrounding Winchester suggested to him the fear that the Federalists would occupy the range of hills to the left of the turnpike and southwest of the town so as to command his approaches. He therefore determined to press them all night in the hope of seizing the . . . heights during the darkness. Without a moment's pause for food or sleep, the army marched forward in perfect order, some of the brigades enlivening their fatigues from time to time with martial music, while ringing cheers passed like a wave down the column for four miles, until their sound was lost in the distance. The last time Jackson's division had passed over this road, they were making their slow and stubborn retreat from the bloody field of Kernstown; and they were now eager to wipe out the disgrace of that check.

"The night was calm but dark. All night long the General rode at the front, amidst a little advanced guard of cavalry, seeking the enemy's bleeding haunches with the pertinacity of a bloodhound. Again and again he fell . . . into ambuscades of their riflemen posted behind the stone fences which here line the road almost continuously. Suddenly the fire appeared, dancing along the top of the wall, accompanied by the sharp explosion of the rifles, and the bullets came hissing up the road. The first of these surprises occurred soon after the burning wagons were passed. No sooner had the fire begun than the General, seeing his escort draw rein and waver, cried in a commanding tone: 'Charge them! Charge them!' They advanced unsteadily a little space, and then, at a second volley, turned and fled past him, leaving him in the road with his staff alone. But the enemy, equally timid, also retired, seemingly satisfied with their effort. The conduct of these troopers filled Jackson with towering indignation; and turning to the officer next to him, he exclaimed: 'Shameful! Did you see anybody struck, sir? Did you see anybody struck? Surely they need not have run, at least until they were hurt!'

"Skirmishers from the 33rd Virginia infantry . . . were now thrown into the fields right and left of the turnpike, and, advancing abreast with the head of the column, protected it for a time from similar insults. But as it approached Barton's Mills, five miles from Winchester, the enemy, posted on both sides of the road, again received it with so severe a fire that the cavalry advance retired precipitately out of it, carrying the General and his attendants along with them and riding down several cannoneers who had been brought up to their support. So pertinacious was the stand of the Federalists here . . . the affair grew to the dimensions of a night combat before they gave way. A similar skirmish occurred at Kernstown also, in which a few of the enemy were killed and captured.

"The army was now not far from its goal; and the General, commanding the skirmishes to continue a cautious advance, caused the remainder to halt and lie down upon the roadside for an hour's sleep. He himself, without a cloak to protect him from the chilling dews, stood sentry at the head of the column, listening to every sound from the front. Meanwhile, the wearied skirmishers pressed on with a patient endurance past all praise, drenched with the dews, wading through the rank fields of clover and wheat and stumbling across ditches until their tired limbs would scarcely obey their wills. When the early dawn came . . . the heights commanding Winchester were in sight. . . . The town . . . is seated upon ground almost level; and such also is the surface south and east of it, through which the great roads from Strasburg and Front Royal approach. . . . But toward the southwest a cluster of beautiful hills projects itself for a mile toward the left, commanding the town, the turnpike, and the adjacent country. . . . Why the enemy did not post their powerful artillery upon the foremost of these heights, supported by their main force, can only be explained by that infatuation which possessed them . . . throughout these events." Using the dawn as his signal, "General Jackson, in a quiet undertone, gave the word to march, which was passed down the column; and the host rising from its short sleep, chill and stiff with the cold night-damps, advanced to battle."

Jackson found the commanding heights occupied by Federal skirmishers only. Banks had chosen to place his two brigades, the one under George Gordon and the other under Colonel Dudley Donnelly, on a set of ridges nearer the town. Jackson formed for his attack on a broad front semicircling the position, he himself commanding on the left, and Richard Ewell on the right. Banks was outnumbered more than two to one. Although determined to make a stand, he was also prepared to continue his retreat.

In Winchester, the Unionists had gone to bed retaining their hope. This extended even to some of the newsmen who had accompanied the retreat from Strasburg. In the words of an unnamed writer who had taken a room in a Confederate home: "By daybreak . . . the voices of cannon and the rattle of musketry, coming in through my open window, brought me suddenly to the consciousness that another day must be broken of its peaceful quiet by the fierce and unnatural pursuits of war. I listened to the sounds and saw the smoke which rose from the hills but three miles distant. The people with whom I remained were gazing thitherward as upon an interesting spectacle, rejoicing that Jackson was again coming to free them from the Northern yoke. During my breakfast I heard the tramping of horses upon the road and the heavy rolling of artillery over the pavements. Certainly, I thought, there can be no haste; we shall not be compelled to leave Winchester. I ordered, however, my horse to be immediately saddled, and continued sipping my coffee with very little concern."

Mary Denison, the Bostonian, did not share the newsman's calm. It seemed to her that the retreat had already begun in earnest. "Winchester presented a strange sight. Vehicles of every description, crowded with sick soldiers and citizens, came by the door. The contrabands [whom Banks was protecting] flocked by, each with his little bundle. Whole families of Negroes, some with huge packs strapped on head and shoulders, little children almost too small to walk, lean horses carrying two and three, went following the train."

As the battle began, Dabney relates, "General Jackson rode forward, followed by two field officers . . . to the very crest of the [first] hill, and, amidst a perfect shower of balls, reconnoitred the whole position. Both the officers beside him were speedily wounded, but he sat calmly upon his horse until he had satisfied himself concerning the enemy's dispositions." The fighting soon became general. For about two hours Banks managed to hold his own, and Jackson's ranks took some punishment. Finally, says Dabney, "the battle . . . reached a stage which General Jackson perceived to be critical. . . . The enemy were evidently moving . . . towards the wooded heights which commanded his extreme left. He now sent for the fine brigade of General Taylor, which was at the head of the column of reserve."

Taylor takes up: "A staff officer approached at full speed to summon me to Jackson's presence and move up my command. A gallop of a mile or more brought me to him. Winchester was in sight, a mile to the north. To the east Ewell with a large part of the army was fighting briskly. . . . On the west a high ridge, overlooking the country to the south and southeast, was occupied by a heavy mass of Federals with guns in position. . . . Jackson, impassive as ever, pointed to the ridge and said, 'You must carry it.' I replied that my command would be up by the time I could inspect the ground, and rode to the left for that purpose. . . . There was scarce time to mark [its] features before the head of my column appeared, when it was filed to the left, close to the base of the ridge for protection from the plunging fire. . . . Riding on the flank of my column, between it and the hostile line, I saw Jackson beside me. This was not the place for the commander of the army, and I ventured to tell him so; but he paid no attention to the remark. We reached [a] shallow depression . . . where the enemy could depress his guns, and his fire became close and fatal. Many men fell, and the whistling of shot and shell occasioned much ducking of heads in the column. This annoyed me no little, as it was but child's play to the work immediately in hand. . . . Forgetting Jackson's presence, [I] ripped out, 'What the hell are you dodging for? If there is any more of it, you will be halted under this fire for an hour.' The sharp tones of a familiar voice produced the desired effect, and the men looked as if they had swallowed ramrods; but I shall never forget the reproachful surprise expressed in Jackson's face. He placed his hand on my shoulder, said in a gentle voice, 'I am afraid you are a wicked fellow,' turned, and rode back to the pike.

"The proper ground gained, the column faced to the front and began the ascent. . . . It was a lovely Sabbath morning, the 25th of May, 1862. The clear, pure atmosphere brought the [adjacent mountain ranges] almost overhead. Even the cloud of murderous smoke from the guns above made beautiful spirals in the air, and the broad fields of luxuriant wheat glistened with dew. It is remarkable how, in the midst of the most absorbing cares, one's attention may be fixed by some insignificant object, as mine was by the flight past the line of a bluebird . . . bearing a worm in his beak, breakfast for his callow brood. . . .

"As we mounted [the slopes] we came in full view of both armies, whose

efforts in other quarters had been slackened to await the result of our movement. I felt an anxiety amounting to pain for the brigade to acquit itself
handsomely; and this feeling was shared by every man in it. About halfway
up, the enemy's horse from his right charged; and to meet it I directed
Lieutenant Colonel Nicholls, whose regiment, the 8th, was on the left, to
withhold slightly his two flank companies. By one volley, which emptied
some saddles, Nicholls drove off the horse, but was soon after severely
wounded. Progress was not stayed by this incident. Closing the many gaps
made by the fierce fire . . . and preserving an alignment that would have
been creditable on parade, the brigade . . . swept grandly over copse and
ledge and fence, to crown the heights from which the enemy had melted
away. Loud cheers went up from our army, prolonged to the east, where
warm-hearted Ewell . . . led forward his men with renewed energy."

With the Federal defense collapsing everywhere, Jackson barked to his
staff officers, "Order forward the whole line; the battle's won!" The general
himself galloped among the leading pursuers and urged them on. He paused
for a moment to grasp Dick Taylor by the hand, a gesture that Taylor found
"worth a thousand words from another."

In Winchester, says Mary Denison, "the cry went forth that the rebels
were driving our forces. We had engaged a carriage, but it failed us. As the
shells began to pour into the doomed city, we availed ourselves of the offer
of some sick soldiers, who had already crowded an old army wagon, and,
leaving everything behind us, we took passage in the retreating train. . . . By
the time we were one mile from the city, many of the buildings were in
flames. Our men . . . fired the houses of storage and blew up the powder
magazines." The Union newsman was still in Winchester, not far from a fire
giving off "heavy columns of smoke," and the sight impelled him to action.
"I took to my horse with all speed now, for the enemy were in the other end
of the town, as the rattle and echo of the musketry up the streets and between the houses most plainly indicated. All the streets were in commotion.
Cavalry were rushing disorderly away, and infantry, frightened by the rapidity of their mounted companions, were in consternation. All were trying
to escape faster than their neighbors, dreading most of all to be the last. . . .
Some shells fell among our men, and the panic was quite general for a short
time. One round shot, a 6-pounder, passing near me, went directly over the
shoulder of my companion, and, brushing the blanket of the one next to me,
fell to the ground. Guns, knapsacks, cartridge boxes, bayonets, and bayonet
cases lay scattered upon the ground in great profusion, thrown away by the
panic-stricken soldiers. . . . But this confusion and disorder was not of long
duration. General Banks, riding continually among the men and addressing
them kindly and firmly, shamed them to a consideration of their unbefitting
consternation. At length, stationing himself and staff with several others
across a field [north of the town] through which the soldiers were rapidly

fleeing, the men were ordered to stop their flight, were formed into line, and made to march on in a more soldier-like manner. What occurred in the extreme rear of the column I am unable to state with much confidence."

The unenviable position in the rear was occupied by the 2nd Massachusetts Volunteers of George Gordon's brigade. Their retreat was harassed not only by Jackson's army but also by Winchester's citizens. "Males and females," Gordon attests, "vied with each other in increasing the number of their victims by firing from the houses, throwing hand grenades, hot water, and missiles of every description." At this same time, other citizens were forming into bucket brigades to extinguish the fires the Federals had started, while still others were providing a welcome for the surging Confederates. Dabney gloried in the moment. "The sidewalks and doorways were thronged with children, women, and old men who rushed out, regardless of the balls, to hail the conquerors. Of these, some ran in among the horses as though to embrace the knees of their deliverers; many were wildly waving their arms or handkerchiefs and screaming their welcome in cheers and blessings, while not a few of the more thoughtful were seen standing upon their doorsteps with their solemn faces bathed in tears and spreading forth their hands to heaven in adoration."

Dick Taylor observed a vignette of an earthier nature. "A buxom, comely dame of some five and thirty summers, with bright eyes and tight ankles, and conscious of these advantages, was especially demonstrative. . . . Whereupon a tall creole . . . sprang from the ranks . . . clasped her in his arms, and imprinted a sounding kiss on her ripe lips. . . . A loud laugh followed and the dame, with a rosy face but merry twinkle in her eye, escaped."

The army's enjoyment of its glorification was brief, for Jackson lost no time in passing the order: "Forward to the Potomac!" Unfortunately for the general's purposes, his cavalry was presently disorganized and ineffectual. Dabney laments: "After pursuing for a few miles with infantry and artillery, General Jackson perceived that the interval between his men and the enemy was continually widening. The warm midday was now approaching, and since the morning of the previous day the troops had been continually marching or fighting, without food or rest. Nature could do no more. At every step some wearied man was compelled to drop out of the ranks by overpowering fatigue. The General therefore ordered the infantry to cease their pursuit and return to the pleasant groves of Camp Stevenson, three miles north of Winchester, for rest and rations, while the cavalry, which had now arrived, assumed the duty of pressing the enemy."

Since the unsupported cavalry was not a mortal threat to his security, Banks began to breathe easier. There was not, however, much easy breathing among the citizens of the Union on this May sabbath. Many were in a state of wildest excitement. There was tumult in the streets as newsboys who had only lately been hawking papers predicting Richmond's early capture raised the cry, "Washington in danger!" Estimates of Jackson's numbers ranged as high as 60,000. A feverish Edwin Stanton spent the day ordering the loyal states to help meet the emergency. The governor of Massachusetts received this telegram: "Intelligence from various quarters leaves no doubt that the enemy in great force are marching on Washington. You will please organize and forward immediately all the militia and volunteer force in your state." Within the hour, the governor issued the following proclamation: "Men of Massachusetts! The wily and barbarous horde of traitors to the people, to the Government, to our country, and to liberty menace again the national capital. They have attacked and routed Major General Banks, are advancing on Harpers Ferry, and are marching on Washington. The President calls on Massachusetts to rise once more for its rescue and defense. The whole active militia will be summoned by a general order . . . to report to Boston Common tomorrow. They will march to relieve and avenge their brethren and friends, and to oppose with fierce zeal and courageous patriotism the progress of the foe. May God encourage their hearts and strengthen their arms, and may he inspire the Government and all the people!" The proceedings in Massachusetts that day were matched in other loyal states. At the same time, Washington took military possession of the Union's railroads to prepare for a quick transportation of the new troops.

Lincoln, whose concern rivaled Stanton's, spent a part of the day sending wires to McClellan at Richmond. "General Banks . . . probably is broken up and in total rout. . . . Stripped bare as we are here, I will do all we can to prevent [the enemy from] crossing the Potomac at Harpers Ferry or above. McDowell has about 20,000 of his forces moving back to the vicinity of Front Royal, and Frémont, who was at Franklin [in western Virginia], is moving to Harrisonburg; both these movements intended to get in the enemy's rear. One more of McDowell's brigades is ordered through here to Harpers Ferry; the rest of his forces remain for the present at Fredericksburg. We are sending such regiments and dribs from here and Baltimore as we can spare to Harpers Ferry, supplying their places in some sort, calling in militia from the adjacent states. . . . If McDowell's force was now beyond our reach we should be entirely helpless. Apprehensions of something like this, and no unwillingness to sustain you, has always been my reason for withholding McDowell's forces from you. Please understand this, and do the best you can with the forces you have." After sending the message, Lincoln made another assessment of the situation, and McClellan was rushed the following: "I think the [enemy's] movement is a general and concerted one, such as would not be if he was acting upon the purpose of a very desperate defense of Richmond. I think the time is near when you must either attack Richmond or give up the job and come to the defense of Washington.

Let me hear from you instantly." McClellan wired back: "Telegram received. Independently of it, the time is very near when I shall attack Richmond. The object of the [enemy's] movement is probably to prevent reinforcements being sent to me. All the information obtained from balloons, deserters, prisoners, and contrabands agrees in the statement that the mass of the rebel troops are still in the immediate vicinity of Richmond, ready to defend it."

During the afternoon of this tumultuous Sunday, General Banks continued his retreat relatively unmolested and in good order. Banks himself gives the details: "Our march was turned in the direction of Martinsburg, hoping there to meet with reinforcements, the troops moving in three parallel columns, each protected by an efficient rear guard. . . . A few miles from Winchester, the sound of the steam whistle [of a train], heard in the direction of Martinsburg, strengthened the hope of reinforcements and stirred the blood of the men like a trumpet. Soon after, two squadrons of cavalry came dashing down the road with wild hurrahs. They were thought to be the advance of the anticipated support, and were received with deafening cheers. Every man felt like turning back upon the enemy. It proved to be the 1st Maryland Cavalry . . . sent out [from Winchester] in the morning as a train guard. Hearing the guns, they had returned to participate in the fight. Advantage was taken of this stirring incident to reorganize our column, and the march was continued with renewed spirit and ardor.

"At Martinsburg the column halted two and a half hours, the rear guard remaining until seven in the evening . . . and arriving at the river at sundown, forty-eight hours after the first news of the attack on Front Royal. It was a march of fifty-three miles, thirty-five of which were performed in one day. The scene at the river when the rear guard arrived was of the most animating and exciting description. A thousand campfires were burning on the hillside, a thousand carriages of every description were crowded upon the banks, and the broad river was between the exhausted troops and their coveted rest.

"The ford was too deep for the teams to cross in regular succession. Only the strongest horses, after a few experiments, were allowed to essay the passage of the river before morning. The single ferry was occupied by the ammunition trains. . . . The cavalry was secure in its form of crossing. The troops only had no transportation. Fortunately, the train we had so sedulously guarded served us in turn. Several boats belonging to the pontoon train which we had brought from Strasburg were launched and devoted exclusively to their service. It is seldom that a river crossing of such magnitude is achieved with greater success. There never were more grateful hearts in the same number of men than when, at midday on [Monday] the 26th, we stood on the opposite shore."

Among the lucky refugees were many civilians, including Mary Denison and the unnamed newsman. But only a part of the train of contrabands had been ferried across. According to Dabney: "A multitude of helpless blacks were found cowering upon the southern bank. . . . Many of these unhappy victims . . . deserted in the hour of alarm by their seducers, were cared for and brought back [for return] to their homes."

The three days of fighting between Front Royal and the Potomac had cost Jackson 400 men in killed, wounded, and missing. He had diminished Banks by at least 2,500 in killed, wounded, missing, and captured. Large quantities of much-needed stores were taken. A sidelight to these gains is given by Dabney: "Winchester had been the great resort of Federal sutlers who had impudently occupied many of the finest shops upon its streets and exposed their wares for sale in them. The headlong confusion of Banks' retreat left them neither means nor time to remove their wealth. All was given up to the soldiers, who speedily emptied their shelves. It was a strange sight to see the rough fellows, who the day before had lacked the ration of beef and hard bread, regaling themselves with confectionery, sardines, and tropical fruits. Their spoils, however, were about to produce a serious evil. The stores of clothing captured by the men in these shops and in the baggage of the fugitives were so enormous that in a day the army seemed to be almost metamorphosed. The Confederate gray was rapidly changing into Yankee blue. Had this license been permitted, the purposes of discipline would have been disappointed and the dangers of battle multiplied. General Jackson speedily . . . issued an order that every person in Federal uniform should be arrested and assumed to be a prisoner of war going at large improperly. . . . The army became gray again as rapidly as it had been becoming blue. The men either deposited their gay spoils in the bottom of their knapsacks or sent them by the baggage trains which were carrying the captured stores to the rear, and donned their well-worn uniforms again."

Jackson issued another order at this time, one that began by commending the army for routing "the boastful host which was ravaging our beautiful country." The order continued: "The general commanding would warmly express to the officers and men . . . his joy in their achievements and his thanks for their brilliant gallantry in action and their patient obedience under the hardships of forced marches. . . . The explanation of the severe exertions to which the commanding general called the army, which were endured by them with such cheerful confidence in him, is now given in the victory of yesterday. He receives this proof of their confidence . . . with pride and gratitude, and asks only a similar confidence in the future. But his duty today, and that of the army, is to recognize devoutly the hand of a protecting Providence in the brilliant successes of the last three days, which have given us the results of a great victory without great losses, and to make the oblation of our thanks to God for his mercies to us and our country in heartfelt acts of religious worship. For this purpose the troops will remain in camp today, suspending as far as practicable all military exercises; and the chaplains of regiments will hold divine service in their several charges at 4 o'clock P.M." Dabney says that "at the appointed hour the general attended public worship with the 37th Virginia Regiment and presented an edifying example of devotion to the men."

In the Union, the panic subsided when it was learned that Banks had not been destroyed and that Jackson's army was not all-powerful. But Lincoln and Stanton proceeded with their plans to throw troops in Jackson's rear. The Confederate general anticipated the possibility of such a maneuver but was not overly concerned. Instead of retiring, he moved to crown his campaign with a demonstration against Harpers Ferry. He lamented the fact he did not have enough men to attack across the river.

9

---◦◈◦---

FAIR OAKS
AND THE RISE OF LEE

AT THE SAME TIME that Jackson's camps at Winchester were ringing with victory sermons, the chaplains of McClellan's regiments at Richmond were joined in a chorus of protest over something unrelated to military developments. Chaplain Stewart, of the 102nd Pennsylvania Volunteers, wrote the editor of his hometown newspaper: "There is at present the most serious apprehension that the Grand Army of the Potomac is on the eve of a terrible and disgraceful defeat, not from the rebels but from *rum*. An order has been issued . . . and now carried into execution, to issue *each morning to every officer and soldier of the army half a gill of whiskey*. General McClellan is said to be the author of this monstrous wrong, both to soldier and country. Better for a general, in this enlightened age on temperance, to have suffered a dozen defeats than issue such an order. But no matter who be responsible, let an indignant Christian community put such a mark on him or them that they shall hereafter be known as the wholesale drunkard makers, the destroyers of men's souls and bodies, the creators of untold anguish to thousands of mothers, wives, sisters, and daughters, and the breakers down of good morals in the army. All this, too, under profession of kindness to the soldier, a medicine beforehand to prevent him from getting sick! . . . Thousands on thousands of young men and boys not yet inured to tipple will now be induced to swallow their daily glass. . . . Never did I feel so tempted and pressed to relinquish the chaplain service and yield all to the control of Satan."

The complaints about the whiskey ration that reached McClellan's headquarters made little immediate impression, for the general was presently busy with a matter of commanding attention. "I received intelligence that a very considerable force of the enemy was in the vicinity of Hanover Court House, to the right and rear of our army, thus threatening our communications, and in a position either to reinforce Jackson or to impede McDowell's junction, should he finally move to unite with us. . . . It was . . . imperative to dislodge or defeat this force. . . . I entrusted this task to Brigadier General Fitz-John Porter, commanding the 5th Corps, with orders to move at daybreak on the 27th." Porter took 12,000 men against 4,000 under Confederate General Lawrence O'Bryan Branch, and the expedition both defeated and dislodged the enemy, at the same time destroying some rail facilities that might have been used to Confederate advantage. By the time the two-day affair ended, the Federals were in possession of a Confederate cannon, many stands of small arms, and 730 prisoners; and they had buried some 200 enemy dead. The Federals lost 355 men in killed, wounded, and missing. Porter relates: "McClellan joined me on the battlefield, and was well pleased. . . . We returned to our camp on the 29th of May. . . . All rejoiced at the success of our mission in securing for a reasonable time our flank from injury and preparing the whole army for a rapid advance on Richmond." McClellan had his usual trouble gaining the proper applause from Washington. He protested in a wire to Stanton: "From the tone of your dispatches and the President's, I do not think that you at all appreciate the value and magnitude of Porter's victory. . . . It was one of the handsomest things in the war, both in itself and in its results."

Actually, one of the results was decidedly unfavorable to Union interests. Confederate General Joe Johnston could not be certain that Stonewall Jackson's ploy in the Shenandoah Valley had influenced Irvin McDowell's plans to march to Richmond, and Porter's attack seemed meant to clear his way. Johnston felt he must do something before McClellan was reinforced. Although a prompt investigation northward by cavalry trooper Jeb Stuart revealed that McDowell was not, in fact, advancing, Johnston was not dissuaded from taking action.

McClellan was not anticipating any immediate trouble, but he disliked the fact that his army was not deployed as a unit but was in two wings, one on either side of an unpredictable waterway. "The Chickahominy River," he explains, "rises some fifteen miles to the northward of Richmond, and [after making an easterly swing around the city] unites with the James about forty miles below. . . . Our operations embraced the part of the river between Meadow's and Bottom's Bridges, covering the approaches to Richmond from the east. In this vicinity the river, in its ordinary stage, is about forty feet wide, fringed with a dense growth of heavy forest trees and bordered by low, marshy bottomlands varying from half a mile to a mile in width. . . . The firm ground lying above high-water mark seldom approaches the river on either bank, and no place was found . . . where the high ground came near the stream on both banks. It was subject to frequent, sudden, and great variations in the volume of water, and a single violent rainstorm of brief duration would cause a rise of water which overflowed

Union officer addressing captured Confederates

the bottomlands on both sides and for many days made the river absolutely impassable without bridges."

Most of the bridges had been destroyed by the retreating Confederates. "It became necessary," McClellan continues, "not only to rebuild the old bridges but also to construct several additional ones. The [Richmond] bank of the river opposite New, Mechanicsville, and Meadow Bridges was bordered by high bluffs which afforded the enemy commanding positions on which to establish his batteries to enfilade the approaches . . . and to prevent the reconstruction of these important bridges. We were thus obliged to select other less exposed points for our crossings. . . . It became necessary to construct eleven bridges, all long and difficult, with extensive log-way approaches, and often built under fire. . . . I caused work upon the bridges to be . . . pushed forward with the greatest vigor, but heavy rains continued to fall from day to day which flooded the valley and raised the water to a greater height than had been known for twenty years. The bridges first made, together with their approaches, which were not arranged for such unprecedented high water were carried away or rendered impassable. It thus became necessary, with immense labor, to build others."

Under the circumstances, says William Swinton, "McClellan's disposition of his army must be considered a grave fault, and inaction in such a situation was in the highest degree dangerous. . . . For Johnston to omit to strike one or the other of these exposed wings was to neglect that principle which forms the whole secret of war—to be superior to your enemy at the point of collision: it was, in fact, to neglect a unique opportunity of delivering a decisive blow. The Confederate commander was not the man to let slip such an opportunity." Johnston's best bet was to attack the two Federal corps on the Richmond side of the river. Swinton describes this as "a situation in which, by bringing two-thirds of his own force to bear against one-third of the Union force, he might hope not merely to defeat but to destroy the exposed wing."

The narrative is assumed by Union cavalryman F. Colburn Adams, whose unit was among those making up the three corps farthest from Richmond, on the north bank of the river: "The morning of the 30th [of May] came in hot and sultry . . . and about noon heavy storm clouds rolled up in threatening masses and filled the heavens with darkness. Then a fierce wind howled through the forest and over the camps, spreading alarm everywhere. A fearful storm soon broke upon us in all its fury. Vivid flashes of lightning vaulted along the clouds, filled the heavens with a glare of light, then coursed along our batteries from one end of the line to the other until the scene became one grand and sublime picture. Now the lightning has killed two men in a shelter tent; now a battery has been struck and a gun carriage shattered. . . . Then the thunder crashed and rolled fiercely; the animals started and pricked up their ears at each flash of lightning; and the

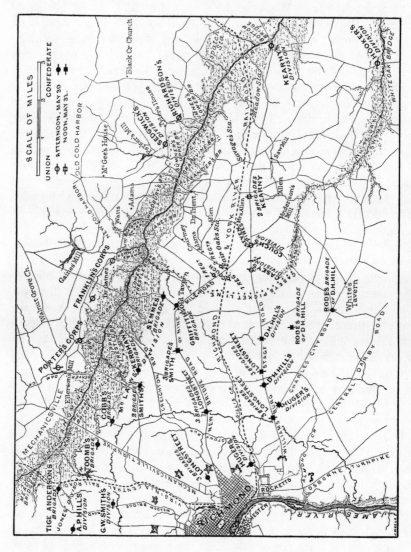

Union and Confederate positions east of Richmond just prior to the Battle
of Fair Oaks, or Seven Pines

roar and violence of the storm increased until the very heavens seemed to be rending asunder. I had witnessed thunder storms in the tropics, but none of them compared with this. A captain of the British army who accompanied General McClellan during the campaign and had been several years in India declared he had seen nothing so violent as this storm.

"When night set in, the rain fell like a deluge . . . accompanied by this violent thunder and lightning. . . . Trees were uprooted, tents blown down, the bridges over the Chickahominy nearly swept away, and the very earth flooded. Never did the prospect look so gloomy for an army. Never did men of stout hearts and iron nerves look with more anxiety, with more changing between hope and fear, to the prospect before them. The enemy could not fail to see his opportunity and take advantage of it. If he could crush our left wing while there was no hope of getting reinforcements over, his victory would give new confidence to his troops and be an advantage from which we should not soon recover."

The Confederates were both encouraged and awed by the storm. "We found it impossible," says South Carolinian Jesse Reid, "to cook anything for supper. I can say for my part that I was wolfishly hungry in consequence. Indeed I could not sleep comfortably with an empty stomach." When the tempest ebbed in the hours before dawn, Reid got up, somehow kindled a fire, and put a pot of dried peas on to cook. "The peas were so black they would have made good ink. About the time they were pretty well done I heard the familiar sound of the long roll beating at General Longstreet's headquarters, and in a few minutes it was beating at the headquarters of the different brigades and regiments. I knew what was up. . . . The sound of galloping hoofs resounded on all sides as couriers dashed away with orders to the different headquarters. . . . In a short time all hands . . . were up and getting on equipments. The order came to be ready to march at daybreak. Everything was in confusion and uproar, but notwithstanding this I ate my peas and felt ready for anything."

The Confederate forces—the divisions of Longstreet, G. W. Smith, D. H. Hill, and Benjamin Huger—were in widespread camps just east of Richmond, from three to six miles from the Federal position they were preparing to attack. The position's front, occupied by Keyes' corps, arced through Fair Oaks and Seven Pines, dots on the landscape about a mile apart. Heintzelman's corps was several miles to the rear. Johnston planned to use the network of roads leading to Keyes' position to launch a coordinated attack on its front and its right flank. The idea was a sound one, but the roads were mired, communications were poor, and there was delay and uncertainty. Coordination failed, and Johnston was unable to exploit his superior power. None of this, however, kept the Battle of Fair Oaks or Seven Pines (as the Confederates preferred to call it) from becoming the greatest battle, thus far, of the war in the East.

Trooper Adams, on the more remote bank of the Chickahominy, rose from his damp bedding to find that "Saturday morning, the 31st, was dull and wet. The storm had ceased, but the roads were flooded, the woods were weeping, and a pale gray mist hung over . . . the long belt of forest on the opposite side of the river. . . . The dark, turbulent waters . . . were rushing and surging through the meadow, filled with wreckwood from the bridges. All eyes were turned instinctively . . . to those woods and fields where our almost isolated left wing stood. By 9 o'clock the fleecy fog began to lift and roll away towards the west, and the houses on the opposite hills took a more distinct and clear outline. At 10 o'clock the mysterious move of a column of the enemy near one of those houses . . . was reported. At fifteen minutes to one o'clock our whole camp was startled by the sudden, crashing sound of infantry and the deep roar of cannon. It seemed as if twenty thousand infantry had discharged simultaneously and repeated in such rapid succession that it were impossible to count the volleys. And this rolling and crashing of infantry and roar of artillery at once indicated the fierceness of the battle that had begun. Then we heard the long roll beating on the opposite hills. 'As I thought,' said General Franklin, who had been nearly washed out of his tent during the night and stood contemplating the scene in front of the door, 'they have attacked us in our weakest point.' In another minute all was bustle and motion at General McClellan's headquarters."

In Richmond, the citizens had known something of Johnston's plans beforehand, and hundreds of men, women, and children had flocked to nearby hills in hopes of getting a glimpse of the battle. Constance Cary Harrison, a teenager, remained in the city but was nonetheless attuned to the situation. "In face of recent reverses, we in Richmond had begun to feel like the prisoner of the Inquisition in Poe's story, cast into a dungeon of slowly contracting walls. With the sound of guns, therefore, in the direction of Seven Pines, every heart leaped as if deliverance were at hand. And yet there was no joy in the wild pulsation, since those to whom we looked for succor were our own flesh and blood, barring the way to a foe of superior numbers, abundantly provided, as we were not, with all the equipments of modern warfare and backed by a mighty nation as determined as ourselves to win. Hardly a family in the town whose father, son, or brother was not part and parcel of the defending army."

Among the residents was the young wife of Colonel John Gordon, commander of the 6th Alabama and one of the leaders of Johnston's attack. Mrs. Gordon was in the company of an elderly uncle, Major John Sutherland Lewis, who was solicitous of her welfare. Lewis relates: "The battle . . . was raging . . . with great fury. The cannonade was rolling around the horizon like some vast earthquake on huge crushing wheels. Whether the threads of wedded sympathy were twisted more closely as the tremendous perils gathered around him, it was evident that her anxiety became more and more intense with each passing moment. She asked me to accompany her to a hill a short distance away. There she listened in silence. Pale and quiet, with clasped hands, she sat statue-like with her face toward the field of battle. Her self-control was wonderful. Only the quick-drawn sigh from the bottom of the heart revealed the depth of emotion that was struggling there."

Tremendous perils had indeed gathered around John Gordon. It was his job to take his Alabamians directly against a section of Union earthworks. "My troops swept over and captured them but at heavy cost. As I spurred my horse over the works with my men, my adjutant, who rode at my side, fell heavily with his horse down the embankment, and both were killed. Reforming my men under a galling fire and ordering them forward in another charge upon the supporting lines, which fought with the most stubborn resistance, disputing every foot of ground, I soon found that Lieutenant Colonel [James J.] Willingham, as gallant a soldier as ever rode through fire and who was my helper on the right, had also been killed and his horse with him. Major Nesmith, whose towering form I could still see on the left, was riding abreast of the men and shouting in trumpet tones, 'Forward men, forward!' But a ball soon silenced his voice forever. . . . I was left alone on horseback, with my men dropping rapidly around me. My soldiers declared that they distinctly heard the command from the Union lines, 'Shoot that man on horseback!' In both armies it was thought that the surest way to demoralize troops was to shoot down the officers."

Jesse Reid's unit—an undermanned battalion—had begun the fight in a similar way. "We marched through a pine thicket along a big road and then through an open field, and right in front of us was a battery of nine cannon, supported by a considerable force of infantry. They were but a few hundred yards in advance of us, and immediately opened fire. Our numbers being so small, we made a flank movement to our left, making for a thick piece of woods that was but a short distance away, as we thought we would be sheltered from the storm of ball and shell which played havoc in our ranks. We were every moment expecting reinforcements. . . . When we had gotten within thirty yards of the woods a large force of the enemy who were hidden in the underbrush raised up as though springing out of the ground, and poured among us the most destructive fire we [had] yet experienced."

Within a matter of minutes, many of the South Carolinians were lying dead or wounded. When the battalion commander himself went down with a wound, someone called out, "Retreat!" There was no response. Again in Reid's words: "My captain, D. L. Hall, and about ten others of my company were all there were left of us. The other companies of the battalion, what was left of them, remained; and we did what shooting we could while laying on the ground amongst our dead and wounded comrades. It was but a short time before the expected reinforcements joined us, when we drove the enemy out of the woods with considerable loss on their side."

Among the troops in the Union lines was the Pennsylvania regiment to which Chaplain Stewart belonged. The opening of the battle found these men in a peculiar position. "No enemy," says Stewart, "appeared in our front, for the reason . . . of an intervening swamp. There we stood . . . listening to that awful rage and din of battle, all the while vexed that we could not see the scene of strife by reason of an intervening wood. At times the earth almost seemed to be tearing open, as ten thousand small arms, with scores of cannon, crashed together and mingled their roar with whizzing bullets, bursting shells, and the shouts and cheers of advancing or retiring columns. Whenever aught especially exciting happened, our whole regiment would send up three grand cheers."

About the time the battle was fully joined, the sky above the Chickahominy became host to a Federal observation balloon. Its suspended "car" was equipped with a field telegraph instrument and was trailing a mile and a half of wire, the far end of which was attached to a ground station. There were two men in the car, master balloonist Thaddeus Lowe and a telegraph operator. This was the beginning of a practice that would be freely employed during the rest of the campaign. The telegrapher explains: "Professor Lowe and myself, with the telegraph . . . reached an altitude of two thousand feet. With the aid of good glasses we were enabled to view the whole affair between these powerful contending armies. As the fight progressed, hasty observations were made by the professor and given to me verbally, all of which I instantly forwarded to General McClellan and division commanders."

At this point McClellan was glad for every shred of information he could get, for his knowledge of the situation was still sketchy. He had learned to his vexation that Heintzelman's corps, stationed several miles behind Keyes and supposed to be rushing aid to the front, was not yet in motion. McClellan was debating the wisdom of trying to send Sumner's corps across the swollen river. According to Trooper Adams: "The only bridges there is any possibility of passing troops over are two built by Sumner, one in front of each of his divisions [their commanders John Sedgwick and Israel B. Richardson]. And the lower one of these, it is reported, cannot be used without serious loss of life. The upper has the appearance of a raft of rough logs, half buried in mud and water, its center forging and surging to the motion of the rapid stream, and only saved from destruction by being fastened and guyed with ropes to the roots and trunks of trees. Such were the slender means of getting reinforcements over—such the frail thread on which hung the fate of the forces engaged in this dreadful struggle with the enemy.

"Two o'clock. The water in the meadows has subsided a little. There is a lull of a few minutes in the battle. The musketry fire is not so rapid and the cannonading at the extreme left has become desultory on our side. Captain

[A. K.] Arnold and myself have stood . . . intently listening to the sound of battle since it commenced, and tracing its changes. He can distinguish the enemy's fire from our own, and his quick, experienced ear tells him that all is not going right . . . with us. He pulls out his watch every few minutes and notes time. 'They have driven us some distance,' he says. 'Unless we get reinforcements over it will go hard with us.' . . .

"The . . . battle . . . has begun again in all its fury. The roll and crash of musketry is even heavier than before, and more incessant; but the cannonading seems to be all on the enemy's side. . . . General Franklin has gone over to General McClellan's headquaraters, where the telegraph is in operation, bringing somewhat confused dispatches from the scene of battle. They bring enough, however, to tell the story that we are being badly cut up over there; that some of our men are fighting with great steadiness and courage but are being pressed back and need help, which Heintzelman does not send. [Keyes' messenger to Heintzelman had traveled with unaccountable slowness, and Heintzelman is only now preparing to respond.] McClellan, Fitz John Porter, and Franklin ride to a point on the bank of the river where they can get but an imperfect view of what is going on in that long belt of woods on the opposite side. 'I must go to Sumner,' says McClellan, and, turning to Franklin, directs him to go to headquarters and take command. In a few minutes more he is plunging through the mud and water, on his way to Sumner. . . . He has not only a fierce and strong enemy to fight, but the elements are all against him.

"At three o'clock, [with] the battle still raging in all its fury, a scene of deep interest might have been witnessed near the log-way approach to Sumner's upper bridge. There stood Sedgwick's division, drawn up in line, ready to cross, in light marching order. A group of officers with serious, thoughtful countenances, and bespattered with mud from head to foot, stand discussing as to whether it is safe to trust the troops on so frail and apparently unsafe a structure. Generals Sumner, Sedgwick, Richardson, and Colonel [Barton S.] Alexander of the engineers, form the prominent figures of the group, which is afterwards joined by General McClellan and a number of his aides. Generals Sumner and Sedgwick are impatient to make the attempt; the engineers are of opinion that the columns cannot cross without serious loss of life. But the fierceness of the battle seems to have suddenly increased, and this hastens a decision. The column is got in motion and moves to the log-way with a quick step as officers of the group watch with breathless anxiety the effect it will have on the loose and swinging structure. Doubt and anxiety soon changes into a feeling of joy. It is found that the weight of the advancing column presses the loose timbers down, fastens them, as it were, to the stumps and mud; and, indeed, increases the strength and solidity of the swinging mass. A half-suppressed cheer now relieves many a heart of its burden. Never before did an army cross a stream under such disheartening circumstances. . . .

"Richardson has made an attempt to cross his division at the lower bridge, but so much has it been damaged by the flood that he has succeeded in getting only a brigade across. He has had to move the other two to the bridge where Sedgwick crossed."

Leading the march of Sedgwick's division was General Willis A. Gorman's brigade. As related by an unnamed private in one of Gorman's regiments, the 15th Massachusetts: "Most of our artillery became so badly mired that we were obliged to proceed without it, but the little battery of 12-pound Napoleon guns, commanded by an energetic regular officer, Lieutenant [Edmund] Kirby, notwithstanding it was continually mired to its axles, was pluckily dragged along by horses and men. Despite the mire, we cracked jokes at each other, shouted and sang in high spirits, and toiled through the morass in the direction of the heavy firing. About 3:30 P.M. we began to meet stragglers from the front. They all told in substance the same story: 'Our companies and regiments are all cut to pieces!' "

These stragglers were members of Silas Casey's division, which had formed the forefront of Keyes' defense. The division had been driven back and its camps were in Confederate hands. Says Southerner Jesse Reid: "We got a good many cannon and small arms. . . . We took between five hundred and one thousand prisoners. . . . We got a great many provisions of all kinds . . . bacon, flour, sugar, coffee (already ground and sweetened), and almost every other kind of dainty, besides several barrels of whiskey, one of which had a bullet hole in it, from which several of the men filled their canteens. My old friend, J. J. Pitts, when he had gotten himself and his canteen both full, thought himself as rich as John Jacob Astor. Among other things I got . . . was a hat—new for me, but somewhat frazzled by its original owner."

Few of the Confederates could take more than a moment or two to enjoy the spoils, for the fighting continued heavy and brutal. Says John Gordon: "Nearly or quite half the line officers of [my] twelve companies had by this time fallen dead or wounded. . . . Still I had marvellously escaped, with only my clothing pierced. As I rode up and down my line, encouraging the men forward, I passed my young brother, only nineteen years old but captain of one of the companies. He was lying with a number of dead companions near him. He had been shot through the lungs and was bleeding profusely. I did not stop; I could not stop; nor would he permit me to stop. There was no time for that, no time for anything except to move on and fire on. At this time my own horse, the only one left, was killed. He could, however, have been of little service to me any longer, for in the edge of this flooded swamp heavy timber had been felled, making an abatis quite impassable on horseback, and I should have been compelled to dismount.

"McClellan's men were slowly being pressed back into and through the Chickahominy swamp, which was filled with water, but at almost every

Kirby's battery on the way to the battlefield

step they were pouring terrific volleys into my lines. My regiment had been in some way separated from the brigade, and at this juncture seemed to reach the climax of extremities. My field officers and adjutant were all dead. Every horse ridden into the fight . . . was dead. Fully one-half of my line officers and half my men were dead or wounded. A furious fire still poured from the front, and reinforcements were nowhere in sight. . . .

"In water from knee- to hip-deep, the men were fighting and falling, while a detail propped up the wounded against stumps or trees to prevent their drowning. Fresh troops in blue were moving to my right flank and pouring a raking fire down my line and compelling me to change front with my companies there. In ordering Captain [Thomas H.] Bell, whom I had placed in command of that portion of my line, I directed that he should beat back that flanking force at any cost. This faithful officer took in at a glance the whole situation, and, with a courage that never was and never will be surpassed, he and his Spartan band fought until he and nearly all his men were killed; and the small remnant . . . were fighting still when the order came at last for me to withdraw. Even in the withdrawal there was no confusion, no precipitancy. Slowly moving back, carrying their wounded comrades with them and firing as they moved, these shattered remnants . . . took their place in line with the brigade. The losses were appalling. . . . Of forty-four officers of the line, but thirteen were left for duty. Nearly two-thirds of the entire command were killed or wounded. My young brother . . . was carried back with the wounded." (The youth would make a complete recovery, only to die of an almost identical wound later in the war.)

It was now about 4 P.M. In spite of some setbacks, the Confederates were exerting heavy pressure on the second Federal defense line, which was manned by General Darius Couch and his division. It was during this part of the fight that Chaplain Stewart and his fellow Pennsylvanians were called from their safe spot behind the swamp and sent into action. "Away went the boys with a shout; yet into what a fearful place were they so quickly hurried! By this time the enemy, in overwhelming numbers, were pressing back our confronting column, seizing our batteries, all the horses of which were killed, while a number of our regiments were in very serious disorder. Our object was to hold the enemy in check. . . . A scene of horrid carnage immediately ensued. To fall back soon became a necessity, else either all be killed or taken prisoners. This was accomplished without haste or serious disorder. In doing so, the saddest thing to me was the seeming necessity of leaving our dead on the bloody field, to be trodden by an insulting foe; and some of those dead were my dearest, best young Christian friends. . . . Sad and melancholy yet precious would have been to me the privilege of assisting to bury, with befitting ceremony, those dear mangled bodies. But no matter into what ditch an insulting foe may cast them, they belong to Christ. . . . I was the last one of our regiment to retire from the scene of carnage; and, so far as could be discovered, none of our wounded were left on the field—though the smoke and horrid rage of cannon and musketry, the shouts and groans, with the strange, unearthly music of a thousand passing missiles of death, may have prevented the discovery of some poor fellow, who would thus fall living into the tender mercies of the rebels."

The Federal reinforcements were at last beginning to reach the field. First came elements of Phil Kearny's division of Heintzelman's corps, who rushed in to bolster the diminished left. Then Gorman's brigade of Sumner's corps arrived on the right, just in time to help counter the advance of a fresh Confederate division, that of G. W. Smith, urged on by Joe Johnston in person. According to the unnamed Union private in Gorman's brigade: "As we came up through a stumpy field we were greeted with the quick *crack*, *crack* of the infantry in our front. The smoke of battle hung in clouds over the field, and through it could be seen the flashes of the artillery. The *ping*, *zip*, *zip* of bullets, and the wounded men limping from the front or carried by comrades were a prelude to the storm to come. We formed on the left of [General John J.] Abercrombie's shattered brigade . . . and were welcomed with hearty cheers. Presently there was a terrible explosion of musketry, and the bullets pattered around us, causing many to drop. A line of smoke ahead showed us where this destructive fire came from. Kirby's five Napoleon guns came up, and in the angle of the woods opened with splendid precision upon the Confederate columns. The recoil of the pieces was often so great as to bury the wheels nearly to the hub in mud.

"Soon the 'rebel yell' was heard as they charged on the right of Kirby's battery, which changed front to the right and delivered a destructive fire of canister. This caused the enemy to break in confusion and retreat to the cover of the woods. Shortly afterward the enemy developed a greater force in our front, and the hum of shot and shell was almost incessant; but in a few minutes the fire slackened and the Confederate lines came dashing upon us with their shrill yells. We received them with a volley from our rifles, and the battery gave them its compliments. The gray masses of the enemy were seen dimly through the smoke, scattering to cover. Presently the order ran down the line, 'Fix bayonets!' While waiting the moment for the final order, John Milan said, 'It's light infantry we are, boys, and they expect us to fly over them crisscross fences.' Then the final order came, 'Guide right— Double-quick— Charge!' Our whole line went off at double-quick, shouting as we ran. Some scattering shots were fired by the enemy as we struggled over the fences, and then their line broke and dissolved from view."

During the late afternoon and early evening, according to a Union newsman writing for the Cincinnati *Commercial*, "the battle raged . . . with unremitting fury. The rebels found it impossible to break our inflexible lines, and we found it difficult to shake them off. . . . The [Federal] officers were all in their places, animating and encouraging the men by their example. . . . The men were delivering their fire with admirable coolness and regularity. . . . The enemy, too, fought rapidly and well. . . . The sun . . . set grimly, flinging his last rays feebly through the thick smoke which hovered over field and forest."

Joe Johnston, who had begun to realize that his grand plan was failing, now became a casualty. "About seven o'clock I received a slight wound in the right shoulder from a musket shot, and, a few moments after, was unhorsed by a heavy fragment of shell which struck my breast. Those around had me borne from the field in an ambulance; not, however, before the President, who was with General Lee not far in the rear, had heard of the accident and visited me, manifesting great concern." Johnston's breast wound was serious; some ribs were broken and a lung damaged. But he had been wounded several times during his long prewar career in the Federal service, and was therefore somewhat accustomed to shocks like this. While in the ambulance he discovered that his sword was missing, and he exclaimed to an attendant, "I would not lose my sword for ten thousand dollars! My father wore it in the War of the Revolution." The valued item was retrieved.

Meanwhile, the battle continued. Again in the words of the Union newsman: "Darkness . . . enveloped the fearful spectacle, only to add gloom to its horrors. The enemy still clung in masses to the thick woods, now and then dashing out at a battery, only to be driven back with cruel punishment. Thousands of muskets in streaming volleys, with the sonorous roar of cannon and the hoarse screams of the combatants, created an uproar as if fiends had been unleashed to prey upon each other. Storms of bullets and canister tore wide passages through the trees and mangled the bodies of men. . . . There was a fringe of flame blazing on the skirts of the thickets. . . . It was past eight o'clock before the carnage ceased." McClellan was now on the field, and his presence gave the troops a timely boost in morale.

In the Confederate lines, as the blesssed quiet descended and campfires were kindled and lanterns lighted, a correspondent representing the Richmond *Dispatch* took a look around. "What pen can describe the scene presented on every side? Friend and foe scattered far and wide in death or in last agonies. Here and there are deserted [Federal] camps; dead and dying fill the tents. Horses wounded and lame rush to and fro. Here are artillerymen, some Federals, some Confederate, wounded or dead, within a few feet of each other. Every wound known to the human body is seen in ghastly reality. All [of the wounded] crave water, and, crawling through the mud, lap the bloodstained and slimy flood. Some curse, some moan and turn their eyes toward heaven sadly. Rebels hand around water to their late foes, and eyes glisten in thankfullness. Squads of prisoners are seen issuing from the woods in divers places, and scowl upon their captors ominously, while others whistle and joke along the road as if infinitely gratified at being captured [rather than having been killed]. Here comes a stalwart Alabamian, left hand shattered and in a sling, carrying off triumphantly the colors of the 5th Pennsylvania Volunteers, keeping a watchful eye on the standard bearer at his side. . . . Our wounded truly are very numerous, but they trudge along quite philosophically."

One of the field hospitals for the Federal wounded was established at Savage's Station, less than two miles behind the lines. Chaplain J. J. Marks was on the scene. "During the entire night the wounded were brought in, until they covered the grounds around the house of Mr. Savage, and filled all the outhouses, barns, and sheds. Lying alongside of our wounded were many Confederate soldiers and officers. . . . The rebels were uniformly treated as kindly as the Union soldiers. All night the surgeons were occupied in amputations; and . . . they found it impossible to look after those whose condition demanded immediately, to revive them, food and stimulants. Wounded men suffer greatly from cold, and shiver as in winter, or with an ague. It was therefore essential to lift them from the damp ground and cover them as far as possible. In the course of the evening twenty or thirty soldiers from different regiments, who had borne in upon their shoulders their wounded comrades, permitted me to organize them into a corps of nurses. Colonel [Samuel] McKelvy, than whom no man was more active for the relief of our men, furnished twenty bales of hay, a thousand blankets, and permitted me to draw on the Commissary Department for coffee, sugar, and crackers to an indefinite amount. The nurse-soldiers soon spread down this hay, and many a shivering, wounded man, when lifted from the damp earth and placed upon the soft grass bed with a blanket spread over him, poured out his gratitude in a thousand blessings. When this was done we followed with hot coffee, and found our way to every suffering man. Everywhere we were compelled to place our feet in streams of blood. One spectacle of anguish and agony only succeeded another. The mind was overwhelmed and benumbed by such scenes of accumulated misery. . . . Great must be the cause which demands such a sacrifice.

"Here and there over the grounds were seen through that night a circle of lanterns waving around the tables of amputators. Every few moments there was a shriek of some poor fellow under the knife. And one after another the sufferers were brought forward and laid down before the surgeons on stretchers, each waiting his turn. And then again one with face as white as marble and every line telling that he had passed through a suffering the utmost which human nature could endure, was borne away and laid down for some kindhearted man to pour into his lips a few drops of brandy . . . and give him the assurance of life and sympathy. There a brother knelt and wept over a dying brother. . . . There a father held up in his arms a dying son and was receiving his last message to mother, sister, and brother. Here a group of sympathizing soldiers stood around a dying companion who was loudly bewailing his early death, and that he should never again see his native hills. There four or five holding in their strong arms one whose brain,

238

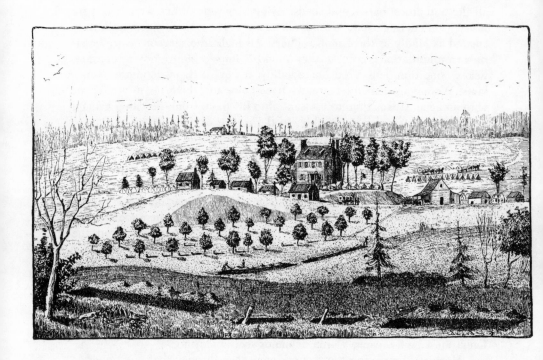

Savage's Station as a Federal hospital complex; burial trenches in foreground

having been pierced with a ball and deprived of reason, was strong in the frantic energy of madness. Here a beckoning hand urged me to come and . . . sit down by [a sufferer's] side and tell him what he must do to be saved. . . . Another begged me to come early in the morning and write a line to father or wife. Others entreated that they should not be compelled to submit to the knife of the operator but that their limbs might be spared them. . . . Others begged that some board might bear their names and be placed at the head of their graves. . . .

"At one place where a wounded soldier was panting his last I was summoned. He begged me to pray for him, and, taking from his finger a gold ring, he asked me to send it to his wife, who had given it him on the day of their marriage. . . . In a few minutes the last battle was fought, and the soldier was asleep. . . . In another group of sufferers I found a little boy apparently not more than twelve years of age. The long hair thrown back from a beautiful forehead enabled me to see by the lantern light a very childlike face. His right leg had been amputated above his knee, and he was lying motionless and apparently breathless, and as white as snow. I bent over him and put my fingers on his wrist, and discovered to my surprise a faint trembling of a pulse. I immediately said to my attendant, 'Why, this child is alive!' 'Yes, sir,' said he, opening his eyes, 'I am alive. Will you not send me to my mother?' 'And where is your mother,' said I, 'my child?' 'In Sumterville, South Carolina,' he replied. 'Oh, yes, my son! We will certainly send you to your mother.' 'Well, well,' said he, 'that is kind. I will go to sleep now.'

"Sabbath, June 1st. It was understood that the battle would be renewed this morning; and with the first dawn of the day I saw Generals Keyes and Heintzelman leave the headquarters of the latter at Savage's Station. They rode, surrounded by their aides, across the field leading to the Williamsburg Road [which coursed toward Richmond]. I had heard during the night that a hospital had been created about a mile from the Station towards the battlefield. I started to find it, and in a short time reached the house, in and around which were lying a multitude of our dying and wounded. . . . Ambulances were here removing the disabled to Savage's Station. Mingled with the great number of wounded were many dead, who, having been brought in, did not survive the night. . . .

"Our men were in line of battle about one hundred yards in advance of this house, in the edge of the forest. It was now about seven A.M. The firing was very brisk and steady all along our front lines, but having none of the regularity and continuous roar of battle, but lively skirmishing. While I was aiding the wounded into the ambulances, I heard loud shouts to our right, and turned to look for the cause. I saw coming out though the forest . . . a large body of our troops. This was General Sumner's corps, which had crossed the Chickahominy on the previous evening and reached the right of our wing in season to prevent our right flank being turned, and consequent defeat; and now, with the true instinct of a loyal and brave commander, he was bringing his men to the scene of the greatest danger. I felt certain, when I saw this magnificent corps move along with the steady step of veterans that the day was ours. As regiment after regiment passed . . . with waving banners and music, they were hailed and cheered with the loudest shouts. They turned up the Williamburg Road, and were immediately followed by General Heintzelman and his corps.

"For a few moments there was the ominous calm which often precedes battle. Taking advantage of this, I ran up along the Williamsburg Road in pursuit of the army, and in a few moments reached our breastworks, which extended along our entire front from the Chickahominy to the White Oak Swamp. Our batteries were in position, and on the breastworks themselves were planted many fieldpieces. Within the entrenchments was a long line of men, as far as the eye could reach, every man bending on his knee and resting his gun on the embankment, silent and motionless, intently looking for the enemy. The gunners stood around the cannon, equally alert and watchful. In front of this line of entrenchments were open fields extending two miles on each side of the road. The open ground in front of us was probably about one-fourth of a mile wide, and then again was interrupted by forests. On the opposite side of this field the enemy was posted under the covert of the woods. . . .

"I saw the troops of General Sumner's corps, and those of General Heintzelman under General Hooker, march into the field, deploying to the right and left; and with a steady quick step they commenced advancing on the enemy. Before they reached the center of the field their march became double-quick. Continually firing as they ran, they dashed forward on the enemy. Occasionally I could see a gap in our lines . . . but in a moment this was not perceptible and the men were marching on as brisk as ever. Very soon our troops reached the edge of the forest, and I trembled in apprehension of the sanguinary contest; but nothing could resist the energy and determination of our soldiers. The struggle was but for a moment, and the tide of battle rolled into the forest and our front line was lost to view, except an occasional gleam of arms that came out from the openings amongst the trees. Then the din and the clash and the roar went up into the heavens more distinctly from the field beyond. By climbing into the trees we could see the enemy pushed back . . . and gradually the rattle of musketry ceased. We heard only the cannon firing on the retreating foe."

The Federals had not really secured a victory; they had merely regained most of the ground they had lost the previous day. But the Confederates had had enough. They withdrew to their lines around Richmond. Within the city itself, according to Constance Cary Harrison, the day was one of horror and sadness. "Ambulances, litters, carts, every vehicle that the city could produce, went and came with a ghastly burden. Those who could walk limped painfully home, in some cases so black with gunpowder they passed

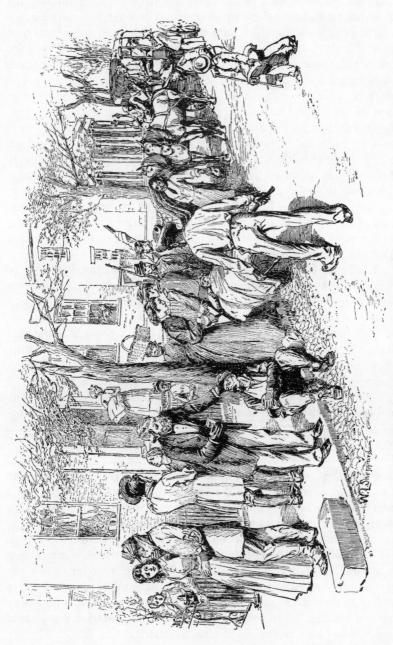

Confederate casualties from Fair Oaks in the streets of Richmond

unrecognized. Women with pallid faces flitted bareheaded through the streets searching for their dead or wounded. The churches were thrown open, many people visiting them for a sad communion service or brief time of prayer. The lecture rooms of various places of worship were crowded with ladies volunteering to sew, as fast as fingers could fly, the rough beds [i.e., pads] called for by the surgeons. Men too old or infirm to fight went on horseback or afoot to meet the returning ambulances, and in some cases served as escort to their own dying sons. . . .

"To find shelter for the sufferers, a number of unused buildings were thrown open. I remember, especially, the St. Charles Hotel, a gloomy place, where two young girls [the narrator and a relative] went to look for a member of their family, reported wounded. We had tramped in vain over pavements burning with the intensity of the sun, from one scene of horror to another, until our feet and brains alike seemed about to serve us no further. The cool of those vast dreary rooms of the St. Charles was refreshing. But such a spectacle! Men in every stage of mutilation lying on the bare boards, with perhaps a haversack or an army blanket beneath their heads—some dying, all suffering keenly, while waiting their turn to be attended to. To be there empty-handed and impotent nearly broke our hearts. We passed from one to the other, making such slight additions to their comfort as were possible, while looking in every upturned face in dread to find the object of our search. This sorrow, I may add, was spared, the youth arriving at home later with a slight flesh wound. The condition of things at this and other improvised hospitals was improved . . . by the offerings from many churches of pew cushions, which, sewn together, served as comfortable beds. . . . To supply food for the hospitals, the contents of larders all over town were emptied into baskets; while [wine] cellars long sealed and cobwebbed, belonging to the old Virginia gentry who knew good Port and Madeira, were opened. . . .

"There was not much going to bed that [first] night. . . . I remembered spending the greater part of it leaning from my window to seek the cool night air, while wondering as to the fate of those near me. There was a summons to my mother about midnight. Two soldiers came to tell her of the wounding of one close of kin; but she was . . . on duty elsewhere. . . . Up to that time the younger girls had been regarded as superfluities in hospital service; but on Monday two of us found a couple of rooms where fifteen wounded men lay upon pallets around the floor, and, on offering our services to the surgeons in charge, were proud to have them accepted and to be installed as responsible nurses under the direction of an older and more experienced woman. The constant activity our work entailed was a relief from the strained excitement of life after the battle."

Fair Oaks had cost the Confederates 6,134 casualties, the Federals 5,031. The tragedy of this extravagant bloodshed was heightened by the fact that it accomplished nothing; the fight was a drawn one. It did, however, in-

Food for the Confederate wounded

clude one occurrence of great moment: the wounding of Joe Johnston. When the general reached Richmond on his stretcher, an elderly man of classic Virginia lineage came to him and said, "Not only do we deplore this cruel affliction upon you, but we feel it to be a national calamity." Johnston raised himself on the elbow of his good arm and responded firmly, "No, sir! The shot that struck me down was the best ever fired for the Southern Confederacy, for I possessed in no degree the confidence of this government, and now a man who does enjoy it will succeed me and be able to accomplish what I never could."

Jefferson Davis gave Robert E. Lee verbal authority to assume command of the army almost as soon as Johnston was wounded. In the words of Fitzhugh Lee, the general's nephew and one of his cavalry officers: "At last, one year after the commencement of the war, Robert E. Lee was in active command of a large army in the field. His task was difficult, his responsibility great. The opposing hosts were thundering at the city's gates. . . . Upon his shoulders rested the safety of his capital. With quiet dignity he assumed his duties."

As for McClellan, he was presently in a confident mood. To Ellen he wrote: "I only regret that the rascals were smart enough to attack when the condition of the Chickahominy was such that I could not throw over the rest of the troops." He published the following address: "Soldiers of the Army of the Potomac! I have fullfilled at least a part of my promise to you. You are now face to face with the rebels, who are held at bay in front of their capital. The final and decisive battle is at hand. Unless you belie your past history, the result cannot be for a moment doubtful. If the troops who labored so faithfully and fought so gallantly at Yorktown, and who so bravely won the hard fights of Williamsburg, West Point, Hanover Court House, and Fair Oaks, now prove worthy of their antecedents, the victory is surely ours. The events of every day prove your superiority. Wherever you have met the enemy you have beaten him. Wherever you have used the bayonet he has given way in panic and disorder. I ask of you now one last crowning effort. The enemy has staked his all on this issue of the coming battle. Let us meet and crush him here in the very center of the rebellion. Soldiers, I will be with you in this battle and share its dangers with you. Our confidence in each other is now founded upon the past. Let us strike the blow which is to restore peace and union to this distracted land. Upon your valor, discipline, and mutual confidence that result depends."

McClellan wrote Stanton: "I only wait for the river to fall to cross with the rest of the force and make a general attack. Should I find them holding firm in a very strong position, I may wait for what troops I can bring up from Fortress Monroe. [Lincoln had just placed the fort's garrison, some 5,500 men, under McClellan's command.] But the morale of my troops is such that I can venture much. I do not fear for odds against me."

10

---❖---

DENOUEMENT IN THE VALLEY

STONEWALL JACKSON'S army—presently mumbering about 15,000 effectives, had come upon precarious times. The army was demonstrating against Harpers Ferry on the morning of May 30 when Jackson learned he was about to be cut off by a pincer movement in the Strasburg–Front Royal area, forty miles to his rear. Frémont, coming from western Virginia, was only twenty miles from the westerly town of Strasburg; and, worse yet, James Shields of McDowell's corps had already occupied Front Royal, ten miles southeast of Strasburg, driving out the small garrison Jackson had left there during his charge toward the Potomac. The two Federal armies were only thirty miles apart. Their combined strength was 25,000 men, and 10,000 more of McDowell's men were on their way to reinforce Shields. Frémont and Shields, however, were each uncertain of the other's situation, and of Jackson's, and they now began to move hesitatingly. This, of course, worked to Jackson's advantage, particularly since his troops had become so adept at making forced marches they had dubbed themselves "Jackson's foot cavalry." By the afternoon of May 30 the army was in full swing toward the pike that led through Winchester to Strasburg.

Jackson, as usual, kept his plans to himself; and, also as usual, this frustrated many of his officers. A young lieutenant of cavalry came riding up to the general and asked. "Sir, are the troops going back?" Jackson replied, "Don't you see them going?" The other persisted, "Yes, but are they all going?" Jackson scowled and snapped to one of his aides, "Arrest that man as a spy!" Senior cavalry commander Turner Ashby came riding up and urged Jackson to forgive the lieutenant, since he hadn't much sense, and Jackson relented.

According to an officer named John G. Gittings, the march was not without its lighter moments. "As our troops debouched from a narrow crossroad into the turnpike, we saw a carriage drawn up by the wayside, in which were seated an elderly gentleman and three young ladies. As we rode by, the old gentleman halted us and inquired anxiously for General Jackson. It at first occurred to us that he had news of importance to communicate to the general, but the young ladies soon made it apparent that their only object in being there was to look upon this now famous officer, whom they had never seen. They paid little heed to any other officer or soldier of the passing column. The old man 'only wanted to see Jackson once before he died,' and the young ladies were 'just crazy to see him!' Soon thereafter, a post quartermaster rode by. His bright uniform presented a striking contrast to the dust-begrimed regimentals of the officers of the column; and the young ladies were sure this fine-looking soldier must be the great Stonewall, the hero of their imaginations. Finally, when General Jackson did appear on the scene, it was difficult to make these ladies believe that the travel-stained horseman, with his faded cap drawn low over his sunburned, bearded face, was the famous Stonewall whose name had wrought so great a spell in that valley."

The main body of the army reached Strasburg on the evening of May 31. In the words of General Dick Taylor: "Jackson sat some time at my campfire that night, and was more communicative than I remember him before or after. He said Frémont, with a large force, was three miles west of our present camp and must be defeated in the morning. . . . The importance of preserving the immense trains, filled with captured stores, was great, and would engage much of his personal attention; while he relied on the army, under Ewell's direction, to deal promptly with Frémont. This he told in a low, gentle voice, and with many interruptions to afford time, as I thought and believe, for inward prayer. The men said that his anxiety about the wagons was because of the lemons among the stores.

"Dawn of the following day . . . was ushered in by the sound of Frémont's guns. Our lines had been early drawn out to meet him. . . . Much cannonading, with some rattle of small arms, ensued. The country was densely wooded, and little save the smoke from the enemy's guns could be seen. My brigade was in reserve a short distance to the rear and out of the line of fire; and here a ludicrous incident occurred. Many slaves from Louisiana had accompanied their masters to the war. . . . They were now, some scores, assembled under a large tree, laughing, chattering, and cooking breakfast. On a sudden, a shell burst in the treetop, rattling down leaves and branches in fine style, and the rapid decampment of the servitors was most amusing.

"But I must pause to give an account of my own servant, Tom Strother, who deserves honorable and affectionate mention at my hands. . . . My paternal grandmother was Miss Sarah Strother of Virginia, and from her estate came [the] Strother Negroes. Tom, three years my Senior, was my foster brother and early playmate. His uncle, Charles Porter Strother . . . had been body servant to my grandfather, Colonel Richard Taylor, whom he attended in his last illness. He then filled the same office to my father [Zachary Taylor], following him through his Indian and Mexican campaigns. . . . Tom served in Florida and Mexico as 'aide de camp' to his uncle, after which he married and became father of a large family. On this account I hesitated to bring him to Virginia, but he would come, and was a model servant. Tall, powerful, black as ebony, he was a mirror of truth and honesty. Always cheerful, I never heard him laugh or know of his speaking unless spoken to. He could light a fire in a minute under the most unfavorable conditions and with the most unpromising material, made the best coffee to be tasted outside of a Creole kitchen, was a 'dab' at camp stews and roasts, groomed my horses (one of which he rode near me), washed my linen, and was never behind time. Occasionally, when camped near a house, he would obtain starch and flatirons and get up my extra shirt in a way to excite the envy of a professional clear-starcher; but such red-letter days were few.

"I used to fancy that there was a mute sympathy between General Jackson and Tom as they sat silent by a campfire, the latter respectfully withdrawn; and an incident here at Strasburg cemented this friendship. When my command was called into action, I left Tom on a hill where all was quiet. Thereafter, from a change in the enemy's dispositions, the place became rather hot; and Jackson, passing by, advised Tom to move; but he replied, if the General pleased, his master told him to stay there and would know where to find him, and he did not believe the shells would trouble him. Two or three nights later, Jackson was at my fire when Tom came to give me some coffee; whereupon Jackson rose and gravely shook him by the hand. . . .

"To return [to the skirmish with Frémont]. Cannonading continued without much effect, and Ewell summoned me to his presence. . . . Jackson, busy with his trains, was not at the moment on the field. . . . To reach Ewell, it was necessary to pass under some heavy shelling, and I found myself open to the reproach visited previously on my men. Whether from fatigue, loss of sleep, or what—there I was, nervous as a lady, ducking like a mandarin. It was disgusting. . . . I reached Ewell, and told him I was no more good than a frightened deer. He laughed and replied, 'Nonsense! 'Tis Tom's strong coffee. Better give it up. Remain here in charge while I go out to the skirmishers. I can't make out what these people are about, for my skirmish line has stopped them. They won't advance, but stay out there in the wood, making a great fuss with their guns; and I do not wish to commit myself to much advance while Jackson is absent.' With this, he put spurs to his horse and was off, and soon a brisk fusillade was heard, which seemed gradually to recede. During Ewell's absence, surrounded by his staff, I contrived to sit my horse quietly. Returning, he said, 'I am completely puzzled. I have just driven everything back to the main body, which is large. Dense wood everywhere. Jackson told me not to commit myself too far. At this rate, my attentions are not likely to become serious enough to commit anyone. I wish Jackson was here himself.' I suggested that my brigade might be moved to the extreme right, near the Capon road, by which Frémont had marched, and attempt to strike that road, as this would enable us to find out something. He replied, 'Do so. That may stir them up. . . . I am sick of this fiddling about.' Had Ewell been in command, he would have 'pitched in' long before; but he was controlled by instructions not to be drawn too far from the pike.

"We found the right of our line held by a Mississippi regiment, the colonel of which told me that he had advanced just before and driven the enemy. Several of his men were wounded, and he was bleeding profusely from a hit in his leg, which he was engaged in binding with a handkerchief. . . . The brigade moved forward until the enemy was reached. . . . Sheep would have made as much resistance as we met. . . . Our whole skirmish line was advancing briskly as the Federals retired. I sought Ewell and reported. We had a fine game before us, and the temptation to play it was great; but Jackson's orders were imperative and wise. He had his stores to save, Shields to guard against, Lee's grand strategy to promote. . . . He could not waste time chasing Frémont. But we, who looked from a lower standpoint, grumbled and shared the men's opinion about the *lemon wagons*."

Chief of Staff Robert Dabney says that "General Jackson now resumed a deliberate retreat, with his rear covered by his cavalry; seeking some position in the interior where he could confront his foes without danger to his flanks. . . . The object immediately demanding his attention was the rescue of his army from its perilous situation. . . . He was aware that Shields had been for nearly two days at Front Royal. The fact that he had not attempted an immediate junction with Frémont suggested the suspicion that he was moving for a point farther [to the south] . . . by way of Luray and New Market Gap. To frustrate this design, General Jackson now sent a detachment of cavalry to burn the White House Bridge across the South Shenandoah, by which the Luray turnpike passed the stream, and also the Columbia Bridge, a few miles [farther on]. He knew that Shields had no pontoon train . . . and the rivers were still too much swollen to be forded. Having taken this precaution, he retreated [southward along] the Valley turnpike in his usual stubborn and deliberate fashion, with his cavalry and [a] light battery in the rear. . . .

"General Frémont, having ascertained that the Confederates were withdrawing, pursued with spirit. . . . On the 2nd of June the enemy succeeded in taking position where their artillery was able to cannonade the

Confederate rear. The cavalry was thrown into disorder by the shells, and fled, carrying a part of its supporting battery with them. The Federal cavalry now pushed forward to reap the fruits of this success, when Ashby displayed that prompt resource and personal daring which illustrated his character. Dismounting from his horse, he collected a small body of riflemen . . . and posted them in a wood near the roadside. Awaiting the near approach of the enemy, he poured into their ranks so effective a fire that a number of saddles were emptied and a part of the survivors retired in confusion. The remainder . . . broke through the ranks of the rear regiment in a brigade of infantry . . . commanded . . . by Colonel J. M. Patton. . . . That officer . . . gave them a volley which terminated their audacity. Only one of the party returned alive to his comrades, the remainder being all killed or captured.

"Colonel Patton, while reporting the events of the day to the General at nightfall, remarked that he saw this party of foes shot down with regret. . . . After the official conversation was ended, [Jackson] asked, 'Colonel, why do you say that you saw those Federal soldiers fall with regret?' It was replied that they exhibited . . . vigor and courage . . . and that a natural sympathy with brave men led to the wish that . . . their lives might have been saved. The General drily remarked, 'No; shoot them all. *I* do not wish them to be brave.' It was thus that he . . . meant to . . . show that such sentiments of chivalrous forbearance, though amiable, are erroneous. Courage in the prosecution of a wicked attempt does not relieve, but only aggravates, the danger to the innocent party assailed and the guilt of the assailants. . . .

"On the 3rd of June, the Confederate army placed the north fork of the Shenandoah behind it, and General Ashby was entrusted with the duty of burning the bridge by which it passed over. Before this task was completed, the Federalists appeared on the opposite bank, and a skirmish ensued in which his horse was struck dead and he himself very narrowly escaped. The necessity of replacing this bridge arrested Frémont for a day, and gave the tired Confederates a respite, which they employed in retiring slowly and unmolested to Harrisonburg. A mile south of that village General Jackson left the Valley road and turned eastward towards Port Republic, a smaller place upon the south fork of the Shenandoah and near the western base of the Blue Ridge. It was not until the evening of June 6 that [Frémont's] advance overtook his rear guard, which was still within two miles of Harrisonburg, posted at the crest of a wooded ridge commanding the neighboring fields. General Ashby, as usual, held the rear; and the division of General Ewell was next.

"In part of the Federal army was a New Jersey regiment of cavalry commanded by one of those military adventurers whose appetite for blood presents so monstrous and loathsome a parody upon the virtues of the true soldier. A subject of the British Crown and boasting of his relationship to some noble English house, this person had offered his services to the Federal Government, siding with the criminal and powerful aggressors against the heroic and righteous Patriots. . . . It had been his blustering boast that at the first opportunity he would deal with the terrible . . . Ashby. . . . His opportunity was now come. He advanced his regiment to the attack, when General Ashby, taking a few companies of his command, met them in the open field, and at the first charge routed them and captured their colonel with sixty-three of his men. The remainder fled into Harrisonburg in headlong panic. . . .

"The sound of the firing now brought General Ewell to the rear; and General Ashby, assuring him that the Federal attack would be speedily renewed in force, asked for a small body of infantry and proposed a plan . . . for turning their onset into a defeat. General Ewell entrusted to him the 1st Maryland Regiment . . . and the 58th Virginia. . . . Ashby disposed the Marylanders in the woods so as to take the Federal advance in flank, while he met them in front at the head of the 58th. . . . The enemy's infantry advanced, and a fierce combat began. They, approaching through the open fields, had reached a heavy fence of timber; whence, under the partial cover, they poured destructive volleys into the ranks of the 58th. . . . Ashby, seeing at a glance their disadvantage, galloped to the front and ordered them to charge and drive the Federals from their vantage ground. At this moment his horse fell; but, extricating himself from the dying animal and leaping to this feet, he saw his men wavering. He shouted, 'Charge, men! For God's sake, charge!' and waved his sword—when a bullet pierced him full in the breast and he fell dead. The regiment took up the command . . . and rushed upon the enemy, while the Marylanders dashed upon their flank. Thus pressed, the Federals gave way. The Confederates . . . poured successive volleys into the fleeing mass. . . . If blood . . . could have paid for that of the generous Ashby, he would have been fully avenged. . . .

"With this repulse, the combat ceased, resulting in a loss to the Confederates of seventeen killed and fifty wounded. . . . The place where it occurred was not the one selected by General Jackson to stand the brunt of a general action, and it was therefore necessary to remove the wounded and the dead at once. The oversight of this humane task he entrusted to General Ewell. All the wounded who could bear a hasty removal were set on horses and carried to a place of safety. A few remained whose hurts were too painful to endure the motion; and of these General Ewell was seen taking a tender leave, replenishing their purses from his own that they might be able to purchase things needful of their comfort in captivity, and encouraging them with words of good cheer." Turner Ashby's "glorious remains" were borne away for a special burial.

The main body of the army was soon assembled at Port Republic. Jackson was now where he wanted to be in order to offer battle both to Frémont

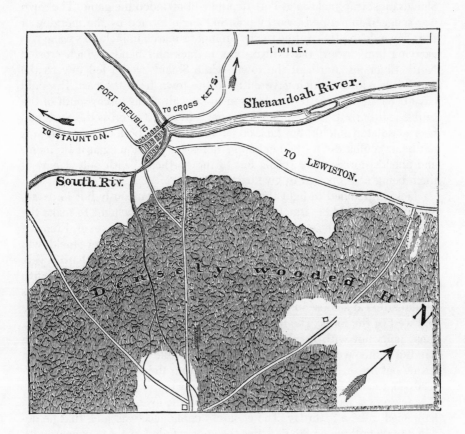

The river junction at Port Republic

and Shields, who were still separated by the northerly flowing Shenandoah, thanks to Jackson's destruction of another bridge, that at Conrad's Store, a dozen miles northeast of Port Republic. There was a bridge and a set of fords at Port Republic itself, and these offered the Federal columns their first accommodations for a junction after Conrad's Store. Frémont and Shields must trap Jackson at Port Republic or abandon the game. The town was snugged into an eastwardly pointing angle formed by the merging of the Shenandoah's two source rivers. Frémont's march in Jackson's wake was carrying him toward the bridge, now in Jackson's hands, which crossed North River just north of the town, while Shields' route led toward the South River fords, which gave entry to the town from the east. It would have been an easy matter for Jackson to take all of his forces south of the bridge and burn it, thus eluding Frémont, afterward to cross the fords and face an isolated Shields. But Jackson intended to fight both columns. He was not being foolhardy, for he held a fine defensive position against Frémont; and Shields' forces were strung out to the northeast, with only a part of them being near enough to give battle.

Jackson planned to fight the columns not simultaneously but in detail. Shields' van would be attacked first, since its weakness ought to make the fight a quick one. To set the stage for this confrontation, however, Frémont had to be given a check. His final defeat could be arranged after Shields was disposed of. The task of checking Frémont was assigned to Richard Ewell, who posted his men on some advantageous heights three or four miles north of Port Republic, near a place called Cross Keys. Jackson himself made his headquarters at a house in Port Republic, which put him south of the bridge and west of the fords. The main body of his army was north of the bridge, those units not with Ewell occupying positions nearer the town. Only a handful of men were with Jackson personally, while his precious trains were strung out on the road leading southward from the town, their guards already in a van position a mile or two beyond.

Jackson's dispositions were completed by the evening of June 7, which happened to be a Saturday. The general's confidence was such that he decided to do nothing on Sunday. But the enemy failed to act in concert with his plans. The commander of Shields' foremost brigade, Colonel S. S. Carroll, was ordered to try to cross the fords and capture the bridge. Carroll's men were a plucky lot. Unfortunately for Jackson's security, the Confederate horsemen supporting the handful of infantry pickets on the enemy's side of the fords were not first-rate troops. Not only were Jackson's plans disrupted, but his burgeoning career was nearly brought to humiliation. Dabney tells the story:

"The morning of June 8, which was the Sabbath day, dawned with all the peaceful brightness appropriate to the Christian's sacred rest; and General Jackson, who never infringed its sanctity by his own choice, was preparing himself and his wearied men to spend it in devotion. But soon after

the sun surmounted the eastern mountains the pickets next the army of
Shields came rushing to headquarters in the village in confusion, with the
Federal cavalry and a section of artillery close upon their heels. So feeble
was the resistance that was offered, the advance of the enemy dashed across
. . . South River almost as soon as they, and occupied the streets. The General had barely time to mount and gallop towards the bridge with a part of
his staff when the way was closed. Two others of his suite, attempting to
follow him a few moments after, were captured in the street; and one or
two, perceiving the hopelessness of the attempt, remained with the handful
of troops thus cut off. . . .

"As the captured Confederate officers stood beside the commander of
the Federal advance, some of his troopers returned to him and pointed out
the long train of wagons hurrying away, apparently without armed escort,
just beyond the outskirts of the village. He immediately ordered a strong
body of cavalry in pursuit; and the hearts of the Confederates sank within
them, for they knew that this was Jackson's ordnance train, containing the
reserve ammunition of the whole army, and that all its other baggage was
equally at the mercy of the enemy. But as the eager Federals reached the
head of the village they were met by a volley of musketry, which sent them
scampering back; and when they returned to the charge two pieces of artillery opened upon them, to the equal surprise and delight of their anxious
captives, and speedily cleared the streets with showers of canister. The explanation was that one of the officers separated from the General's suite,
seeing the impossibility of joining him, had addressed himself to rallying a
handful of the fugitive picket guards, and with these and a section of raw
artillerists from the reserves, had boldly attacked the enemy. Thus the
trains were saved and a diversion was made until the General could bring
forward more substantial succors.

"Nor was it long before these were at hand. Galloping across the bridge
and up the heights to the camp of the 3rd and 1st Brigades of his own division, he ordered the long roll to be instantly beaten and the artillery to be
harnessed. The horses were still grazing in the luxuriant clover fields and
the men were scattered under the shade of the groves, but in a few moments
the guns were ready for action and two or three regiments were in line.
Jackson ordered [three batteries] to crown the heights overlooking the
river; and, placing himself at the head of the leading regiment of the 3rd
Brigade, the 37th Virginia . . . rushed at a double-quick toward the all-im-
portant bridge, now in the enemy's possession. When he approached it, he
saw the village beyond crowded with Federal cavalry, but now checked in
their pursuit of his trains, while one of their two fieldpieces was replying to
the Confederate artillery and the other was placed at the mouth of the
bridge, prepared to sweep it with murderous discharges of grape. One lightning glance was enough to decide him. Ordering Captain Poague to engage
with one of his pieces the gun at the southern end of the bridge, he led the

37th Regiment . . . marching by the flank. Without pausing to wheel them into line as they came within effective distance, he commanded them . . . to deliver one round upon the enemy's artillerists and then rush through the bridge upon them with the bayonet. They fired one stinging volley, which swept every cannoneer from the threatening gun, and then dashed with a yell through the narrow avenue.

"As soon as Jackson uttered his command he drew up his horse; and, dropping the reins upon his neck, raised both his hands toward the heavens, while the fire of battle in his face changed into a look of reverential awe. Even while he prayed, the God of battles heard. . . . The bridge was gained and the enemy's gun was captured. . . . To clear the village of [the Federals] was now the work of a moment, for the batteries frowning [from] the opposite bank rendered it untenable to them. . . . Their retreat was so precipitate that they left their other piece of artillery behind them also, and dashed across the fords of South River by the way they came."

Only one of the Confederate prisoners had been retained, and he would soon escape and return to Port Republic. As the Federal column retired northeastward along the Shenandoah, the Confederates moved several of their fieldpieces to new heights on their side of the river and hurried the defeated men along with some well-directed shots. Dabney says that Jackson ordered these weapons kept in place as a deterrent to another advance. "When it was argued with him that, surely, General Shields would not suffer the critical hour to pass without attempting again to cooperate with Frémont by a more serious and persistent attack, his only answer was to wave his hand towards the commanding positions of his artillery and say, 'No, sir! No! He cannot do it. I should tear him to pieces.' And he did not do it!"

Jackson's Sabbath had been broken, and it remained so, for at 10 A.M. Frémont's Federals moved against Ewell at Cross Keys. The attack, however, was a halfhearted affair. Frémont seemed more concerned with avoiding a defeat than with gaining a victory. He was easily stopped, and in the middle of the afternoon he began drawing back. Ewell did not press him far, for Jackson's orders precluded such a move. Jackson was mightily pleased with the day's work. Now it seemed safe for him to leave a small force facing Frémont while the rest of the army was thrown across the fords for an attack on Shields. Jackson hoped to make quick work of Shields the next morning, recrossing the fords in time for a decisive afternoon attack on Frémont.

Jackson decided to cross his troops dryfooted by building a bridge of wagons with planks laid over, and the project was achieved after the moon rose at midnight. The bridge was supposed to be uniformly wide enough to carry the men marching several abreast; but, unknown to Jackson, there was a grave flaw at the center. Two of the wagons had been poorly aligned and were also unmatched in elevation. This disrupted the planking; only one plank was stable enough for vigorous use. In effect, the entire structure was capable of accommodating only single-file traffic. "This bridge," says Dabney, "furnished an instance of the truth that very great events may be determined by very trivial ones."

Busy not only with the pioneers who constructed the bridge but with tactical consultations, Jackson got but scant time to sleep. An hour before dawn, Colonel John Imboden, who had charge of a battery of howitzers packed by mules and who needed instructions, reported to the house the general was using as his headquarters. "Not wishing to disturb him so early, I asked the sentinel what room was occupied by 'Sandy' Pendleton, Jackson's adjutant-general. 'Upstairs, first room on the right,' he replied. Supposing he meant our right as we faced the house, I went up, softly opened the door, and discovered General Jackson lying on his face across the bed, fully dressed, with sword, sash, and boots all on. The low-burnt tallow candle on the table shed a dim light, yet enough by which to recognize him. I endeavored to withdraw without waking him. He turned over, sat up on the bed, and called out, 'Who is that?' He checked my apology with, 'That is all right. It's time to be up. I am glad to see you. Were the men all up as you came through camp?' 'Yes, General, and cooking.' 'That's right. We move at daybreak. Sit down. I want to talk to you.' I had learned never to ask him questions about his plans, for he would never answer such to anyone. I therefore waited for him to speak first. He referred very feelingly to Ashby's death and spoke of it as an irreparable loss. When he paused, I said, 'General, you made a glorious winding-up of your four weeks' work yesterday.' He replied, 'Yes, God blessed our army again yesterday, and I hope with his protection and blessing we shall do still better today.' Then . . . he outlined the day's proposed operations." These did not include a definite job for Colonel Imboden's battery, but he was told to take it to the field and find a safe place in the rear to await the possibility of a summons to action.

The crossing was begun at the appointed time. Jackson himself negotiated the waters on horseback in company with the cavalrymen, who went over first, and he remained unaware of the flaw in the bridge. He had planned for some six or eight thousand troops to follow him in a hurry, but the anticipated speed did not develop. Chief of Staff Dabney had been assigned the task of supervising the crossing, and he soon became frustrated. "Proposals to arrest the passage of the troops long enough to remedy [the defect] effectually, or else to disuse the bridge and force the men through the water, were all neglected by the commanders of the brigades." The first unit to complete the crossing was the original Stonewall Brigade of Bull Run fame, now commanded by Brigadier General Charles S. Winder. Dick Taylor's brigade started across next. Winder had hardly got his units organized before Jackson led them along the road to Lewiston. He was getting a somewhat slower start then he had planned upon, but he expected supports to follow in ample numbers and in ample time. The Federals at Lewiston, commanded by Major General E. B. Tyler, numbered only about 3,500. Shields and the main body were still making their approach from the north, too far away to come to Tyler's aid. Undaunted, that officer prepared to meet Jackson's attack.

"The position occupied by General Tyler," says Confederate staff officer William Allan, "was an admirable one, on the second terrace from the Shenandoah. His center was near [the Lewis farm buildings], his right extending through the open fields towards the river, while his left rested in the dense wood east of the main road at the site of an old coal pit. The ground held by the left and center was elevated and commanded all the available approaches from Port Republic. Especially was this the case on his left, which was the key to the whole position. Here he had six guns planted. A dense and almost impenetrable forest protected this flank."

Jackson was already deploying Winder's 1,200 men in front of the Federals by the time Dick Taylor's troops completed their crossing. Those who had crossed first were sitting in groups along the river's grassy margin. Taylor relates: "The sun appeared above the mountain. . . . Suddenly . . . was heard the din of battle, loud and sustained, artillery and small arms. The men sprang into ranks, formed column, and marched; and I galloped forward a short mile to see the . . . Federal lines, their right touching the river . . . advancing steadily, with banners flying and arms gleaming in the sun. A gallant show, they came on. Winder's . . . brigade, with a battery [Poague's], opposed them. This small force was suffering cruelly. . . . As my Irishmen predicted, 'Shields' boys were after fighting.' [Behind us,] Ewell was hurrying his men across the bridge, but it looked as though we should be doubled up on him ere he could cross and develop much strength."

Jackson had begun his attack with a maneuver to his right against the Federal guns, but the troops were repulsed. As usual, the general was everywhere, issuing orders and offering encouragement. He repaired a break in the line by leading the faltering men forward with the cry, "The Stonewall Brigade never retreats!" He paused in his rounds to check on Colonel Imboden's howitzer-laden mules, temporarily ensconced in a ravine near the center of the line, behind Poague's battery. In Imboden's words: "I was having a remarkable time with our mules. . . . Some of the shot aimed at Poague came bounding over our heads, and occasionally a shell would burst there. The mules became frantic. They kicked, plunged, and squealed. It was impossible to quiet them, and it took three or four men to hold one mule from breaking away. Each mule had about three hundred pounds weight on him, so securely fastened that the load could not be dislodged by any of his capers. Several of them lay down and tried to wallow their loads off. The men held these down, and that suggested the idea of throwing them all on the ground and holding them there. The ravine sheltered us so that we were in no danger from the shot or shell which passed over us. Just about the time that our mule circus was at its height . . . Jackson . . . passed on the brink of our ravine. His eye caught the scene, and, reining up a moment, he accosted me with, 'Colonel, you seem to have trouble down there.' I made some reply which drew forth a hearty laugh, and he said, 'Get your mules to the mountain as soon as you can, and be ready to move.' Then he dashed on." Imboden did as directed, but his battery was left unemployed.

Jackson seemed to find his perilous situation enjoyable. At about 8 A.M. he was obliged to accept the fact that his grand plan for the day had been frustrated. He had expected to be driving the Federals by this time, to have reached the point at which he could turn back, recross the fords, and go over the bridge after Frémont. Now, with his old brigade bleeding and imperiled, Jackson sent word to General Isaac R. Trimble, commander of the small force left in front of Frémont, to fall back to Port Republic and burn the bridge. Trimble was, in fact, already retiring slowly, for Frémont had begun to press him. It is almost certain that Trimble could have delayed Frémont the necessary time if Jackson's plan had worked. Dabney laments: "Thus three ill-adjusted boards cost the Confederates a hard-fought and bloody battle, and delivered Frémont from a second defeat far more disastrous than that of the previous day."

Dick Taylor says that when he reached Lewiston "Jackson was on the road, a little in advance of his line where the fire was hottest, with reins on his horse's neck, seemingly in prayer. Attracted by my approach, he said in his usual voice, 'Delightful excitement.' I replied that it was pleasant to learn he was enjoying himself, but thought he might have an indigestion of such fun if the six-gun battery was not silenced. He summoned a young officer from his staff and pointed up the mountain. The head of my approaching column was turned short [to the right] up the slope, and speedily came to a path. . . . We took this path, the guide leading the way. From him I learned that the plateau occupied by the battery had been used for a charcoal kiln; and the path we were following, made by the burners in hauling wood, came upon the gorge opposite the battery. Moving briskly, we reached the hither side a few yards from the guns. Infantry was posted near, and riflemen were in the undergrowth on the slope above. Our approach, masked by timber, was unexpected. The battery was firing rapidly. . . . The head of my column began to deploy under cover for attack, when the sounds of battle to our rear appeared to recede, and a loud Federal cheer was heard, proving Jackson to be hard pressed. It was rather an anxious moment, demanding instant action.

"Leaving a staff officer to direct my rear regiment—the 7th, Colonel [Harry T.] Hays—to form in the wood as a reserve, I ordered the attack, though the deployment was not completed and our rapid march by a nar-

row path had occasioned some disorder. With a rush and shout the gorge
was passed and we were in the battery. Surprise had aided us, but the
enemy's infantry rallied in a moment and drove us out. We returned, to be
driven a second time. The riflemen on the slope worried us no little, and
two companies of the 9th Regiment were sent up the gorge to gain ground
above and dislodge them, which was accomplished. The fighting in and
around the battery was hand to hand, and many fell from bayonet wounds.
Even the artillerymen used their rammers in a way not laid down in the
manual, and died at their guns. . . . I called for Hays, but he, the promptest
of men, and his splendid regiment, could not be found. Something unexpected had occurred, but there was no time for speculation. With a desperate rally, in which I believe the drummer boys shared, we carried the
battery for the third time, and held it. Infantry and riflemen had been
driven off, and we began to feel a little comfortable."

The relief was quickly replaced by a new concern. Looking down toward the enemy on the plain, Taylor saw that he was forming for an uphill
attack. "He . . . came into full view of our situation. . . . With colors advanced, like a solid wall he marched straight upon us. There seemed nothing left but to set our backs to the mountan and die hard. At the instant,
crashing through the underwood came Ewell, outriding staff and escort. He
produced the effect of a reinforcement and was welcomed with cheers. The
line before us halted and threw forward skirmishers. A moment later a shell
came shrieking along [the line], loud Confederate cheers reached our delighted ears, and Jackson, freed from [the threat of the guns], rushed up like
a whirlwind, the enemy in rapid retreat. We turned the captured guns on
them as they passed, Ewell serving as a gunner.

"Though rapid, the retreat never became a rout. Fortune had refused
[them] her smiles, but Shields' brave boys preserved their organization and
were formidable to the last; and had Shields himself, with his whole command, been on the field, we should have had tough work indeed. Jackson
came up, with intense light in his eyes, grasped my hand, and said the brigade should have the captured battery. I thought the men would go mad
with cheering. . . . While Jackson pursued the enemy without much effect
[for some miles] . . . we attended to the wounded and performed the last offices to the dead, our own and the Federal. I have never seen so many dead
and wounded in the same limited space. . . . Ere long my lost 7th Regiment,
sadly cut up, rejoined. This regiment was in rear of the column when we left
Jackson to gain the path in the woods, and before it filed out of the road his
thin line was so pressed that Jackson ordered Hays to stop the enemy's rush.
This was done, for the 7th would have stopped a herd of elephants, but at a
fearful cost. Colonel Hays was severely wounded, among many others, and
the number of killed was large. . . . Many hours passed in discharge of sad
duties to the wounded and dead, during which Frémont appeared on the

opposite bank of the river [north of the burning bridge] and opened his guns; but observing, doubtless, our occupation, he ceased his fire, and after a short time withdrew."

Port Republic cost Jackson 816 men killed and wounded. The Federals lost only 460 in killed and wounded, but about 450 became Jackson's prisoners, while at least 100 more had to be listed as missing. That evening Jackson led his tired troops eastward to the mouth of Brown's Gap in the Blue Ridge, where they began a period of rest. Frémont and Shields got orders from Washington to end their pursuit, and Jackson's Valley Campaign was over. Although the general's plans had miscarried at Port Republic, the campaign was to enter history as a marvel of its kind. Between May 8 and June 9 Jackson's command, limited both in manpower and in other resources, had marched nearly 400 miles, skirmished almost daily, fought five battles and defeated three armies, one of them twice, and had captured about twenty pieces of artillery, some 4,000 prisoners, and great quantities of valuable stores. The campaign had kept Washington in a state of nervous confusion and had robbed McClellan of major reinforcements. Now Jackson rested and awaited orders regarding further participation in the fight to save Richmond.

Not much had happend in the Richmond theater since the Battle of Fair Oaks. Both sides were adding to their defenses. The Prince de Joinville says that "the Federal army neither wished to offer, nor to invite another such battle as that of Fair Oaks till its bridges should be [completed] and its two wings put into communication with each other.... We hastened to entrench ourselves along our whole line. This was a tremendous piece of work.... Redoubts and embankments had to be raised, rifle pits had to be dug, and all this under a broiling sun [or under generous rains]. We had furthermore to cut down the trees on the site selected, and [in order to create a field of fire] for several hundred yards in advance. In some places no earthworks were erected, but it was thought sufficient to cut down the forest into the contour of a regular fortification. The thickest part of the woods, left standing and salient in the midst of a vast abatis, played the part of a bastion. The artillery and the sharpshooters [were] placed in this wood....

"All these labors were executed with admirable energy and intelligence. In this aspect the American soldier has no rival. Patient of fatigue, rich in resources, he is an excellent digger and ditcher, an excellent woodman, a good carpenter, and even something of a civil engineer.... It is impossible to give an idea of the celerity with which work of this kind was done. I [saw] a grove a hundred acres in extent, of ancestral oaks and other hardwood trees cut down in a single day by a single battalion. Nevertheless, all this work was not done without much fatigue, both moral and material, as the natural consequence of incessant toil under an incessant fire. In these vast and pathless woods, where you run a constant risk of being surprised, it is

A Federal battery in the Richmond lines

impossible to throw out one's advance very far. So we form . . . a picket line
. . . supported by strong reserves. . . .

"The two armies were now so near together, and so determined to cede
no inch of ground, that their pickets were stationed within hailing distance
of one another. Generally they got along very amicably together and contented themselves with a reciprocal watchfulness. Sometimes friendly communications took place between them. They trafficked in various trifles and
exchanged the Richmond newspapers for the New York *Herald.* It even
happened one day that some Federal officers were invited by their Confederate comrades to a ball in Richmond, on condition that they would suffer
their eyes to be bandaged in going and returning.

"But a single shot would disturb these good relations. The firing would
last a greater part of an hour, and a hundred men perhaps be killed or
wounded before they became quiet again. At other times the troops were
surprised in their tents by a shower of shells, coming nobody knew where
from, over the heads of the pickets. This was a disagreeable reveille when it
happened at night. If it took place in the daytime the men would clamber
up into some high tree to spy out the spot from which the firing came. This
would be betrayed by the smoke, and sometimes a Confederate soldier
would be seen perched in some towering tree, himself directing the fire of
the artillerymen. Then the Federals would reply and make great efforts to
bring down the aerial gunner. These isolated annoyances, whether of picket
firing or long-range shelling, troubled nobody but the troops immediately
exposed."

De Joinville enjoyed riding around in the Federal encampments and
making observations. He was generally entertained by what he saw, but in
one of the camps he was shocked by "the disagreeable spectacle of the gigantic posters which an embalmer exhibited . . . and in which this trades-
man, speculating at once upon the losses of the army and on the domestic
affections of their friends, promised to embalm the slain and send them
home at a reasonable rate." To his surprise, De Joinville learned that the
vulgarity was not without a redemption. "This enterprising [man] . . . saved
the life of a colonel who, having been thrown into a prolonged swoon by the
explosion of a shell, was supposed to be dead, and, having been committed
to the embalmer, recovered his consciousness during the operation."

Chaplain Stewart of Pennsylvania, quartered in a tent near Fair Oaks,
wrote home on June 9: "So far as I can understand, each army occupies
substantially the same position held previously to the battle. . . . The past
week . . . has had a most debilitating influence upon many of our regiments. . . . As ours [is] encamped in a mud hole close beside the bloody
ground—every alternate day and night drenched with torrents of rain, together with very inadequate shelter—the hot, sultry weather—putrefying
malaria from the blood of men and horses—and not a drop of water within

262

Exchanging coffee for tobacco

reach fit either to drink or use in cooking—the only marvel is all are not on the sick list. Should the present condition of things long continue, the number of invalids must be fearfully swelled. The tocsin for another battle would in an instant produce a great change for the better—more effective far than all the abominable whiskey with which our poor soldiers are still daily poisoned."

No tocsin for another battle was imminent. On June 10 McClellan informed Washington: "I am completely checked by the weather. The roads and fields are literally impassable for artillery, almost so for infantry. The Chickahominy is in a dreadful state. . . . I wish it to be distinctly understood that, whenever the weather permits, I will attack with whatever force I may have, although a larger force would enable me to gain much more decisive results." McClellan's strength had been diminished by the Battle of Fair Oaks and by sickness. Washington was somewhat more receptive to his pleas for reinforcements now: Stonewall Jackson was no longer threatening the line of the Potomac. McClellan wrote Ellen that "the Secretary and President are becoming quite amiable of late. I am afraid that I am a little cross to them, and that I do not quite appreciate their sincerity and good feeling. . . . How glad I will be to get rid of the whole lot!" Washington released the troops in modest numbers. The largest body, 9,500 men, was McCall's division of McDowell's corps. For the showdown fighting, McClellan would have about 115,000 effectives. He continued to believe— or at least professed to believe—that Lee had about 200,000. In actuality, Lee was building toward 90,000. This number included Jackson's army in the Shenandoah Valley. Lee intended to call Jackson to Richmond for the campaign's climax; but now, in order to keep McClellan and Washington guessing as to Jackson's role, Lee sent him, with ostentation, three extra brigades, as though reinforcing him for another drive toward the Potomac.

Lee had not yet earned the confidence of his officers or of Richmond's anxious citizens. James Longstreet says that "General Lee's experience in active field work was limited to his West Virginia campaign . . . which was not successful. His services on our coast defenses were known as able, and those who knew him in Mexico as one of the principal engineers of General Scott's column, marching for the capture of the capital of that great republic, knew that as a military engineer he was especially distinguished; but officers of the line are not apt to look to the staff in choosing leaders of soldiers, either in tactics or strategy. There were, therefore, some misgivings as to the power and skill for field service of the new commander." Adds Richmond editor Edward Pollard: "There was an early popular supposition that Lee was rather too much of the Fabian stamp of a commander and disinclined to the risks of battle. . . . His quiet manners, the absence of all bustle about him, and a singular appearance of doing nothing when, in fact, he was most busy, confirmed the popular impression of his slowness and un-

willingness to deliver battle, and inclined the people of Richmond to believe that he was awaiting the attack of the enemy. . . . They little imagined
that he was meditating taking the initiative himself and putting the insolent
enemy on the defensive. The quiet, thoughtful commander never admitted
an improper person into his confidence; he was annoyed by politicians and
Congressional delegations who wanted information of his plans, but never
obtained it; he was assailed by foolish clamors of demagogues whose interest in the Confederacy appeared to be enclosed within the boundaries of
their Congressional districts or counties, and who complained that particular parts of the country had been stripped of troops to defend Richmond; he
was pursued by popular impatience for battle; but to all he was the imperturbable gentleman, opposing to curiosity and clamor a placid manner and
a polite but supreme reticence. Each day he was seen on horseback about
the lines, dressed in a plain suit of gray, with a scanty attendance of officers. . . . Each day his army was busy in strengthening their defensive
works; and people wondered at McClellan's silence and Lee's apparent un-
concern, and speculated when the great battle would be delivered."

Curiously enough, Mrs. Robert E. Lee was still at the White House on
the Pamunkey River, deep inside McClellan's lines. The manner of Mrs.
Lee's egress is explained by a Confederate officer, W. Roy Mason: "One day
in June, 1862, General Lee rode over to General Charles W. Field's headquarters at Meadow Bridge and asked for me. (I would say here that on
leaving home to enter the army I carried a family letter of introduction to
General Lee; and on account of that, and also my relationship to Colonel
Charles Marshall, an aide on his staff, my visits at army headquarters were
exceptionally pleasant). When General Lee approached me on this occasion, he said, 'Captain, can General Field spare you a little while?' I replied,
'Certainly, General; what can I do for you?' 'I have some property,' he answered, 'in the hands of the enemy, and General McClellan has informed
me that he would deliver it to me at any time I asked for it.' Then, putting
aside his jesting manner, he told me that his wife and Miss Mary Lee, his
daughter, had been caught within the Federal lines at the White House, the
residence of W. H. F. Lee, his son, and he desired me to take a courier and
proceed with a flag of truce to Meadow Bridge and carry a sealed dispatch
to General McClellan. At the Federal headquarters I would meet the ladies,
and escort them to Mrs. Gooch's farm, inside our lines.

"I passed beyond the [Confederate] pickets to the second bridge, where
I waved my flag of truce, and was asked by the Union officer of the guard to
enter. When I reached the picket, the officer said he had been ordered not
to pemit any flag of truce to pass through his lines until he had communicated with the headquarters of General McClellan. I waited on the bridge,
and when the courier returned he had orders to bring me before the general. The officer insisted on blindfolding me, and positively forbade my cou-

rier accompanying me. I was then led through the camps, where I could hear the voices of thousands laughing, talking, or hallooing. After riding an hour, a distance, as I supposed, of three or four miles, I reached headquarters and was relieved of my bandage.

"The general came out and gave me a hearty welcome; and when he heard that I had been blindfolded he was so indignant that he placed the officer, my guide, under arrest. I had never seen him so excited. He asked me into the house, produced his liquors, and gave me a dinner of the best, after which we discussed the situation at length. He asked me no questions which it would compromise our cause to answer, but we calmly reviewed the position of things from our separate points of view, and he inquired anxiously after all his old friends. (General McClellan and my brother-in-law, General Dabney H. Maury, C.S.A., formerly captain, U.S.A., had been classmates and devoted friends, and the general had visited my father's house and my own at Fredericksburg.)

"About 3 o'clock in the afternoon, looking down the road, we saw a carriage approaching. The curtains were cut off, and it was drawn by a mule and a dilapidated old horse, driven by a Negro of about ten or twelve years, and followed by a cavalry escort. General McClellan, jumping up hastily, said, 'There are Mrs. Lee and Miss Mary now.' As the carriage stopped before the door, General McClellan, greeting the ladies with marked cordiality, at once introduced me, and remarked to Mrs. Lee that the general (her husband) had chosen me as her escort through the lines, and that by a strange coincidence he (McClellan) had found in me a personal friend. He offered to accompany us in person to the river, but this was declined by Mrs. Lee as entirely unnecessary.

"When we reached Mrs. Gooch's farm and our own pickets, cheer after cheer went down the long line of soldiers. Near the house we were met by General Lee and a large number of officers [who had] assembled to honor the wife and daughter of their chief.

"Before leaving for Richmond, Mrs. Lee handed me from a basket under the carriage seat two fine tomatoes, the finest I had ever seen, remarking that she supposed such things were scarce in the Confederacy. (The seeds of these tomatoes I preserved, and, some years after the war, General Lee ate some tomatoes at my table and praised them; whereupon we told him, to his astonishment, that those were the Lee tomatoes, and that they had been distributed all over the state under that name, from the seed of those given me by his wife.)"

Found tacked to the front door of the White House after Mrs. Lee's departure was this notice: "Northern soldiers who profess to reverence the name of Washington, forbear to desecrate the home of his early married life, the property of his wife, and now the home of her descendants. —A granddaughter of Mrs. Washington."

11

---❖---

STUART'S RIDE AROUND
McCLELLAN

WHEREAS Joe Johnston had attacked McClellan's left wing, which lay on the Richmond side of the Chickahominy, Lee decided to move against the wing on the far side of the river, thus threatening McClellan's contact with his supplies, which were being brought ashore at the White House for railroad or wagon transport a dozen miles westward to the army's positions. It would be strategically expedient for Lee to march a column northward from Richmond for an easterly swing across the Chickahominy's headwaters and a descent upon McClellan's right flank. First, however, it would be necessary to gather some information. In the words of cavalry officer Fitzhugh Lee, the general's nephew: "His enemy's right was the place to attack, but where was it located and how was it defended? Were the roads leading to it obstructed, and were the woods 'slashed,' or would the attacking column have to assault lunettes, redans, irregular pentagons, and enclosed redoubts? How was he to ascertain all this? Fortunately, he had the very officer in his army who could obtain replies to these important questions, and he was the commander of his cavalry . . . Jeb Stuart . . . a soldier from the feathers in his hat to the rowels of his spurs. . . . His brilliant courage, great activity, immense endurance, and devotion to his profession had already marked him as a cavalry commander of unquestioned merit. . . . He was a Christian dragoon—an unusual combination. His Bible and tactics were his textbooks. He never drank liquor, having given a promise to his mother to that effect when a small boy, but when wet from the storm and wearied from the march he would drink . . . the contents of a tin quart cup of strong coffee. Duty was his guiding star. Once when on the eve of an expected battle he was telegraphed that his child was dying and urged to go to her, he replied, 'I shall have to leave my child in the hands of God; my duty requires me here.' Lee knew him well. He had been a classmate at the

266

Jeb Stuart

United Military Academy of his eldest son, and was his aide-de-camp when
John Brown was captured. Such was the man who stood before his commander . . . to receive his instructions."

This was on June 10. Stuart was delighted with the assignment. In his
enthusiasm, he told Lee that he would do more than investigate McClellan's right flank; he would ride entirely around his army and return to Richmond from the south. Lee neither approved the idea nor flatly rejected it.
The next day Stuart received written orders enjoining caution: "The utmost
vigilance on your part will be necessary to prevent any surprise to yourself. . . . You will return as soon as the object of your expedition is accomplished, and you must bear constantly in mind, while endeavoring to
execute the general purpose of your mission, not to hazard unnecessarily
your command or to attempt what your judgment may not approve; but be
content to accomplish all the good you can without feeling it necessary to
obtain all that might be desired. I recommend that you only take such men
and horses as can stand the expedition, and that you take every means in
your power to save and cherish those you do take."

Stuart selected 1,200 troopers and a section of horse artillery. Among his
subordinate commanders was not only Lee's nephew, Fitzhugh Lee, but
also one of the general's sons, William H. F. "Rooney" Lee. Stuart's staff officers included the huge but light-footed and aristocratic Heros von Borcke,
a former Prussian dragoon who had just lately reached the Confederacy
aboard a blockade runner. Von Borcke begins the story: "June 12, 1862. It
was two o'clock in the morning, and we [of the staff] were all fast asleep,
when General Stuart's clear voice awoke us with the words, 'Gentlemen, in
ten minutes every man must be in his saddle!' In half the time all the members of the staff were dressed . . . and the ten minutes was scarcely up when
we galloped off to overtake the main body. . . . None of us knew where we
were going. . . . Nevertheless everyone followed our honored leader with
perfect confidence."

According to another staff officer, John Esten Cooke, the moon was
bright and Stuart was "a gallant figure to look at. The gray coat buttoned to
the chin; the light French saber balanced by the pistol in its black holster;
the cavalry boots above the knee, and the brown hat with its black plume
floating above the bearded features, the brilliant eyes, and the huge mus-
tache which curled with laughter at the slightest provocation—these made
Stuart the perfect picture of a gay cavalier. . . . Catching up with his column . . . Stuart pushed on northward [throughout the day] . . . and, reaching
the vicinity of Taylorsville, near Hanover Junction, went that night into
bivouac."

The column was now twenty-two miles north of Richmond. It was time
to turn right for a southeasterly swing around McClellan's flank. Says Stuart
himself: "Our noiseless bivouac was broken early next morning, and with-

Confederate cavalryman

out flag or bugle sound we resumed our march, none but one knew whither. I, however, immediately took occasion to make known my instructions and plans confidentially to the regimental commanders. . . . Scouts had returned, indicating no serious obstacles to my march . . . to Old Church. . . . I proceeded . . . via Hanover Court House."

John Esten Cooke explains that Hanover Court House was approached with caution. "We looked upon . . . its old brick court house, where Patrick Henry made his famous speech against the parsons, its ancient tavern, its modest roofs, the whole surrounded by the fertile fields waving with golden grain—all this we looked at with unusual interest. For in this little bird's nest . . . some Yankee cavalry had taken up their abode. Their horses stood ready saddled in the street, and this dark mass we now gazed at furtively from behind a wooden knoll, in rear of which Stuart's column was drawn up, ready to move at the word. Before he gave the signal, the General dispatched Colonel Fitz Lee round to the right to flank and cut off the party. But all at once [our] scouts in front were descried by the enemy. Shots resounded. And, seeing that his presence was discovered, Stuart gave the word and swept at a thundering gallop down the hill. The startled 'bluebirds' . . . did not wait. The squadron on picket at the court house . . . hastily got to horse—then presto! they disappear in the dense cloud of dust from which echo some parting salutes from their carbines.

"Stuart pressed on rapidly, took the road to Old Church, and . . . in a thickly wooded spot was suddenly charged himself. It did not amount to much, and seemed rather an attempt at a reconnaissance. A Federal officer at the head of a detachment came on at full gallop, very nearly ran into the head of our column, and then, seeing the dense mass of gray coats, fired his pistol, wheeled short about, and went back at full speed with his detachment. Stuart had given, in his ringing voice, the order 'Form fours! Draw saber! Charge!' And now the Confederate people pursued at headlong speed, uttering shouts and yells. . . . The men were evidently exhilarated by the chase, the enemy just keeping near enough to make an occasional shot practicable.

"A considerable number of the Federal cavalrymen were overtaken and captured, and these proved to belong to the [prewar] company in which Colonel Fitz Lee had . . . been a lieutenant. I could not refrain from laughter at the pleasure which Colonel Fitz . . . seemed to take in inquiring after his old cronies. Was Brown alive? Where was Jones? And was Robinson a sergeant still? Colonel Fitz never stopped until he found out everything. The prisoners laughed as they recognized him. Altogether . . . the interview was the most friendly imaginable.

"The gay chase continued until we reached the Totopotomoy, a sluggish stream dragging its muddy waters slowly between rush-clad banks [and] beneath drooping trees; and this was crossed by a small rustic bridge. . . . The

Union cavalry bugler

picket at the bridge had been quickly driven in, and disappeared at a gallop; and on the high ground beyond, Colonel W. H. F. Lee, who had taken the front, encountered the enemy. The force appeared to be about a regiment, and they were drawn up in line of battle in the fields to receive our attack. It came without delay. Placing himself at the head of his horsemen, Colonel Lee swept forward at the *pas de charge,* and with shouts the two lines came together. The shock was heavy, and the enemy—a portion of the old United States Regulars commanded by Captain [William B.] Royall— stood their ground bravely, meeting the attack with the saber. Swords clashed, pistols and carbines banged, yells, shouts, cheers resounded. Then the Federal line was seen to give back and take to headlong flight. . . . But . . . Captain [William] Latané, of the Essex Cavalry, had been mortally wounded in the charge, and as the men of his company saw him lying bloody before them, many a bearded face was wet with tears."

As a close pursuit began, Lieutenant W. T. Robins and five others, riding together, became enmeshed in the fleeing column. Robins relates: "Although the Federal cavalry both in front and rear were in full retreat, our situation was perilous in the extreme. Soon we were pushed by foes in our rear into the ranks of those in our front, and a series of hand-to-hand combats ensued. To shoot or to cut us down was the aim of every Federal as he neared us, but we did what we could to defend ourselves. Every one of my comrades was shot or cut down, and I alone escaped unhurt. After having been borne along by the retreating enemy for perhaps a quarter of a mile, I leaped my horse over the fence into the field, and so got away. Now came the rush of the Confederate column, sweeping the road clear and capturing many prisoners. . . . The Federals did not attempt to make a stand until they reached Old Church. Here their officers called a halt, and made an attempt to rally to defend their camp."

Heros von Borcke tells what happened: "Their lines were broken by our furious attack. They fled in confusion, and we chased them in wild pursuit across an open field, through their camp, and far into the woods. When we had returned to their camp the work of destruction began. Everyone tried to rescue for himself as much as possible of the articles of luxury with which the Yankees had overloaded themselves. But few succeeded in the end; for, in accordance with the well-laid plan of our leader, flames flashed up, now in one place, now in another, and in a few minutes the whole camp was enveloped in one blaze, hundreds of tents burning together presenting a wonderfully beautiful spectacle."

According to W. T. Robins, this was the end of organized resistance on the part of the Federal cavalry. "We had surprised them, taken them in detail, and far outnumbered them at all points. . . . We halted for a short time at Old Church, and the people of the neighborhood . . . came flocking out to greet us and wish us Godspeed. They did not come emptyhanded, but brought whatever they could snatch up on the spur of the moment, rightly supposing that anything to allay hunger or thirst would be acceptable to us. Some of the ladies brought bouquets and presented them to the officers as they marched along. One of these was given to General Stuart, who, always gallant, vowed to preserve it and take it into Richmond."

The confederate troopers had now accomplished their mission, had located McClellan's right flank and had determined that it was not forbiddingly fortified. But Stuart was too pleased with the way things were going to want to turn back. Deciding to try to make it all the way around, he harbored "the hope of striking a serious blow at a boastful and insolent foe which would make him tremble in his shoes. . . . In a brief and frank interview with some of my officers I disclosed my views, but while none accorded a full assent, all assured me a hearty support in whatever I did. . . . There was something of the sublime in the implicit confidence and unquestioning trust of the rank and file in a leader guiding them straight, apparently, into the very jaws of the enemy, every step appearing to them to diminish the faintest hope of extrication."

Cooke says that "from Old Church onward it was *terra incognita*. What force of the enemy barred the road was a question of the utmost interest, but adventure of some description might safely be counted on. In about twenty-four hours I, for one, expected either to be laughing with my friends within the Southern lines, or dead, or captured. . . . At a steady trot now, with drawn sabers and carbines ready, the cavalry, followed by the horse artillery . . . approached Tunstall's Station on the York River Railroad, the enemy's direct line of communication with his base of supplies at the White House. Everywhere the ride was crowded with incident. The scouting and flanking parties constantly picked up stragglers and overhauled unsuspecting wagons filled with the most tempting stores. In this manner a wagon stocked with champagne and every variety of wines . . . fell a prey to the thirsty graybacks. . . . The men [on the flanks] were many of them from the region, and for the first time for months saw their mothers and sisters. These went quite wild at sight of their sons and brothers. They laughed and cried, and on the appearance of the long gray column instead of the familiar blue coats of the Federal cavalry, they clapped their hands and fell into ecstasies of delight."

It was only now, in the middle of the afternoon, that the first reports of the Confederate raid began reaching McClellan's main army, on the Chickahominy ten miles to the west. Trooper F. Colburn Adams relates: "Our camp was thrown into an intense state of excitment by a report that the enemy was approaching in force from the direction of Hanover Court House, his advance guard being composed of several regiments of cavalry and two batteries of artillery. One had it that his force was at least thirty thousand. Another said it was Stonewall Jackson with forty thousand. . . .

General McClellan had removed his headquarters to near Trent's house on the [Richmond] bank of the Chickahominy, and Franklin was absent from his. I believe he was with General McClellan. This increased the excitement. Then Captain Royall of the 5th Regular Cavalry came in with a severe saber cut wound on his head and covered with blood. This gave rise to rumors of the most ridiculous kind, which were not long in finding their way through every camp. Of course we were all under arms at once, and had our horses saddled, ready to move."

But no move was ordered, and the Confederates continued on their way unmolested. "The column," says Cooke, "was now skirting [the west bank of] the Pamunkey, and a detachment hurried off to seize and burn two or three transports lying in the river." These were small vessels at a newly created landing a few miles upstream from the main fleet at the White House. Union newsman Charles Alfred Townsend happened to be riding the road on which the detached Confederates made their approach, driving a fragment of Federal cavalry before them. "I . . . had come to a blacksmith's shop . . . when I was made aware of some startling occurrence in my rear. A mounted officer dashed past me, shouting some unintelligible tidings, and he was followed in quick succession by a dozen cavalrymen, who rode as if the foul fiend was at their heels. Then came a teamster, barebacked, whose rent harness trailed in the road; and . . . some wagons that were halted before the blacksmith's . . . rattled off towards White House. 'What is the matter, my man?' I said to one of these lunatics, hurriedly. 'The rebels are behind!' he screamed with white lips, and vanished. I thought that it might be as well to take some other road, and so struck off . . . in the direction of the new landing." The newsman was appalled to learn that this was the very road the Confederates were seeking. "I heard the crack of carbines behind, and they had a magical influence upon my speed. I rode along a stretch of chestnut and oak wood . . . and when I came to a rill that passed by a little bridge . . . turned up its sandy bed and buried myself in the underbrush. A few breathless moments only had intervened when the roadway seemed shaken by a hundred hoofs. The imperceptible horsemen yelled like a war party of Comanches, and, when they had passed, the carbines rang ahead as if some bloody work was being done at every rod."

The firing was more theatrical than punishing, and the detachment swept on to the river and ignited the transports. With the flames and smoke soaring up, the Confederates galloped back to the main column, which continued southward. Now Jeb Stuart, who was riding in front, sent for Lieutenant Robins, who relates: "I found the general, and was directed by him to take thirty men as an advance guard and to precede the column by about half a mile. Further, I was directed to halt at the road running . . . to the White House long enough to cut the telegraph wire on the road; thence to proceed to Tunstall's Station on the York River Railroad, at which place, the prisoners had informed the general, a company of Federal infantry was posted. . . . I was directed to charge the infantry, disperse or capture them, cut the telegraph and obstruct the railroad. Here was our point of danger. Once across the railroad, we were comparatively safe. But in possession of the railroad . . . the enemy could easily throw troops along its line to any given point. However, no timely information had been furnished to the Federal general. We moved with such celerity that we carried with us the first news of our arrival. Pushing forward at a trot, and picking up straggling prisoners every few hundred yards, the advance guard at length reached the telegraph road. At this point we overtook an ordnance wagon, heavily loaded with canteens and Colt revolvers. The horses had stalled in a mud hole, and the driver, cutting them out from the wagon, made his escape. The sergeant in charge stood his ground and was captured. Here was a prize indeed. . . .

"In order to save time, a man furnished with an ax was sent to cut the telegraph wire while the rest of the party was engaged in rifling the wagon. While these operations were in progress a body of Federal cavalry, suddenly turning a bend in the road, made their appearance. As soon as the Federal officer in command saw us he called a halt, and, standing still in the road, seemed at a loss to know what to do. His men drew their sabers, as if about to charge, but they did not come on. By this time the telegraph had been cut and the wagon disposed of. Our men were hastily mounted and formed into column of fours, with drawn sabers, ready for any emergency. There we stood, eying each other, about two hundred yards apart, until the head of the main Confederate column came in sight, when the Federals retreated down the road leading to the White House. One man of the Federal party was sent back along the road to Tunstall's Station, now only about half a mile off. I supposed, of course, that this messenger was sent to warn the Federal troops at Tunstall's of our approach. I was, however, afterward informed that he galloped through Tunstall's but never stopped, and when someone called to him, 'What's to pay?' he dashed along, calling out at the top of his voice, 'Hell's to pay!'

"The road now being clear, we marched on briskly, and arriving near the station, charged down upon it with a yell. We could see the enemy scattered about the building and lounging around before we charged them. The greater part scattered for cover and were pursued by our people. I pushed straight for the station house, where I found the captain of the company of infantry, with thirteen of his men, standing in front of the building, but with no arms in their hands. Only one of them seemed disposed to show fight. He ran to the platform where the muskets were stacked, and, seizing one of them, began to load. Before he could ram his cartridge home, a sweep of the saber, in close proximity to his head, made him throw down his gun; and, jumping into a ditch, he dodged under the bridge over the railroad and made his escape. I had no time to pursue him; but, turning to look after the others, met the captain, who, sword in hand, advanced and surrendered himself and his company as prisoners of war.

"I then proceeded to obstruct the railroad. To do this effectually, I caused a tree to be cut down which was standing on the side of the road. It fell across the railroad. In addition to this, I placed across the tracks an oak sill about a foot square and fourteen feet long. I had barely time to do this before a train from the direction of Richmond came thundering down. At this time General Stuart, with the main body, arrived at the station. The engine driver of the coming train, probably seeing the obstructions on the track and a large force of cavalry there, suspected danger; and, being a plucky fellow, put on all steam and came rushing down. The engine, striking the obstructions, knocked them out of the way and passed on without accident. General Stuart had dismounted a number of his men and posted them on a high bank overlooking a cut in the road, just below the station, through which the train was about to pass. They threw in a close and effective fire upon the passing train, loaded with troops. Many of these were killed and wounded."

The engineer himself had been hurt, but he rushed the train through to the White House, its whistle shrieking. Among the Federals there at the time was Chaplain J. J. Marks. "When the wounded and dead were brought in on these cars, and the many officers and soldiers sprang out to tell the story, the scene of excitement beggars description. Hundreds of Negroes, running back to their miserable shanties, gathered up their little effects; sutlers packed their goods and hastened them to the vessels that were about slipping their cables; numbers of officers ran to and fro to gather men to repel an attack; others were busy securing the papers and goods of their departments and issuing orders which no one obeyed. And any observer could see how easy it is for a few men, acting in concert, to scatter ten thousand acting without a plan or head."

Stuart's activities inspired nothing very much better in the main Federal camps on the Chickahominy. "Let us see," says F. Colburn Adams, "what we did to intercept or cut off this bold raider. Everybody wanted to go in pursuit of him, and yet nobody was ready to go. . . . Stuart had a father-in-law in our army, a bold trooper withal, and what could be better than to send him in pursuit of his rebel son? If they came to sabers and one got killed, why it would be all in the family, and in civil war such things do occur at times." As it happened, Stuart's father-in-law, Brigadier General Philip St. George Cooke, was commander of McClellan's cavalry reserve, and it was quite in his place to deal with the problem Stuart was posing. But Cooke could get no clear information on the situation, and his pursuit was poorly organized and sluggishly activated. "The gallant father," Adams opines, "seems to have had some grave apprehensions of being captured and entertained by his rebel son."

After the ambush at Tunstall's, says John Esten Cooke, "Stuart . . . reflected for a single moment. The question was, should he . . . attack the White House, where enormous stores were piled up? It was tempting, and he afterwards told me he could scarcely resist it. But a considerable force of infantry was posted there . . . and the attempt was too hazardous. The best thing for that gray column was to . . . keep moving, well closed up, both day and night, for the lower Chickahominy. So Stuart pushed on. Beyond the railroad appeared a world of wagons, loaded with grain and coffee, standing in the road abandoned. . . . They were all set on fire. . . . In a field . . . thirty acres were covered with them. They were all burned. The roar of the soaring flames was like the sound of a forest on fire. . . . The sky overhead, when night descended, was bloody-looking in the glare."

The wagons had been searched in vain for ready-to-eat rations. Again in the words of W. T. Robins: "It was now the second night since leaving camp, and the well-filled haversacks with which we started from camp had long since been empty. The march had been so rapid that there was little opportunity of foraging for man or beast. Except a little bread and meat brought out to the column by the country people as we passed along, we had had nothing since daybreak. The men were weary and hungry and the horses almost exhausted by the long fast and severe exercise. . . . Down through New Kent County to a place called [Talleysville] we marched as rapidly as our condition would permit. I was still in the command of the advance guard, marching some distance ahead of the column, and had orders to halt at this point and await the coming up of the main body. Fortunately, an enterprising Yankee had established a store here. . . . He had crackers, cheese, canned fruits, sardines, and many other dainties dear to the cavalryman, and . . . we of the advance were made new men."

Stuart with the head of the main column soon reached Talleysville, where he made a halt of about three hours to permit his stragglers to close up. According to Union Chaplain J. J. Marks: "We had a hospital near to this place, and to this General Stuart and the principal surgeon connected with his staff rode over. Their conduct was humane and gentlemanly, the surgeon coming in . . . and borrowing a small quantity of medicines, the general not permitting any of his officers to enter the house, saying he did not wish to alarm the sick men. He placed guards around the premises to prevent any of our men leaving . . . and communicating with our army. Though General Stuart said he did not wish to alarm our sick men, yet that night was fatal to more than one. It is easy, in a certain stage of the typhoid fever when the whole nervous system is at the lowest depression, to destroy a patient by an alarm or shock. Of the sick in this hospital was one noble young man from Indiana County, Pennsylvania, Ralston Hoover, who died that night. He had been sick three weeks, and was thought to be recovering,

A Yankee sutler's shop

and was deemed at this time to be out of danger. In his pocket, after his death, were found some of the most touching and beautiful letters from a child sister and a little brother, telling him how much they missed him, how they longed for his return, how they counted the days until he might come back, but, above all, telling how proud they were of their soldier brother."

Leaving Talleysville, Stuart's column, now encumbered with many prisoners riding on captured mules, headed southward through Mount Olive Church toward Sycamore Spring, the site of a ford over the lower Chickahominy. "The highway lay before us," recounts John Esten Cooke, "white in the unclouded splendor of the moon. . . . The exhaustion of the march now began to tell on the men. Whole companies went to sleep in the saddle, and Stuart himself was no exception. He had thrown one knee over the pommel of his saddle, folded his arms, dropped the bridle, and—chin on breast, his plumed hat drooping over his forehead—was sound asleep. His surefooted horse moved steadily, but the form of the General tottered from side to side. . . . The column thus moved on during the remainder of the night, the wary advance guard encountering no enemies and giving no alarm."

The ford at Sycamore Spring was reached between dawn and sunrise. "Here," says W. T. Robins, "our real troubles began. To our chagrin, we found the stream swollen by recent rains almost out of its banks and running like a torrent. No man or horse could get over without swimming, and it happened that the entrance to the ford on our side was below the point at which we had to come out on the other side. Therefore, we had to swim against the current. . . . The 9th Cavalry made the trial. After repeated efforts to swim the horses over we gave up, for we had crossed over only seventy-five men and horses in two hours."

The commander of the 9th, W. H. F. Lee, announced, "I think we are caught!" And the sentiment was shared by most of those who heard him. Everyone looked to Stuart. In Cooke's words: "I had never been with him in a tight place before, but from that moment I felt convinced that he was one of those men who rise under pressure. . . . He was not excited. All I noticed in his bearing to attract attention was a peculiar fashion of twisting his beard. . . . Otherwise he was cool and looked dangerous. . . . Ordering his column to move on, [he] galloped down the stream to a spot where an old bridge had formerly stood. Reaching this point, a strong rear guard was thrown out, the artillery placed in position; and Stuart set to work vigorously to rebuild the bridge. . . . The stone abutments remained, some thirty or forty feet only apart, for the river here ran deep and narrow between steep banks. . . . A skiff was procured; this was affixed by a rope to a tree in the mid-current just above the abutments, and thus a movable pier was secured in the middle of the stream. An old barn was then hastily torn to pieces and robbed of its timbers. These were stretched down to the boat and up to the opposite abutment, and a footbridge was thus ready. Large numbers of the men immediately unsaddled their horses, took their equipment over, and then returning, drove or rode their horses into the stream and swam them over. In this manner a considerable number crossed; but the process was much too slow. There, besides, was the artillery, which Stuart had no intention of leaving. A regular bridge must be built without a moment's delay. . . .

"Heavier blows resounded from the old barn; huge timbers approached, borne on brawny shoulders; and, descending into the boat anchored in the middle of the stream, the men lifted them across. They were just long enough. The ends rested on the abutments, and immediately thick planks were hurried forward and laid crosswise. . . . Standing in the boat beneath, Stuart worked with the men, and as the planks thundered down and the bridge steadily advanced the gay voice of the General was heard humming a song. He was singing carelessly, although at every instant an overpowering force of the enemy was looked for. . . . At last the bridge was finished. The artillery crossed amid hurrahs from the men, and then Stuart slowly moved his cavalry across the shaky footway.

"A little beyond was another arm of the river, which was, however, fordable . . . and through this, [and] through the interminable sloughs of the swamp beyond, the head of the column moved. The prisoners, who were numerous, had been marched over in advance of everything, and these were now mounted on [their] mules. . . . Mounted often two on a mule, they had a disagreeable time, the mules constantly falling in the treacherous mudholes and rolling their riders in the ooze. When a third swamp appeared before them, one of the Federal prisoners exclaimed, with tremendous indignation, 'How many damned *Chicken*hominies are there, I wonder, in this infernal country!' "

Three more hours had passed, and it was now early afternoon. The serious pursuit feared by the Confederates had not developed. But as Stuart's bridge was being burned by a detail under W. T. Robins, a small party of Federals made a furtive approach through the woods across the torrent. Robins was unsuspecting. "The men were lounging about on the ground. . . . I was seated under a tree on the bank of the river, and at the moment that the hissing of the burning timbers of the bridge let me know that it had fallen into the water, a rifle shot rang out from the other side, and the whistling bullet cut off a small limb over my head, which fell into my lap. . . . With a thankful heart for [the] bad aim, I at once withdrew the men and pushed on after the column. . . . Soon the column was in sight, and the march across Charles City County to the James River was made as vigorously as the jaded horses were able to stand. The men, though weary and hungry, were in fine spirits. . . . About sunset we neared the James. . . . Here we rested for about two hours, having marched into a field of clover, where the horses ate their fill. In the twilight, fires were lighted to cook the rations just brought in by our foragers.

"We were now about twenty-five miles [southeast of] Richmond, on the James River Road. Had the enemy been aware of our position, it would have been easy for him to throw a force between us and Richmond, and so cut us off. But the Federal general was not well served by his scouts, nor did his cavalry furnish him with accurate information of our movements. Relying upon the mistakes of the enemy, Stuart resolved to march straight on into Richmond. . . . Accordingly, I was ordered to take the advance guard and move out. . . . Although in the saddle and in motion, and aware that the safety of the expedition depended on great vigilance in case the enemy should be encountered . . . I was constantly falling asleep and awaking with a start when almost off my horse. . . .

"The full moon lighted us on our way . . . and frequently the windings of the road brought us near to and in sight of the James River, where lay the enemy's fleet. In the gray twilight of the dawn . . . we could see the masts of the fleet, not far off. Happily for us, the banks were high, and I imagine they had no lookout in the rigging, and we passed by unobserved. The sight of the enemy's fleet had aroused us somewhat, when 'Who goes there?' rang out on the stillness of the early morning. The challenger proved to be a vidette of the 10th Virginia Cavalry, commanded by Colonel J. Lucius Davis, who was picketing that road. Soon I was shaking hands with Colonel Davis and receiving his congratulations."

Stuart, with his casualties totalling one man killed and a number wounded, reported directly to an anxious Lee, while the troopers returned to their camps, where they were greeted as heroes and showered with questions. That evening, according to a writer for the Richmond *Examiner,* "the Negroes, mules, and Yankees captured by General Stuart . . . were marched up Main Street under an escort of cavalry. The Yankees, on foot, marched first, between files of horsemen; the Negroes came next, some on foot and others in wagons; while the mules, to the number of two hundred, unbridled and of their own accord followed the procession in a drove. At the corner of Eighteenth Street, the Yankees and Negroes were wheeled to the left and conducted to Libby Prison, while the mules were sent to stables in another direction."

That night Judith McGuire penned in her diary: "General Stuart has just returned to camp after a most wonderful and successful raid. . . . We are all full of excitement and delight, hoping that he discovered much about the Federal army which may be useful, but which, of course, is kept from the public. . . . General Stuart must have gone, it is said, within a few miles, perhaps nearer, of his father-in-law, the Federal General Cooke. I wonder what the old renegade Virginian thinks of his dashing son-in-law? If he has

The gunboats on the James River

a spark of proper feeling left in his obdurate heart, he must be proud of him."

General Cooke's true feeling was one of mortification. Not only had he been made to look foolish; he had also earned stern disapproval in a report written by Fitz John Porter, top commander on the Federal right now that McClellan had moved his headquarters to the Richmond side of the Chickahominy. As for McClellan himself, he made light of the raid, but he was nevertheless chagrined by it. Its timing, however, was such that he had something of equal magnitude on his mind at the same moment. He had got the remarkable notion that Davis and Lee might be willing to participate in a truce, that the time might be right for settling the war by conference.

It must not be supposed that McClellan consulted with Washington before taking action on this idea. As his country's savior, he must do whatever he himself believed the situation required. He initiated his efforts on June 15, the last day of Stuart's ride. The thing was easy enough to manage. It was incorporated with a meeting that had been arranged for the purpose of discussing an exchange of prisoners. The principals were McClellan's aide-de-camp Colonel Thomas M. Key and Confederate General Howell Cobb.

In Key's words: "I was ordered to proceed with a flag of truce to the bridge crossing the Chickahominy upon the Mechanicsville Road, where I would be met by General Cobb at 11 o'clock A.M. for the purpose of a conference in regard to an exchange of prisoners, my instructions being to learn the views of the rebel government and report them to General McClellan, making arrangements for a second meeting. I also received permission to converse with General Cobb upon the general subject of the existing contest, informing him, however, that all such conversation was purely personal and not in any respect of an official or representative character. I went to the place appointed, and there was met upon the bridge by General Cobb. We availed ourselves, as suggested by General McClellan, of the shelter of a little hut made by our pickets a few feet from the bridge, and talked together for several hours. . . .

"Our personal conversation began by my saying to him that I was pleased to meet him upon a peaceful errand, and that nothing was so desired by me as that we might soon meet in permanent peace. He replied that permanent peace could at any time be established in half an hour. I told him I would like to hear his views on that subject, and in return I would give him mine. . . . He then began speaking, and . . . the drift of the discourse was that the invasion of the seceding states, with its consequent slaughter and waste, had created in the Southern mind such feelings of animosity and spirit of resistance that the war could only end in separation or extermination. . . . I told him briefly in reply that his statement surprised and grieved me . . . that I had hoped and supposed that the Confederate leaders at least had been impressed by a sense of the hopelessness of the struggle. That the unequal character of the contest, our greater numbers, wealth, credit, and resources of all kinds; the unanimity of the Free States . . . the Union sentiment manifested . . . in greater or less degree throughout the South; the hopelessness of foreign intervention; the complete establishment of sea and river blockade; the loss of position after position in the interior, and the certainty of our irresistible advance had satisfied them that continued resistance must be unavailing.

"To this he said he would reply *seriatim*, and he did so at great length . . . denying that there was any Union sentiment left in the planting region. . . . He said that food and arms made sufficient material for war; that the slaves had never been so tractable as now; that slave labor was directed almost exclusively to the production of food, especially in districts remote from military operations, and that every state had its manufactories of arms and powder. He claimed that the military strength of Confederate States was as yet unbroken; that our army before Richmond was not strong enough to force an entrance into it; that . . . we could only take it when they saw fit to abandon it. He asserted that if we took Richmond and every other important point in the Confederate States . . . it would require years to suppress organized resistance, and that at last we would be compelled to hold the country by military occupation. . . .

"I told him in reply that such a state of things as he had at last described would involve on the part of the United States measures of military necessity and security not now contemplated . . . that I did not believe the people of the South, meaning free white citizens, were opposed to the United States Government; that I believed that the secession movement proceeded from a class of men who had arrogated to themselves superior social position, and who intended to frame a government in which they could grasp and hold political power; and that in my opinion . . . it might become necessary to disorganize that condition of society which gave rise to that class of men. . . .

"Here we ceased conversation on general matters and returned to the particular subject of our meeting [the exchange of prisoners]. . . . I subsequently said to him, 'Every day's experience must show to your intelligent men that your people are fighting their friends; that neither the President, the army, nor the people of the loyal states have any wish to subjugate the Southern States or to diminish their constitutional rights. Our soldiers exhibit but little animosity against yours; the prevailing sentiment among them is a conviction of duty. I cannot understand the grounds upon which your leaders continue this contest.'

"He said, 'The election of a sectional President, whose views on slavery were known to be objectionable to the whole South, evinced a purpose on the part of the Northern people to deprive the people of the South of an equal enjoyment of political rights. We cannot now return without degradation or with security. The blood which has been shed has washed out all feelings of brotherhood. We must become independent or conquered.'

"I replied, 'Mutual bravery shown in battle never yet of itself permanently alienated the combatants; it produces mutual respect. A return to the Union ... would not involve degradation. The security of the South would be greater than before. . . . No political organization at the North would be in respectable numbers which proposed Federal legislation or action in violation of the Constitution or in excess of its powers.' I told him that, speaking for myself alone, I would express the opinion that this wretched strife should be at once ended by submission on the one side and amnesty on the other. . . . He replied that no Confederate leader could openly advocate such a position and continue to live. . . . He said that the South might suffer much but would ultimately succeed; that the struggle has but begun."

Cobb's sentiments, which left no grounds for the establishment of peace talks, were at odds with the Northern view that the Confederacy would collapse with the capture of Richmond. But Cobb spoke with the confidence of a man undefeated. There is little doubt that the fall of the Confederate capital at this time would have been a critical blow to Southern morale. And if the fall had been accompanied by the destruction or surrender of their principal army, the seceded states might well have considered returning to the Union, especially since Lincoln, at this stage of the war, was prepared to offer them generous terms.

Thomas Key, disturbed by Cobb's intransigence, closed his report on the parley with a personal comment on the war as a whole: "It may be found necessary ... to destroy the class which has created this rebellion by destroying the institution [slavery] which has created them." This was not the sort of thing McClellan wanted to hear. Indeed, the entire report disappointed him deeply. He sent it to Washington, and soon heard from an umbraged Stanton: "It is not deemed proper for officers bearing flags of truce in respect to the exchange of prisoners to hold any conference with the rebel officers upon the general subject of the existing contest or upon any other subject than what relates to the exchange of prisoners."

Convinced by Key's report that Lee had determined upon a stubborn defense of Richmond, McClellan reconsidered the direction of his approach. The Prince de Joinville heard him speak of an alternate plan. "It was to transport the whole army seventeen miles from its position at that time, to abandon the line of communications on the York River, and to seek, with the assistance of the navy, a new base on the James River. If this movement could be successfully and secretly made, the chances of a great battle fought on the river bank with the cooperation of the gunboats covering one flank of the army would be much more favorable to the Federals. But the movement had dangers of its own, and it was not easy of accomplishment in the face of the enemy; not to mention the undesirableness of an apparent retreat. The plan was . . . renounced, or at least adjourned. . . . The General wished to carry out the operations already commenced; but he nevertheless took the wise precaution of sending to City Point on the river James vessels loaded with ammunition, provisions, and supplies of all sorts."

Although McClellan expected Lee to be a firm adversary, he had no idea that his old Mexican War associate was planning to take the offensive. In McClellan's opinion, Lee was not capable of that kind of boldness. It seemed a safe bet that he would remain inactive until attacked. McClellan wrote Ellen: "Look on the maps I sent you . . . and find Old Tavern on the road from New Bridge to Richmond. It is in that vicinity that the next battle will be fought. I think that they see it in that light, and that they are fully prepared to make a desperate resistance. I shall make the first battle mainly an artillery combat. As soon as I gain possession of the Old Tavern I will push them in upon Richmond and behind their works; then I will bring up my heavy guns, shell the city, and carry it by assault. I speak very confidently, but if you could see the faces of the troops as I ride among them you would share my confidence. They will do anything I tell them to do. I could not help laughing when, on the day of the last battle [Fair Oaks], I was riding along in front, a man jumped out in an interval of the cheering and addressed me quite familiarly, saying, 'Halloo, George! How are you? You are the only one of the whole crowd of generals that is worth a ———.' I won't fill up the last word, but the whole command shouted, 'That's so!' I think there is scarcely a man in this whole army who would not give his life for me." If this was an exaggeration, the fact remains that the majority of the enlisted men still had every confidence in their cherished Little Mac. He had managed to keep them convinced that all of their trials in this endless campaign could be laid at Washington's doorstep.

At about the same time that Ellen was reading her husband's message, Lee was writing to Stonewall Jackson in the Valley: "Frémont and Shields are apparently retrograding, their troops are shaken and disorganized, and some time will be required to set them again in the field. If this is so, the sooner you unite with this army the better. McClellan is being strengthened. . . . There is much sickness in his ranks, but his reinforcements by far exceed his losses. The present, therefore, seems to be favorable for a junction of your army and this. . . . To be efficacious, the movement must be secret. . . . The country is full of spies, and our plans are immediately carried to the enemy. . . . Unless McClellan can be driven out of his entrenchments he will move by positions under cover of his heavy guns within shelling distance of Richmond. I know of no surer way of thwarting him than that proposed. I should like to have the advantage of your views and be able to

Union workers completing one of the bridges over the Chickahominy

confer with you. Will meet you at some point on your approach to the Chickahominy."

Lee needed time to mature his plans, and McClellan, of course, cooperated by continuing to move with his customary deliberation. Ellen was told on June 17: "The weather yesterday and today has been splendid. It is clear and bright. . . . The roads and fields are drying beautifully. The river is falling rapidly; our bridges are nearly finished, and we shall soon be on the move." McClellan spent the next day conducting a general review. He rode about briskly, all the while nodding, smiling, and doffing his hat in response to cheering of such a volume as to make the Confederates wonder what was happening. It was probably a calculated appearance, made to bolster morale.

"The sick," says Chaplain Marks, "increased by hundreds, and all the hospitals were crowded. . . . Everything began to wear the appearance, to my eye, of despondency in the army. Rumors came to us daily of the great increase of the Confederate forces, while ours were evidently rapidly diminishing." The worst illness, according to Federal newsman George Alfred Townsend, continued to be typhoid fever. The victims "seemed to wither and shrivel away; their eyes became at first very bright, and afterward lusterless; their skins grew hard and sallow; their lips faded to a dry whiteness; all the fluids of the body were consumed; and they crumbled to corruption before life had fairly gone from them. . . . The number of persons that died . . . was fabulous. . . . The embalmers were now enjoying their millennium, and a steam coffin manufactory was erected at the White House, where twenty men worked day and night turning out hundreds of pine boxes."

By this time the medical people had decided that the daily whiskey ration was not retarding the progress of the fever, and the order was rescinded. Chaplain Stewart wrote home: "Let us bless the Lord together. . . . Should no additional blindness induce the powers-that-be to renew the whiskey ration, we will, while in our present condition, have an absence of drunkenness among our rank and file. Get it here they cannot. Would that a similar necessity rested upon officers of every grade. Although difficulty is frequently experienced in getting forward sufficient army supplies through the limited channels which have been opened, yet it is said and believed that whole wagon-loads of boxes filled with champagne, brandy, and whiskey for 'headquarters' find preference in *public* conveyance."

For those officers in the various headquarters sections who were accustomed to using alcohol as a tranquilizer, a time had come when this aid was sorely needed. The campaign was obviously approaching a climax, and things were disturbingly hazy as to the direction this momentous event would take. Some of the officers who knew Robert E. Lee did not share McClellan's belief in his timidity. They saw the "outnumbered" Union army, divided by the Chickahominy and dependent upon the York River for its supplies, as being in an untenable position; and they felt that McClellan should either attempt a strong move against Richmond at once or seek unity and security to the south, on the bank of the James.

Even those officers who had kept their faith in McClellan's ability, joining him in blaming Washington for every failure to date, could no longer take him altogether seriously. To his intimates he spoke of himself as an instrument of God, but he did not seem to know what God wanted him to do. One day he was disdainful of the "terrible odds" against him; the next he was bitter about his "weakness." He spoke of launching great battles but fought only when action was forced upon him, and he kept returning to musings about winning Richmond and the war by skillful maneuvering rather than by fighting. What he would have preferred above all, apparently, was for Washington to send him reinforcements in such numbers as to awe Davis and Lee into surrendering.

McClellan the professional soldier did not understand the war as well as Lincoln and Stanton the military amateurs. Said Lincoln to a group of Northern ladies who paid him a visit: "General McClellan thinks he is going to whip the rebels by strategy, and the army has got the same notion. They have no idea that the war is to be carried on and put through by hard, tough fighting, and that it will hurt somebody; and no headway is going to be made while this delusion lasts." It was McClellan's failure to accept the realities of the war and to pursue victory boldly that had got him into his present predicament. While his army was before Washington the previous autumn, McClellan outnumbered Joe Johnston, then at Manassas, at least three-to-one. A smashing advance might well have carried the Union army straight through to Richmond. Drawn up before Yorktown, McClellan initially had at least a six-to-one advantage. He could have marched over John Magruder and hurried to Richmond before Johnston had time to organize an adequate defense. The argument that McClellan was not aware of his great numerical superiority must be answered with the assertion that he himself was responsible for the state of his intelligence system, and that he was all too eager to believe exaggerated reports. It was as though he wanted an excuse for inaction, or wanted Washington to take alarm at the reports and send him a preponderance of power.

In his present situation, it must be admitted, McClellan could have used more troops. He had given the Confederates too much time to reinforce themselves and to improve their fortifications. His 25,000-man edge over Lee was not enough to ensure the success of an immediate frontal assault upon Richmond. Of course, in spite of his brave talk to Ellen, McClellan's intention was to soften the city's defenses with siege operations before assaulting. And his numbers were sufficient for this course of action, even if the Confederates did not stand still for it; he could launch countermeasures.

But the pressures of the situation were beginning to exhaust McClellan's nerve.

The general's most consistently loyal associates and friends, who saw him as he saw himself, found it incredible that Washington should continue to be so stupid as to deny this brilliant strategist the kind of support he requested. "When will the nation learn," wrote a nurse stationed on a hospital ship at the White House landing, "that it is in the hands of its greatest man, and wait calmly for *his* results, only taking care in the meantime to strengthen his hands?" People like this clung to the belief that if McClellan had been permitted to keep McDowell's corps in the beginning he would have stormed into Richmond. There is precious little evidence to support this viewpoint. McClellan was McClellan. Even if he had deemed 150,000 men to be an adequate force (which is doubtful), he would almost certainly have found another reason, or a whole set of reasons, for advancing slowly and cautiously, and thus would have ended up as he was now.

While making his preparations to move in force against Old Tavern on the Richmond side of the Chickahominy, McClellan called Franklin's corps from the far side, where Lee was planning to attack. The march to the bridge, according to Trooper Adams, was made over a rise that afforded a view to the rear. "More than one general officer looked back over that long thin line we called our right with feelings of misgiving. The line extended from near where we stood to Mechanicsville, a distance of five miles, and was left with Fitz John Porter's corps and McCall's division of Pennsylvania Reserves and Stoneman's cavalry to hold it." With Franklin's arrival, McClellan had about three-fourths of his army with him on the Richmond side of the river.

During this period the skirmishing grew hotter, partly because Lee was probing the Union lines. The digging continued apace. Southerner Jesse Reid wrote home: "It really seems to me that McClellan as well as some of our own generals had better handle the spade than the sword. Both sides are ditching every day. I think if we had fewer ditches and more Stonewalls it would be better for us. . . . I don't see the sense of piling up earth to keep us apart. If we don't get at each other sometime, when will the war end? My plan would be to quit ditching and go to fighting."

On Sunday afternoon, June 22, McClellan wrote his wife: "I am as anxious as any human being can be to finish this war. Yet when I see such insane folly behind me I feel that the final salvation of the country demands the utmost prudence on my part, and that I must not run the slightest risk of disaster, for if anything happened to this army our cause would be lost. I got up some heavy guns today, and hope to give secesh a preliminary pounding tomorrow and to make one good step next day. The rascals are very strong and outnumber me very considerably. They are well entrenched also, and have all the advantages of position, so I must be prudent. But I will yet suc-

One of the artillery batteries left on north bank of river. Gunners are harassing a Confederate position on south bank.

ceed, notwithstanding all they do and leave undone in Washington to prevent it. I would not have on my conscience what those men have for all the world."

It was on the day after McClellan wrote this that Lee made the final arrangements for his attack. In the words of Confederate General Daniel H. Hill: "While encamped about noon on Monday, the 23rd of June, 1862, on the Williamsburg Road about a mile from the battlefield of Seven Pines, in command of a division of the Confederate Army, I received an order from General Lee to report immediately at his quarters on the Mechanicsville Road. On approaching the house which the general occupied, I saw an officer leaning over the yard-paling, dusty, travel-worn, and apparently very tired. He raised himself up as I dismounted, and I recognized General Jackson, who till that moment I had supposed was confronting Banks and Frémont far down the Valley of Virginia. He said that he had ridden fifty-two miles since one o'clock that morning, having taken relays of horses on the road. We went together into General Lee's office. General Jackson declined refreshments courteously tendered by General Lee, but drank a glass of milk. Soon after, Generals Longstreet and A. P. Hill came in, and General Lee, closing the door, told us that he had determined to attack the Federal right wing and had selected our four commands to execute the movement."

According to Longstreet, "The general explained the plan briefly . . . then excused himself to attend to office business, asking that we talk the matter over for our better comprehension. Turning to Jackson, I said, 'You have distance to overcome, and in all probability obstacles will be thrown in the way of your march by the enemy. As your move is the key of the campaign, you should appoint the hour at which the connection may be made cooperative.' He promptly responded, 'The morning of the 25th.' I expressed doubt of his meeting that hour, and suggested that it would be better to take a little more time, as the movements of our columns could be readily adjusted to those of his. He then appointed the morning of the 26th."

Jackson was in such a fog of fatigue at this time that he was unable to think intelligently. Even the second date he set was too tall an order for his "foot cavalry," still fifty miles northwest of Richmond. The great Stonewall's reputation, just now rising to international heights, was to undergo a retrogression during Lee's fight to save Richmond, a phenomenon destined to intrigue military analysts ever after. Jackson's failure to come up to expectations was probably based on a combination of things: a physical and moral fatigue that affected his judgment; a similar fatigue in his men that made them unable and even unwilling to drive themselves as hard as they had in the Valley, especially since they knew that Lee had thousands of other troops to work with; and the circumstance that the Richmond area was unfamiliar territory, which impeded celerity of movement. But Jackson's very approach to the field had its effect on events, for it prompted McClellan to begin thinking entirely in defensive terms. Lee had enjoined Jackson to secrecy in his march to Richmond, but the Confederate cause was not harmed by the fact that secrecy was not preserved.

The news broke in the Union lines on June 24. Trooper Adams gives the details: "Our scouts have brought in a man dressed in dirty gray clothes. He turns out to be a very intelligent man, and after giving various accounts of himself finally confesses to be a deserter from Jackson's army, which he describes as advancing slowly in the direction of Hanover Court House. There is no doubt now in the minds of some of our generals as to where the enemy intends to make his real attack, and what part Stonewall Jackson is to play. Now is the time to prepare for it, to send back troops to strengthen our right at Mechanicsville and to guard against Jackson's attempt on our rear. But General McClellan still hesitates, is still uncertain as to what the enemy's real intentions are."

McClellan was at first unwilling to credit the deserter's story because such a development seemed unlikely. It was true that Banks and Frémont had proved singularly inept in their campaign to trap and destroy Jackson, but surely they had the power and the ability to hold him in the Valley! If the deserter was telling the truth, Jackson had not only cost McClellan a large body of reinforcements but was about to compound the damage by strengthening Lee. The thought was appalling. McClellan fired off a telegram to Stanton: "I would be glad to learn, at your earliest convenience, the most exact information you have as to the position and movements of Jackson, as well as the sources from which your information is derived, that I may the better compare it with what I have."

While awaiting a reply, McClellan made the opening thrust in his planned movement upon Old Tavern. "Between eight and nine o'clock on the morning of the 25th," he explains, "the advance was begun by General Heintzelman's corps. The enemy were found to be in strong force all along the line, and contested the advance stubbornly, but by sunset our object was accomplished." This was McClellan's first step toward Richmond, and also his last, the beginning of what became known as the Seven Days' Campaign. Returning to his headquarters that evening, McClellan found the expected message from Stanton, and it was anything but reassuring. Nobody in Washington had any definite information on Jackson's whereabouts, but it was believed he had 40,000 men. (The actual number was 18,000.) Stanton had evaluated all the conflicting intelligence about the mysterious general and was induced "to suspect that his real movement now is towards Richmond." One might begin to feel sorry for McClellan at this point except for the knowledge that the new crisis was still another result of his aversion to expeditious action, of his incurable habit of giving the enemy every advantage of *time*.

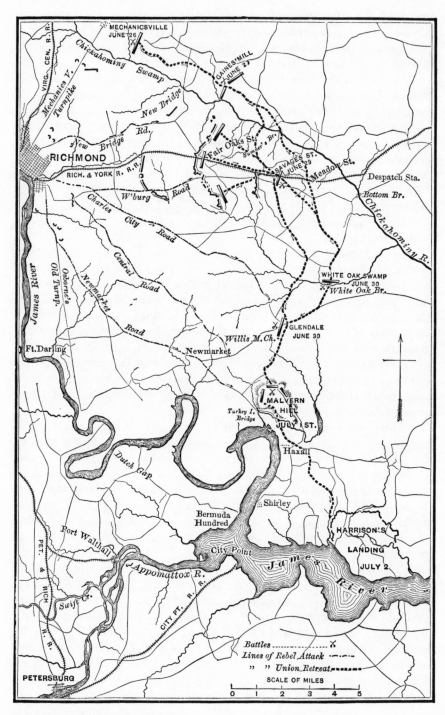

Battlefields of the Seven Days

"I have just returned from the field," McClellan replied to Stanton, "and found your dispatch in regard to Jackson. . . . I incline to think that Jackson will attack my right and rear. The rebel force [in its entirety] is stated at 200,000. . . . I shall have to contend against vastly superior odds if these reports be true. But this army will do all in the power of men to hold their position and repulse any attack. I regret my great inferiority in numbers, but feel that I am in no way responsible for it, as I have not failed to represent repeatedly the necessity of reinforcements; that this was the decisive point and that all the available means of the government should be concentrated here. I will do all that a general can do with the splendid army I have the honor to command, and, if it is destroyed by overwhelming numbers, can at least die with it and share its fate. But if the result of the action, which will probably occur tomorrow or within a short time, is a disaster, the responsibility cannot be thrown on my shoulders; it must rest where it belongs. Since I commenced this [dispatch] I have received additional intelligence. . . . I shall probably be attacked tomorrow, and now go to the other side of the Chickahominy to arrange for the defense on that side. I feel that there is no use in my again asking for reinforcements."

McClellan did not tell Stanton that his arrangements for the defense of his right were combined with a flurry of preparations for a general retreat, or, as he preferred to call it, a "change of base." He explained later: "The dangerous position of the army had been faithfully held to the last moment. . . . I decided then to carry into effect the . . . plan of abandoning the Pamunkey and taking up the line of the James. The necessary orders were given for the defense of the depots at the White House to the last moment and its final destruction and abandonment. It was also ordered that all possible stores should be pushed to the front while communications were open. The ground to the James had already been reconnoitered with reference to this movement."

In his own eyes, McClellan was about to do something not only necessary but praiseworthy. He was certainly not as self-assured, however, as these words written in later years seem to indicate: "Such a change of base, in the presence of a powerful enemy, is one of the most difficult undertakings in war, but I was confident in the valor and discipline of my brave army, and knew that it could be trusted equally to retreat or advance, and to fight the series of battles now inevitable, whether retreating from victories or marching through defeats; and, in short, I had no doubt whatever of its ability, even against superior numbers, to fight its way through to the James and get a position whence a successful advance upon Richmond would again be possible."

It had taken McClellan eleven months to make his preparations and to fight his way to Richmond's gates. Now he was about to fight to leave them in order to make new preparations to fight his way back.

12

LEE BREAKS THE SIEGE

LEE'S ATTACK PLAN was one of great daring. Employed against an abler adversary, it might have been turned against him. Only the commands of John Magruder and Benjamin Huger, a total of 25,000 men, were to be left in the Richmond defenses. McClellan had about three times that many troops on the Richmond side of the Chickahominy. Lee's intended march with his main body—northward from the city, eastward over the river's headwaters, then southeastward along the bank to Fitz John Porter's lines—would take him out of contact with the city's defenders; and these troops would remain imperiled until Lee restored contact by driving Porter far enough to uncover some of the lower crossings. Jefferson Davis wasn't quite sure what to think of Lee's plan. "I pointed out to him that our force and entrenched line between [the Federal left] and Richmond was too weak for a protracted resistance, and, if McClellan was the man I took him for when I nominated him for promotion in a new regiment of cavalry, and subsequently selected him for one of the military commissions sent to Europe during the War of the Crimea, as soon as he found that the bulk of our army was on the north side of the Chickahominy he would not stop to try conclusions with it there but would immediately move upon his objective point, the city of Richmond. If, on the other hand, he should behave like an engineer officer and deem it his first duty to protect his line of communication, I thought the plan was not only the best but would be a success." Lee, as a former engineer himself, responded with a small smile that he did not think that engineer officers were any more likely than other officers to make mistakes. Then he assured Davis that the plan was feasible. From Northern newspapers that had reached Richmond, Lee had learned of McClellan's misapprehensions about Confederate numbers, and he knew that this was a decided advantage.

Fitz John Porter's main defense lines were at Beaver Dam Creek, which flowed into the Chickahominy. His front was manned by McCall's division, with John Reynolds' brigade on the right, and Truman Seymour's on the left at Ellerson's Mill. The outposts were at Mechanicsville, about a mile from the main body. Porter relates: "The morning of Thursday, June 26, dawned clear and bright. . . . The formation of the ground south of the Chickahominy opposite Mechanicsville and west to Meadow Bridge largely concealed from view the forces gathered to execute an evidently well-planned and well-prepared attack upon my command. For some hours, on our side of the river all was quiet, except at Mechanicsville and at the two bridge crossings. At these points our small outposts were conspicuously displayed for the purpose of creating an impression of numbers and of an intention to maintain an obstinate resistance. We aimed to invite a heavy attack, and then, by rapid withdrawal, to incite such confidence in the enemy as to induce incautious pursuit. . . . The position selected on Beaver Dam Creek for our line of defense was naturally very strong. The banks of the valley were steep, and forces advancing on the adjacent plains presented their flanks as well as their front to the fire of both infantry and artillery, safely posted behind entrenchments. The stream was over waist-deep and bordered by swamps."

Although Porter could not see the enemy on his left-front, his right-front offered a long view across the countryside. "In the northern and western horizon vast clouds of dust arose, indicating the movements of Jackson's advancing forces. They were far distant, and we had reason to believe that the obstacles to their rapid advance placed in their way by detachments sent for that purpose would prevent them from making an attack that day. . . . We did not fear Lee alone. We did fear his attack, combined with one by Jackson on our flank. But our fears were allayed for a day."

As a result of Jackson's tardiness, the troops under Longstreet and the two Hills (who, incidentally, were not related) remained inactive throughout the morning and into the early afternoon. It was a situation that gave Lee considerable concern for the safety of Richmond. Magruder, with Huger on his right, had been charged with defending the city at all hazards, and "Prince John" had undertaken the responsibility, expecting an attack and harboring the hope that the pressure would ease off as soon as the guns opened across the river and divided McClellan's attention. Thus far no attack had developed, but one still seemed likely, and the continued silence at Mechanicsville made Magruder fidgety. His fears, of course, were groundless. At noon McClellan, then at the Trent house in front of Richmond, wired Washington: "All things very quiet on this bank of the Chickahominy. I would prefer more noise." It did not seem to occur to him that he had enough power in his left wing to make all the noise he wished, and that, in fact, he ought to be using the wing to make a great deal. Running true to

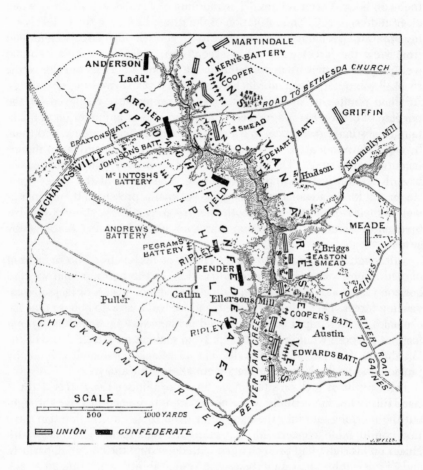

Battle of Mechanicsville (or Beaver Dam Creek)

form, he merely kept this vast array in readiness to defend itself if attacked. Talks with his front-line generals, some of whom had been infected by his repeated references to the enemy's "superiority" and had themselves begun to see troops that weren't there, convinced McClellan the Richmond defenses held 100,000 men. The fact that Lee had divided his army seemed proof that he was as strong as had been supposed. McClellan would have been incredulous at the knowledge that Lee had not only left the Richmond lines thinly manned but had also ordered these troops to *pursue closely* if the Federals began moving toward the river bridges after the firing began at Mechanicsville.

The reason it was important for Lee to await Jackson's arrival before attacking was that the action was supposed to begin with a march by Jackson against Porter's right-rear, thus turning the Federal general out of his strong position and making him easy game for the combination of Confederate forces. But finally A. P. Hill, who had been selected to initiate Lee's advance upon word from Jackson that he was closing in, decided to wait no longer. He was convinced that Jackson, with his reputation for fast marching, just had to be somewhere near and would shortly be ready to do his part. Hill was two miles from Lee at this time and did not consult him about moving. As a result, Lee's first step in his campaign to save Richmond was a disaster.

Fitz John Porter tells how the fight began: "About two o'clock . . . the boom of a single cannon in the direction of Mechanicsville resounded through our camps. This was the signal which had been agreed upon to announce the fact that the enemy were crossing the Chickahominy. The curtain rose; the stage was prepared for the first scene of the tragedy. . . . About three o'clock the enemy . . . in large bodies commenced rapidly to cross the Chickahominy almost simultaneously at Mechanicsville, Meadow Bridge, and above, and pushed down the . . . bank along the roads leading to Beaver Dam Creek. In accordance with directions previously given, the outposts watching the access to the crossings fell back after slight resistance to their already designated position on the east bank of Beaver Dam Creek, destroying the bridges as they retired."

Both sides now opened with artillery fire. The roar was deafening near at hand, and it was heard loudly even in Richmond. The Mechanicsville region was visible from high spots in the city and its environs, and hundreds of citizens hurried to take a look. Governor John Letcher and a select group went to the roof of his mansion, and almost every other tall building bearing on the scene was soon capped with huddles of people. The flashes of some of the guns could be seen against the bright blue horizon.

Returning to Fitz John Porter: "After passing Mechanicsville the attacking forces were divided, a portion taking the road to the right to Ellerson's Mill, while the larger body directed their march to the left into the valley of Beaver Dam Creek, upon the road covered by Reynolds. Apparently unaware, or regardless, of the great danger in their front, this force moved on with animation and confidence, as if going to parade or engaging in a sham battle. Suddenly, when halfway down the bank of the valley, our men opened upon it rapid volleys of artillery and infantry, which strewed the road and hillside with hundreds of dead and wounded, and drove the main body of the survivors back in rapid flight. . . . On the extreme right a small force of the enemy secured a foothold on the east bank, but it did no harm. . . . The forces which were directed against Seymour at Ellerson's Mill made little progress. Seymour's direct [fire] and Reynolds' flank fire soon arrested them and drove them to shelter, suffering even more disastrously than those who had attacked Reynolds. Late in the afternoon, greatly strengthened, they renewed the attack with spirit and energy, some reaching the borders of the stream, but only to be repulsed with terrible slaughter."

In Richmond, as the fighting continued into the dusk, the number of observers increased. Diarist Judith McGuire says that "the commanding hills from the President's house to the Almshouse were covered, like a vast amphitheater, with men, women and children witnessing the grand display of fireworks—beautiful, yet awful—and sending death amid those whom our hearts hold so dear. . . . The brilliant light of bombs bursting in the air and passing to the ground, the innumerable lesser lights emitted by thousands and thousands of muskets, together with the roar of artillery and the rattling of small arms, constituted a scene terrifically grand and imposing." Adds Edward Pollard: "Barns, houses, and stacks of hay and straw were in a blaze; and by their light our men were plainly visible rushing across the open spaces through infernal showers of grape."

There were Richmond citizens who deliberately avoided looking toward the battlefield. Among them was Mrs. Roger A. Pryor, whose husband was one of Lee's generals. "I shut myself in my darkened room. At twilight I had a note from Governor Letcher . . . inviting me to come to the Governor's mansion. From the roof one might see the flash of musket and artillery. No! I did not wish to see the infernal fires. I preferred to . . . wait alone in my room. The city was strangely quiet. Everybody had gone out to the hills to witness the aurora of death. . . . As it grew dark a servant entered to light my candles, but I forbade her. Did I not mean to go to supper? I would have coffee brought to me. God only knew what news I might hear before morning. I must keep up my strength."

General Pryor was safe when the battle ended with full darkness, but nearly 1,500 other Confederates had been killed or wounded. Fitz John Porter lost about 360 men. News of the victory raced through the Federal camps on the Richmond side of the Chickahominy. According to Surgeon Stevens, the reaction was electric. "Men who had, by constant hardships and by continually looking on death, almost forgotten the feelings of joy now broke out in loud shouts of gladness; and for the first time in many weeks the bands played those heart-stirring national airs which in times past had been wont to fill the hearts of the soldiers with enthusiasm. . . . A renewal of the attack might be expected at any moment. Still, the men of the whole of the left wing were exulting in the glad hope that in the morning we were to march into Richmond almost without opposition. . . . The prize which they had so often been promised seemed almost within their grasp. Men shook hands with each other, sang patriotic songs, and shouted in greatest glee. Bands continued to ring out their notes of gladness until long after nightfall. General officers rode about announcing a grand victory . . . and the men lay down upon their arms to dream of reveling in the streets of Richmond before another night."

The army's instincts were better than McClellan's. Although the dauntless Lee decided to continue with his original plan, his campaign was presently in disorder. He had not only lost his first battle but had also failed to uncover the crossings he needed to make contact with Magruder. That officer found his own position extremely worrisome, and he moved his headquarters close to the front that evening so as to keep a personal watch on the multitudinous foe. McClellan, of course, was unable to see his advantage, for he had chosen to believe that the Confederates had 100,000 men on either side of the river. Beaver Dam Creek gave him only a momentary feeling of elation. He wired Stanton at 9 P.M.: "Victory of today complete and against great odds. I almost begin to think we are invincible." The mood was quickly replaced by renewed worries about Jackson, and the preparations for the retreat to the James were not interrupted. Even while the left wing of the army was celebrating the prospect of entering Richmond, the medical director at the White House, Dr. Thomas T. Ellis, was writing: "There is a general movement of all the vessels, that have so long been lying in the Pamunkey River, towards the mouth. Everything possible to be moved has been, or will be, sent down to Cumberland or West Point. All the tugs and steam vessels have been busy as bees, and things look rather lively on the water. . . . On the land there has been quite a general clearing out. Quartermasters and other officers have placed their effects, private or official, upon steamers, ready for an instant start so soon as the rebel bayonets gleam near us. The woods lining the shores of the river have been cut down to give the gunboats a chance to work."

McClellan had made so many pronouncements about taking Richmond against all odds that few people with the army realized that he was planning a general retreat. Some of the White House personnel believed that he had decided to assemble his entire force on the Richmond side of the river for an immediate attack, a maneuver that naturally required the abandonment of his Pamunkey base and the transmission of his supplies around to the mouth of the James for easy delivery up to the gates of the city. McClellan slept little that night, for he had to perfect his retirement plans. To gain the additional time he needed both to start his artillery and wagon trains overland toward the James and to destroy the stores for which there was no room on the wagons or ships, he would have to order his friend Fitz John Porter to fight another battle. At Beaver Dam Creek, however, Porter's right flank was dangerously vulnerable to Jackson's approach. At about 3 A.M. McClellan sent word for Porter to withdraw down the Chickahominy to Gaines' Mill and set up a new defense line with his back toward a set of bridges that would provide him direct contact with the main army.

"Before sunrise of the 27th," Porter relates, "the troops were withdrawn from Beaver Dam Creek and sent to their new position east of Powhite Creek, destroying the bridges across it after them. Some batteries and infantry skirmishers, left as a ruse at Beaver Dam Creek, by their fire so fully absorbed the attention of the foe that our purpose suddenly and rapidly to abandon the entrenchments seemed unsuspected. But when they discovered our withdrawal their infantry pressed forward in small detachments, the main body and the artillery being delayed to rebuild the bridges."

At 10 A.M. McClellan, then at his headquarters on the Richmond side of the river, sent his first wire of the day to Stanton, reporting that Porter's change of position had been "beautifully executed under a sharp fire, with but little loss. The troops on the other side are now well in hand, and the whole army so concentrated that it can take advantage of the first mistake made by the enemy." This, of course, was only talk. The enemy had already made a mistake—his attack at Beaver Dam Creek—that could have been taken advantage of. "There is little doubt," says analyst Swinton, "that a direct march of the whole army on Richmond on the morning of the 27th would have had the effect to call Lee to the defense of his own communications and the Confederate capital, which was defended by only 25,000 men. McClellan held the direct crossings of the Chickahominy . . . and Lee would have been compelled to make a detour of at least a day to rejoin the force in front of Richmond. Why, therefore, did not General McClellan execute this operation? He [later answered] this question by a reference to the limited quantity of supplies on hand; but this cannot be accepted as valid, for the army had at this time rations for many days, and large stores had . . . to be burnt previous to the retreat. The real reason is that the operation overleaped, by its boldness, the methodical genius of the Union commander."

The tragedy of McClellan's leadership was fast reaching its climax. Fitz John Porter knew that his commander had made plans for a "change of base," but he believed these plans to be merely precautionary. He was not aware that his corps was being put at great peril for the sole purpose of gaining McClellan extra time to get the retreat organized. Porter believed his mission to be a nobler one. "I . . . determined to hold my position at least long enough to make the army secure. Though in a desperate situation, I was not without strong hope of some timely assistance from the main body of the army, with which I might repulse the attack and so cripple our opponents as to make the capture of Richmond by the main body of the army, under McClellan, the result of any sacrifice or suffering on the part of my troops or of myself. I felt that the life or death of the army depended upon our conduct in the contest of that day, and that on the issue of that contest depended an early peace or a prolonged, devastating war."

As for the men on the Richmond side of the river, Surgeon Stevens says that "their astonishment ... on discovering ... that Porter's corps had fallen back was only equaled by their mortification and disappointment as they saw the long lines of rebels advancing in the gray of the morning against our retreating column. They had believed, when [the previous] night came on, that our arms had achieved the first of a series of victories which was to give us the rebel capital. Now they saw that our army was already in retreat, and they gazed at the long train of artillery and wagons, which had parked near us, with downcast faces. [This was Porter's train, which had been brought over during the night.] From our camp, Porter's corps could be distinctly seen, and we could watch the movements of the rebels as they arrived upon the highlands, formed their line on the range of hills opposite Porter, and planted their guns near the large barn on Dr. Gaines' farm."

It was another bright blue day, and the sun grew hot. Noon came, and the battle was not yet joined. Longstreet and the Hills were still making their dispositions. In addition, Jackson was having trouble finding his way to Old Cold Harbor, near which lay the foe's right wing, where he was supposed to unite with D. H. Hill. "While General Lee waited to get all his divisions in hand," explains Edward Pollard, "he made his temporary headquarters at a farmhouse near the battlefield. . . . He sat entirely alone on the rear portico . . . while the foreground and the adjoining orchard were occupied by general officers, aides, couriers, and prisoners [taken during the morning's advance], making an animated scene of war. Officers who in a few moments were to stand face to face with death chatted as gaily as if they were going to a picnic. Some sat under the shady trees, making a hasty repast. . . . General Lee . . . awaited an hour on which hung mighty and untold destinies as calmly as a signal for the ordinary duties of the day."

The Confederate commander might have been frowning had he known what was presently happening at the White House. General Silas Casey, who was in charge of the evacuation measures, had been obliged to subject the Lee property to rough usage. A number of axemen were busy on the front lawn. "The chopping," relates Medical Director Ellis, "is plainly heard as, one by one, the lofty trees of a century's growth—oaks, elms, and pines—topple over and fall with a fearful crash. Others are engaged in the

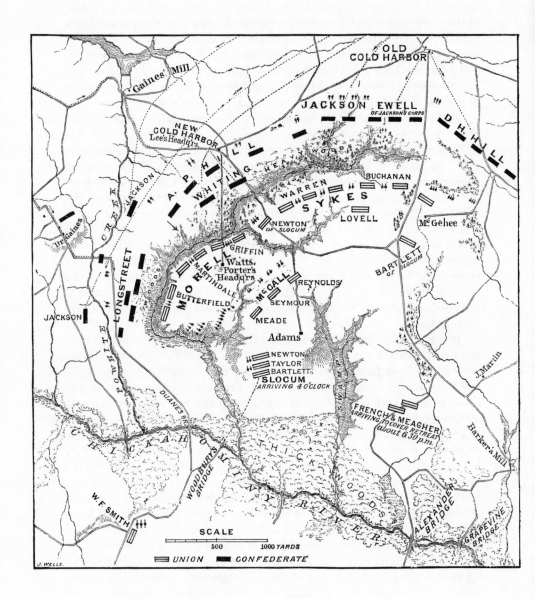

Battle of Gaines' Mill

erection of a high signal station, from which the movements of the enemy can be watched, and a lofty cupola on the roof of the White House or Lee House, from which a splendid view of the river for its full length and the surrounding country can be had. A detachment of the signal corps from the gunboats are now stationed in both of these, to give notice to General Casey's headquarters and the vessels on the river, so that they can act in concert, and, if necessary, drop down beyond the reach of the enemy's guns.

"Other active preparations for departure are going on: the freight-laden schooners and transports are, one by one, starting for Fortress Monroe, and many exclamations of surprise issue from the lips of those ignorant of the order to evacuate, but as yet little or no panic exists. The railroad over which so many hundred wounded have been carried, with its locomotives and hundred freight cars, and which carried all the supplies, men, and horses to the advance, is now busily engaged in bringing back such supplies and wagons as can be shipped down the river and are not required in the purported change of front by the army. These active preparations have not escaped the notice of the hundreds of sutlers and camp followers. The bustle soon becomes general, and vessels of every kind are being rapidly loaded at the wharves. . . . The contrabands are being put on board of canalboats. The order was sent this noon to their camp, about an eighth of a mile from here, and with their camp equipage they are busily hurrying to and fro from the boats. . . . Soon all of the three or four thousand . . . will bid farewell to this part of Dixie. . . . I think they don't regret their exodus from the Old Dominion. . . . The excitement has increased so much that many of the [contraband] laborers, panic-stricken, refuse to work, fearing to be taken prisoners. Colonel Butler has a band playing airs around the camp, which seems to inspire them with confidence as to their safety."

While awaiting Lee's attack on Porter, the nervous McClellan prepared to defend himself also on the Richmond side of the river, for the Confederate lines there were exhibiting a disturbing restlessness. Chaplain Stewart's regiment was one of those on picket that day. "The enemy, in large force, were so near that every ordinary word spoken by them could be distinctly heard." A similar situation on another part of the field is described by Private Warren Goss: "One of my comrades, while on picket, heard orders given as if to a large body of men, 'From right of companies to rear in a column, right face! Don't get into a dozen ranks there! Why don't they move forward up the path?' These commands excited our vigilance. What puzzled us was that we could not hear the tramp of men, which is usual in moving large bodies of troops, when near enough to hear their voices. Later we knew that the Confederates . . . were keeping up a big show with a small number of troops." The head showman, of course, was Prince John Magruder, who was conducting a replay of his successful Yorktown trick. He was quite as successful this time. When McClellan informed the generals in front of Richmond that they might be required to send some of their troops to help Porter, most reacted with apprehension for their own security.

It was about 12:30 when the Battle of Gaines' Mill opened with heavy skirmishing as the Confederates improved their deployments. The part played by the 1st South Carolina Volunteers is described by one of the unit's officers, J. F. J. Caldwell: "We moved forward and drove a strong skirmish [line] from a pine thicket just beyond the mill, at the double-quick. A brigade commander in our division afterwards said that it was the most beautiful advance he had ever seen. . . . We shot down several of the enemy as they retreated across the open field; but one of them, after lying a moment, rose and attempted to follow his flying comrades. By this time the uninjured ones had passed out of sight; so this unfortunate was left to the fire of our whole line. The excitement became intense. A perfect shower of balls was hurled after him, striking up the dust before, behind, and all around him. But still he staggered on, striving but the more vigorously as the danger increased. Cries of 'Kill him!' 'Shoot him!' 'Down with the fellow!' and others of rougher cast resounded from every side; but shoot as we would, he succeeded in reaching a clump of pines, where we found him soon after, exhausted by fatigue and loss of blood."

When the main action began about two o'clock, Stonewall Jackson was not yet on the scene; but, as at Beaver Dam Creek, he was momentarily expected. Again, A. P. Hill opened the attack, this time by Lee's order. Hill occupied the Confederate center. Longstreet was on his right, and D. H. Hill on his left. Jackson was moving not only to merge with D. H. Hill but also to function as senior commander on that part of the field. Fitz John Porter was watching as A. P. Hill's widespread lines, with banners waving, emerged from a belt of woods in the face of a storm of opposition from the Union defenses. "Dashing across the intervening plains, floundering in the swamps, and struggling against the tangled brushwood, brigade after brigade seemed almost to melt away before the concentrated fire of our artillery and infantry; yet others pressed on, followed by supports as dashing and as brave as their predecessors, despite their heavy losses and the disheartening effect of having to clamber over many of their disabled and dead, and to meet their surviving comrades rushing back in great disorder from the deadly contest. For nearly two hours the battle raged. . . . The fierce firing of artillery and infantry, the crash of the shot, the bursting of shells, and the whizzing of bullets, heard above the roar of artillery and the volleys of musketry, all combined was something fearful. Regiments [on the Union side] quickly replenished their exhausted ammunition by borrowing from their more bountifully supplied and generous companions. Some withdrew, temporarily, for ammunition, and fresh regiments took their places ready to repulse, sometimes to pursue, their desperate enemy for the purpose of retaking ground from which we had been pressed and which it was necessary to occupy in order to hold our position."

Private John W. Urban of McCall's Pennsylvania Reserves gives a specific incident of the action: "The regiments belonging to the division of the Pennsylvania Reserves were sent to combat where their services would be the most needed, and were frequently in the severest parts of the battle. One of the fiercest conflicts that occurred . . . was fought by Colonel [Hiram] Duryea's regiment of Zouaves [the 5th New York Infantry] and a large force of rebels. . . . A rebel column six-or-eight-men deep . . . charged with frantic yells on the Union regiment. The Zouaves poured into their ranks a deadly fire, and then, with a wild shout, charged bayonets. . . . Then ensued a conflict as terrible as human beings can make it.

"When the fighting was the severest, our regiment was ordered forward to reinforce the gallant Zouaves; and, as we advanced for that purpose, we could distinctly see the desperate nature of the fighting. Neither side appeared to think of loading their muskets, but depended entirely on the bayonet. We advanced as fast as possible to the assistance of the Zouaves, but by the time we reached the ground the gallant fellows had beaten the rebels back into the woods and out of sight. They had however, paid dearly for their victory, as about 300 of this heroic band lay dead or terribly wounded on the field. The regiment was completely disorganized. . . .

"For a few minutes after we arrived on the field, there was a lull in the fighting, and Colonel [R. Biddle] Roberts ordered the regiment to advance over the ground so hotly contested a few moments before. As we advanced, I had a good opportunity of seeing the terrible character of the conflict. The ground was so thickly covered with the dead and wounded that it was with the utmost difficulty we could advance without treading on them. . . . The regiment was compelled to break ranks and get over the ground as best they could. . . . The red uniforms of the Zouaves, showing more conspicuously than the gray of the enemy, gave us at first the impression that the Union loss was the severer; but a closer inspection of the field revealed the fact that the loss of the enemy was even greater. The nature of the wounds inflicted proved the close proximity in which the combatants contested for the mastery. Some of the dead had their heads broken in by blows from butts of rifles, and others lay dead with bayonets thrust through them, the weapon having been left sticking in their bodies. Some of the wounded begged piteously to be helped to the rear; and altogether it was the most sickening sight I had ever witnessed."

Local vicitories such as achieved by the Zouaves were repeated all along the line; and finally, according to Fitz John Porter, "the enemy were repulsed in every direction. An ominous silence reigned." Somewhat earlier, Porter had sent a message across the river asking for reinforcements. William Swinton says that "General McClellan, at half-past three, sent him Slocum's division of Franklin's corps, which increased his force to 35,000 men. It was evident, however, that beyond this, Porter could expect little or no aid, for the troops on the south bank of the Chickahominy had at the same time their attention fully engaged by the demonstration of Magruder."

The afternoon's action saw Union newsmen making the rounds on both sides of the river. Up to this time George Alfred Townsend, recuperating from typhoid fever in a house on the Richmond bank, had been making no rounds at all; but now, during the period of silence on Porter's field, Townsend mounted his horse and rode across Grapevine Bridge. "It was with difficulty that I could make my way along the narrow corduroy, for hundreds of wounded were limping from the field to the safe side, and ammunition wagons were passing the other way, driven by reckless drivers who should have been blown up momentarily. Before I had reached the north side of the creek, an immense throng of panic-stricken people came surging down the slippery bridge. A few carried muskets, but I saw several wantonly throw their pieces into the flood; and, as the mass were unarmed, I inferred that they had made similar dispositions. Fear, anguish, cowardice, despair, disgust were the predominant expressions of the upturned faces. . . . I reined my horse close to the side of a team, that I might not be borne backward by the crowd; but some of the lawless fugitives seized him by the bridle, and others attempted to pull me from the saddle. 'Give up that hoss!' said one. 'What business you got with a hoss?' 'That's my critter, and I am in for a ride; so you get off!' said another. I spurred my pony vigorously with the left foot, and with the right struck the man at the bridle under the chin. The thick column parted left and right, and though a howl of hate pursued me I kept straight to the bank, cleared the swamp, and took the military route . . . toward the nearest eminence. At every step of the way I met wounded persons. A horseman rode past me, leaning over his pommel, with blood streaming from his mouth and hanging in gouts from his saturated beard. . . . In one place I met five drunken men escorting a wounded sergeant. The latter had been shot in the jaw, and when he attempted to speak the blood choked his articulation. . . . A mile or more from Grapevine Bridge, on a hilltop, lay a frame farmhouse with cherry trees encircling it. . . . The house was now a surgeon's headquarters, and the wounded lay in the yard and lane, under the shade, waiting their turns to be hacked and maimed. I caught a glimpse through the door of the butchers and their victims. Some curious people were peeping through the windows. . . . At the top of the next hill sat many of the Federal batteries, and I was admonished by the shriek of [Confederate] shells that passed over my head and burst far behind me that I was again to look upon carnage and share the perils of the soldier."

The shellfire signaled the resumption of the action. By this time Stonewall Jackson's Valley troops were filtering to the field, some joining D. H. Hill, who had been waiting for Jackson on the left, others moving to support the battered A. P. Hill in the center, and a few even becoming reserves for Longstreet on the right. Operating personally on the left, Jackson found himself confused not only by the unfamiliar terrain but also by the configuration of the Federal right. Lee had informed him that McClellan would probably throw this flank out in such a way as to try to prevent a Confederate thrust toward the White House, but the flank was bent back toward the Chickahominy. Lee did not know that McClellan planned to abandon the White House, pull the survivors of Porter's stand to the Richmond side of the river, and retreat toward the James. The unexpected situation cost Jackson time as he maneuvered his left to adjust to it.

Confederate cavalry officer John Esten Cooke, who served with Jackson's forces that day, explains that "General Lee had joined General A. P. Hill at New Cold Harbor, and now listened with anxiety for the sound of Jackson's guns on the left. . . . To relieve General Hill, meanwhile . . . General Longstreet was directed to make a feint on the right against the enemy's left . . . and this he proceeded to do without loss of time. The batteries on the south side of the Chickahominy, as well as those in front, were sweeping the approach, but the men advanced with great coolness to the assault, and were now close upon the Federal position. Its enormous strength was now for the first time discovered; and, finding that he could effect nothing by a feint, General Longstreet determined to turn the movement into a real attack, and made his preparations without delay.

"Such was the aspect of affairs on the field about five in the evening. The Federal troops had repulsed every assault, and the descending sun threatened to set upon a day memorable in the annals of the South for bloody and disastrous defeat. . . . General Lee, as we have said, awaited anxiously near New Cold Harbor the noise of guns upon his left. . . . Suddenly the hearts of all throbbed fiercely; and cheers rose and ran along the shattered lines of Hill as the welcome sound was heard. From the woods on the left came the rattle of small arms mingled with the roar of artillery. . . . General Lee pushed on in the direction of the sound and saw Jackson coming to meet him. 'Ah, General,' said Lee. 'I am very glad to see you. I hoped to have been with you before.' Then pausing a moment and listening to the long-streaming roar in the woods, he added, 'That fire is very heavy. Do you think your men can stand it?' Jackson turned his head to one side, as was his custom, listened, and then said in his brief tones, 'They can stand almost anything. They can stand that!' After a brief interview, he then returned to the command of his corps. His appearance . . . was in strong contrast to that of General Lee, who is very erect and graceful on horseback. Jackson leaned forward like a tyro . . . and wore his famous old sun-scorched cap drawn down low upon the forehead. He was sucking a lemon, and rode about slowly . . . listening . . . to the continuous roar of musketry from the woods. His position . . . was near the Old Cold Harbor House."

Because Jackson's troops had been so long in their approach, it was nearly 7 P.M before Lee completed his dispositions for a general attack. The smoke of the battlefield was a lurid canopy in the evening sunlight as both wings were at last advanced. Southerner J. F. J. Caldwell says that "the terror of the struggle during this time . . . is inconceivable to those who have never witnessed a great battle. From far back on our right, where Longstreet stormed batteries and breastworks . . . to the extreme left, where D. H. Hill swept [forward] . . . the air was filled with the incessant roll of musketry and the thunder of cannon. I was sent back some distance during the heat of the engagement, and had thus an opportunity of seeing and hearing [that is] rarely enjoyed by a participant in a battle. In every direction I could see columns hurrying into action along the dusty roads, and lines moving under fire, with waving banners and wild cheers. . . . The great Lee seemed to be ubiquitous, here sending in a fresh brigade, here dispatching couriers to various quarters of the field, here rallying and reassuring a disordered regiment, constantly in motion but always sublimely brave and calm."

For a time, Fitz John Porter's troops managed to stand fast. Porter had called again for reinforcements, and the brigades of Generals Thomas Meagher and William French, Sumner's corps, were on the way. McClellan had dispatched these units with great reluctance, for John Magruder had begun demonstrating furiously toward the end of the day. Allowing himself to be totally deceived, McClellan wired Stanton from his headquarters in front of Richmond: "Attacked by greatly superior numbers in all directions on this side. We still hold our own, though a very heavy fire is still kept up on the [other] bank of the Chickahominy. The odds have been immense. We hold our own very nearly. I may be forced to give up my position during the night. . . . Had I 20,000 fresh and good troops we would be sure of a splendid victory tomorrow." The last line, intended as a dig at the administration, must have left the Secretary somewhat confused. If the odds against McClellan were really immense, they would not have been greatly changed by 20,000 reinforcements.

The odds against Porter that evening were nearly two-to-one. "Each party," relates Union newsman George Alfred Townsend, "was now straining every energy—the one for victory, the other against annihilation. The darkness was closing in, and neither cared to prolong the contest after night. The Confederates . . . aimed to finish their success with the rout or capture of the Federals, and the Federals aimed to maintain their ground till nightfall. The musketry was close, accurate, and uninterrupted. Every second was marked by a discharge." Adds the Prince de Joinville: "Now in their turn come up the Confederate reserves. They deploy regularly into line against the Federal left, which gives way, breaks, and disbands. The disorder grows from point to point. . . . In vain do the generals, the officers of

Federal artillery during final moments of Gaines' Mill action

the staff, among them the Count of Paris and the Duke of Chartres, ride sword in hand into the melee to stop their disorderly movement. The Battle of Gaines' Mill is lost. . . . The enemy . . . was advancing on the plain still in the same order . . . and every minute he was closing in upon the confused masses of the Federals. Such is the fury of the cannonade and the musketry fire that the cloud of dust struck up from the ground floats steadily over the battle. Then came the order for [our] cavalry to charge. I happened at this moment to be near its position. I saw the troopers draw their swords with the sudden and electrical impulse of determination and devotion. . . . The charge failed against the dense battalions of the enemy, and the broken regiments galloping [back] through the artillery and the flying infantry only increased the general disorder. The artillery horses were killed, and I saw, with painful emotion, the men working with the courage of desperation at guns which could no longer be removed. They dropped one after another. Two alone were left at last, and they continued to load and fire almost at point-blank range. . . . Then the deepening twilight hid the scene. All these guns were lost."

"Meanwhile," says the special correspondent of the New York *Tribune*, Charles A. Page, "the panic extended. Scores of gallant officers endeavored to rally and re-form the stragglers, but in vain, while many officers forgot the pride of their shoulder straps and the honor of their manhood, and herded with sneaks and cowards. . . . That scene was not to be forgotten: Scores of riderless, terrified horses dashing in every direction; thick-flying bullets singing by, admonishing of danger; every minute a man struck down; wagons and ambulances and cannon blocking the way; wounded men limping and groaning and bleeding amid the throng; officers and civilians denouncing and reasoning and entreating, and being insensibly borne along with the mass; the sublime cannonading; the clouds of battle smoke, and the sun just disappearing, large and blood-red." To this general description, Page adds: "During the stampede, for a moment the attention of hundreds was attracted to a horse galloping around carrying a man's leg in the stirrup—the left leg, booted and spurred. It was a splendid horse, gayly caparisoned."

The Prince de Joinville resumes: "Happily, night came on, and, after losing a mile of ground, the army reached the fresh brigades of Meagher and French, which were formed in good order. These brigades sent up a vigorous hurrah, and a few guns put anew in battery opened their fire upon the enemy, who paused at last, checked by this final and determined resistance. As the last guns of this action were firing, we heard a lively rattle of musketry from the direction of Fair Oaks on the other side of the river. It came from the Confederates who were attacking the Federal works; but the attack, which was probably only a demonstration, was vigorously repelled. The day had been severe. In the main battle, that of Gaines' Mill, 35,000

Federals had failed to defeat 60,000 Confederates, but they had held them in check. More could not have been expected."

Porter's casualties in killed, wounded, captured, and missing were 6,837. Lee's were 8,750. He lost 1,000 men in the final charge alone. General John Hood's 1st Texas Brigade (which included units from Virginia and Georgia) had suffered shockingly while doing some of the evening's most effective work. Laments an unnamed survivor: "It was indeed a sad sight to look at the old regiment, a mere squad of noble men, gathered around their tattered colors. I could not realize that this little band of fifty or sixty men was the 4th Texas. But it was even so. Out of 530 men who went into the fight, there were 256 killed, wounded, or missing, while many were completely broken down, and nearly everyone was struck or grazed."

In the words of Colonel B. Estvan, a Prussian officer serving in Lee's ranks: "The soldiers were so fearfully exhausted by the day's struggle that many of them sank down from their places in the ranks upon the ground. Although I, too, could scarcely keep in the saddle, so great was my fatigue, I hastened with one of my aides to that quarter of the field where the struggle had raged the most fiercely. The scene of ruin was horrible. Whole ranks of the enemy lay prone where they had stood at the beginning of the battle. The number of wounded [Confederates] was fearful, too, and the groans and imploring cries for help that rose on all sides had, in the obscurity of the night, a ghastly effect that froze the blood in one's veins. Although I had been upon so many battlefields in Italy and Hungary, never had my vision beheld such a spectacle of human destruction. The preparations for the transportation of the wounded were too trifling, and the force detailed for that purpose was either too feeble in numbers or had no proper knowledge of its duties. Even the medical corps had, by the terrors of the situation, been rendered incapable of attending to the wounded with zeal and efficiency. With inconceivable exertion I at length succeeded, with the assistance of some humane officers, in bringing about some kind of order amid this frightful confusion. By the happiest chance, I found some Union ambulances, had all our men who could drive and knew the way pressed into service, and set to work to get the wounded into Richmond."

Many of the men who had been hurt earlier in the day were already in Richmond hospitals. At 10 P.M. Judith McGuire sat down at her desk and wrote in her diary: "Another day of great excitement in our beleaguered city. From early dawn the cannon has been roaring around us. Our success has been glorious! The citizens—gentlemen as well as ladies—have been fully occupied in the hospitals. Kent, Paine & Co. have thrown open their spacious buildings for the use of the wounded. . . . Visions of the battlefield have haunted me all day. Our loved ones, whether friends or strangers—all Southern soldiers are dear to us—lying dead and dying; the wounded in the hot sun, the dead being hastily buried. McClellan is said to be retreating. Praise the Lord, O my soul!"

At about the same time Judith McGuire was writing, Union trooper F. Colburn Adams was viewing a sad scene near McClellan's headquarters on the grounds of the Trent house. "The wounded from the battlefield, to the number of several thousand, had been brought over and laid in rows on the ground, so thick that it was with difficulty you could pick your way through them. . . . Although very many were suffering from the severest of wounds, and but little care could be given to them, scarcely a murmur or complaint was heard. Now and then one, in seeing a passer-by, would raise his head and inquire how the battle resulted. Another would request him to tell somebody to bring him a drink of water. General McClellan's head-quarter tents were all struck, and the general was laying down under a booth made of the branches of a tree, worn out with fatigue, for he had not slept for forty-eight hours and had been almost constantly in the saddle."

McClellan shortly bestirred himself, for his corps commanders were arriving for a council of war. Among the witnesses to the ensuing scene was George Alfred Townsend. "The young commander sat in a chair. . . . Heintzelman was kneeling upon a fagot, earnestly speaking. De Joinville sat apart, by the fire, examining a map. Fitz John Porter was standing back of McClellan, leaning upon his chair. Keyes, Franklin, and Sumner were listening attentively. Some sentries paced to and fro, to keep out vulgar curiosity. Suddenly there was a nodding of heads, as of some policy decided." With that, the corps commanders mounted and rode off to rejoin their respective units. McClellan made the first move in his personal retreat, transferring his headquarters several miles along the Chickahominy to Savage's Station.

At 12:30 A.M. the Young Napoleon sent the following dispatch to Secretary Stanton: "I now know the full history of the day. On this side of the river (the right bank) we repulsed several strong attacks. On the left bank our men . . . were overwhelmed by vastly superior numbers. . . . Had I 20,000, or even 10,000 fresh troops to use tomorrow I could take Richmond; but I have not a man in reserve, and shall be glad to cover my retreat and save the material and personnel of the army. . . . I have lost this battle because my force was too small. I again repeat that I am not responsible for this, and I say it with the earnestness of a general who feels in his heart the loss of every brave man who has been needlessly sacrificed today. I still hope to retrieve our fortunes; but to do this the Government must view the matter in the same earnest light that I do. You must send me very large reinforcements, and send them at once. . . . I know that a few thousand more men would have changed this battle from a defeat to a victory. As it is, the Government must not and cannot hold me responsible for the result. I feel too earnestly tonight. I have seen too many dead and wounded comrades to feel otherwise than that the Government has not sustained this army. If you do not do so now, the game is lost. If I save this army now, I tell you plainly that I owe no thanks to you or to any other persons in Washington. You have done your best to sacrifice this army." Stanton and Lincoln never saw the last two lines of this dispatch. They were deleted by the supervisor of military telegrams in Washington, who was appalled at McClellan's flagrant disrespect for the nation's top leaders.

It wasn't until sunrise of the day following the battle that all of Fitz John Porter's depleted units had joined the main army on the Richmond side of the river. From that moment, explains William Swinton, the army had a radically altered goal. "It was no longer a question of taking Richmond, but of making good the retreat to the James with a victorious enemy in the rear. McClellan had still, however, a certain advantage of his opponent. He had a determinate course of action . . . already in process of execution, while Lee remained still in doubt as to his adversary's design. He saw that McClellan might still throw his united force to the north side of the Chickahominy and give battle to preserve his communications by the White House; and he saw that, holding the lower bridges of the Chickahominy, he might retreat down the Peninsula over the same route by which Johnston had retreated up the Peninsula. In either case, it was necessary to hold his entire force in hand on the north side of the river. Yet McClellan had adopted neither of these courses, but one different from either, and which his adversary had not divined."

Lee had no choice that morning but to await McClellan's next move. While doing so, the Confederate general took the time to attend to a personal matter. One of his sons, Robert E. Lee, Jr., had participated in the Battle of Gaines' Mill as a private in one of Stonewall Jackson's artillery batteries; and, having had no word as to how the youth had fared, the general rode to that part of the field where Robert's unit was encamped. The younger Lee recounts: "Most of the men were lying down, many sleeping, myself among the latter number. To get some shade and to be out of the way, I had crawled under a caisson and was busy making up many lost hours of rest. Suddenly I was rudely awakened by a comrade, prodding me with a sponge-staff, as I had failed to be aroused by his call, and was told to get up and come out, that someone wished to see me. Half awake, I staggered out, and found myself face to face with General Lee and his staff. Their fresh uniforms, bright equipments, and well-groomed horses contrasted so forcibly with the war-worn appearance of our command that I was completely dazed. It took me a moment or two to realize what it all meant, but when I saw my father's loving eyes and smile it became clear to me that he had ridden by to see if I was safe and to ask how I was getting along. I remember well how curiously those with him gazed at me, and I am sure that it must have struck them as very odd that such a dirty, ragged, unkempt youth could have been the son of this grand-looking, victorious commander."

If Lee and his generals were uncertain of McClellan's intentions that day, they could at least be sure he was about to do *something*. In the words of D. H. Hill: "While we were lying . . . idle . . . the clouds of smoke from the burning [stores] in the Federal camps and the frequent explosions of magazines indicated a retreat; but Whiting kept insisting upon it that all this was but a *ruse de guerre* of McClellan preparatory to a march upon Richmond. I made to him some such reply as that once made to General Longstreet, when a cadet at West Point, by Professor Kendrick. The Professor asked Longstreet, who never looked at his chemistry, how the carbonic acid of commerce was made. Longstreet replied, 'By burning diamonds in oxygen gas.' 'Yes,' said Professor Kendrick, 'that will do it; but don't you think it would be a *leetle* expensive?' 'Don't you think,' I said to Whiting, 'that this ruse of McClellan is a *leetle* expensive?' The old West Point yarn had a very quieting effect upon his apprehensions."

In Washington that morning, President Lincoln was in a state of alarm. He had read the dispatch to Stanton in which McClellan claimed he was going to have a hard time saving his army and was in desperate need of reinforcements. Although the President was dubious about the great strength McClellan claimed for Lee, he could not be sure the picture was not a true one, and he was obliged to respond: "Save your army at all events. We will send reinforcements as fast as we can." McClellan wired back: "It is impossible to tell where reinforcements ought to go, and I am yet unable to predict result of approaching battle. It will probably be better that they should go to Fort Monroe and thence according to the state of affairs when they arrive. It is not probable that I can maintain telegraphic communications more than an hour or two longer." His alarm increasing, Lincoln wired the Army and Navy headquarters at Fort Monroe to try to establish contact with McClellan, determine his situation, and report back to Washington. Thus did McClellan's unwarranted retreat begin to throw not only Washington but also the entire Union into a fit of dismay.

In the Army of the Potomac itself, according to Surgeon Stevens, "the feelings of the men underwent a terrible revolution. . . . Our brave fellows had looked with sad faces at Porter's retreating column, but that was felicity compared with what they now experienced. Even when the right wing was forced across the river they still had faith that their bravery was to be rewarded with victory. . . . And now the siege of Richmond was to be abandoned, and the men who but two days before had exulted in the glad hope of a speedy entrance into the city, which even now lay just within our grasp, were to turn their backs as *fugitives* before their enemies! It was a time of humiliation and sorrow. Every man was weighed down with a terrible anxiety. Officers hurried to and fro . . . hastily forwarding the preparations for the retreat." Only one corps, that of Erasmus Keyes, started southward that first day. With the aid of area blacks who served as guides, these troops crossed White Oak Swamp and took up a position as the army's advance guard on the opposite side. The thousands of wagons making up the army's trains began to follow.

It was another busy day at the White House depot, which the Confederates had not yet molested. Medical Director Ellis says that activities began with the removal of the sick from his general hospital. "Many of them being well able to walk to the river, [they] were permitted to do so. The remainder, several hundred in number, were carried in ambulances or on litters, as their cases required. The whole number were quietly and comfortably removed, and by the arrangements I had made were well accommodated on the hospital transports. . . . General Stoneman [with his cavalry command] has just arrived from Tunstall's Station . . . and is now holding a consultation with General Casey at his tent on the lawn in front of the White House. [Stoneman] . . . says he can hold the enemy in check until we have all left here. At the same time he recommends all possible dispatch.

"The gunboat *Commodore Barney* has been added to our fleet. The *Currituck* is about a mile above the railroad bridge. The others are in position below, with everything in readiness for an attack, should the enemy force our protecting lines. The signal gun for all to embark has just been fired; and hundreds, taking advantage of it, are making a fierce onslaught on the sutlers' stores, stripping them of drygoods, groceries, and whiskey. . . . The officers interfered to prevent this . . . but too late. . . . The commissary stores, to a great extent, were got on board; but a large amount, stored in a wooden building, were destroyed, as they were said to be partially damaged. The building, outside, was heaped up with bales of hay, on which whiskey was spilled to hasten its destruction. . . .

"The postoffice and quartermaster's tents, the officers' and sutlers' tents, the Negro quarters and railroad shanties, then the White House itself, were given to the flames. The flame, smoke, and noise from the crackling and falling timbers made the scene one of the grandest imaginable, throwing a lurid glare for miles around and over the river, in strange contrast with the sunlight. Added to this was the frequent explosion of shells and other ammunition. The light from the fire continued until after dark and lit up the heavens, making visible for miles the scene of the destruction. The White House itself, situated as it was on a high bluff, must have been seen blazing at a great distance. Many mourned its destruction, which, I learn, was contrary to the orders of General Casey, but the torch was set to it by someone of the many who for a long time complained of its being so jealously guarded by Union sentries, and it the property of a rebel leader. . . .

"The work of destruction being nearly complete, including the explosion of three splendid locomotives and the burning of over one hundred railroad cars, General Casey, with his staff, are getting on board the *Knickerbocker*. Colonel Ingalls [of the quartermaster corps] and his department have gone on board the *Circassian;* and we start down the river, which is filled with the transports. As we turn the winding of the crooked stream, forests of masts can be seen, bound for Fortress Monroe. Looking back at the White House, we can still see the bright flames flying upward, lighting up the banks of the muddy stream."

In the Richmond arena, General John Magruder was beginning another worrisome night. "I considered the situation of our army as extremely critical and perilous. The larger portion of it was on the opposite side of the Chickahominy, the bridges had all been destroyed, but one was rebuilt . . . which was commanded fully by the enemy's guns . . . and there were but 25,000 men between [McClellan's] army of 100,000 and Richmond. I received repeated instructions during Saturday night from General Lee's headquarters enjoining upon my command the utmost vigilance, directing the men to sleep on their arms and to be prepared for whatever might occur. These orders . . . were also transmitted to General Huger, on my right. I passed the night without sleep and in the superintendence of their execution. Had McClellan massed his whole force in column and advanced it against any point of our line of battle, as was done at Austerlitz under similar circumstances by the greatest captain of any age, though the head of his column would have suffered greatly, its momentum would have insured him success, and the occupation of our works about Richmond, and consequently of the city, might have been his reward. His failure to do so is the best evidence that our wise commander fully understood the character of his opponent."

McClellan began pulling his units out of their entrenchments toward Savage's Station at 3 A.M. Sunday, June 29. "The men," says Surgeon Stevens, "slung their knapsacks and quietly moved off. A scene of desolation met their view as they passed along. Tents cut to pieces, commissary stores thrown upon the ground or burning in heaps, blankets and clothing piled promiscuously about . . . all indicating a retreat under the most disastrous circumstances. . . . The endless streams of army wagons, artillery trains, and ambulances were all pouring down the roads from the various camps and crowding into the narrow paths that led to the opposite side of the Peninsula [by way of White Oak Swamp]. Porter's infantry mingled with the trains, and thousands of cattle driven along through the woods by the roadside made a strange scene. Franklin's, Sumner's, and Heintzelman's corps were to guard the rear."

It was about dawn of that day when Lee came to the conclusion that McClellan was almost certainly retreating toward the James, and he got confirmation of this from Jeb Stuart, whose cavalry command had spent the night encamped a few miles from the White House. In Stuart's words: "The conflagration raged fearfully at the White House during the entire night, while explosions of shells rent the air. . . . Early next morning I moved cautiously . . . down . . . till, coming in plain view of the White House at a distance of a quarter of a mile, a large gunboat was discovered lying at the landing. I [had] . . . proceeded to this point with a small party and one piece of artillery. Colonel W. H. F. Lee, the proprietor of this once-beautiful estate, now in ashes and desolation, described the ground and pointed out all the localities to me, so that I was convinced that a few bold sharpshooters could compel the gunboat to leave. I accordingly ordered down about seventy-five. . . . They advanced boldly on this monster, so terrible to our fancy, and a body of sharpshooters were sent ashore from the boat to meet them. Quite a determined engagement of skirmishers ensued, but our gallant men never faltered in their determination to expose this Yankee buggaboo called gunboat. To save time, however, I ordered up the howitzer, a few shells from which, fired with great accuracy and bursting directly over her decks, caused an instantaneous withdrawal of sharpshooters and precipitate flight under full headway of steam down the river. . . . The command was now entirely out of rations and the horses without forage, and I had relied on the enemy at the White House to supply me with these essentials. I was not disappointed, in spite of their efforts to destroy everything. Provisions and delicacies of every description lay in heaps, and the men regaled themselves on the fruits of the tropics as well as the substantials of the land. Large quantities of forage were left also. An opportunity was here offered for observing the deceitfulness of the enemy's pretended reverence for everything associated with the name of Washington, for the dwelling-house was burned to the ground, and not a vestige left except what told of desolation and vandalism. . . . During the morning I received a note from the commanding general directing me to watch closely any movement of the enemy in my direction, and to communicate what my impressions were in regard to his designs. I replied that there was no evidence of a retreat of the main body from the position before Richmond down the Williamsburg roads, and that I had no doubt the enemy . . . was endeavoring to reach the James as a new base."

Lee's operations against the retreating McClellan got under way slowly. Although Stonewall Jackson (with D. H. Hill continuing under his command) occupied a position on the Chickahominy that was close to the left flank of the Federal march southward through Savage's Station, the bridge Jackson needed had been destroyed and he was obliged to spend the day rebuilding it. Longstreet and A. P. Hill had to cross the river too far to the north for an expeditious attack. Their mission, in fact, was to start westward around White Oak Swamp in preparation for an attack on McClellan's column later in his march. It was Magruder whom Lee sent in direct pursuit of the Federals that morning; and, anxious to the point of sickness over his inferior numbers, Prince John moved so cautiously as to spend most of the day preparing the attack he had been ordered to make on the column's rear.

It was mid-afternoon when McClellan's rearmost troops reached Savage's Station. "Here," says Surgeon Stevens, "trains and troops were crowded together in wonderful confusion. Immense heaps of commissary stores, arms, and ammunition were waiting destruction. . . . The work . . . went on at a marvelous rate. Boxes of hard bread, hundreds of barrels of flour, rice, sugar, coffee, salt, and pork were thrown upon the burning piles. . . . One heap of boxes of hard bread as large as a good sized dwelling made a part of the sacrifice. Boxes of clothing and shoes were opened, and every man as he passed helped himself to whatever he thought worth carrying away. . . . It was easy thus to dispose of commissary and quartermaster's stores, but to destroy the immense magazines of cartridges, kegs of powder, and shells required more care. These were loaded into [railroad] cars. A long train was filled . . . and then, after setting fire to each car, the train was set in motion down the steep grade. With wildest fury the blazing train rushed, each revolution of the wheels adding new impetus to the flying monster, and new volumes to the flames. The distance to the bridge [across the Chickahominy] was two miles. On and on the burning train thundered like a frightful meteor. Now, the flames being communicated to the contents of the cars, terrific explosions of shells and kegs of powder lent new excitement to the scene. The air was full of shrieking, howling shells, the fragments of which tore through the trees and branches of the forest; and huge fragments of cars were seen whirling high in the air. At length the train reached the river; and such was its momentum that, notwithstanding the bridge was burned, the engine and the first car leaped over the first pier in the stream, and the cars hung suspended."

Even before the work of destruction was completed, many of the army's regiments began marching from Savage's Station to take up the route through White Oak Swamp. Chaplain J. J. Marks, on duty at the station's field hospital, witnessed some poignant scenes among the 2,500 sick and wounded men who, by McClellan's order, were to be abandoned to the Confederates. Marks himself, along with a number of surgeons and male nurses, had decided to remain with these unfortunates; and the chaplain watched with the deepest emotion as some of the army's able-bodied officers and soldiers stopped by the hospital for last-minute visits. "Many a manly cheek was wet with tears as they bade farewell to those whom they never expected to meet again. Fathers had to drag themselves away from the couches of their sons; and, after they had gone a few steps, would return to look once more and to renew the oft-repeated instruction to nurse and surgeon. There were many sad partings. Up to this time the disabled had not known that they were to be left behind; and when it became manifest that such was to be their fate, the scene could not be pictured by human language. Some wounded men . . . struggled through the grounds exclaiming they 'would rather die than fall into the hands of the rebels!' I heard one

Casualties at Savage's Station just before their abandonment to the Confederates

man crying out, 'O my God! Is this the reward I deserve for all the sacrifices I have made, the battles I have fought, and the agony I have endured from my wounds?' Some of the younger officers wept like children; others turned pale, and some fainted. . . .

"About four o'clock we saw moving over the plain . . . the last of the ambulances and wagons, retiring in the distance, and the light of the evening sun was reflected in dazzling brilliance from the guns of the departing regiments. Here and there was a horseman galloping through the dust; but the great throng of dashing officers, of plumed cavalry, of regiments with waving banners and music, had passed away like the dream of a brilliant tournament. We were not, however, yet quite abandoned. Opposite to Savage's Station, looking north, is a large plain of several hundred acres. . . . On this field were standing in line of battle 20,000 men under General Sumner, the rear guard of the army, left to hold in check the enemy until our troops were safe beyond White Oak Swamp. . . .

"About five o'clock . . . we saw rising up in the field towards the Chickahominy a great cloud of dust. Very soon afterwards there burst upon us the thunder of artillery, and from the upper rooms of the Savage House we could see the approaching columns of the enemy. . . . Shell met shell in the heavens from the contending cannon, and battery responded to battery, until it was one continued and unceasing roar of the mightiest thunder. For an hour not a musket was fired. . . . Suddenly the whole mass of the enemy's forces sprang forward with wild yells and screams. . . . At this moment . . . I could see long streams of fire, like serpents' tongues, dart from our many thousand muskets, and louder than the roar swelled up the shout of defiance. Beaten back by this leaden storm, the enemy wavered and retreated a few steps. . . . But soon after, troops coming up behind them pressed the front line once more into the field. Again there leaped from ten thousand guns the fiery blast, and yell answered yell."

Among the troops John Magruder employed in the fight was J. B. Kershaw's brigade of South Carolinians, the unit to which Sergeant D. Augustus Dickert belonged. Dickert was then nearing his eighteenth birthday, and he was nearly robbed of the privilege of making it. "I was struck by a minnie ball in the chest, which sent me reeling to the ground. . . . While I lay in a semi-unconscious state, I received another bullet in my thigh, which I had every reason to believe came from someone in the rear. . . . When I came to consciousness . . . the first thing that met my ears was the roar of musketry and the boom of cannon, with the continual swish-swash of the grape and canister striking the trees and ground. I placed my hand in my bosom, where I felt a dull, deadening sensation. There I found the warm blood that filled my inner garments and now trickled down my side as I endeavored to stand upright. I had been shot through the left lung, and as I felt the great gaping wound in my chest, the blood gushing and spluttering out at every breath, I began to realize my situation. I tried to get off the field the best I could, the bullet in my leg not troubling me much, and as yet I felt strong enough to walk. My brother, who was a surgeon . . . in the ranks, came to my aid and led me to the rear. . . . As I sat upon the fallen trunk of a tree, my brother made a hasty examination of my wound. . . . He pronounced my wound at first as fatal . . . but after probing . . . with his finger he gave me the flattering assurance that, unless I bled to death quite soon, my chances might be good. . . . I thought sure I was dying then and there, and fell from the log in a death-like swoon.

"But I soon revived, having only fainted from loss of blood, and my brother insisted on my going back . . . to a farmhouse . . . where our surgeons had established a hospital. The long stretch of wood we had to travel was lined with the wounded, each wounded soldier with two or three friends helping him off the field. . . . I will never forget the scene that met my eyes as I neared the house where the wounded had been gathered. There the torn and mangled lay, shot in every conceivable part of the body or limbs—some with wounds in the head, arms torn off at the shoulder or elbow, legs broken, fingers, toes, or foot shot away. . . . The great mass were stretched at full length upon the ground, uttering low, deep, and piteous moans that told of the great sufferings or a life passing away. The main hall of the deserted farmhouse, as well as the rooms, were filled to overflowing with those most seriously wounded. The stifling stench of blood was sickening in the extreme. The front and back yards, the fence corners, and even the outbuildings were filled with the dead and dying. Surgeons and their assistants were hurrying to and fro. . . . Here they would stop to probe a wound, there to set a broken rib, bind a wound, stop the flow of blood, or tie an artery. But among all this deluge of blood, mangled bodies, and the groans of the wounded and dying, our ears were continually greeted by the awful, everlasting rattle of the musketry, the roar of the field batteries, and the booming, shaking, and trembling of the siege guns."

Union narrator Marks had continued watching the fight from an upstairs window of the Savage House. "Now the whole field was so covered with the pall of battle we could see nothing but the vivid flash from the cannon, like the lightning darting out of a cloud, and the muskets in the hands of our men . . . still vomiting forth streams of flame. . . . The clash of arms was occasionally interrupted by the coming into the field of fresh regiments, cheering their companions with loud shouts. The dullest ear could perceive the difference between the voices of our men and those of the enemy. Ours shouted in clear, ringing, and manly tones, while the enemy's sounded like the scream of the panther and the yell of the savage. . . . Nobly and grandly were they repulsed; and when the final cheer of victory arose from our columns . . . there was not a solitary derisive cry in answer. The victory was complete. Well did our rear guard fulfil their trust and hurl back the forces which were pressing from behind to throw us into confusion. . . . The repulse of that evening enabled our columns and baggage trains to place between us and the enemy the difficult . . . White Oak Swamp.

"Never was there a more impressive spectacle than that presented by this retreat of the Grand Army. This vast body of men, well trained, fully equipped, and equalling in courage any army which the world has ever seen, eager for the fight, asking but for generals to lead them to victory, was, after having almost knocked at the door of the rebel stronghold, retreating in haste—at the command of one man—who, however distinguished for ability in one department of military science [that of organization], in every hour of danger was a *child,* and in every great emergency was oppressed with conscious incapacity.

"After the enemy was repulsed at the Battle of Savage's Station, General Sumner sent to General McClellan for, as he expressed himself, 'orders to push the enemy into the Chickahominy.' General McClellan's reply was that 'the rear guard will follow the retreat of the main body of the army.' On the reception of this command, the greatest consternation and displeasure reigned among both officers and men. Many . . . wished to sacrifice themselves in any way rather than by a disgraceful retreat. But at length . . . the rear guard took up their line of march . . . and the gray light of dawn found them safe beyond the White Oak Swamp."

13

─◆─

FINALE AT MALVERN HILL

IN RICHMOND, the citizens had entered upon a period of increased anxiety over the perils of the Confederate soldiery. "There was scarcely a family," explains Sallie Putnam, "that had not some one of its numbers in the field. Mothers nervously watched for any who might bring to them news of their boys. Sisters and friends grew pale when a horseman rode up to their doors, and could scarcely nerve themselves to listen to the tidings he brought. Young wives clasped their children to their bosoms, and in agony imagined themselves widows and their little ones orphans. . . . A horseman rode up to the door of one of our houses . . . and cried out to an anxious mother, 'Your son, madam, is safe, but Captain ——— is killed!' On the opposite side [of the street], on the portico of her dwelling, a fair young girl, the betrothed of Captain ———, was said to have been sitting at the moment, and thus heard the terrible announcement!"

The wounded and sick who kept arriving in the city were placed in the various improvised hospitals, where they were cared for and fussed over by an abundance of volunteers. Mrs. Roger Pryor says that "the women who worked in Kent & Paine's hospital never seemed to weary. . . . The wise matron assigned us hours, and we went on duty with the regularity of trained nurses. My hours were from seven to seven during the day, with the promise of night service should I be needed. Efficient, kindly colored women assisted us. Their motherly manner soothed the prostrate soldier, whom they always addressed as 'son.' . . . Every morning the Richmond ladies brought for our patients such luxuries as could be procured. . . . It was at this hospital, I have reason to believe, that the little story originated which was deemed good enough to be claimed by other hospitals, of the young girl who approached a sick man with a pan of water in her hand and a towel over her arm. 'Mayn't I wash your face?' said the girl. . . . 'Well,

325

lady, you may if you want to,' said the man wearily. 'It has been washed fourteen times this morning. It can stand another time, I reckon.' . . .

"I used to veil myself closely as I walked to and from my hotel, that I might shut out the dreadful sights in the street—the squads of prisoners, and, worst of all, the open wagons in which the dead were piled. Once I *did* see one of these dreadful wagons! In it a stiff arm was raised, and shook as it was driven down the street, as though the dead owner appealed to Heaven for vengeance, a horrible sight never to be forgotten."

A common sound in the street, according to Constance Cary Harrison, was "the wailing dirge of a military band preceding a soldier's funeral. One could not number those sad pageants; the coffin crowned with cap and sword and gloves, the riderless horse following with empty boots fixed in the stirrups of an army saddle; such soldiers as could be spared from the front marching after with arms reversed and crape-enfolded banners; the pass-ers-by standing with bare, bent heads. Funerals less honored outwardly were continually occurring. . . . The green hillsides of lovely Hollywood were . . . upturned to find resting places for the heroic dead. So much taxed for time and for attendants were those who officiated that it was not unusual to perform the last rites for the departed at night."

In her dairy, Judith McGuire recorded the situation's brighter side: "McClellan certainly retreating. We begin to breathe more freely. But he fights as he goes. Oh, that he may be surrounded before he gets to his gun-boats!" These lines were written on Monday, June 30, the day after the Battle of Savage's Station. Early that morning, Lee launched measures in-tended to put the Federal army in the kind of predicament Mrs. McGuire beseeched. The general began the day by sending a request for Stonewall Jackson, whose troops were now across the river, to meet him at Savage's Station. Robert Stiles of the Richmond Howitzers happened to be sitting at the base of a huge pine tree near the appointed spot at the appointed time, and he experienced an unforgettable moment. "Hearing the jingle of cav-alry accoutrements toward the Chickahominy, I looked up and saw a half-dozen mounted men, and riding considerably in advance a solitary horse-man, whom I instantly recognized as the great wizard of the marvelous Valley Campaign which had so thrilled the army and the country. Jackson and the little sorrel stopped in the middle of the road, probably not fifty feet off, while his staff halted perhaps a hundred and fifty yards in his rear. . . . Horse and rider appeared worn down to the lowest point of flesh consistent with effective service. . . . A ghastly scene was spread across the road hard by. The 17th and 21st Mississippi . . . had been ordered into the woods about dusk the evening before, and . . . the poor fellows ran into a Federal brigade and were shocked and staggered by a deadly volley. . . . Almost every man struck was killed, and every man killed shot through the brain. Their comrades had gone into the woods as soon as it was light, brought out the bodies and laid them in rows, with hands crossed upon the breast, but eyes wide-staring . . . and every forehead stained with ooze and trickle of blood. Men were passing through the silent lines, bending low, seeking in the distorted faces to identify their friends.

"Jackson glanced a moment toward this scene. Not a muscle quivered as he resumed his steady gaze down the road toward Richmond. . . . A moment later, and his gaze was rewarded. A magnificent staff approached from the direction of Richmond. . . . General Lee . . . rode forward with a courier, his staff halting. As he gracefully dismounted, handing his bridle rein to his attendant, and advanced, drawing the gauntlet from his right hand, Jackson flung himself off his horse and advanced to meet Lee, the little sorrel trotting back to the staff. . . . The two generals greeted each other warmly, but wasted no time upon the greeting. . . . Jackson began talking in a jerky, impetuous way, meanwhile drawing a diagram on the ground with the toe of his right boot. He traced two sides of a triangle . . . then . . . began to draw a third . . . slowly and with hesitation, alternately looking up at Lee's face and down at his diagram, meanwhile talking earnestly; and when at last . . . the triangle was complete he raised his foot and stamped it down with emphasis, saying, 'We've got him'; then signaled for his horse and . . . vaulted awkwardly into the saddle and was off. Lee watched him a moment, the courier brought his horse, he mounted, and he and his staff rode away."

One is left to wonder at the meaning of Jackson's triangle, but it was related to Lee's plans for a two-pronged move against McClellan, with Jackson's wing of the army marching in direct pursuit through White Oak Swamp, and the other wing, under Longstreet, completing its westerly swing around the swamp in order to come in on the Federal flank. McClellan had foreseen the likelihood of such a combination against him, and he prepared to receive it by deploying three of his corps—those of Sumner, Heintzelman, and Franklin—on a three-mile front with his western flank near the hamlet of Glendale and his eastern just south of White Oak Bridge, which he rendered a ruin. McClellan did not remain on the field; he retired toward Harrison's Landing and the gunboat fleet in order to further the arrangements for his new base.

Once again, Lee's plans did not work out. Stonewall Jackson may have seemed alert and competent to Robert Stiles that morning, but he was still lagging in performance. He and his troops reached the north bank of White Oak Creek, at the southern edge of the swamp, around noon. At first the Federals on the south side of the stream—those of Franklin's corps—believed they were in for a fierce fight, for Jackson deployed twenty-eight pieces of artillery along the bank and made a formidable beginning. According to Unionist F. Colburn Adams: "We could distinctly see the gunners busy among their batteries, preparing for the work of death. Their infantry yet remained concealed in the rear, covered by the dense foliage.

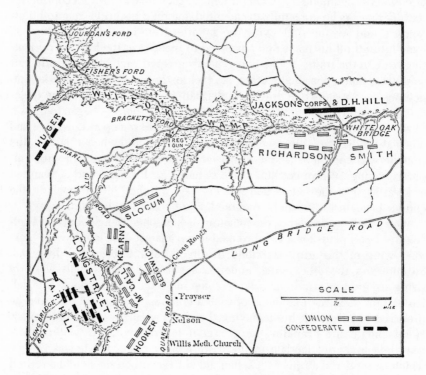

Battle of White Oak Swamp (or Glendale, or Frayser's Farm)

Our artillery line was formed. . . . Both armies stood now for some time in silence, as if watching each other and hesitating as to which should begin the work of death first. An open field intervened between the two lines, and on a bit of rising ground near its center stood the house General McClellan had used for his headquarters. The owner's wife, a smart, talkative [young] woman with strong Southern sympathies, had made herself very uncomfortable at the presence of so many soldiers about her premises, and had several times remonstrated against the liberties they took with her fruit trees. She had also expressed great anxiety as to who was to compensate her for the loss of her fences and crop. The Confederate artillery answered that question, I think, in a rather summary manner, having trained at least two batteries on the house. . . . They opened along their whole line with a crash that made the very earth tremble. . . . The infantry dropped and hugged the ground . . . and some of our batteries were struck. . . . The house settled to the ground as if it had been cut suddenly from its foundation, and the fruit trees around it were splintered to pieces. The enemy evidently thought General McClellan still occupied the house. . . . A number of orderlies around [it] probably led to the error." The sharp-tongued young woman, carrying her two-year-old child, had fled before the barrage began; but her elderly husband, unwilling to leave his ducks and chickens unprotected from Yankee appetites, had remained behind. Losing a leg to a shell, he quickly bled to death. As General Franklin said later, "he had sacrificed himself for his poultry."

Franklin's Federals expected Jackson's infantry to follow the barrage with an attack across the creek, but Jackson allowed himself to be stopped by the ruined bridge. He learned that the stream had fordable spots, but he made little effort to use the information. About all that his troops accomplished in the vicinity of the bridge was the capture of a drunken Irishman who had strayed from his unit, and even this triumph was only temporary. The captive put up his fists and offered to fight it out. Although at least one of his captors felt that the Yankee ought to be shot, he was turned loose. This obstreperous fellow later boasted of the incident, adding the claim that, given another quart of whiskey, he could have held the bridge single-handedly all day. As for Jackson, he soon lay down in the shade of a tree and went to sleep, and the fight never developed into anything more serious than skirmishing and artillery dueling.

The Confederate effort from the west was composed of two columns, the main one under Longstreet, seconded by A. P. Hill. The lesser column, headed by Benjamin Huger, was several miles to Longstreet's left. Huger was expected to reach the field in time to fire the first shots, with Longstreet joining in at once. At the same time, some 6,000 recently drafted troops, together with cavalry and artillery, were sent down along the bank of the James with instructions to find a spot where they might harass the Federals

Federal forces at White Oak Bridge

when they resumed their retreat. Led by General Theophilus Holmes, this mission came to nothing, at least partly because of an unexpected development, one that spawned an anecdote that was later repeated throughout the Confederate army. It was D. H. Hill who put the story on record: "As General Holmes marched down the river, his troops became visible to the gunboats, which opened fire upon them, throwing those awe-inspiring shells familiarly called by our men 'lamp posts' on account of their size and appearance. Their explosion was very much like that of a small volcano and had a very demoralizing effect upon new troops, one of whom expressed the general sentiment by saying, 'The Yankees throwed them lamp posts about too careless like.' The roaring, howling gunboat shells were usually harmless to flesh, blood, and bones, but they had a wonderful effect upon the nervous system. . . .

"General Holmes, who was very deaf, had gone into a little house concealed from the boats by some intervening woods and was engaged in some business when the bellowing of the 'lamp posts' began. The irregular cavalry stampeded and made a brilliant charge to the rear. The artillerists of two guns . . . were also panic-struck, and cutting their horses loose, mounted them, and, with dangling traces, tried to catch up with the fleet-footed cavaliers. The infantry troops were inexperienced in the wicked ways of war, having never been under fire before. The fright of the fleeing cavalry would have pervaded their ranks also with the same mischievous result but for the strenuous efforts of their officers, part of whom were veterans. Some of the raw levies crouched behind little saplings to get protection from the shrieking, blustering shells. At this juncture General Holmes, who, from his deafness, was totally unaware of the rumpus, came out of the hut, put his hand behind his right ear, and said, 'I thought I heard firing.' "

As for Longstreet, he was in position to attack from the west, his lines facing McCall's Pennsylvania Reserves, at 11 A.M., even before Jackson arrived at White Oak Bridge. Huger, however, had found the road on Longstreet's left to be a perfect tangle of trees felled by the Federals, and he was moving by inches. Lee's well-conceived combination was dwindling to a single effective column. In Longstreet's words: "Everything was quiet on my part of the line, except occasional firing between my pickets and McCall's. . . . About half-past 2 o'clock artillery fire was heard on my left, evidently at the point . . . where Huger was to attack. [These were Federal guns greeting Huger's arrival, and he allowed them to keep him at bay.] I very naturally supposed this firing to be the expected signal, and ordered some of my batteries to reply, as a signal that I was ready to cooperate. While the order to open was going around to the batteries, President Davis and General Lee, with their staff and followers, were with me in a little open field near the rear of my right. We were in pleasant conversation, anticipating fruitful results from the fight, when our batteries opened. Instantly the Federal batteries responded most spitefully. It was impossible for the enemy to see us as we sat on our horses in the little field, surrounded by tall, heavy timber and thick undergrowth; yet a battery by chance had our range and exact distance, and poured upon us a terrific fire. The second or third shell burst in the midst of us, killing two or three horses and wounding one or two men. Our little party speedily retired to safer quarters. The Federals doubtless had no idea that the Confederate President, commanding general, and division commanders were receiving point-blank shot from their batteries.

"Colonel Micah Jenkins was in front of us, and I sent him an order to silence the Federal battery, supposing that he could do so with his long-range rifles. He became engaged, and finally determined to charge the battery. That brought on a general fight. . . . The enemy's line was broken and he was partly dislodged from his position . . . but our line was very much broken up by the rough ground we had to move over, and we were not in sufficiently solid form to maintain a proper battle. . . . At times, when vigorous combinations were made against us, McCall regained points all along his line. Our counter-movements, however, finally pushed him back again. . . . Other advances were made, and reinforcements came to the support of the Federals, who contested the line with varying fortune, sometimes recovering batteries we had taken, and again losing them."

The fight over two of McCall's batteries, those of Captains Mark Kerns and James Cooper, is described from the Federal side by Private John Urban, a member of one of the infantry regiments, the 1st, that was helping to support them: "Kerns' battery was running out of ammunition, and its brave commander, who had in vain been trying to get a new supply, was compelled to withdraw his guns. . . . The enemy, mistaking the movement for a retreat of the Union forces, immediately . . . charged on the now defenseless battery, and it would have fallen into their hands, had not the prompt measures of Colonel Roberts prevented it. . . . When the enemy with cries of exultation rushed forward . . . his voice rang out, 'First Regiment, forward, charge bayonets!' And with a loud cheer we rushed on the advancing enemy. We did not fire a shot, but relying on the bayonet we charged with an impetuosity that broke the rebel line, when we poured a deadly volley into their backs and pursued them over the fields. Unfortunately the momentum of the charge carried us too far, and it soon became evident that we had got ourselves into a bad fix. A column of fresh rebel troops flanked us, and we were soon in the most imminent danger of being surrounded and cut off by them. We had also suffered fearfully in the charge. Our gallant Captain, George H. Hess, and a large number of officers and men of the regiment had fallen, and we were compelled to fall back in confusion to the edge of the wood in the rear of Cooper's battery.

"The enemy in strong force now rushed on the battery, and, capturing

A Confederate attack at Glendale

it, were on the point of turning the guns on our lines when Colonel Roberts ordered us to take cover behind the trees and open on the enemy. We immediately opened a deadly fire ... and for a short time we would tumble them as fast as they could lay hands on the battery; but we could not accomplish impossibilities, and the immense hordes of the enemy would soon have dislodged us and secured the battery, had we not at that most critical moment received reinforcements. The 9th Regiment was hastening from the left for that purpose, and when informed that Cooper's battery was in the hands of the enemy they demanded to be led against them for the purpose of recapturing it. The battery was a great favorite with the Reserves.... The noble 9th Regiment, joined by our regiment, with a tremendous cheer now charged upon the enemy, and a most terrific conflict ensued. Both sides discharged their pieces, and then with the most frantic yells of rage rushed on each other. Never was battle more severely contested.... No time could be secured for loading, so all had to rely on the bayonet or such weapons as they might have in their possession. Bayonet thrusts were frequently given, muskets clubbed, and even knives were used in this fearful struggle. The dead bodies of men and horses and broken caissons were literally piled up around the guns of the battery, and in some cases afforded barricades for the contestants.

"On the left, the charge of the four regiments under the gallant [Colonel Senaca G.] Simmons had cleared the field, and on our right [Lieutenant A. M.] Randol's battery of regulars, supported by the 4th and 7th Pennsylvania Reserves, were sweeping the enemy like chaff from the field, so the rebels in our front could expect no relief from that quarter; and the desperate fighting of the 9th and 1st Regiments, who now appeared to be seized with a supernatural frenzy, was at last too much for them, and they broke and fled from the field. With shouts of rage we pursued them ... thinning their ranks at every step, until compelled by our officers to halt.... The battery was now recaptured and the enemy was driven from the field, but at a fearful cost, and we looked with dismay on our thinned ranks and listened with horror to the pitiful pleadings of our wounded comrades who were lying around us."

Returning to Confederate narrator James Longstreet: "Ten thousand of A. P. Hill's division had been held in reserve in the hope that Jackson and Huger would come up on our left, enabling us to dislodge the Federals, after which Hill's troops could be put in fresh to give pursuit and follow them down to Harrison's Landing.... As neither Jackson nor Huger came up, and as night drew on, I put Hill in to relieve my troops.... He formed his line and followed up in [their] position.... By night we succeeded in getting the entire field, though all of it was not actually occupied.... As the enemy moved off they continued the fire of their artillery upon us from various points, and it was after 9 o'clock when the shells ceased to fall. Just before dark General McCall, while looking up a fragment of his division, found us where he supposed his troops were, and was taken prisoner. At the time he was brought in, General Lee happened to be with us. As I had known General McCall pleasantly in our service together in the 4th Infantry, I moved to offer my hand as he dismounted. At the first motion, however, I saw he did not regard the occasion as one for renewing the old friendship, and I merely offered him some of my staff as an escort to Richmond."

Although Longstreet may have ended the day in possession of much of the disputed ground, Lee's grand plan had received a major setback. In the words of D. H. Hill: "It had been a gallant fight . . . but as an obstruction to the Federal retreat . . . amounted to nothing." William Swinton says that the Federal stand "insured the integrity of the army, imperilled till that hour." General McClellan had spent the afternoon on one of the gunboats down the river. He could hear the sounds of battle, but had no certain knowledge as to what was happening. As usual, he anticipated the worst. He was in touch with Washington again, and two hours before the fighting ended he wired Stanton: "We are hard pressed by superior numbers. I fear I shall be forced to abandon my material to save my men under cover of the gunboats. You must send us very large reinforcements by way of Fort Monroe. . . . If none of us escape, we shall at least have done honor to the country. I shall do my best to save the army. Send more gunboats."

Even as this hysterical message was being dispatched, the wagons carrying McClellan's material were continuing along their route to safety. As for the army, it was not harassed during its withdrawal from the battlefield. According to Trooper Adams, however, the Federals were in a state of anxiety as the result of "all sorts of wild rumors, some asserting that we were cut off from the river, and that, as our supplies were exhausted and our ammunition nearly so, the whole army would be compelled to surrender in the morning. . . . There was a still more serious and damaging rumor . . . to the effect that General McClellan had abandoned the army, gone on board a gunboat, and had left for Washington. Absurd as this rumor was, it gained belief and had a serious effect on the troops. Officers were heard to say that a general, to gain victories . . . must be present, watch the tide of the battle, and know when to take advantage of it. That he must be prepared to take all risks, never let up when he had begun to fight, and to follow up advantages until they turned into substantial results. Others argued that an indomitable will was more necessary to a successful general than intelligence, which was apt to become oppressed with a fancied magnitude of the enemy. . . . So great was the alarm and excitement caused by the rumors . . . and so bad their effect on the spirits of the troops that many sincerely believed we could not fight another day and must surrender to the enemy or break up and find our way to Fort Monroe as best we could."

The army, of course, held together, and the coming of daylight found it making its way toward Malvern Hill, a few miles to the south. Says Private Warren Goss: "Acres and acres of waving grain, ripe for the reapers, were seen on every side. The troops marched through the wheat, cutting off the tops and gathering them into their haversacks, for . . . they were . . . hungry, as well as lame and stiff from marching. The bands . . . began playing patriotic airs, with a very inspiring effect. As they neared James River and caught sight of our gunboats, a cheer went up from each regiment. . . . They took position on the Malvern plateau. . . . Our stragglers, their courage revived by sight of the gunboats, came up the hill seeking their regiments. One squad . . . came in with a Confederate wagon in which were several wounded comrades rescued from the battlefield. Another squad had their haversacks filled with honey, and bore marks of a battle with bees. During the morning, long lines of men with dusty garments and powder-blackened faces climbed the steep Quaker Road. Footsore, hungry, and wearied . . . these tired men took their positions and prepared for another day of conflict."

Like the Federals, the Confederates had begun stirring from their camps at dawn. One of the witnesses to their march was Union soldier John Urban. Shot in the arm near the close of the previous day's fighting, he had taken refuge at a house being used as a hospital, and the enemy had seized it, making prisoners of Urban and numerous others. "The house we were at stands but a few steps from the road on which most of the rebel army marched in advance on the Union position at Malvern Hill. . . . I secured a good position, and for hours watched the rebels marching along. Most of the regiments appeared to be well equipped and drilled, and under any other circumstances I might have enjoyed the sight; but under the present circumstances I felt so vexed and chagrined that it was anything but a pleasant sight to me. To look at the long lines of armed men marching along with secession flags flung to the breeze and in pursuit of my comrades and the dear old flag, and to realize that I was a helpless prisoner among them made me feel most wretched. . . . The rebel . . . emblems of treason were a great annoyance to the Union wounded lying on the ground. 'Look at their dirty rags,' and similar expressions could be heard frequently, and some of the boys cared very little who heard them. The finest body of rebel troops that marched along this road was General Magruder's division. . . . The regiments had from seven to nine or ten hundred men. I counted seventeen regiments. . . . As the rebel army marched past, some of their men were constantly coming inside of the yard for water, and some of them sometimes stopped and exchanged a few words with us. After Magruder's troops had passed . . . an officer who was surrounded with a numerous staff came riding into the yard, and I soon came to the conclusion that he was some leading officer of the rebel army. Directly after riding into the yard, one officer came dashing up and handed him a paper. . . . After reading it, he galloped rapidly down the road, followed by his escort, in the direction of the front. . . . A rebel soldier who was standing close to me asked if I knew who he was. On my replying in the negative, he informed me that it was Stonewall Jackson."

The paper Urban saw was doubtless an order from Lee regarding troop dispositions for the planned attack. Jackson was soon conducting a personal survey of McClellan's position. "His reconnaissance," explains Robert Dabney, "showed him the enemy most advantageously posted upon an elevated ridge in front of Malvern Hill, which was occupied by several lines of infantry, partially fortified [with fresh-made earthworks], and by a powerful artillery. In short, the whole army of McClellan . . . was now, for the first time, assembled on one field, determined to stand at bay . . . while the whole Confederate army was . . . converging around it, under the immediate eye of the Commander-in-Chief and the President. The war of the giants was now to begin indeed. . . . The position of the Federalists had been selected by McClellan himself, with consummate skill. His line fronted north, covering the river road behind it and presenting a convex curve toward the Confederates. His right was covered by a tributary of Turkey Creek, and his left by the fire of his gunboats. . . . The ground occupied by him dominated, by its height, over the whole landscape. . . . The country before him was not only of inferior altitude but covered with woods and thickets, save within a few hundred yards of his own lines. And here the open fields sloped gently away, offering full sweep to his murderous fire. . . . General Lee . . . assigned the left to Jackson and the right to Magruder, supported by Huger and Holmes. Longstreet and A. P. Hill, with their wearied divisions, were held in reserve."

Lee believed that after his failure at Glendale and White Oak Bridge he had no choice but to make this difficult attack, which some of his officers opposed. The attack offered Lee his last chance to shatter the Federals before they settled under the full protection of their fleet and were united with a new line of supply and reinforcement. Lee based his hopes for success on the belief that the enemy was demoralized. The belief would have been strengthened if Lee had seen a wire that McClellan sent to Washington that morning. "My men are completely exhausted, and I dread the result if we are attacked today by fresh troops. If possible, I shall retire tonight to Harrison's Bar. . . . Permit me to urge that not an hour should be lost in sending me fresh troops. More gunboats are much needed. . . . I now pray for time. . . . Our losses have been very great. I doubt whether more severe battles have ever been fought. We have failed to win only because overpowered by superior numbers."

Lee's deployments proceeded slowly, for they were impeded by a poor knowledge of the roads and paths through the woods and the vine-tangled

Battle of Malvern Hill

swamps. It was hot work, even though the rays of the July sun were splintered by the foliage. On the Union side, according to Captain William B. Weeden of the 1st Rhode Island Artillery, the time was spent in perfecting the defense and waiting. "Meanwhile, the gunboats from the James River and our heavy guns posted in the rear threw great shells over our heads. These shells sometimes accidentally damaged ourselves, but generally they burst in the woods where the rebels were forming, or along the line of their march. . . . To be dressed for an evening party and to wait a half hour for the guests is not easy; to be ready and to wait five or six hours when the guests bring Miniés and the chance of a bayonet thrust tries all the powers of man. The line of privates were kept at their fixed posts. . . . Every bit of shade, a steep bank, closed and deserted houses, fence covers, single trees—each became a coign of vantage where groups of waiting officers could while away the weary interval. . . . There was a farmhouse over on the left and just in rear of the line of batteries. The ice-house had been opened, a pitcher and glasses had been seized from the household, [which had been] abandoned by the housekeeper, and thirsty warriors cooled themselves with the best of all drinks. . . . Even whiskey or the strength-giving brandy could not compete with ice-water here. . . . The day wears on. A breeze from the river tempers the fierce heat of the Southern sun. The sound of our great guns mingles with the scattering shots of skirmishers, and the stealthy bullets of rebel sharpshooters now begin to take effect as the intervals lessened."

One of the scenes on the Confederate left at this time is detailed by D. H. Hill: "I saw Jackson helping with his own hands to push [Captain James] Reilly's North Carolina battery farther forward. It was soon disabled, the woods around us being filled with shrieking and exploding shells. I noticed an artilleryman seated comfortably behind a very large tree, and apparently feeling very secure. A moment later a shell passed through the huge tree and took off the man's head. This gives an idea of the great power of the Federal rifled artillery."

"Soon," says the Union's Chaplain Stewart, "two hundred pieces of artillery were belching forth their awful thunders and scattering solid shot, shells, and canister among the rebels. . . . Nor were *they*, in the meantime, idle. Bold and unflinching, they opened on us. . . . At first their balls, shells, and canister flew and whizzed and screamed and burst over our heads, or fell far beyond, yet soon obtaining such accuracy of range as to make each one feel that between him and death there might be but a moment. Yonder, a cannonball tore through the ranks, dashing to pieces one, two, or three soldiers. There, a horse and rider were knocked down together. Here, a shell exploded, tearing off the head of one, the arm of a second, and leg of a third."

It wasn't until late afternoon that anything like close action began to develop. A single Confederate brigade, that of Colonel George T. Anderson,

A Union gun at Malvern Hill

was ordered to assault one of the nearer Federal batteries. In the words of Unionist Charles Weeden: "The woods bordering our main field swarmed with gray and butternut coats, and regiments stepped briskly forward, firing as they moved. Our batteries spoke quick and often. . . . Here and there a wide rent opens in the ordered files. It never closes, for another gap disorders the men who would try to fill the first. . . . Our infantry . . . add their galling fire to the crash of the shells. . . . No troops can stand such a fire, and the rebel brigade fell back under cover of the woods after half an hour or more of courageous effort. They came out singly and picked up the wounded. . . . This was a smart little action, but only the prelude to the Battle of Malvern Hill."

Because of the difficult terrain and the confusion it caused, Lee never got his army in hand, and the attack that developed was foreign to his intentions. The efforts of Jackson's wing on the Confederate left were led by D. H. Hill. John Gordon, now commanding one of Hill's brigades, was heavily involved. He relates: "The hour for the general assault which was to be made . . . by the whole Confederate army had come and passed. . . . Some of the divisions had not arrived upon the field; others, from presumably unavoidable causes, had not taken their places in line; and the few remaining hours of daylight were passing. Finally a characteristic Confederate yell was heard far down the line. It was supposed to be the beginning of the proposed general assault. General Hill ordered me to lead the movement of the right [of his division], stating that he would hurry in the supports to take their places on both my flanks and in rear of my brigade. I made the advance, but the supports did not come. Indeed, with the exception of one other brigade, which was knocked to pieces in a few minutes, no troops came in view. Isolated from the rest of the army and alone, my brigade moved across this shell-ploughed plain toward the heights, which were perhaps more than half a mile away. Within fifteen or twenty minutes the center regiment, 3rd Alabama, with which I moved, had left more than half of its number dead and wounded along its track, and the other regiments had suffered almost as severely. One shell had killed six or seven men in my immediate presence. My pistol . . . had the handle torn off; my canteen . . . was pierced, emptying its contents . . . on my trousers; and my coat was ruined by having a portion of the front torn away; but . . . I was still unhurt.

"At the foot of the last steep ascent, near the batteries, I found that McClellan's guns were firing over us; and, as any further advance by this unsupported brigade would have been not only futile but foolhardy, I halted my men and ordered them to lie down and fire upon McClellan's standing lines of infantry. I stood upon slightly elevated ground in order to watch for the reinforcements, or for any advance from the heights upon my command. In vain I looked behind us for the promised support. Anxiously I looked forward, fearing an assault upon my exposed position. . . . As a retreat in daylight promised to be almost or quite as deadly as had been the charge, my desire for the relief which nothing but darkness could now bring can well be imagined. In this state of extreme anxiety a darkness which was unexpected and terrible came to me alone. A great shell fell, buried itself in the ground, and exploded near where I stood. It heaved the dirt over me, filling my face and ears and eyes with sand. I was literally blinded. Not an inch before my face could I see. But I could think, and thoughts never ran more swiftly through a perplexed mortal brain. Blind! Blind in battle! Was this to be permanent? Suppose reinforcements now came, what was I to do? Suppose there should be an assault upon my command from the front? Such were the unspoken but agonizing questions which throbbed in my brain. . . . The blindness, however, was of short duration. The delicate and perfect machinery of the eye soon did its work. . . .

"Large bodies of troops had been sent forward, or, rather, led forward, by that intrepid commander, General Hill, but . . . unavoidable delay . . . and other intervening difficulties prevented them from ever reaching [our] advanced position. . . . In the hurry and bustle of trying to get them forward . . . they were subjected to the same destructive fire through which my troops had previously passed."

While he struggled to coordinate his division's attack, getting no help from Jackson's other units, Hill was temporarily encouraged by the sight of a general movement on the part of Lee's right wing. "I never saw anything more grandly heroic than the advance after sunset of the nine brigades under Magruder's orders. Unfortunately, they did not move together and were beaten in detail. As each brigade emerged from the woods, from fifty to one hundred guns opened upon it, tearing great gaps in its ranks; but the heroes reeled on and were shot down by the reserves at the guns, which a few squads reached. . . . It was not war—it was murder." The darkness desired by John Gordon (and thousands of others) came at last, and the Confederates of both wings began withdrawing. On the Union side, according to Trooper Adams, "cheer after cheer went up; shouts of triumph mingled with the peals of cannon and the clash of arms . . . reverberating . . . along the lines and closing the terrible tragedy with an halo of inspiration, grand and affecting."

The pyrotechnics that flared against the evening sky of July 1, 1862, gradually diminishing until replaced by the quiet stars, marked the end of the costly Battles of the Seven Days. Casualties in killed, wounded, captured, and missing were nearly 16,000 for the Federals and more than 20,000 for the Confederates. The additional thousands who fell victims of sickness went unlisted. As for the climactic contest at Malvern Hill, it staggered Lee's army. Robert Stiles explains: "The effect of these repeated bloody repulses can hardly be conceived. One fearful feature was the sudden and awful revulsion of feeling among our soldiers, inspired by six days

Union sharpshooters in Malvern wheatfield

of constant victory and relentless pursuit of a retreating foe. The demoralization was great, and the evidences of it palpable everywhere. The roads
and forests were full of stragglers. Commands were inextricably confused,
some, for the time, having actually disappeared. Those who retained sufficient self-respect and sense of responsibility to think of the future were
filled with the deepest apprehension. I know that this was the state of mind
of some of our strongest and best officers."

A notable exception was Stonewall Jackson. When the battle ended, he
sought his headquarters encampment and went to sleep. But soon a party of
his generals came for the purpose of telling him that if McClellan should
decide to attack in the morning they would be unable to offer resistance.
Jackson's medical director, Dr. Hunter McGuire, was at headquarters when
the group arrived. "It was difficult," says McGuire, "to wake General Jackson, as he was exhausted and very sound asleep. I tried it myself, and after
many efforts, partly succeeded. When he was made to understand what was
wanted, he said, 'McClellan and his army will be gone by daylight,' and
went to sleep again."

In McClellan's view, Malvern Hill was not so much a victory as another
escape from disaster. Whereas the Confederates feared he would take advantage of their disorganization and attempt to march upon Richmond, he
had no thought but to continue his retreat to Harrison's Landing. The withdrawal was begun as soon as the fighting ended, with only the rear guard,
led by Colonel William W. Averell, still on Malvern as a foggy dawn broke.
"Our ears," states the colonel, "had been filled with agonizing cries from
thousands before the fog was lifted, but now our eyes saw an appalling
spectacle upon the slopes down to the woodlands half a mile away. Over
five thousand dead and wounded men were on the ground in every attitude
of distress. A third of them were dead or dying, but enough were alive and
moving to give to the field a singular crawling effect. The different stages of
the ebbing tide are often marked by the lines of flotsam and jetsam left
along the seashore. So here could be seen three distinct lines of dead and
wounded marking the last front of three Confederate charges of the night
before. Groups of men, some mounted, were groping about the field."

McClellan's retreat from victory prompted some of his officers to protest angrily. One-armed Phil Kearny went so far as to tell his staff that the
commanding general was guilty either of cowardice or of treason. The enlisted men, according to Warren Goss, did "a deal of growling . . . but most
of them seemed to think Little Mac knew what he was about."

Union newsman Joel Cook explains that Harrison's Point "was the spot
chosen for the encampment of the army and its restoration from the ex-
cessive fatigue it had undergone. The hundreds of vessels laden with supplies which had left the White House were there, and everything was in
readiness to provide for the wants of the soldiers. Wednesday morning, July

2, was ushered in by a severe and unrelenting northeast storm which converted everything into mud and mire. As the weary troops arrived, they were forced to pitch their little shelter-tents upon this disagreeable surface. Rain fell in torrents. The sick and wounded . . . were feebly and slowly tramping through the mud, to lie down in it, the rain beating upon them whilst they waited for the hospital boats. . . . Regiment after regiment of troops had their hearts touched, and generously gave up their tents for the wounded to creep under . . . and many a grateful look showed the gratitude of the poor fellows who had given health and strength to their country.

"The rain fell faster and the mud grew deeper. One could scarcely walk. And Wednesday night lowered upon the army, perhaps the saddest and dreariest since it entered the field. On that day and the next, all labored at shipping the wounded and landing commissary stores. Steamboat after steamboat passed down the James River, filled to overflowing with unfortunate victims of the week of battle. Craft of all kinds landed food which was at once sent to the regiments. . . . The enemy, too, on Thursday attacked the camp, but were worsted . . . [This was a minor incursion conceived and led by the impulsive Jeb Stuart.] The rain did not stop until noon of that day, and the condition of the encampment was most sorrowful. Sunset, however, was clear, and better weather could be safely prophesied. The Fourth of July found the army fully protected by gunboats and earthworks, and prepared to hold its position against all odds. . . . During the afternoon General McClellan reviewed the troops, and was received everywhere with the most enthusiastic demonstrations."

An address composed by the general was read before the assembled units. "Attacked by superior forces, and without hope of reinforcements, you have succeeded in changing your base of operations by a flank movement, always regarded as the most hazardous of military expedients. . . . Upon your march you have been assailed day after day with desperate fury by men . . . skilfully massed and led. . . . You have, in every conflict, beaten back your foes with enormous slaughter. Your conduct ranks you among the celebrated armies of history. . . . On this our nation's birthday we declare to our foes, who are rebels against the best interests of mankind, that this army shall enter the capital of the so-called Confederacy." The hearers responded with cheers and applause.

The reality of McClellan's position at this time was that he had failed to take his objective, had fled in near panic from inferior numbers, had amassed thousands of needless casualties (including 1,734 dead), and had abandoned or destroyed millions of dollars' worth of government property. But, thanks to the general's announcements to the newspapers, not only the greater part of the army but also a large segment of the Northern public saw the Seven Days as he saw them. One of his subordinate officers explains: "The official statements that Lee commanded 180 or 200,000 men, while

General McClellan had only 75,000; the failure of the former to capture the extensive trains of wagons that filled every road, or penetrate the lines in a single instance, after suffering enormous losses—inspired confidence in the general, who had won the glory of saving the whole force from destruction."

The administration at Washington saw nothing glorious in McClellan's situation. For President Lincoln, the failure of the Peninsula Campaign was a crushing blow. "I was as nearly inconsolable as I could be and live." Lincoln's gloom was not relieved when McClellan's chief of staff, General R. B. Marcy (his father-in-law), arrived in Washington with a letter that stated: "The army is thoroughly worn out, and requires rest and very heavy reinforcements. Our losses have been very great, for the fighting has been desperate. . . . I hope that we shall have enough breathing space to reorganize and rest the men . . . before the enemy can attack again. . . . I doubt whether there are today more than 50,000 men with their colors. To accomplish the great task of capturing Richmond and putting an end to this rebellion, reinforcements should be sent to me rather much over than much less than 100,000 men. I beg that you will be fully impressed by the magnitude of the crisis in which we are placed." Lincoln did not take too seriously McClellan's claim that his numbers were down to 50,000, even though he knew that sickness and absenteeism were as much a factor as battlefield losses. It was a matter of record that, in all, 160,000 men had been sent to the Peninsula. But, no matter how severely McClellan had been diminished, his request for 100,000 reinforcements was unrealistic. Such a number was simply not available. General Marcy shocked both Lincoln and Stanton by saying that if McClellan did not get the troops he asked for he might be forced to capitulate to Lee. Lincoln flustered Marcy by allowing himself a flash of anger: " 'Capitulate' is a word not to be used in connection with our army!" The interview, together with the defeatist letter, convinced the President that he must pay a visit to McClellan at Harrison's Landing as soon as he could get away.

The mood in Richmond that first week in July was considerably better than that in Washington, but there was nothing akin to ecstasy. Although the people were enormously relieved that McClellan was now twenty-five miles distant, they were disappointed that he hadn't been dealt a decisive defeat. Lee himself was disappointed, but he made no charges against Jackson or anyone else. "Regret that more was not accomplished gives way to gratitude to the Sovereign Ruler of the Universe for the results achieved." Jackson, who could still take satisfaction in his earlier contributions to the campaign, felt that God deserved "undying gratitude . . . for this great victory, by which despondency increased in the North, hope brightened in the South, and the capital of Virginia and the Confederacy was saved." Lee felt out McClellan's new lines, found them unassailable, and took his troops

back to the Richmond defenses "to afford them the repose of which they
stood so much in need." Jefferson Davis issued an address thanking the men
for "skillfully and heroically" preserving the South's "just cause."

On July 7, accompanied by a small party of aides, Abraham Lincoln
boarded the steamer *Ariel* for the journey to Harrison's Landing. As the
paddle-wheeled ship, trailing a roll of smoke, throbbed its way down the
scenic Potomac and Chesapeake, the President had much to think about.
McClellan's failure had destroyed all hopes for a quick end to hostilities and
a restoration of the Union as it had been. The President believed he had no
choice now but to pursue a war of conquest, ignoring the wishes of the
Peace Democrats, who were soft on slavery, and allying himself with the
Republican party's abolitionist wing. A proclamation of emancipation
seemed necessary for the reasons he had anticipated: to give a new thrust to
the Union cause and to provide the war with a moral issue designed to dis-
courage foreign intervention in favor of the South. During that overnight
voyage, Lincoln was also obliged to ponder what should be done with
McClellan's army, and how to deal with the frustrating general himself.
Should the army be reinforced for a new drive upon Richmond, or should it
be withdrawn to Washington for an advance on the Confederate capital
from the north? The latter move could be made in cooperation with a new
army Lincoln had created by combining the troops of McDowell, Banks,
and Frémont under the pugnacious and bombastic Major General John
Pope. The question of replacing McClellan was a ticklish one, for his extraordinary popularity with the enlisted men had to be considered. Would
the general's removal have a devastating effect on morale? Would the men
rise in mutiny against the change? Not the least of the President's concerns
during the voyage was that he could not even be sure how his visit to the
army would be received, since he knew that McClellan had imbued a great
many of the troops with an angry distrust of the administration.

Lincoln arrived off Harrison's Landing at about four o'clock in the afternoon on July 8, his appearance coming as a surprise to the people on the
Union vessels anchored about. In the words of Katharine Prescott Worme-
ley, a volunteer nurse from Newport, Rhode Island, who was then aboard
the hospital ship *Wilson Small:* "While we were at dinner someone said,
chancing to look through a window, 'Why, there's the President!' and he
proved to be just arriving on the *Ariel,* at the end of the wharf close to
which we were anchored. I stationed myself at once to watch for the coming of McClellan. The President stood on deck with a glass with which,
after a time, he inspected our boat, waving his handkerchief to us. My eyes
and soul were in the direction of general headquarters, over where the great
balloon was slowly descending. Presently a line of horsemen came over the
brow of the hill through the trees, and first emerged a firm-set figure on a
brown horse, and after him the staff and bodyguard. As soon as the General

reached the head of the wharf he sprang from his horse, and in an instant every man was afoot and motionless. McClellan walked quickly along the thousand-foot pier, a major general beside him, and six officers following. He was the shortest man, of course, by which I distinguished him. . . . When he reached the *Ariel,* he ran quickly up to the afterdeck, where the President met him and grasped his hand. . . . He is stouter than I expected, but quicker, and more *leste.* He wore the ordinary blue coat and shoulder straps; the coat, fastened only at the throat and blowing back as he walked, gave to sight a gray flannel shirt and a—suspender! They sat down together, apparently with a map between them, to which McClellan pointed from time to time with the end of his cigar. We watched the earnest conversation which went on, and which lasted until 6 P.M. Then they rose and walked side by side ashore—the President, in a shiny black coat and stovepipe hat, a whole head and shoulders taller, as it seemed to me, than the General. Mr. Lincoln mounted a led horse of the General's, and together they rode off, the staff following, the dragoons presenting arms and then wheeling round to follow, their sabers gleaming in the sunlight. And so they . . . passed over the brow of the hill . . . the cannon . . . firing salutes."

The President spent the evening reviewing the troops and he was encouraged by the reception he received. A soldier from Pennsylvania, Oliver Willcox Norton, explained in a letter to his family: "Old Abe . . . did not get round to us till 9 o'clock . . . but it was beautiful moonlight, and as he went galloping past, riding beside Little Mac, everyone could tell him by his stovepipe hat and his unmilitary acknowledgment of the cheers which everywhere greeted him. His riding I can compare to nothing else than a pair of tongs on a chair back, but notwithstanding his grotesque appearance, he has the respect of the army." According to Norton, many of the troops had come to the conclusion that it wasn't Lincoln who was responsible for McClellan's misfortunes, that it was the abolitionists, "the men who have been using their influence to prevent his being reinforced, to secure his defeat, and in some way to so prolong the war as to make the abolition of slavery a military necessity. Curses loud and deep are heaped on such men." Norton and the others who held this view did not realize that, even though the abolitionists were not above thinking in such terms, McClellan had possessed the power to capture Richmond and thus devitalize the abolitionist cause. Nor were these troops aware that McClellan's failure had forced Lincoln himself to turn to abolitionism.

McClellan had believed all along that the President, because of intellectual weakness and political cowardice, was fair game for abolitionist domination. Now, during the executive visit to Harrison's Bar, the general handed Lincoln a letter designed to set him straight. "The time has come when the Government must determine upon a civil and military policy covering the whole ground of our national trouble. The responsibility of deter-